Comparative Public Policy

Comparative Public Policy

Anneliese Dodds

palgrave
macmillan

First published 2013 by
PALGRAVE MACMILLAN

Palgrave Macmillan in the UK is an imprint of Macmillan Publishers Limited,
registered in England, company number 785998, of Houndmills, Basingstoke,
Hampshire RG21 6XS.

Palgrave Macmillan in the US is a division of St Martin's Press LLC,
175 Fifth Avenue, New York, NY 10010.

Palgrave Macmillan is the global academic imprint of the above companies
and has companies and representatives throughout the world.

Palgrave® and Macmillan® are registered trademarks in the United States,
the United Kingdom, Europe and other countries

ISBN 978-0-230-31942-4   hardback
ISBN 978-0-230-31943-1   paperback

This book is printed on paper suitable for recycling and made from fully
managed and sustained forest sources. Logging, pulping and manufacturing
processes are expected to conform to the environmental regulations of the
country of origin.

A catalogue record for this book is available from the British Library.

Library of Congress Cataloging-in-Publication Data
Dodds, Anneliese.
Comparative public policy / Anneliese Dodds.
p. cm.
ISBN 978–0–230–31943–1 (pbk.)
1. Comparative government.   2. Policy sciences.   I. Title.
JF51.D63 2012
320.6—dc23   2012024722

10 9 8 7 6 5 4 3 2 1
22 21 20 19 18 17 16 15 14 13

Printed in China

Contents

List of Illustrative Material

Figures

Tables

Boxes

Acknowledgements

I would like to thank my colleagues at both King's College London and Aston University for their support during the production of this book, particularly John Meadowcroft, Karen West, Naonori Kodate, Pam Lowe, Simon Green and Crispian Fuller. Especial thanks are due to Ken Young for having first suggested this project and for his kind support during its execution.

I must also acknowledge the input of successive generations of King's and Aston public policy students. Their insightful comments and committed engagement with comparison have fed directly into the production of this book. I am also grateful to Frank Castles for first introducing me to this stimulating subject.

My editors at Palgrave Macmillan, Steven Kennedy and latterly Helen Caunce, have been extremely encouraging and helpful throughout. I am also heavily indebted to those who anonymously reviewed the text. Their meticulous and constructive engagement has improved the book immeasurably. I am also – as always – indebted to Mark Thatcher and Richard Parry for their inspiration and encouragement, as well as to Keith, Jean, Angus and Jen. Above all, however, I must thank Ed Turner for his many helpful ideas, optimism, and saintly levels of patience.

ANNELIESE DODDS

List of Abbreviations

AFDC	Aid to Families with Dependent Children
AIE	Access to Information on the Environment
ALMP	Active Labour Market Policies (also known as AMS)
ANAES	Agence Nationale d'Accréditation et d'Évaluation de la Santé (French: National Agency for Accreditation and Evaluation in Health)
BRICs	Brazil, Russia, India and China
CEDAW	Convention on the Elimination of All Forms of Discrimination against Women
CME	coordinated market economy
CNE	Comité National d'Évaluation (French: National Evaluation Committee)
EARP	Environmental Assessment Review Process
EIA	environmental impact assessment
EMS	European Monetary System
EPA	Environmental Protection Agency
GATT	General Agreement on Tariffs and Trade
GDP	gross domestic product
GMO	genetically modified organism
IAEA	International Atomic Energy Agency
IB	International Baccalaureate
ICC	International Criminal Court
ICTR	International Criminal Tribunal for Rwanda
ICTY	International Criminal Tribunal for the Former Yugoslavia
IEN	Inspecteurs de l'Éducation Nationale (French: National Education Inspectorate)
ILO	International Labour Organization
IMF	International Monetary Fund
IPCC	Intergovernmental Panel on Climate Change
IPR	Inspecteur Pédagogique Régional (French: Regional Education Inspector)
ISI	import-substituting industrialization
LDC	least developed country
LMD	licence, master, doctorat (French: undergraduate degree, master's degree, doctorate)
LME	liberal market economy
NAFTA	North American Free Trade Agreement
NEPI	new environmental policy instrument

NGO	non-governmental organization
OECD	Organisation for Economic Co-operation and Development
PES	Principal Economic Status
PISA	OECD's Programme for International Student Assessment
RMOs	références médicales opposables (French: best practice recommendations regarding a medical condition)
TANF	Temporary Aid for Needy Families
TCC	transnational capitalist class
TNC	trans-national corporation
UN	United Nations
UNCED	UN Conference on Environment and Development
UNESCO	United Nations Educational, Scientific and Cultural Organization
USAID	US Agency for International Development
VAT	value added tax
WHO	World Health Organization
WTO	World Trade Organization

Introduction

The purpose of this text is to provide an introduction to the subject of, and scholarship within, comparative public policy. The book combines information about public policies in different countries with an explanation of the different frameworks that have been used to analyse these policies. It provides a detailed overview of the nature and variations in policy between states, across a range of key policy areas. These variations are analysed by separating government use of financial resources, powers of organization, use of authority and provision of information.

The investigation of different policy areas provides the background for a comparison and evaluation of the main explanations for similarities and variations in public policy between nation states. The book also considers the nature and pitfalls of policy learning between nation states, and the emergence and impact of policy-making processes at global and regional level, beyond the nation state. Key theoretical and empirical research contributions are highlighted throughout the text.

The coverage of individual subject areas in this book – economic, welfare, health, education and environmental policy – is not intended to be exhaustive. Governments obviously make policies in many other areas, from foreign policy to cultural policy to immigration policy. In addition, it is not possible in one volume to do justice to all the complicated aspects of government policy-making across even just this restricted range of policy areas. Instead, the policy area chapters indicate the patterns that exist across different policy sectors, providing a foundation of empirical knowledge before more theoretical matters are examined in subsequent chapters.

By comparing government use of policy tools across five policy areas, this text provides an integrated assessment of public policy developments across different fields and countries. This departs from usual approaches to comparative public policy analysis, which have generally focused on specific fields, policy types or questions, rather than investigating government use of different policy instruments in a more coordinated and holistic manner. There have been some attempts to adopt Christopher Hood's (1986; 2007) typology of policy types to analyse public policies across countries, an approach which is also used here. However, previous attempts have generally been used to examine discrete policy areas within a relatively small number of countries (see, for example, Margetts, 1999), rather than the broader approach taken in this book.

To keep tables and figures intelligible, I have selected a range of broadly representative core countries for comparison throughout – Australia, Denmark, France, Germany, Italy, Japan, Sweden, the United Kingdom and the United States, although other countries are brought in or used as examples where particularly interesting and/or salient. This follows the approach taken by most scholarship within the field, and most teaching on this subject. Nonetheless, Chapter 13 considers the implications of this relatively narrow choice of nations, which excludes the 'Majority World' of 'emerging', 'developing' and 'post-communist' nations.

The book considers both the impact of domestic factors and international factors on the development of public policy. Numerous approaches have been put forward to classify domestic factors. Gough (2008), for example, isolates 'five Is' – 'industrialization', 'interests', 'institutions' and 'ideas' which all mediate the impact of 'internationalization'. Hassenteufel (2008: 104) distinguishes the three 'analytical levels' of 'actors' (covering individual and group resources, ideas and interests), their 'interactions', and the 'contexts' within which interactions occur. Bovaird and Loffler (2003: 14–6) identify no fewer than thirty factors that can be seen as driving public policy change, depending on the policy in question, covering economic, political, social, technological, environmental and legal/legislative issues.

This book adopts the 'three Is' framework of 'interests', 'ideas' and 'institutions', with all three factors being considered in detail. Often, interests and ideas will be seen as the key motivators for public policy-making, whilst institutions merely shape the development of policies. Some have argued that ideas might only change slowly and be responsible for long-term change, whereas interests may tend to affect policy-making relatively quickly, and the impact of institutions might only be felt over the medium term (Palier and Surel, 2005: 29–30). This book instead adopts a contextual approach that acknowledges that the different factors may be important at different stages of the policy process, but that this is likely to differ depending on the policy under investigation, and can only be considered through empirical investigation (*ibid*.: 27).

How this book is structured

This book is organized in such a manner that readers can either select various parts or chapters to read, or can progress through the book from beginning to end. Chapter 1 discusses the value in comparing public policies. Those who are particularly interested in concrete differences between public policies in different policy sectors should focus on Chapters 2 to 7. Those who are interested in theoretical approaches to comparing public policies should concentrate on Chapters 8, 9, 10, 11,

12 and 14. Finally, those who are already engaged in comparative public policy research and are interested in methodological issues should focus on Chapters 13 and 14.

Chapter 1 considers the rationale behind comparative public policy analysis. It sets out reasons why it is both practically and theoretically useful to examine policies across countries, and the deepened understanding that can result from this. It also considers whether comparative public policy research should be viewed as a separate field of enquiry, or whether the comparative method underlies all approaches to research in the social sciences. Going into greater detail, the chapter then considers how comparative public policy can be defined, and what it actually compares. Finally, the chapter summarizes some of the challenges for comparative public policy research in the face of increasing international pressures on policy-makers.

Chapter 2 provides a systematic consideration of the ways in which policies can differ across nations. It examines how governments can exert control over economic means, regulation and information within different policy areas. It also considers how government can relate to other actors within different policy sectors, including non- and quasi-governmental actors. It then examines theories which suggest that governments' use of these policy mechanisms, and interactions with these other actors during the policy process, vary systematically across nations. Following this, the chapter sets out the framework that will be used to analyse governments' use of policy instruments during Chapters 3 to 7. Finally, the chapter also examines the scope of public policy-making: to what extent can governments intervene in the lives of their own population, and that of other states?

Chapters 3 to 7 of the book adopt the framework set out in Chapter 2 to make a comparative examination of five policy sectors: economic, welfare, health care, education and environmental policy.

Each chapter first defines the policy area and the scope of the chapter, before surveying the most salient and influential approaches to comparing public policies in each sector. It then details how policies can differ between nations in the sector concerned, in terms of their use of financial resources, organization, authority and the provision of information. The chapter goes on to consider differences in the 'scope' of policies in each area – that is, who they affect, and how.

Chapters 8, 9 and 10, consider in detail why systematic variation in public policies occurs by examining cross-national differences in three contextual variables affecting policy-making – institutions, interests and ideas. Each chapter first defines the variable concerned. It then details and analyses those theories which suggest that each variable, either singly or in combination with the others, plays a role in determining why public policies differ across nations.

Whilst Chapters 8 to 10 mainly concentrate on domestic factors influencing policymaking, Chapters 11 and 12 consider the growing importance of the international policy context. Chapter 11 considers the prospects for policy transfer across nations and learning, and how these processes can be detected and researched. Chapter 12 then examines policy-making beyond the nation state, including how cross-national processes such as globalization and Europeanization impact on public policy-making.

As noted, much of the text focuses on nations which are longstanding members of the OECD: democracies which have been subject to extensive industrialization.

Chapter 13 surveys public policy-making in developing and post-communist nations. Whilst some have attempted to apply existing approaches to policy analysis to these nations, others have argued that new approaches are necessary which better reflect the different interests, ideas and institutions influencing policy-making in these countries. This chapter reviews these arguments, and also draws lessons from the study of developing and post-communist nations for public policy-analysis more generally.

The final chapter, Chapter 14, provides a thorough introduction to how comparative research can be carried out in practice. It first presents and discusses the different choices researchers must make when carrying out comparative public policy research. It then examines some of the most salient problems affecting comparative research and explains how each can be overcome. Finally, it briefly considers the logistical issues which comparative public policy researchers need to take into account.

Chapter 1

Why Compare Public Policies?

The comparative approach to investigating policy processes, outputs and outcomes, is an important, if under-used, tool for researchers and policy-makers. It can, of course, help us understand policy-making and its consequences in foreign nations, but can also illuminate policy processes in our own country. It provides 'free lessons' on how to make policy differently, and awakens us to the contingency of 'how things are done' in our own country. Comparing policy in different nations can also provide us with a deeper and richer understanding of the fundamental drivers of policy-making and how it impacts on the world.

This chapter has four aims. First, it provides a more detailed justification for why researchers and policy-makers should be prepared to engage in comparing policies across nations. Second, it considers the status of comparative public policy within social science as a whole and, in particular, whether comparative research constitutes a separate field of enquiry to other forms of research. Third, the chapter provides a brief history of comparative public policy. Fourth, it explains what comparative public policy is and what it is not: how comparative public policy can be defined, what is being compared, and how comparative public policy can be conducted in an increasingly interconnected world.

Given that much public policy analysis adopts a national focus, and seems to assume this is sufficient, why should researchers and policy-makers be interested in investigating other nations' policy-making systems?

As this book explains, policies, the stakeholders involved in designing and delivering them, and policy outputs and outcomes, vary significantly across nations. This might be anticipated in the fields of culture or language, which could reasonably be expected to be governed in multifarious ways in different nations. Similarly, we might expect policy difference between nations which are able to extract significant funds from their populations through taxation when compared with poorer countries. Yet, even amongst relatively similar countries with apparently identical aims, we find radically divergent policy approaches.

One example, developed in Chapter 5, is the field of health care policy. All modern governments state they want to see improved population health and high-quality health care. None, professedly, wants the health of their population to deteriorate or the quality of health care to diminish. Despite these similar basic aims across countries, health care is delivered in manifold ways across nations. In some countries, health care is provided entirely by private organizations; in others, provision is almost entirely undertaken by public organizations. It is paid for through universal taxation in some countries, through social insurance in others, through private insurance in yet other nations, and through payments 'at the point of use' of health care in others. In some countries, medical interest groups drive policy-making on health care; in others, their policy-making role is considerably less significant. As mentioned, this diversity persists even given similar basic policy aims.

National, regional and local governments thus adopt a bewildering variety of approaches towards similar policy problems. In turn, the impacts of analogous policies vary significantly depending on their societal, cultural and national context. Politics and policy 'work' in distinctive ways in different nations, regions and towns.

This highlights the contrast between social research (including the study of public policy) and the study of the natural sciences. Causal relationships in the natural sciences are always the same, provided the relevant parameters are held constant: hence, gravity always 'works' in the same way, no matter where one is in the world. In contrast, human societies are so diverse and idiosyncratic that there is no such thing as a universal 'social law' within the social sciences (Dogan, 2002). Comparative public policy can help us to understand and explain why divergent policies are adopted in different contexts, and why they lead to a variety of outcomes.

The desire to understand policy and its outcomes is often particularly strong in contexts of rapid societal and political change. Comparison has often been used as a means to arbitrate in contexts of conflict between political groupings representing opposing political values, norms and interests (Richter, 1969: 132). It has also been spurred by exposure to different societies through actual or threatened cultural or military colonization, or domestic turmoil.

An example of this comes from the Moroccan scholar Muhammad As-Saffãr. Saffãr's account of his observations during a diplomatic journey to Paris illustrates the concerns of Moroccan rulers in the 1840s, confronted as they were by seemingly insuperable Western military and political power (Saffãr and Miller, 1992). Similarly, Tocqueville's detailed analysis in *Democracy in America* (published in 1835) could be seen as spurred by concerns within his home country, France, given its 'difficult transition from aristocracy to democracy' (Browers, 2003: 8). Other comparative studies have been spurred not by threat but by emulation, as with scholarly attempts to better understand 'classical antiquity or primitive Christianity' during the 'Renaissance and the Reformation' (Richter, 1969: 132). Currently, China and India's public policies are viewed by some as revealing possible 'lessons' to be taken on board by other nations (Kelly *et al.*, 2006).

The need for comparative analysis has become stronger following reactions to the 2008 financial crisis. This has led to a 'collapse' in the 'easy consensus on policy which typified the last years of the age of liberalization – roughly, the three decades from 1978 to 2008' (Coen and Roberts, 2012: 5). Widespread civil unrest, the fall of governments and radical drops in government spending and living standards have led many to question previous assumptions that external pressures such as globalization and Europeanization would lead inexorably to policy convergence. Orthodoxies such as central bank and regulatory independence have been brought into question, state ownership has been extended, and debate rages about the relative merits of austerity and stimulus (*ibid.*).

In this context, comparison can act as an 'import-mirror' on our own society and polity (May, 2003: 208–9). A particular policy approach which appears 'inevitable' or 'taken for granted' can be shown to be socially or culturally contingent following comparative investigation. Comparison thus places the status quo in perspective. One example of this comes from educational benchmarking by the OECD's Programme for International Student Assessment (PISA) which ranks different nations according to the educational skills and proficiency of 15-year-olds. Poor scores in PISA have promoted calls for educational reform in a number of nations. PISA implicitly places nations in competition with each other over their respective educational standards. This highlights the ambiguous nature of benchmarking (Cox *et al.*, 1997), which stresses collaboration amongst participants to enhance overall performance, but also leads to competition between those nations being benchmarked. Such 'competition' may be rather illusory, if the financial and institutional constraints applying in different countries render reform impracticable, or even impossible. This 'embeddedness' of different policy systems is considered in greater detail in Chapter 10.

In addition to this 'benchmarking' role, comparison can open our eyes to new insights which we would never have considered if closeted within the confines of a purely domestic frame of reference. Adopting a comparative perspective can result in a radically altered understanding of what is achievable (and, sometimes, impossible) through the policy process.

As well as shedding light on existing policies and phenomena, comparative analysis can also highlight new ways of dealing with domestic policy problems. This use of comparative analysis by policy 'entrepreneurs' to generate 'new' policy ideas has had a very significant impact, particularly in criminal justice and welfare policy.

Placing domestic policies in comparative context can therefore lead us to question the *status quo* and consider adopting new policy approaches. Comparative analysis can also fundamentally alter our understandings of the nature of certain phenomena, and our views on how and why they arise.

For example, comparative analysis can indicate the diverse ways in which a particular phenomenon can arise across nations, regions or social groups, and whether there is any 'essential basis' for the matter in question. For instance, 'slavery' has existed in a variety of incarnations over history and across different nations. Engaging in comparative analysis would enable us to specify what precisely distinguishes cases of slavery from oppression and other uses of coercive power (Elder, 1976: 211–12). Such analysis has also been used to generate 'ideal types', approximations of prevalent phenomena created by accentuating and combining their recurrent characteristics. This approach was instigated by Max Weber (1961), who used it to develop a typology of 'legitimation strategies' (legal–rational, traditional and charismatic domination) used by rulers in different nations.

Finally, comparative analysis has also been promoted as part of political attempts to build understanding across nations. This has been particularly the case within the European Union. The European Union's civil service, the European Commission, has devoted substantial funds to building research cooperation across Europe and beyond, in both the physical and social sciences. This collaboration has involved financial support for joint research projects and European-level research observatories and centres, and 'pump-priming' funds to increase communication between European scholars by creating networks, websites and conferences (Hantrais and Mangen, 1996a). Participation in these, and similar, initiatives enables scholars to learn from colleagues from very different intellectual traditions – often, in the process, creating innovative conceptual approaches as well as generating important new research findings.

Is comparative research a separate field of enquiry?

Historically, many authors have been keen to single out comparison as an especially valuable intellectual endeavour. Hence, Montesquieu maintained that comparison could be viewed as 'the single most valuable capacity of the human mind', whilst Tocqueville 'shared this high estimate' with his view that the 'mind can gain clarity only through comparison' (Richter, 1969: 136). Max Weber (1980 [1925]) argued that every social phenomenon could be examined both in and of itself, and in contrast with other similar (and different) social phenomena – that is, comparatively.

It has also been suggested that the social sciences are in some sense inherently comparative; that comparative studies are not merely constitutive of one branch of the discipline, but the discipline itself, as Durkheim argued of sociology (Jowell, 1998). This position was developed by the philosopher Alasdair Macintyre when he suggested that there simply could not be any type of political 'science' apart from comparative political science. For Macintyre (1984: 261), the fact that comparative methods underlay all political science research explained why the comparative politics section of the American Political Science Association had ceased to exist as a separate body. Indeed, Neumann (1957) suggests that the American Political Studies Association was itself created in 1903 as 'an outgrowth of a movement looking toward a National Conference on Comparative Legislation'. In the same vein, Harold Lasswell, often viewed as the 'founder' of policy studies, suggested that comparison was unavoidable within social scientific research, a position also adopted by Gabriel Almond, well-known for his cross-national studies of civic culture (Lijphart, 1971: 682).

In contrast, Peter Mair has suggested that comparative political science, at least, involves a combination of both substance (content) and method (comparison). For Mair (1996: 311), this combinative character of comparative research distinguishes it from other types of research which may use the comparative method, but fail to compare similar phenomena across two or more units. On the contrary, Lijphart (1971: 682) has suggested that comparative politics 'indicates the how but does not specify the what of the analysis'; that describing a study as 'comparative' makes claims about methods but not content. For Lijphart (*ibid.*), 'the comparative method can be distinguished from three others: the experimental, statistical, and case study methods'.

Others have adopted a more subtle approach, suggesting that comparative research can, but need not necessarily, involve the use of distinctive approaches to distinctive subject matter. Hence, May quotes Øyen's description of four types of comparative researchers, ranging from 'purists' to 'ignorants', 'totalists' and 'comparativists'. Of these groups, only 'comparativists' view comparative research as distinctive, are aware of the specific problems facing comparative work, and view it as a discrete topic. Purists come at the other extreme, viewing comparative research as completely assimilable with other types of research and not requiring any additional attention to methodological or theoretical issues. Between these two extremes are the 'ignorant' and 'totalist' comparative researchers. 'Ignorants' are described as nationally-centred researchers who are insensitive to social, historical and cultural context. 'Totalists', for their part, are aware of methodological and theoretical issues affecting comparative research, but nonetheless fail to alter how they operationalize concepts and frame research questions to take these issues into account (May, 2003: 207).

In summary, whilst comparative analysis can be viewed as fundamental to all social research, some commentators suggest that its methods and subject matter render it separable from other research strategies. Which position we take may depend, as Øyen suggests, on our awareness of the particular challenges facing comparative research, which are dealt with in detail in Chapter 14.

Comparative public policy in historical perspective

Modern comparative public policy can be seen as growing out of comparative approaches to politics and sociology, which were arguably in evidence from the beginnings of each discipline.

A variety of works were produced from the classical period onwards which placed various nations' political institutions and policy approaches in international perspective, as part of an attempt to move beyond nationally-specific views. One of the first such attempts was Aristotle's *The Politics*, which included a typology of several political regimes drawn from Greece and beyond, their specific institutional features, and how these could be seen as relating to their domestic social, economic and cultural context (Aristotle, 350BC). Montesquieu (1989) [1750] adopted a similarly wide-ranging approach in his study of republics, monarchies and despotic governments in the eighteenth century, and how these related to the 'national character'.

Much of this early work investigating foreign nations and their politics was highly normative, being designed to illustrate how the writer's own culture was superior to the others being described (Sica, 2006). Even those scholars who were generally open to criticisms of their own society sometimes proved unable to move beyond 'taken-for-granted' assumptions. Hence Montesquieu, who had adopted the novel device of seeing France through foreigners' eyes in his *Persian Letters*, written in 1721, was keen to describe the Orient as the 'natural home of despotism'. Similarly, Tocqueville, despite his awareness of the specificity of American attitudes towards indigenous populations, failed to use the same awareness in relation to French activities in Algeria (Richter, 1969: 131).

In addition to studies of national constitutional arrangements, comparative methods were seized upon by the new discipline of sociology from the eighteenth century onwards. Some early sociological scholars were extremely ambitious for their new discipline. Auguste Comte, viewed by many as the founder of sociology, aspired to compare societies over history and prehistory, but also to compare human societies with animal ones (Sica, 2006). Although restricted to human societies, Max Weber's analysis (1930) of the links between religion and economic activity and structure was similarly ambitious in its attempt to explain very wide-ranging macro-social trends.

The desire to develop encompassing theories based on abstractions from numerous domestic contexts continued to motivate much comparative work as the twentieth century wore on. This was particularly the case from the 1950s onwards, where scholars attempted to broaden their analyses from the study of Western societies to cover developing nations as well. This 'global scope' necessitated a shift away from the previous focus on formal representative institutions. Henceforth, many scholars were also keen to examine non-state institutions, which in some undemocratic societies wielded extensive political power (Finer 1970: 5; Almond 1990: 192; Browers, 2003: 9). These cross-national analyses often involved the creation and testing of hypotheses linking macrosocial trends. One such hypothesis was the so-called 'Wagner's law', based on the German academic and politician Alfred Wagner's hypothesis that growth in national wealth would lead to growth in the size and scope of state activity.

From the 1970s onwards, scholars' attention began to shift away from global ambitions and hypothesis-testing towards more circumscribed goals. This process could be seen as partly inevitable; as Dogan (2002) notes in relation to sociology (but which is equally applicable to other forms of social research), the process of adding to knowledge within the discipline unavoidably leads to the compartmentalizing and delimiting of fields of investigation. As a result, the discipline becomes more developed and mature by segmenting and dividing-up what is studied. In addition, the advent of 'Reaganomics' in the 1980s, as well as other 'radical' public policy responses to the oil crisis, undermined theories of modernization which had presaged public policy convergence.

Henceforth, rather than attempt global abstract analyses, studies of democracy tended to focus on specific regions and to stress the political and institutional processes involved in democratic breakdown and consolidation, as well as its social and economic context (see, for example, Linz and Stepan, 1978). As Mair (1996) notes, the work of Arendt Lijphart offers a good illustration of these broad developments in comparative analysis. Lijphart shifted from analysing the societal and economic prerequisites for democratic regimes towards investigating the consequences of different political systems (particularly, of 'Westminster' as against 'consociational' political systems). This represents a move away from investigating what makes politics 'the way it is' towards a concern with what politics 'does'.

This new focus on the outputs of politics (i.e. on policy) has opened up space for the field of comparative public policy to emerge. It has been simultaneously accompanied by a reduction in the scope of analysis, in terms of both the policy areas and national contexts examined.

One relatively early – and influential – example of what could be described as 'comparative public policy' came from a study by Titmuss

(1970) of the provision of blood for transfusions in the USA and Britain. Titmuss claimed that commercial blood donation led to reduced efficiency and lower quality blood compared with donation (or 'gift') based systems. In the context of widespread debate about the appropriateness of state intervention and marketization, this argument was highly influential. Numerous more modern examples of so-called 'small-N', sectorally-specific studies abound. This style of comparison, involving research into how a small number of countries deal with similar policy problems, has since been very popular within comparative public policy research. Two prominent examples from this very wide field are Peter Hall's (1986) text on economic policy in Britain and France and Michael Moran's (1999) work on the governance of the health care state in Britain, Germany and the USA. As will be discussed in the next section, however, many strategies have been adopted by comparative public policy analysts when deciding what to compare, and across which units.

Indeed, the field of contemporary comparative public policy is extremely diverse and it would be mistaken to view developments in a linear fashion. Browers (2003: 10) has noted that many comparativists in political science appear 'content to be part of a "messy center" that combines "diverse conceptual lenses" and is driven not by method but by "real world puzzles"', and the same is surely true for many comparative analysts of public policy.

Comparative public policy is an inherently interdisciplinary exercise. Heidenheimer *et al.* (1983: 89), in their textbook of comparative public policy written in the mid-1980s, suggested that it was 'located at a busy cross-roads in the social sciences' between political science, sociology, history and economics. Contemporary comparative public policy has also drawn on theories and approaches from anthropology and public management. The 'messy centre' has continually expanded as new research areas have been explored by intrepid public policy researchers.

Comparative public policy, as with the study of public policy in general, both benefits (through greater richness and explanatory power) and suffers (through centripetal tendencies) from this interdisciplinarity. It has also become easier to undertake than ever before, given advances in transport and communications. As a result, the field of comparative public policy research is growing in size and scope as every year passes.

Six years before this book was written, Charles Lees (2006) argued that comparative research would come to dominate political science completely, and that single-country scholars were becoming increasingly isolated. More recently, Christopher Pollitt (2011: 120, 125) considered the internationalization of public administration, and argued that the 'scene' had become increasingly populated and various over recent years – to the extent that comparative public administration was 'dangerously fashionable'.

Arguably, the interdisciplinary field of public policy analysis has internationalized considerably, with core journals such as the *Journal of Public Policy*, the *Journal of Public Administration Research and Theory* and *Public Administration* adopting a considerably more comparative approach. There is a vast and growing range of comparative analyses of public policy, coming from a broad span of theoretical angles and covering a plethora of policy areas. This book does not attempt to offer a survey of this very extensive field. Instead, it provides readers with a clear, concise and contemporary understanding of influential approaches to comparing public policies across nations, and illustrates these in relation to some core policy areas.

Defining comparative public policy research

This book defines comparative public policy as the use of the comparative approach to investigate policy processes, outputs and outcomes. The two halves of this definition, 'comparative approach' and 'policy processes, output and outcomes' both require further specification.

Taking a 'comparative approach' to social research may sound relatively straightforward. Comparison's etymological roots suggest the 'bringing together' of two or more units in order to see how alike or equal they are, placing them 'in contest'. As is discussed in the next section, a wide variety of policy-related units can be subjected to comparison, such as interest groups, political parties, local governments, government agencies, policy sectors and, most commonly, different nations.

Some authors have suggested that only certain types of studies qualify as 'truly' comparative. Hantrais and Mangen (1996b: 1), for example, argue that, in order to be genuinely comparative, a cross-national research study needs to involve data being collected on certain issues or phenomena from two or more countries, 'using the same research instruments', with the express intention of then comparing that data within a cross-national research team. This book adopts a more expansive definition, whereby any research which either explicitly or implicitly contrasts policy processes, outputs or outcomes from one or more units counts as 'comparative public policy'. Under this expansive definition, cross-national research qualifies as genuinely 'comparative', even if it is based entirely on secondary analysis of research produced by separate nationally-based researchers.

Moving to the second half of the definition, demarcating the object of research as 'policy processes, output and outcomes' enables the examination of not only the 'positive' activity of decision-making, but also of decisions which are not made (since these are also part of the policy process).

This book thus follows Feldman's (1978: 300) injunction that 'inaction is policy', since it, as with policy-making, involves the use of government control. For the purposes of this book, 'policy' is not restricted to the activities of governments but includes the activities of non- or quasi-state actors, where these are sanctioned by governments. The book follows Parsons (1996: 14) in distinguishing policy, 'an attempt to define and structure a rational basis for action or inaction', from 'administration', which need not be impelled by such an explicit intention.

Some have argued that policy studies are inherently normative – that is, 'value-laden'. Hence, Goodin *et al.* (2008: 5) describe policy studies as 'academic works that attempt to do the real political work: contributing to the betterment of life, offering something that political actors can seize upon and use'. For these authors (*ibid.*), policy studies are 'unabashedly value laden'. Such an argument has also been put forward by some comparative public policy analysts. Hence, Lipson (1957) argues that the 'aim of comparison . . . is evaluation'. For Lipson, it is both inevitable and desirable that researchers should 'pass judgment' on the way in which their research subjects have dealt with particular policy problems.

Some commentators would argue that the process of undertaking social research inevitably involves us 'taking sides' (Becker, 1967); that the choice of research topic is a value-laden activity, but not the conduct of research itself (Weber, 1948b); or, contrarily, that the use of certain research methods, such as survey interviewing, is inherently normative (Oakley, 1981).

This book does not take a position on the question of whether comparative public policy is – or should be – normative, or should instead avoid making value judgements. Nonetheless, it should be noted that much research does appear to adopt comparison as a means of promoting a particular policy position. For example, Hodge and Bowman (2010: 223) use a comparison of 'policy and dialogue activities' concerning nanotechnology in the UK and Australia to suggest that the Australian government should follow the UK in promoting 'wide-ranging public debate' about the new technology.

As already stated, a judgement on whether comparative public policy is, or should be, normative is beyond the scope of this book. Any reader should, however, be wary of work which appears to assume a particular normative position as 'taken for granted', or which advocates a move towards a particular comparator policy model, without explaining why this should occur.

Many scholars of comparative public policy focus exclusively on comparison between *countries* (Heidenheimer *et al.*, 1983; Castles, 1998). These scholars take different decisions about the number of nations to analyse, and how to select nations for examination. Some try to generate globally valid results, often through the use of cross-national surveys –

such as Ronald Inglehart's 'World Values Survey' (undated). Others examine nations which are members of international groupings, such as the Organisation for Economic Cooperation and Development (OECD) (e.g. Castles, 1998; Swank, 2002). Another branch of cross-national analyses focuses on smaller numbers of nations sharing specific characteristics, such as small European capitalist states which entered world markets in the late nineteenth or early twentieth centuries (Katzenstein, 1985), small nations which are members of the European Union (Panke, 2010), or nations which have undergone class-based social revolutions (Skocpol, 1979). Bollen *et al.* (1993) coined the term 'macrocomparative studies' to describe such comparison between two or more nations.

For other authors, the unit of analysis has comprised different *groupings of nations*. Hence, Joseph Nye (1971) compared regional integration processes across Africa, the Middle East, Latin America and Europe in his work *Peace in Parts*. As the European Union has developed to become the world's most integrated trading bloc, research focusing on its internal dynamics has proliferated. However, even if the EU is in some senses unique, it can still usefully be analysed in comparison with other integration processes and institutions (Caporaso, 1997). Bernhard Ebbinghaus (1998) has argued that supranational institutions and transnational processes, such as the EU, can be compared not only with other international developments, but also with those at national level. As an example, he cites Fritz Scharpf's work, which has examined similarities between the so-called 'joint-decision making trap' (affecting the relations between German *Länder* and the federal state), and relations between supranational EU institutions and member states.

Apart from comparing national- or supranational-level units, comparativists have also studied policy-making within *sub-national geographically-defined units*, such as regions, cities or towns. This approach is particularly valuable when studying very diverse nations, where 'a national study can be just as challenging as a cross-national comparative study' (Hakim, 2002: 200). The nation of Nigeria, for example, harbours peoples speaking no less than 514 languages, whilst Indonesia is home to 719 linguistic groups (Lewis, 2009). Together, the two countries represent 18 per cent of the world's linguistic diversity, despite possessing only 5 per cent of its population. Treating Nigeria or Indonesia as coherent units in comparison with other more homogeneous nations may cause significant methodological problems unless the nations' linguistic and cultural diversity is taken into account. One way of avoiding such problems would be through comparing regions within each country with each other, which would enable the research project explicitly to acknowledge, and deal with, such diversity. Adopting sub-national areas as the unit of analysis can, therefore, help researchers deal with 'super-diverse' national populations when carrying out comparative research.

In addition to using this technique to aid with cross-national comparative analysis, some theorists have also compared sub-national units within only one country. Such comparison between different localities within one nation can help 'screen out' intervening variables such as national administrative culture, which might prevent the appropriate identification of causal processes (Yetano, 2010: 169).

Aside from comparing sub-national geographical units, researchers have also compared *exemplars of certain organizational categories* with each other. For example, *sub-national governments* and their approaches to different policy problems have been extensively compared (e.g. Bartlett *et al.*, 1999). Similarly, the development, activities and relative power of *political parties* in the policy process has been examined, both by comparing different types of party (as with, for example, Herbert Kitschelt's work on 'ecological' and 'radical right' parties) (Kitschelt 1989; Kitschelt with McGann 1995), and by examining different national party systems (e.g. Lipset and Rokkan's work (1967) on social cleavages). Different *types* or *forms* of organization have also been compared with each other, such as private and public sector organizations (Rainey and Bozeman, 2000).

Comparison between different *policy sectors* has also been used to generate important findings about the nature of the policy process. Hence, scholars have examined which stakeholders are involved in decision-making in particular sectors, and how they relate to government and form 'policy networks' or 'communities' (Atkinson and Coleman, 1989; Marin and Mayntz, 1991; Marsh and Rhodes, 1992; Le Galès and Thatcher, 1995; Marsh, 1998). Policy networks have been compared in a variety of fields, from agriculture (Montpetit, 2002) to water policy (Bressers *et al.*, 1995).

Finally, as well as comparing different nations, regions, geographical sub-units, members of organizational categories, and policy sectors, comparativists have also compared the policy process across *different time periods*.

Such comparison may be longitudinal and cross-sectional, as with Frank Castles' (1998) analysis of public policy change within the members of the Organisation for Economic Cooperation and Development. Alternatively, comparison may be 'diachronic' rather than continuous, where certain delimited time periods in one or more nations are compared with each other. Lijphart (1971) describes a study by Charles Freye as falling into this category of diachronic comparison, which focused on relationships between political stability and the party and interest group systems in Germany during two different time periods, the Weimar and Bonn republics. A variant of this approach is provided by studies of attempts to introduce similar policies during different time-periods. For example, Curran and Hollander (2010: 483) compared the policy processes surrounding two attempts to build new pulp mills in Tasmania, one in 1989 and another twenty years later.

BOX 1.1   A comparison across time: two attempts at liberalization in the UK higher education sector

In Dodds (2011), I compared two cases where UK governments had attempted to institute markets in higher education which were ten years apart. The cases were examined using a combination of documentary analysis of press reports and the papers of key organizations and individuals, and basic statistical analysis. The resultant findings were then tested during semi-structured interviews with governmental officials, politicians and interest group actors.

The first case of attempted liberalization was successful: the UK government did manage to introduce full-cost fees for international students and competition between universities to attract these students. In the second, unsuccessful case, government failed to introduce a 'bidding' system for additional domestic student numbers.

I considered three possible reasons to explain the differential success of the two attempts:

- a market-favouring logic of action must be established before a market can be created;
- a threshold of competitive behaviour must be reached before a collective institution tips into a market; and
- the strategic position of different actors within institutions will affect the extent to which a market can be created.

The article suggested that all three approaches helped explain why liberalization occurred in one case and not the other, but none was sufficient to explain this on its own. As a result, the article concluded by arguing against simplistic approaches to institutional change.

Another type of comparison across time is described by Dogan (2002) as 'asynchronic', involving a double comparison which compares different time periods from different contexts. Dogan cites Forrest's (1994) work in this connection, comparing the weak state in post-colonial Africa with that operating in the nations of Europe during the Middle Ages.

Separately, scholars of politics and public policy have debated extensively whether work focusing on individual cases can legitimately be described as 'comparative'.

Some researchers, although focusing on one particular unit, develop what could be described as an 'unbalanced' comparison, contrasting features of other similar units against their chosen unit to provide some context. Hence, Ernst Haas (1961) focused on European integration, but contrasted this with a variety of similar processes across the globe.

Some have argued that not merely 'unbalanced' comparisons, but even explicitly 'single case' studies, can be classified as 'comparative'. For example, the use of 'ideal types' (abstractions from different exemplars of a particular phenomenon) in order to contextualize single cases could be seen as involving comparison (Ragin, 1987: 4).

Charles Ragin argues, in addition, that '[m]any area specialists are thoroughly comparative because they implicitly compare their chosen case to their own country' (*ibid.*). Others reject claims that researching a foreign country will automatically involve scholars in comparison. Hence, Peter Mair (1996: 310) criticizes the view that whilst 'an American scholar working on, say, Italian politics is usually regarded by her national colleagues as a "comparativist" . . . an Italian scholar working on Italian politics is regarded by her national colleagues as a "non-comparativist"', claiming that this 'makes nonsense of the definition' of comparative research.

In a recent contribution to this debate, Charles Lees (2006: 1097) has cogently argued for the need for more comparative work by those who would otherwise be drawn to single-country studies. He suggests that focusing uniquely on one case can lead researchers to inappropriately 'stretch' concepts and develop 'incompatible definitions and uses of the same models'. In summary, concepts and models are often applied 'vertically' onto different national cases by single-country scholars. Lees suggests here that this 'vertical' process should be accompanied by more 'horizontal' analyses of the use of such concepts and models, to examine whether they are being applied in a coherent manner.

Second, Lees (*ibid.*: 1098) suggests that single-country scholars are prone to describing 'their' cases as 'culturally exceptional', when comparative analysis might indicate genuine similarities between their nation and others. Whilst Lees (*ibid.*: 1096) accepts the difficulties of moving beyond single-country studies, given the 'sunk costs [for researchers] of not only learning another language but also acculturating themselves into the warp and weft of their specialist country's political culture', he suggests that their frequent use of 'implicit . . . comparison across time' is a poor substitute for rigorous comparative analysis.

Conversely, other commentators have suggested that single-country case studies may be not only desirable but necessary as a means of generating knowledge and understanding of less-researched areas. Bradshaw and Wallace (1991) suggest that single-case studies should be used within comparative research in contexts where newly-researched or unique situations are being investigated, and where existing theories are unlikely to offer much explanatory purchase.

This book focuses on research which explicitly compares policy processes, outputs and outcomes across two or more units (generally, but not exclusively, different countries). Readers should, however, be aware that some single-country studies, and studies which draw on findings from a range of different countries as part of a less formal comparison, are also viewed by some commentators as part of the comparative canon.

Comparing public policies in an interconnected world

A final, rather complex, question for comparative public policy concerns the extent to which the factors we use to explain differences across countries can be separated from international processes. Traditionally, domestic and international policy-making were seen as two separate realms, of 'low'/domestic politics, and 'high' politics/foreign affairs. Scholars examining these realms worked either within the field of political science and public policy, or in international relations, with little interaction between the two approaches. Each involved very different underlying assumptions about policy-making processes. Whilst domestically-focused scholars viewed societies as if they were hermetically sealed 'islands', international relations scholars, on the contrary, focused on the relationships between sovereign states (Ebbinghaus, 1998).

This division, and how it has started to break down since the 1970s, can be explained by considering the debate over the 'second image' of international relations. Kenneth Waltz (1954) suggested that the study of international relations was dominated by three 'images' of the causes of international politics. The first image focused on individual or psychological factors, the second on domestic political regimes, and the third on systemic (i.e. international-level) factors.

Waltz's 'second image' thus viewed domestic politics as influencing international politics, but not vice versa. This began to be questioned by comparative scholars who suggested the causal relationship between international and domestic policy-making could also flow in the opposite direction. According to what Peter Gourevitch (1978) described as the 'second image reversed', the structure of domestic policy-making could be viewed as a consequence of international politics – not just its cause. International-level trade policies, for example, could impact on the political power of different interest groups (Rogowski, 1986), particularly the balance of power between capital and labour (Hiscox, 2001).

Some comparative scholars have suggested, however, that simply 'reversing' causal attributions (by viewing international processes as influencing domestic policy-making, rather than the other way around) offers too simplistic a notion of how the domestic and international policy-making levels interact (Thatcher, 2007). Policy-makers are involved in two simultaneous 'games', one at the domestic level and one at the international, and will attempt to use each game in an effort to advance their preferences in the other (Putnam, 1988). Furthermore, involvement in the 'transnational game' may affect policy-makers' perceptions of what their preferences are in the first place (Callaghan, 2010: 577).

This insight has been a central concern of the developing literature on Europeanization. As Claudio Radaelli (2003: 34) puts it, 'European policy is not a mysterious deus ex machina situated "up there". Instead it originates from processes of conflict, bargaining, imitation, diffusion, and interaction between national (and often subnational) and EU level actors'. At the same time, developments at EU level may be drawn upon by domestic actors (Radaelli, 2003; Bulmer and Burch, 2001).

To conclude, whilst comparative public policy can be separated from the study of international relations, it often involves the examination of how domestic and international pressures interrelate to shape policy-making processes. Separating international from domestic pressures has become increasingly challenging, as interconnections between nations both deepen and multiply (a problem examined in detail in Chapter 14). Despite this difficulty, numerous scholars of comparative public policy have tenaciously attempted to provide a clearer understanding of how policy-making operates at national and international levels, and the relationship between these levels. Examples of this innovative research covering different policy sectors and nations are discussed at various points throughout this book.

Summary

❑ Comparing public policies across nations can help us understand policy developments and related phenomena in our own country, as well as in other countries.

❑ Whilst comparative analysis can be viewed as fundamental to all social research, some (but not all) commentators suggest that its methods and subject matter render it separable from other research strategies.

❑ Political scientists and sociologists have been comparing public policies for hundreds of years, although in the past comparison was often used as a means of legitimation for domestic policies, rather than for strictly scholarly purposes.

❑ Comparative public policy is defined here as the use of the comparative approach to investigate policy processes, outputs and outcomes.

❑ We can compare different nations, multinational groupings of countries, subnational units within countries, members of organizational classes, policy sectors, and time periods.

❑ The traditional distinction between the study of domestic policy-making (or 'low' politics), and international policy-making (or 'high' politics/foreign affairs) is starting to break down, with increasing numbers of studies in comparative public policy examining how domestic and international pressures on policy-making interrelate.

Chapter 2

Differences between Public Policies: An Introduction

Public policies currently have a significant impact on virtually everyone in both developed and developing societies, even if that impact is sometimes indirect. Everyone who has been born with the help of any kind of medical staff, received medical care at any time, gone to school, travelled or migrated into or out of a country, been employed, paid income or sales tax, or even just been required to leave a pub or bar at a certain time in the evening, has already had his or her life shaped by public policies.

This chapter examines in a systematic manner the differences that can arise between nations and sectors in the delivery of public policies in all these areas and beyond. First, it considers the *resources* drawn on in producing and implementing public policies, and then the types of *instruments* used by public policies. The most influential approaches which have been put forward to classify and categorize these instruments are summarized here.

This provides the context for the development of the approach used in this book. This text systematically examines five policy areas (economic, welfare, health, education and environmental policy) by separating them according to different types of policy instruments: the use of financial resources, authority, organization, and the provision of information. The chapter describes the way in which these different instruments can be categorized, and indicates the framework adopted within Chapters 3 to 7.

In addition to each of the empirical chapters considering the use of different policy instruments, the scope of public policy is also examined: who is involved in deciding on and delivering public policy, and how they interact with different policy instruments, as well as who is affected by public policy. This chapter provides some preliminary suggestions about the impact of different types of policy instruments on different groups of citizens. It also indicates how understanding the scope of public policy-making requires an awareness of the impact of public policy on non-nationals within the domestic territory, as well as populations beyond the national territory (through cross-border and international policy-making).

Finally, the chapter considers whether there are systematic differences between nations in their use of policy instruments and the involvement of certain groups of actors – whether we can discern what have been described as different *policy styles* in different countries, as well as whether the use of policy instruments has varied systematically between policy sectors and over time. As the chapter indicates, whilst some general trends can be discerned, it is difficult to generalize across different nations and sectors in their use of policy instruments. This necessitates the differentiated approach to analysing the functions and scope of public policy that is adopted throughout the rest of this book.

Public policy resources

Many attempts to classify and examine the development of public policies across nations and sectors have begun with a consideration of the *resources* available for public action. Harold Lasswell (1950) called on examples from China, the USA, and a range of other countries as part of his historical disquisition on 'the methods of the influential', the governing elites. For Lasswell, these elite methods included the use of 'symbols' (such as ideology and propaganda), 'violence' (wars, revolutions and assassinations), 'goods' (rationing, pricing, bribing), and 'practices' (governing procedures). Lasswell argued that these strategies used by governors involved the 'management' of certain 'value assets' – that is, certain resources. Similarly, the analysis of the 'technologies' involved in policy-implementation undertaken by Bardach (1980) rested on a categorization of four different resources: money, political support, administrative complexity and creative leadership.

One systematic survey cites ten different resources which are available to public policy actors (Knoepfel *et al.*, 2007). These comprise:

- *force* – the traditional prerogative of the state;
- the *law* – like force, 'mainly (but not exclusively) at the disposal of public actors';
- *personnel* or human resources;
- *money* or financial means;
- *information*;
- *organization* – the structures of interaction between policy actors and policy targets;
- *consensus* – 'between the political-administrative actors, the end beneficiaries and target groups with respect to the production modalities and contents of implementation measures (outputs)';
- *time* – covering the time that can be consecrated to make and enact policy, and the benefits that come from sustained involvement in a particular policy area;

- *infrastructure* – 'the 'property' resource: all of the tangible goods or property at the disposal of the different actors, including public actors, whether the actors are the owners of these goods or have acquired a right of use to them (by means of a rental contract, for example)';
- *political support* – 'or the 'majority' resource' (*ibid*.: 51–79).

In addition to these ten resources, *social* resources (individual actors' 'social status and relational networks') may also be important in explaining the power of individual public actors (Hassenteufel, 2008: 106). To an extent, these resources may be exchangeable: hence, for example, it may be possible for consensus to be lacking in relation to a particular area (such as French nuclear policy in the 1970s) but for policy actors to be able to access a sufficient amount of political support for the lack of consensus to be unimportant (Knoepfel *et al.*, 2007: 83).

How governments act: policy instruments

How these resources are put to use is the subject of a ballooning literature on policy instruments. Policy instruments can be defined as 'the set of techniques by which governmental authorities [or their proxies, acting on behalf of governmental authorities] wield their power in attempting to ensure support and effect or prevent social change' (Vedung, 1998: 21, 50). Numerous approaches have been developed in the classification of such instruments.

A bewildering number and variety of types of policy instruments have been identified. For example, the economist Kirschen and colleagues (1964) distinguished 64 different types of instruments. Howlett and Ramesh (2003: 88) suggest that the 'variety of instruments available to policy-makers to address a policy problem is limited only by their imaginations', although, of course, it is also limited by the resources available.

Some approaches divide groups of instruments up according to certain spectra – such as, for example, the degree to which they involve government expenditure or otherwise, are coercive and direct (focused on a specific population) or otherwise, or the degree to which they affect actors inside or outside government. Others have focused on the intended outputs of policy instruments as a means of classifying them. These approaches are, broadly, based on 'investigators' induction' – that is, they rely on the 'reconstructive logic' of analysts, often drawing on findings gleaned from policy-makers themselves concerning the matters they find important to take into account when designing policies (Linder and Peters, 1989).

Theories used elsewhere in the social sciences can also provide an underlying rationale for policy instrument classification. Such deductive, theory-based, approaches have drawn on public finance, social psychology and anthropology. These approaches are drawn upon to set out the four categories of policy instruments used to structure the empirical chapters in this book – use of financial resources, authority, organization, and the provision of information.

Policy instruments as coercive and direct

Some of the most intuitive approaches to classifying policy instruments place them in relation to ranges of what at least *appear* to be relatively simple and easily assessed attributes, such as the degree to which instruments involve government action (or are based on inaction, such as reliance on market mechanisms) (*ibid.*, 1989: 55), the amount of public expenditure they require (Mosher, 1980), the extent of government coercion they involve (Cushman, 1941; Doern and Wilson, 1974; Anderson, 1977), the extent of coercion they involve *and* the degree to which individuals are targeted by policy (directness) (Lowi, 1964; 1972), or the degree to which they focus on internal (governmental) or external (societal) targets (Bemelmans-Videc, 1998; Howlett and Ramesh, 2003).

The degree to which policy instruments involve the 'coercion' of target populations formed the well-spring of some of the earliest attempts at classification. For example, Robert Cushman's (1941) work on independent regulatory commissions in the USA focused on the degree to which government chose to regulate certain activities (or not), and then on the degree to which any regulation was coercive or otherwise. Robert Dahl and Charles Lindblom's (1976) classic analysis of methods of social organization also distinguished the 'intrusiveness' of policy instruments from other factors – such as the degree to which they depended on other structures for their success, such as state bodies or markets.

Perhaps the most sustained and influential development of this position, however, came from Theodore Lowi's analysis of public policy types which, for our purposes, can be assimilated to types of public policy instruments.

Lowi argued that initially three (1964), and then four (1972), categories of public policies could be discerned: distribution, regulation, redistribution, and constitutive policies. These four categories represented different combinations of two factors: the degree to which coercion was likely to occur through the policy instrument concerned, and the degree to which any sanctions which might be applied related either to individuals' characteristics or, alternatively, to the 'environment of conduct' of targeted groups. This latter dimension referred to the extent to which policy instruments focused explicitly on individuals and their behaviour, or, instead, changed the environment within which behaviour took place – that is, the *directness* of the policy instrument.

For example, Lowi (1972: 299) indicates how a 'general rule covering all fraudulent advertisers' could only be applied to 'individual advertisers' (applied to individual characteristics). In contrast, some other types of policy do not 'need to wait for a particular behaviour, but rather do not touch behaviour directly at all'. These include, for example, a 'minor change in the Federal Reserve discount rate'. This would significantly affect individuals' 'propensity to invest', but 'no official need know of' the existence of the people thus affected- the impact is entirely indirect and applies only to the environment of conduct.

For Lowi, *distributive policies* involve 'most contemporary public land and resource policies; rivers and harbors (pork barrel) programs; defense procurement and research and development; labor, business and agricultural 'clientele' services; and the traditional tariff'. Such policies are, for Lowi (1964: 690), 'virtually not policies at all but ... highly individualized decisions that only by accumulation can be called a policy', given that they are created in relation to specific schemes, individuals or groups. *Regulative policies* are similar to distributive ones as they affect individual conduct rather than the environment of conduct, but can involve significant coercion (e.g. through fines or disqualification). Such coercion is applied to specific individuals who have been found to be transgressing the regulation concerned; hence, regulation involves 'a direct choice as to who will be indulged and who deprived' (*ibid.*).

Redistributive policies have an immediate impact, as with regulation, but this impact relates to the environment of conduct (the position of an individual within a group), rather than to specific named individuals. Hence, its 'categories of impact' are 'much broader' than regulatory policies, 'approaching social classes' (*ibid.*). *Constitutive policies* relate to how all the other types of policy are enacted, and concern the creation and/or reorganization of institutions (Lane, 2000: 50). They operate as 'collective indirect constraints' which set the parameters for the use of public power (Hassenteufel, 2008: 11). An example of 'constitutive' policies would be the adoption of 'contractual' policies in France, which involve the agreement of contracts between the central state and local regions (*contrats de plan État-région*) (*ibid.*), or the creation in Britain of an Office for Budget Responsibility to offer expert assessment of government finances and the economy, ahead of budget announcements.

Although influential, approaches such as Lowi's, which focus primarily on the degree to which policy instruments involve coercion, can be challenged on a variety of fronts. First, relationships between individuals and governing authorities, and governing activities in general, are often not assimilable to coercion and restraint. One example of this is the creation of nationalized industries, whereby the state substitutes itself for either existent or non-existent private sector actors. These 'policies of direct intervention' are not easily characterized in terms of the degree to which they are 'coercive'. Similarly, public policy actors may often attempt not to coerce subjects but, instead, to persuade them of the merits of a particular type of behaviour or course of action (*ibid.*: 12).

Internal (and external) policy instruments

Rather than focusing on coerciveness and directness, policy instruments can also be classified according to the degree to which they focus on government itself, or on effecting change outside it – on society. This emphasizes Lowi's distinction between 'constitutive' policies and other types of policy. Hence, Howlett and Ramesh (2003) distinguish between 'substantive instruments' – which provide goods or services 'in society', and 'procedural instruments' – which 'alter aspects of policy deliberations' (see also Bemelmans-Videc, 1998: 3–4).

Some public policy studies have focused entirely on such 'internal', 'procedural' instruments. For example, William Gormley (1989) analysed the use of controls within the US bureaucracy. Gormley suggested that three types of controls could be distinguished: catalytic controls, or 'prayers', which use external catalysts to provoke particular responses (such as environmental impact statements, or freedom of information acts); coercive tools, or 'muscles', which directly impact on behaviour (such as orders or prohibitions); and hortatory tools (which use threats or persuasion to promote bureaucracies to comply with policy).

One other work which attempted to analyse the use of control within government comes from Christopher Hood's analysis within *The Art of the State* (1998). This draws on the anthropologist Mary Douglas's cultural theory and her conceptualization of 'grid' and 'group' principles of organization. Broadly, 'grid' 'denotes the degree to which our lives are circumscribed by conventions or rules', with 'high grid' referring to cultures strictly constrained by conventions and/or rules, as compared with 'low grid' cultures which lack such constraints. 'Group', on the other hand, 'denotes the extent to which individual choice is constrained by group choice, by binding the individual into a collective body' (Hood, 1998: 8). In 'high group' cultures, individuals are bound into collective bodies, as compared with 'low group', more atomistic, cultures.

Hood then details how different approaches to control tend to be adopted in public organizations subject to different mixtures of 'grid' and 'group' characteristics. Oversight as a method of control is common to hierarchical systems (high grid and group), competition is common to individualist systems (low grid and group), mutuality is common to egalitarian systems (low grid and high group), and forms of randomness are common to 'fatalist' systems (high grid and low group). Although Hood's approach is focused on internal government activities (public management), it has fruitfully been applied to a range of other governing activities (Verweij and Thompson, 2006), extending even to regulation to stamp out 'dodgy kebabs' (Lodge *et al.*, 2010).

Policy instruments as linked to different outputs

Instruments can also be classified according to their imputed or intended outputs. Hence, Elmore (1987) attempted to classify different strategies for government intervention, delineating different types of instruments as 'mandates' (providing rules which constrain behaviour), 'inducements' (providing funds to incentivize certain behaviours), 'capacity-building' (providing funds to enable agencies to act in order to change behaviour), and 'system changing' instruments (which change how agencies are organized to implement policies).

Schneider and Ingram's approach (1990) also arguably rests on a consideration of intended outputs – in particular, on the desired behaviour change from particular instruments, which itself rested on a view of the behavioural assumptions underlying each type of instrument (Salamon, 2002: 22; Stewart, 2009: 88). Schneider and Ingram delineate five different types of instruments: *authority, incentive, capacity, symbolic and hortatory,* and *learning*.

Authority tools, first, are 'statements backed by the legitimate authority of government that grant permission, prohibit, or require action under designated circumstances'. *Incentive* tools, on the other hand, 'rely on tangible payoffs, positive or negative, to induce compliance or encourage utilization' – such as sanctions or force (Schneider and Ingram, 1990: 515). *Capacity* tools, unlike the first two categories, 'assume that the target groups will have sufficient incentive or motivation to participate in the activity, or change their behaviour, if they are properly informed and have the necessary resources' (*ibid.*: 518). Hence capacity tools 'provide information, training, education, and resources to enable individuals, groups, or agencies to make decisions or carry out activities' (*ibid.*: 517), with examples including health warnings and training programmes (*ibid.*: 518).

Fourth, *symbolic and hortatory* tools attempt to persuade targets to act in a particular way by altering their views on what is right, wrong, just, and so forth. They operate by altering the perceived importance of an issue; the degree to which a particular policy is consonant with existing values, beliefs and preferences; and the extent to which it is associated with 'positive symbols, labels, images, and events' (*ibid.*: 519–20). An example of such a tool would include drug prevention policy, within which sports personalities have been used as spokespeople, to associate the 'just say no' message with popular, positively-viewed individuals and activities (*ibid.*: 519). Another interesting example comes from the realm of public apologies by governments for past wrongs, which are entirely symbolic in content (Lind, 2008).

Finally, Schneider and Ingram also isolate a category of *'learning tools'*. Whereas the four types of tools described previously all operate in contexts where target groups are either already persuaded, or unpersuaded, of the merits of certain behaviour, learning tools 'are used when the basis upon which target populations might be moved to take problem-solving action is unknown or uncertain' (*ibid.*: 521). Hence, these tools 'assume agencies and target populations can learn about behavior, and select from the other tools those that will be effective' (*ibid.*: 521). Such tools might include mediation or arbitration programmes, hearings, advisory boards or citizen panels (*ibid.*: 521–2).

Schneider and Ingram's approach acknowledges the fact that the properties of an instrument are effectively 'indissociable from the aims attributed to it' (Lascoumes and Le Galès, 2007: 6). However, it is arguable that the same instrument may be associated with different goals by different (or even the same) group. For example, Bezes (2007) examines the use, over time, of a special technique used to calculate the French civil service wage bill. Bezes (2007: 31) describes how this apparently innocuous and technical instrument was variously conceived of as a 'learning instrument', 'instrument of embryonic free-market policy', and 'instrument of social dialogue'. To put this in Schneider and Ingram's terminology, we would need to claim that the technique simultaneously constituted a capacity, an authority and a learning tool, which appears rather confusing.

Deductive approaches to policy instruments

Rather than attempt to classify policy instruments inductively – that is, to first collate information about the use of policy instruments 'in the real world', and then split the instruments up according to what has been revealed as their key characteristics, some authors have used what could be described as a 'deductive' approach. The deductive approach uses theories from other disciplines to specify the dimensions against which policy instruments vary.

A number of authors have adapted schemes from other fields to the study of policy instruments. For example, Richard Musgrave's analysis of three different branches of government (based on allocation, 'the provision of goods and services free or almost free of charge'; redistribution across the population; and stabilization, the conduct of macroeconomic policy), is based on the 'classical public finance approach to the public sector', which itself was based on existing accounting conventions (reported in Lane, 2000: 51).

Carrots, sticks and sermons

One influential approach which draws on pre-existing theory came from the Swedish political scientist Evert Vedung. Vedung's typology of policy instruments draws on the sociologist Amitai Etzioni's theory of different sources of control. For Etzioni (1961), there are three kinds of social control: coercion (again), economic assets and normative values. These kinds of social control can be argued to be 'universals, since they regulate behaviour with regard to three universal potential dysfunctions: interaction among actors who do not share ultimate values and solidary ties; the scarcity of means; and the imperfectability of socialisation' (*ibid.*, 1961: footnote 7).

Vedung (1998: 29) uses Etzioni's approach as a 'point of departure' to develop three categories of policy instruments: economic means, regulations and information – or, in common parlance, carrots, sticks and sermons. *Economic instruments* cover cash-related means such as incentives (transfers, grants, subsidies, reduced-interest loans, loan guarantees, and tax expenditures), loan insurance, investments, taxes, charges, fees, customs duties and tariffs, as well as in-kind incentives such as government provision of goods and services, private provision of goods and services under government contracts, and vouchers (*ibid.*: 43–4). *Regulations* can be unconditional or absolute, conditional with exemptions (as a safety valve for absurd situations), with permissions (concession, permits, licences, authorizations), or with obligation to notify (*ibid.*: 42). Finally, *information instruments* can include mediated transmission (via the television, radio, film, newspapers, printed matter, labels and posters) or, instead, involve interpersonal transmission (direct, personal advice; classroom or on-site education; workshops; conferences; demonstrations; exhibitions, investigation and publicity) (*ibid.*: 48–9).

Each category imposes particular relationships between governors and the governed. Hence, when regulated, 'the governee is obligated to do what the governor tells her to do'. When presented with economic inducements, 'the governee is not obligated to perform an action, but the governor may make action easier or more difficult by adduction of deprivation of material resources'. When presented with information, the relationship may be a 'persuasive' one (*ibid.*: 31). In contrast, the 'defining property of regulation is that the relationship is authoritative, meaning that the controlled persons or groups are obligated to act in the ways stated by the controllers' (*ibid.*: 31). Subjects are not, however, obligated to act in the same way when presented with economic inducements or with information (*ibid.*: 32).

Some of Vedung's descriptions of economic inducements and information go, however, beyond common-sense understandings of these concepts. Hence, he argues that 'economic instruments include non-monetary as well as monetary material resources', with a 'bump in the road to prevent motorists from speeding [constituting] an economic instrument just as a tax levied on gasoline is' (*ibid.*: 32–3) – despite the fact that no money changes hands when one crashes over a speed bump.

Similarly, he maintains that 'in public policy, government can also "inform" the citizenry about what is good or bad, right or wrong', rather than 'informing' being restricted to the transferring of accurate information, as might be expected to be the case (*ibid.*: 33).

Vedung (*ibid*: 35) argues that there is an essential difference between sticks *qua* regulations and carrots *qua* economic inducements: '*in principle* regulation is more constraining than tax, however high', because breaking a regulation will turn an individual into a 'law-breaker', whereas individuals remain 'law-abiding citizen[s]' if they 'take an action in spite of the fact that [they] must pay a tax if [they] do it'.

The significance of this distinction in practice may, however, be culturally-specific. Knoepfel *et al.* (2007: 66) point out that, in certain situations – particularly, for example, in some of the 'former Eastern-bloc countries' – 'over-regulation in the different areas of public intervention led to the absence of respect for law' and widespread non-compliance. As a particularly egregious current example, whilst extensive regulations have been promulgated and enacted to control lobbying in many nations, as in Lithuania, a miniscule number of lobbying associations comply with regulatory imperatives (Kalnins, 2005). It could therefore be argued that *in practice*, if not in principle, legal restrictions may be less (or at least, no more) constraining than economic measures.

It is also arguable that Vedung fails to consider how government can shape behaviour through its powers of organization – by, for example, introducing 'fencing to shape crowd behaviour' (Hood, 2007: 139). Vedung would presumably argue that, as with a road bump, such fencing constitutes an economic disincentive, and hence falls within the 'carrot' category of economic means. For example, a member of the crowd could, if they really wanted to, walk in the opposite direction to that promoted by the fencing, but it would take them much longer to go the same distance, and possibly involve some undignified leaping.

Other choice-shaping activities of the state are perhaps less easily dealt with in terms of economic incentives, however. The recent rise of behavioural economics and finance suggest the widespread recognition that individuals frequently act in irrational ways, and often contradict their economic interests (Ariely, 2008). A 'Consortium of Behavioral Scientists' has even been lauded with ensuring that President Obama won the 2008 US Presidential Election, by harnessing behaviours such as herd instinct to persuade voters to turn out (Grunwald, 2009). However, attempts by politicians to alter behaviour through the selective provision of information or advice have existed for a far longer period.

For example, governing authorities have often attempted to alter the way in which 'freely-chosen' options (such as health insurance schemes or pension plans) are presented to a largely ignorant and time-pressured public (Thaler and Sunstein, 2008). Such 'shaping' or 'nudging' activities could be described in terms of saving individuals' time (and thus constitute 'economic means', i.e. carrots), but this only applies to those cases where individuals would otherwise have made the effort to read all the small print of the hundreds of different schemes available, and hence save time by 'trusting government' to guide them towards appropriate options. After all these qualifications, Vedung's 'carrot' starts to take on a rather mangled shape.

Hood's 'NATO'

Perhaps the most commonly used approach to policy instruments based on existing analytical categories, however, is that developed by Christopher Hood, drawing on categories from control theories used within disciplines such as cybernetics – and, in particular, the difference between information-gathering and action (detecting and effecting). Hood (1986) suggests that public actors operate through the use of the information they have acquired by merit of being central actors ('nodality'), through their legal powers ('authority'), their financial resources ('treasure') and the formal organizations which they can use for their ends ('organization') – thus the acronym 'NATO' (see also Howlett and Ramesh, 2003).

Nodality-related tools include information provision and processing, the provision of advice, advertising, public information campaigns, and the setting-up and operation of policy inquiries, other research into policy areas, or expert bodies or commissions. These tools can affect both individuals' behaviour (e.g. public information campaigns might lead to individuals stopping smoking) and also alter perceptions about policy areas (for example, the findings from an official investigative commission on smoking could buttress views that smoking leads to poor health outcomes, and facilitate a ban on smoking in public places).

In contrast, *authority-related tools* include the use of so-called 'command and control' regulation (regulation undertaken by public bodies where sanctions for non-compliant behaviour are clearly specified in law, or regulations); what is often described as 'regulated self-regula-tion' or self-regulation which operates against the threat of government intervention; delegated regulation; and the creation of consultation processes which lead to some groups becoming 'insiders' to the policy process, whilst others remain 'outsiders'.

The category of *treasure-related tools* covers a number of other activi-ties traditionally closely associated with the state, which involve it in legit-imately transferring or extracting funds. Hence, such tools include the collection of tax and of charges or fees, use of the tax system for spending (such as through tax credits or incentives), the provision of grants and loans (if the interest paid on the latter is lower than the market rate), and the funding of non- or quasi-governmental actors (such as interest groups).

Finally, *organization-based tools* include the direct use of state, non- and quasi-state bodies to promote or induce certain behaviours. Hence, 'organization' covers reorganization and shaping of governmental and non-governmental activities, the use of family and voluntary organizations (either through shaping the conditions in which these organizations operate, or through refraining from action so these bodies can operate), and the direct provision of goods and services through publicly-owned or controlled bodies. This approach implicitly challenges typologies of policy instruments, such as Lowi's, which used coercion by government of other actors as a key variable.

Instead, according to this approach, governments create and sustain the conditions whereby markets can operate. This is obviously the case where governments act to secure property rights and contracts, and other systems of market protection, but even illegal or quasi-legal markets 'owe their existence to governments that attempt to ban the production and sale of these goods or services, thereby creating shortages that can provide high rates of return for those willing to risk punishment and imprisonment for their provision' (Howlett and Ramesh, 2003: 98).

This approach also, as mentioned, considers that government inaction can constitute a policy instrument, where this involves government declining from using its powers of organization to deal with a particular issue, so that other actors (e.g. families, or the voluntary sector) may step in. Vedung (1998: 24), however, argues that it is only appropriate to talk of policy 'tools' in situations 'when governments have decided to actively take action'. Certainly, in the face of pressure to act, governmental non-decision might appropriately be viewed as constituting a policy stance (Heidenheimer *et al.* 1990: 5, in Bemelmans-Videc, 1998: 2), and non-decision can, certainly, have a significant impact on public policy outcomes over time (Bachrach and Baratz, 1962). This book does view government non-decision, in the face of pressure to act, as a form of public policy, but accepts Vedung's cautions that such an approach can pose methodological difficulties for researchers (as considered in Chapter 14).

The approach adopted in this book

As will have been clear from the analysis above, different analysts have proposed a wide variety of means for classifying and understanding the use of different policy instruments. Christopher Hood suggests that this need not prevent us, however, from engaging in the analysis of policy instruments. He argues (Hood, 2007: 141) that differences in approach have arisen often because they 'reflect different purposes, they are ways of doing different kinds of analysis, rather than different ways of doing the same kind of analysis'. For example, some of the approaches focus on how government modifies citizens' behaviour – 'the "change-agent" perspective', whilst others examine the relationship between different institutions and organizations across and beyond government – the 'system' perspective (*ibid.*).

This book uses a policy instruments approach as a tool to aid the examination of public policies across nations and sectors. It separates four categories of policy instruments: those involving the use of financial resources, authority, organization and the provision of information. Innovatively, this book considers the use of each type of policy instrument across the five policy areas of economic, welfare, health, education and environmental policy. Examples of each category, drawn from the empirical chapters, are summarized in Table 2.1.

This book does not suggest, however, that different policy instruments can be easily or simply 'chosen' and 'adopted' by governments as part of a simple policy-making process. Comparing the different policy instruments used across sectors and nations does not entail that policy instruments are in some sense commensurable, or equally available to governments.

This book therefore eschews what has come to be known as the 'policy-design approach'. This approach was motivated by concern at policy-makers' alleged inability to choose the most effective instruments (Linder and Peters, 1984: 257). Theorists of policy design argued that the study of policy instruments was required to provide for policy-makers a 'good overview of the generic forms of [policy] instruments, because the issue of choosing the appropriate combination is one of the most intricate and important in strategic political planning' (Vedung, 1998: 21). Policy design thus constituted a 'pragmatic', 'political and technical approach to solving problems'.

According to this view, the role of policy-makers was to choose from their toolbox the most effective instruments for the job at hand (Lascoumes and Le Galès, 2007: 2–3; Kassim and Le Galès, 2010: 5–8). A deeper understanding of how instruments and the policy process 'works' would, thus, enable more effective intervention (Linder and Peters, 1984: 238). The policy design approach was hostile to sociological explanations of policy-making due to what is viewed as its lack of ability to support instrument choice. For example, for Linder and Peters (*ibid.*: 244), 'macrosociology' is 'as likely to support the shotgun or the sledgehammer as it is the scalpel' – and thus unhelpful.

There are, however, a number of potential problems with the policy design approach. First, its emphasis on choosing the most effective and efficient tools 'for the job' ignores the fact that the goals of any particular policy instrument may not be clear when it is adopted. In some cases, different political actors may support the use of one type of policy instrument without having any agreement on what the goals of policy should

Table 2.1 *Examples of each category of policy instrument*

	Economic policy	Welfare policy	Health policy	Education policy	Environment policy
Resources	Tax incentives to support favoured kinds of economic activity; funding of training activities; provision of public infrastructure	Non-contributory transfers (e.g. unemployment benefit; minimum income guarantees for pensioners)	Payment for publicly-funded health care services; grants to, e.g., pregnant mothers to improve nutrition	Payment for publicly-funded education services; provision of grants to, e.g., poorer learners to support school attendance	Funds to support national parks and conservation areas; tax incentives/grants to support sustainable activities (e.g. renewable energy)
Authority	Licensing and regulation of different economic activities; enforcement of property rights and contracts	Mandating contributory pensions; behavioural conditions imposed on receipt of transfers (e.g. workfare)	Banning of unhealthy behaviours (e.g. smoking); regulation of pharmaceuticals and the provision of health care	Imposition of attendance requirements; imposition of sanctions following poor performance	Banning and regulation of polluting activities; imposition of requirements on land- and ocean-use
Organisation	Creation of tripartite arrangements in corporatist systems; structuring of new markets (e.g. in privatized utilities)	Administration of welfare services and transfers; provision of public sector jobs	Administration and reform of public health care organizations and their interrelationships, including with the private sector	Administration and reform of public educational institutions; organisation of parameters of education (e.g. schooling duration)	Creation of markets in tradable permits (e.g. for carbon); creation of agencies to promote sustainability
Information	Provision of information to support consumer protection by helping tackle information asymmetries between consumers and producers	Provision of information about pension provision and job opportunities; shaping policy narrative surrounding unemployment	Public health campaigns to promote exercise and nutrition; provision of information on survival rates and other 'quality indicators'	Provision of 'school league tables' and inspection reports; provision of information on comparability of degrees across nations	Provision of 'scores' for area cleanliness (e.g. beaches); publication of information on environmental performance

be (Kassim and Le Galès, 2010: 8). This is complicated by the fact that instruments may often be portrayed by politicians in peculiar ways, for symbolic reasons. For example, President Roosevelt 'insisted on including a symbolic employee contribution in the Social Security program so that this program could be characterised as "insurance", which was easier to sell politically, even though it lacks most of the defining features of insurance' (Salamon, 2002: 22). Furthermore, a 'public policy does not necessarily make itself visible immediately by the observer' (Hassenteufel, 2008: 12), given that very often its various dimensions may not have been explicitly set out, including at whom it is targeted (*ibid.*: 13). Finally, it is often unclear which dimensions of a tool truly define it and are not merely peripheral (Salamon, 2002: 19–21).

Instead of following the 'policy design' approach, this book adopts what has been described as a 'sociological approach' to policy instruments. This acknowledges that, first, policy instruments are not necessarily readily available to policy-makers as part of some kind of 'toolbox' from which a selection can be made, related to the policy problem concerned. Instead, the process of choosing and operationalizing policy instruments, or 'instrumentation', emphasizes the frequent need to construct or develop policy instruments, rather than simply pick the most appropriate for the circumstances (Linder and Peters, 1989; Lascoumes and Le Galès, 2004, 2007; Kassim and Le Galès, 2010: 5).

Public policy instruments are devices that are 'both technical and social, that organize . . . specific social relations between the state and those [they are] addressed to, according to the representations and meanings' they carry (Lascoumes and Le Galès, 2007: 4). Particular policy instruments may change in form over time, often not as the result of explicit decision but through, for example, the gradual development and coordination of different interacting policy approaches and areas (Kassim and Le Galès, 2010: 11). Policy instruments may be chosen for a range of reasons (such as power dynamics or social relations) not necessarily connected to their effectiveness. Indeed, authors promoting this approach question the assumption that policy instruments are necessarily chosen as means to achieve a particular goal, since in some cases, the consequences of policy instruments for politics and policy can change (in both unintended and intended ways) over time (*ibid.*: 7–8; Bezes, 2007: 50; Palier, 2007). As such, policy instruments themselves can be seen as constitutive of policy, rather than merely a means of achieving a predetermined goal.

Adopting this more sociological approach requires acknowledging that, in order to understand policy instrument choice and use, we need to go beyond efficiency considerations to consider both the political context and the role of policy instruments as part of governing institutions. This book therefore disaggregates and analyses the ways in which certain ideas, institutions and interests have impacted on public policies, and the policy instruments used to implement them (in Chapters 8, 9 and 10), as well as considering patterns in policy instrument use across nations and within sectors, in the chapters on different policy areas (cf. Peters, 2002).

Trends in the use of policy instruments

Trends across nations

It is arguable that the use of certain policy instruments has changed over time, particularly within the OECD. For example, Lowi (1964: 689) suggested that redistribution and regulation only came into play in the USA from the mid-1800s onwards, with 'constitutive' policies following later. Robert Dahl, in his influential work *Polyarchy* (1971: 66–77), argued that the use of coercion within public policy would diminish as (he suggested) power would become more diffused through the socio-economy.

More recent analyses have broadly agreed, suggesting that 'new' or 'newer' policy instruments are being increasingly invoked, such as 'constitutive' policies and those based on incentives (Hassenteufel, 2008: 15). Some suggest that the extent of such instruments has been so significant that governing arrangements should be described as 'regulatory states', which intervene 'more indirectly than directly', acting 'more in interaction with non-state actors' than on their own. Under this conception, the traditional activities of the so-called 'positive state' (such as taxation and public spending) are less likely to be used, whilst social, economic and administrative regulation are, instead, more frequently adopted as levers of government action (*ibid.*; Majone, 1997). The extent to which nations have developed towards this type of 'regulatory' state is examined in greater detail in Chapter 10, which considers the role of institutions (and, hence, *inter alia*, of rules and regulations) in shaping policy-making.

Policy developments since the 1980s have, certainly, led to the increasing use of indirect policy instruments, relying on non-state actors 'to deliver publicly financed services and pursue publicly authorised purposes' (Salamon, 2002: 2). These non-state actors are not only required to implement policies, but also in many cases, to exercise 'discretion over the use of public authority and the spending of public funds' (*ibid.*: 2). Salamon (*ibid.*: 1, 2) argues that, whereas in the past 'government activity was largely restricted to the direct delivery of goods or services by government bureaucrats, it now embraces a dizzying array of loans, loan guarantees, grants, contracts, social regulation, economic regulation, insurance, tax expenditures, vouchers, and more', constituting a 'revolution in the 'technology' of public action over the last fifty years'.

Many of these 'new' policy instruments are viewed as less 'interventionist' than traditional governmental tools. They typically rely on altering the incentives faced by individuals and private sector bodies, rather than introducing new rules to directly control their activities. One politically popular new approach to policy instruments has argued that governments should reorientate their activities towards 'nudging' or 'persuasion', rather than regulation. This approach, popularized by Thaler and Sunstein's book *Nudge* (2008), led to the setting up of a Behavioural Insights Team by the UK's coalition government in July 2010. Nonetheless, Thaler and Sunstein's central insight – that individuals and organizations do not operate in market situations as expected by theories of neoclassical economics, due to myopia and information and attention constraints – has received less political attention (Chakrabortty, 2010).

Other authors have implicitly linked the use of newer instruments to the development of govern*ance* as opposed to govern*ment*. Although not without its critics (Kjaer, 2011), Rod Rhodes's definition of 'governance' is used frequently. He argues that the term 'refers to self-organizing, inter-organizational networks characterized by interdependence, resource-exchange, rules of the game, and significant autonomy from the state' (Rhodes, 1997: 15).

The spread of govern*ance* thus implies a reduction in the centrality (to use Hood's terminology, the 'nodality') of the state as part of the policy-making and policy-implementing process (Rhodes, 1997). For example, Ringeling (2002: 588) differentiates 'horizontal tools' from 'vertical tools', the traditional tools of public action. Such 'horizontal tools' do not assume that 'government [is] an actor situated above other actors', nor even that 'a central point of governance [is] necessary'. 'Horizontal' tools include networking and other forms of interacting; public–private partnerships; voluntary agreements; and convenants. In a similar vein, Osborne and Gaebler's (1992: 31) breathless study of the 'reinvention' of government stated that no less than 36 'alternatives to standard service delivery' could be found at the point of writing across the USA – many of which involved a reduced role for 'traditional', 'centralizing' government.

Other authors are, perhaps, more sanguine about the significance of these 'new' tools. For example, Rittberger and Richardson (2003) detail how 'old style' regulation continues to dominate approaches within the EU, despite the apparent explosion in the use of 'new' policy instruments relying on economic mechanisms and persuasion. Similarly, Jordan *et al.* (2005: 493) note that not only have 'new' instruments failed to replace 'old' instruments in the field of environment policy, but also that so-called 'new' instruments (such as market-based instruments, eco-labels, environmental management systems and voluntary agreements), in their stress on 'less hierarchical exchange relationships', follow a long tradition of environmental policy-making in the Netherlands, France, Germany and Austria.

Trends within nations

Rather than examining trends in policy instrument use across different countries or sectors, it is also possible to consider trends within particular countries or sectors, over time. As is indicated in the empirical chapters, there is certainly a large degree of 'path dependence' in the use of different policy instruments across countries. For example, ex-Communist countries – where both population and politicians are more used to public policy-making and policy-implementation being concentrated in state-owned organizations – are clearly more predisposed to policies facilitated by extensive state ownership than the USA would be, for example.

In other nations, significant religious conflict may have led to the embedding of both norms and institutions promoting decentralized types of policy-making and implementation. An example of this comes from the development of 'pillarization' in the Netherlands. 'Pillarization' refers to a situation where there are clear distinctions between different groups in society, which hold to different comprehensive worldviews and/or religions (e.g. Calvinist/Dutch Reformed Church, Roman Catholic, or Socialist). With 'pillarization', these groups develop their own institutions, from schools to newspapers and social clubs to hospitals. In the Netherlands, successive governments actively supported many of these institutions, particularly where they formed part of the welfare state (e.g. education and health) (Salamon, 2002: 6). Another example comes from the German concept of 'subsidiarity', whereby the state was required to 'turn first to the "free welfare associations" to address social needs before enlisting state institutions' (*ibid.*).

Drawing on these insights, some authors have gone so far as to suggest that it is possible to discern different national 'policy styles', although as Knoepfel *et al.* (2007: 150) note, these attempts have not been 'altogether successful'. Richardson *et al.* (1982: 2), for example, compared 'policymaking and implementation styles' across a number of countries and sectors. They specified two dimensions across which policies might vary in their style across countries. One dimension was similar to Lowi's 'coercion' dimension – the 'government's relationship to other actors in the policy-making and implementing process', and whether this involved 'consensus or imposition'. The other dimension, however, considered a separate topic: the degree to which governments took an 'anticipatory/active attitude towards societal problems' or, alternatively, 'an essentially reactive approach to problem-solving' (*ibid.* 12–13).

Some cross-national trends in the use of instruments were identified. For example, 'most European countries' were finding it 'increasingly difficult to adopt an anticipatory approach to problem-solving', were subject to 'a high degree of sectorization of policy-making' and were 'finding that policy-making and implementing processes have to accommodate increasing numbers of increasingly active interest groups' (*ibid.*: 197). However, they acknowledged that the 'reality of policy-making and implementation is often too 'messy' for it to exactly fit our simple typology' (*ibid.*: 198).

Another attempt to apply this notion of policy style argued that despite the 'face validity of the concept' of policy styles, it did not prove 'itself to be very robust or effective' when analysing policy areas such as industrial policy and policies to counteract HIV and to regulate financial markets. National policy styles did not explain why particular approaches were adopted to similar problems in different nations. Rather, Bovens *et al.* (2001b: 647) suggested that it was more appropriate to view national policy styles as being produced by 'other political forces rather than [constituting] a more free-standing explanatory concept'. Nonetheless, policy styles might help explain the 'success of policies' and 'their political palatability' (*ibid.*). The use of particular instruments may itself have an impact on governing cultures, including the appropriateness of different instruments in the future (de Vroom, 2001: 526).

Other authors have investigated the degree to which particular sectors display the use of similar sets of policy instruments. This 'policy-sector approach' argues that, *inter alia*, we would be likely to see similar policy instruments adopted in the same policy sector across countries, *contra* the national 'policy styles' approach (Freeman, 1985; Bemelmans-Videc, 1998). A number of studies have been carried out to investigate whether there is indeed an identity, or even just similarity, in the methods adopted by different national public authorities in relation to specific policy sectors. Continuity and change in the use of policy instruments has thus been examined in relation to environmental policy (Rittberger and Richardson, 2003; Knill and Lenschow, 2005; Holzinger *et al.*, 2006); taxation (Radaelli, 2003); and social policy (Wincott, 2003), amongst other policy areas. Chapters 3 to 7 examine the 'policy sectors thesis' in detail, in the realms of economic, welfare, health, education and environmental policy.

The scope of public policies

By formulating and implementing public policies using different policy instruments, public actors not only shape the behaviour of different target groups (by changing the incentives for and barriers to certain types of activity), they can also affect the opportunities for different groups to exercise political power in the future. Lowi's work, referred to above, is often viewed as significant for concluding that 'policy' can determine 'politics' – that is, that the type of policy adopted could have a significant influence on the future of political contestation in a particular policy area (Howlett and Ramesh, 2003: 89). However, the use of certain policy instruments also affects the power of those involved in their creation and development.

Public policy actors

This book examines the activities of a range of different 'public actors' in numerous different policy fields across nations, and considers how these activities can be explained using different theoretical frameworks. The separation of 'public' from 'private' actors is a difficult endeavour. Patrick Hassenteufel (2008: 23) has argued that the concept of 'public policy' should be abandoned for that of 'public action', partly because public policies are becoming less and less 'state-centered'. Given the complexity of public activities in the contemporary world, on this reading it is no longer sufficient to focus on public actors, since many different, new actors and organizations have been brought into the process of policy-making and implementation.

However, this book follows Knoepfel *et al.* (2007: 28) in distinguishing public from private actors, and restricts analysis to the former. Public actors can be viewed as those who belong 'to the political-administrative system', or who otherwise have been granted the 'legitimation to decide or act on the basis of a delegation based on a legal rule'. Such public actors 'by proxy' might include, for example, trade unions or professional organizations which have been granted the authority to run insurance schemes by the state, partially privatized enterprises which fulfil public service missions (e.g. France Télécom), or non-governmental organizations (NGOs) or interest groups incorporated within powerful policy networks. Distinguishing between public and private actors does not imply that the activities of private actors are politically inconsequential. Vast numbers of studies have examined how private actors can influence policy-making without having been explicitly granted authority by governments to do so. Works from this corpus have examined private interests and policy-making in the USA (e.g. Heinz *et al.*, 1993), EU (e.g. Wallace and Young, 1997 or Knill and Lehmkuhl, 2002a), and at global level (Ronit and Schneider, 2000). However, for reasons of parsimony, this book's focus is restricted to those who are either part of the public policy-making and policy-implementing machine, or who have been granted authority by it.

Public policy actors may see their power boosted or diminished by the adoption of particular policy instruments. Groups may lobby for the introduction of instruments which enable them to influence programmes' 'postenactment evolution' (Salamon, 2002: 11) or, alternatively, which put blocks on the role of other, negatively-viewed actors in its future evolution (Knoepfel *et al.*, 2007: 44–5). Actors may have a strong preference for certain types of policy instruments, distinct from any views they may have about policy content.

Rittberger and Richardson (2003: 580) illustrate this in their discussion of industry groups' consistent support 'for enhanced use of economic instruments against "competitiveness-inhibiting", "command and control" regulation' in the environmental policy arena. As another example, Bezes (2007: 24) indicates how top French bureaucrats, faced with highly politicized issues around civil service pay, pushed for the adoption of a less visible, highly complex instrument, which indirectly increased their own power. The use of a highly opaque instrument, of course, also decreased the power of target groups to challenge policy in this area. The role of public policy instruments in affecting target groups, both domestically and abroad, is the subject of the next section.

Public policy targets

Inclusion and exclusion of different groups by public policies
Even public policies which ostensibly affect 'everyone' may still exclude certain categories of the population. As is considered in Chapter 4, 'welfare' policies have often failed to cover certain groups despite apparent universality, such as the lack of implementation of social security and wage protection for Aboriginal people in Australia (Kennett, 2001: 129), despite the fact that Aboriginal peoples were (naturally) citizens of Australia.

In addition, many nations have used restrictive naturalization rules to exclude certain groups from citizenship, and thus from benefiting from public policies. This applies, for example, to the large Korean population in Japan who, until 1982, could not join the Japanese pension scheme, and continue to be barred from holding public office (despite the fact that many are second- or third-generation migrants) (Kennett, 2001: 136). Debates over the conditions under which long-standing migrants can naturalize (and thus be able to participate fully in public life, with its associated rights and responsibilities) have raged in a variety of countries. In Germany, for example, the issue dominated elections in the late 1990s, following proposals from the federal government to enable 'dual nationality', whereby non-Germans could naturalize without losing their other citizenship (Turner, 2011). In some cases, however, rather than being barred from enjoying certain rights, ethnic minority groups may be able to exercise additional rights. For example, Inuit and Indians have been allocated sovereign status in Canada and, in theory, are able to negotiate directly with the federal government (rather than having to go through provincial governments) (Lightman and Riches, 2009: 51).

Different impacts on different groups

Public policies also obviously affect different groups in different ways, a fact which is often obscured because 'target populations' may not be clearly specified. Public policies which ostensibly have an equal impact across different groups may, in reality, affect different groups unequally. For example, given the concentration of British female employment in the public sector, across-the-board cuts in funding to the British public sector disproportionately affect women rather than men, even if this is not an explicit goal of the policy being promulgated.

Lowi suggests that political conflict is minimal in relation to *distributive* policies, due to the fact that it often involves comparatively small sums going to a very large number of individuals, communities or projects, whereas *regulation* is inherently conflictual due to the fact that it will inevitably excite the interests of different affected groups. In contrast, *redistributive* policies will, he suggests, only tend to provoke two sets of opinions, or 'two sides'; and these 'sides are clear, stable and consistent', reflecting the interests of labour and capital (Lowi, 1964: 692, 711). Similarly, Wilson (1980) argued that different policy types were associated with majoritarian, pluralist, elitist and clientelist politics, depending on the degree to which they concentrated benefits.

However, the degree of political conflict may depend not only on the type of policy, but also on its target. Even distributive policies are likely to result in political contestation, if these are targeted at 'unpopular groups' (Schneider and Ingram, 1993: 345). Regulatory policies need not lead to conflict if unpopular groups are targeted, rather than popular (*ibid.*) – for example, criminals and potential criminals, rather than business groups. Different types of instruments are, perhaps, more likely in relation to different populations – such that, for example, transfers to the better-off are normally implemented through less visible types of policy instrument, compared with transfers to serve 'redistributive' goals, which are accompanied with more public fanfare and publicity (Salamon, 2002: 37).

Jenny Stewart investigates this topic in detail in her analysis of 'tough' (coercive, sanction-based) and 'tender' (incentives, persuasion and capacity-building based) policies. She suggests (Stewart, 2009: 90) that the degree to which these types of policy are applied to different target groups will depend upon how they are viewed societally and politically. Further, the type of policies adopted will depend on decision-makers' views of the nature of human behaviour. If such behaviour is viewed as 'stemming from individual calculation and preference, independent of the environment in which the person was brought up', incentives or disincentive-based policies are likely to be invoked, whereas if behaviour is viewed as a 'product largely of' the 'environment in which the [target] person was brought up', policy will more likely be based on 'adaptation, learning and harm minimisation' (*ibid.*: 107).

Non-domestic targets of public policy

In addition to a country's public policies having an impact on its domestic population, they can also affect foreign nationals, either by virtue of foreigners entering domestic territory or due to the cross-border and international effects of certain public policies.

This potentially challenges images of governments as sovereign authorities over their domestic territories. From Max Weber's time onwards, policy analysts have defined the state as being able to monopolize the use of physical force in a specific territory. More recently, states have also been viewed as being able to monopolize the extraction of fiscal resources from that territory (Hassenteufel, 2008: 14). The concept of 'the state' has been very prominent within analyses of public policy, particularly those from continental Europe. Hence, for example, Yves Mény and Jean-Claude Thoenig (1989), in their book on public policies, focus on contributing to theories on the emergence and nature of the state, whilst Bruno Jobert and Pierre Muller's (1987) text on public policy-making is entitled *L'Etat en action* (*The State in Action*).

One policy area which has traditionally been closely associated with state sovereignty is control over national borders. Policies concerning immigration, apart from for purposes of asylum, largely remain the prerogative of national states (although some nations have voluntarily pooled their sovereignty over immigration, as in the European Schengen area). Whilst international bodies may have been highly active in immigration policy to promote policy learning and coordination, such impact has been mainly voluntary (Channac, 2006).

In many other policy areas, however, public policy decisions taken in one domestic context can have a significant impact elsewhere, regardless of the views of the 'receiving' country. This has occurred even in areas closely associated with government's prerogatives to promote internal security. For example, crackdowns on illegal activities in one nation (such as that waged by the Colombian government against its drug cartels) may merely displace such activities to other jurisdictions – as occurred with the subsequent shift of bandits into Venezuela, Brazil, Ecuador and Panama (McKinney, 1991: 244–5).

In addition to promoting the migration of domestic nationals into other jurisdictions, public policies undertaken in one country may promote the migration of people away from another territory. Examples of this come from successive UK governments' promotion of the use of foreign-educated medical staff within its National Health Service. Some have posited the existence of 'welfare tourism' between nation states or localities. The fear of this has in some cases led to reduced levels of public welfare (Schram and Soss, 1998), despite limited evidence that such 'tourism' genuinely exists (Clarke with Piven, 2009: 38; see also Morris, 1998).

Furthermore, when public authorities undertake activities beyond their own borders, there is no guarantee these will not have a domestic impact. Some would argue this was the case with information about British foreign policy being used to radicalize domestic terrorists. Less controversially, given the extent of global travel, few governments can guarantee that, in attacking another country, they will not be inadvertently attacking members of their own population (who might be in the targeted nation for reasons of tourism, education or business) (McKinney, 1991: 245).

Of course, public policies adopted in other nations may affect other countries in a variety of ways beyond population movements, ranging from economic impacts (as the recent financial crisis starkly attests), to environmental impacts (given the uncontainable nature of pollution), to the impact of policy learning on promoting alternative policy approaches (as it becomes easier and easier to learn from, and use, the example of how other nations 'do things').

Aside from the impact of these cross-border pressures, examined in greater detail in Chapter 12, traditional assumptions that governing authorities will be sovereign over their domestic territories can be qualified, given the development of multinational forms of governance, as noted in Chapter 1. Even the ability of states to monopolize force within their borders, for example, has long been circumscribed as a result of international conventions, such as the Geneva Conventions enacted to protect non-combatants and prisoners of war following World War II, as well as treaties and conventions covering trade (such as the World Trade Organization, European Union, NAFTA, and Mercosur).

The interpretation of such conventions and treaties by different states has sometimes been highly controversial. For example, some attacks by British forces on Iraq were argued to have been contrary to the Geneva Convention as they concerned non-military targets, a claim the British government vigorously denied. Another interesting example comes from the US embassy, which has refused to pay the London congestion charge by claiming that it constitutes a tax, which contravenes the Vienna Convention on Diplomatic Relations – an interpretation which has been vigorously denied by successive London mayors.

Despite these caveats, as a result of international-level agreements, it is arguable that modern states no longer exercise a complete monopoly of control over their domestic populations – limiting the scope of national public policies and leading to a 'multilateralisation' of public action (Petitville and Smith, 2006: 362). The field of 'global policy studies', 'the study of international interactions designed to deal with shared public policy problems', focuses on this process (Nagel, 1991: xiii). 'Shared policy problems' include transboundary problems (such as wind- or water-borne pollution, or migrant populations) and common property problems (such as oceans, Antarctica, or the atmosphere). Soroos (1991: 4) argues that 'global' policies have a twofold characterization: they are subject to concern 'throughout much of the world', and they are, or are likely to be, 'taken up by one or more international institutions', such as the UN. Such global policies tend to involve the definition and implementation of global regulations or the creation of 'programs administered by international agencies' (*ibid*: 12).

Aside from dealing with 'shared policy problems', public authorities also engage in the promotion of their nation's own interests, interests which may or may not be shared with other countries, through the mechanism of foreign policy. Lowi argued against including foreign policy within his typology of public policies, for two reasons. First, he felt this would 'overly extend' his analysis, making it less parsimonious. Second, and more substantially, he argued that foreign policy-making was substantially different from other policy areas, precisely because of the fact that it was subject to international pressures. (Rather amusingly in comparison to the balance of global power at the time of writing, Lowi attested that 'foreign policy-making in America' was 'only a subsystem', as 'Winston Churchill, among other foreigners, has consistently participated in our foreign policy decisions'). Lowi (1964: 689, footnote 17) did maintain, however, that he would include within his scheme any 'aspects of foreign and military policy that have direct domestic implications'.

Others have resisted this approach, suggesting that 'external relations' should be included within the scope of public policy analysis (Menon and Sedelmeier, 2010: 76). Menon and Sedelmeier argue that, whilst there are characteristics of foreign policy which 'distinguish it from other sectors', this 'is true, at one level or another, of all sectors' (*ibid.*). Furthermore, the analysis of public policy and the study of international relations are becoming increasingly similar – both in terms of their content and the research methods they adopt – and a useful cross-fertilization is occurring between the two disciplines (Petitville and Smith, 2006). However, for Petitville and Smith, '[c]onvergence is certainly not fusion' between public policy and international relations, not least since many of the most important animating questions for each discipline remain distinct (*ibid.*: 362).

This book follows Petitville and Smith by distinguishing foreign policy from global, regional, national and local public policy. Foreign policy is, therefore, not singled out as an area to be investigated in the empirical chapters, although its influence is examined within the text where relevant. For example, changing policies towards entitlement for those without domestic citizenship is considered in Chapter 4 on welfare. As mentioned in Chapter 1, this book acknowledges the fact that public actors are frequently involved in two simultaneous 'games', at both the domestic and international levels; and that domestic and international pressures interrelate to shape policy-making processes, even in areas which on the surface may appear relatively insulated from exogeneous forces.

Conclusion

Public policies are delivered in a wide range of ways across nations and sectors. This chapter has delineated the resources available to public policy-makers and the different ways in which they can use these resources – that is, the different policy instruments available to them. Policy instruments can be analysed as more or less coercive, and more or less targeted at specific people; as affecting governments themselves, or external actors; or as linked to different policy outcomes. Alternatively, different types of policy instruments can be classified using theories drawn from other disciplines, such as sociology (as with Vedung's 'carrots, sticks and sermons') or anthropology/cultural theory (as with Hood's 'NATO').

This text examines how four different types of policy instruments are used (those relating to the use of financial resources, authority and organization, and to the provision of information) across five policy sectors. As is indicated throughout the book, the use of different policy instruments in different fields depends not only on their efficiency but also on factors such as the interests, ideas and institutions which form the policy context.

Whilst some broad trends are discernable across different countries in the use of policy instruments (particularly, moves towards more indirect instruments), there is less evidence that specific 'policy styles' have developed in different countries. The notion that different policy sectors in different nations are characterized by the use of similar policy instruments is examined in the empirical chapters which now follow.

As well as considering how public policies are made and delivered, this chapter has also considered who is involved in this process, and who is affected by public policies. Whilst we are all, to some extent, affected by public policies, the extent of this effect can depend on a variety of factors, from citizenship status to gender and other attributes. Whilst we most often think of public policies as affecting domestic populations, they can also impact on foreign populations. Partly for this reason, the line between studies of public policy and those of foreign policy is becoming increasingly thin – as is clear from the rest of this text.

As mentioned, Chapters 3 to 7 examine five policy areas: economic, welfare, health, education and environmental policy. After introducing each policy area, each chapter examines the use of different policy instruments, and their scope, in these areas across a wide variety of countries. It then considers theories which attempt to explain the use of such policy instruments – for example, those which claim that convergence is occurring, and those which would suggest that we are likely to see continuing divergence across nations. This is preliminary to a detailed discussion of the various influences on public policy-making, covered in the subsequent chapters.

Summary

❏ There are a wide variety of policy instruments which governments can draw on, depending on political, economic and social circumstances.

❏ Policy instruments can be more or less coercive and direct in their impact. They may be targeted at government itself, or at individuals and organizations outside it.

❏ This book examines how governments use four different types of policy instruments: those involving the use of financial resources, authority, organization and the provision of information.

❏ Some authors have detected a transnational trend away from the use of taxation and spending as levers of public policy-making, and towards the use of indirect methods of policy-making and delivery – such as the provision of incentives and use of regulation.

❏ There is continuing debate over whether different national 'policy styles' can be identified. Whilst some argue for the existence of national specificities in policy processes, others claim that similarities are more evident between policy sectors (e.g. between different nations' health or education systems) than across all of a nation's policy sectors.

❏ Public policies, and the policy instruments used to implement them, can affect different groups in different ways. This impact can be explicit, through the targeting of certain groups, or implicit.

❏ Even ostensibly 'domestic' policies can affect people and organizations based in different countries.

Chapter 3

Economic Policy

Economic policy is often separated from broader discussions of public policy, due to disciplinary barriers between economists and policy analysts. Yet, in all developed nations, 'economics is married, if only at common law, to politics' (Dahl and Lindblom, 1976: xlv). This is, first, because of the continuing influence of states on economic activity, both within and beyond domestic borders. The extent to which competitive markets can arise, consolidate and grow in the absence of (predominantly state) authority has preoccupied political economists for decades (see Hayek, 1988; and Polanyi, 2001 [1944], for contrasting views). Regardless of this, it remains indisputable that, even in those nations traditionally viewed as following a '*laissez-faire*' approach to economic policy, governments and their bureaucracies play an essential role in funding, controlling, organizing and informing economic activity. As this chapter will show, this remains the case despite the influence of globalization.

More than perhaps any other area of policy, economic policy decisions can have wide repercussions on other policy areas. This is because successful (or unsuccessful) economic policies can increase (or reduce) government capacity to finance other policies, by impacting on the ability to raise revenue through taxation. Some have argued that economic policy also differs from other types of policy because its goals are almost universally accepted, as well as the means to achieve them. For these theorists, 'full employment, stable prices, and steady levels of economic growth' can be readily measured and are generally supported as policy aims (Heidenheimer *et al.*, 1990: 134). Others would suggest that whilst '[o]ther things being equal' such goals are indeed 'preferred' by society, in practice, 'these goals are not all positively related' (Keech, 1980: 345). The bulk of material presented in this chapter supports the latter view, and indicates that amongst developed capitalist nations there is apparently considerable divergence concerning the appropriateness of certain economic policies, even if convergence can be observed in some areas.

This chapter focuses on a wide range of economic policies. It examines government use of financial resources (the provision of tax-funded services; taxation itself; tax expenditures), of authority (the prescribing of certain economic activities; the regulation of economic activity and of workers' pay and conditions; controls on flows of goods, services, and workers across domestic borders), of organization (planning; public

49

ownership; the creation of economic policy institutions), and information (the provision of information and advice to the public; and the generating of information to inform policy-making). As such, it goes beyond the examination of 'macroeconomic' policy (attempts 'to control economic aggregates through the manipulation of economic demand') to cover areas traditionally viewed as 'industrial policy' (Grant, 2002: 1).

The context: theories of economic policy development

Until the 1930s, control of the public purse – that is, government use of taxation and spending – was 'regarded simply as a means of paying for the government's own operation, not of regulating overall economic activity' (Heidenheimer *et al.*, 1990: 135). From the end of World War II onwards, however, the influence of public authorities has vastly increased, as the scope of their economic ambitions has widened. This occurred in different ways in different nations, but a clear trend could be discerned up to the mid-1960s of enormous growth in public spending and moves to determine directly 'a large segment of each nation's economic activities' (Shonfield, 1965: 66).

The economist John Maynard Keynes and his followers were successful in advocating an activist role for government in 'smoothing out' the business cycle, to try to reduce the impact on employment and growth of 'booms' and 'busts'. What is known as 'counter-cyclical demand management' – higher taxation and less spending in times of plenty, and vice versa during economic downturns – dominated policy approaches in many countries during the 1950s, 1960s and into the 1970s. Policy-makers during this period were keen to focus on the maintenance of full employment through economic cycles (*ibid.*: 63). Their task became seen as an increasingly technical one, using Keynesian demand-management techniques to achieve 'sustained growth', with 'everyone' potentially 'win[ning]' from the continually strong, and largely stable, patterns of economic growth experienced in most developed nations (Heidenheimer *et al.*, 1990:132, 162).

The Keynesian consensus did not last. The oil price crises of the 1970s and increasing inflation in the 1980s led to a shift in policy priorities away from combating unemployment and towards fighting inflation (*ibid.*: 162, 166). This radical change in policy priorities was also induced by the increasing popularity of 'monetarist' views of economic policy amongst both professional economists and many politicians (Hall, 1993). The 'monetarist revolution' of the late 1970s and 1980s suggested that, rather than focusing on demand, governments should attempt to control the supply of money as a means of preventing inflation, which they argued was harmful to long-term growth.

Accompanying these developments was the widespread exhaustion of socialist forms of economic organization. With the demolition of the Berlin Wall, the 'Cold War dominoes were falling in the opposite direction and, before long, conservative forms of teleology were announcing the final triumph of capitalism's market order' (Peck and Theodore, 2007: 731). Or at least, that was the case until the US subprime crisis grew from 2007 into a credit crunch, then a credit crisis, and finally, triggered worldwide recession. The crisis highlighted not only the inadequacy of purely nationally-based regulatory systems in dealing with 'systemic' financial risks (Claessens *et al.*, 2010: 289), but also the unpredictability of contagion. In a situation where 'much of how crises start and spread remains unknown' (*ibid.*: 271), governments have taken a range of approaches to stimulate domestic growth. This underlines the continuing 'diversity ... at the very heart of a world that has abandoned the need for closed, encompassing [political and economic] systems' (Dahrendorf, 1999: 15).

The influence of interests

A variety of approaches have suggested that economic policies in different nations reflect the influence of different interests. These can be roughly categorized into those prioritizing producer interests and politicians' interests.

The ad hoc influence of producer interests

One particularly stark contrast between different nations' economic policies is drawn by Mancur Olson (1982) in *The Rise and Decline of Nations* – 'RADON'. Olson attempted to explain what he described as the 'national failure' of Britain, pointing out that since 'World War II it has had one of the slowest growth rates of the developed democracies. Its growth rate has indeed lagged behind that of most developed countries since the last two decades of the nineteenth century' (*ibid.*: 3). In contrast to Britain, at that point, stood France, Germany, and Japan, all of which were growing economically. Olson's (1963) explanation for the divergence in economic performance hinges on politicians' responses to organized groups, relating back to his 'theory of collective action'.

Very briefly, Olson had suggested that only certain interest groups would be able to attract members, those which could provide 'selective incentives' from which only members would benefit. These could relate either to side benefits of membership (e.g. cheaper insurance and legal advice for trade union members), or to the effects of campaigning by the group concerned. Not all groups can provide selective incentives from campaigning in this way. A campaign group trying to push for clean air, if successful, would benefit all citizens, regardless of whether they had participated in its campaign. In contrast, a trade association which persuaded the government to erect barriers to entry to new entrants from outside the association *would* be able to provide benefits to each individual member of the association which could not be enjoyed by anyone else.

Olson then claims that certain countries, including Britain, had become dominated by interest groups intent on extracting these kinds of excludable benefits for their members. Such interest groups were not interested in increasing the overall size of the 'economic pie' (i.e. in increasing economic growth), but only their share of the 'pie' (i.e. their 'rent' from the economic system). It was, Olson claimed, possible for interest groups to become sufficiently large and 'encompassing' that their interests paralleled those of society as a whole (e.g. in the case of the large trade union and business federations that characterized some corporatist systems). However, Olson maintained that particularly high numbers of relatively small interest groups appeared to be dominating policy-making processes in nations which had experienced societal and political stability, whereas they had been largely 'swept away' in nations subjected to radical upheaval. Hence the relative success of economic policy-making in Japan, Germany and France compared with Britain and the USA.

Olson's analysis appears to cohere curiously with the approaches taken by many politicians during the 1980s, who aimed at reducing the power of organized groups within the policy-making process (not least in Thatcherite Britain). However, many of his prognoses have been undermined since RADON's publication. Olson described the USA as 'sclerotic', yet it grew faster than Japan throughout much of the 1980s and 1990s, with the latter being subject to a profound economic slowdown. In any case, Olson's characterization of Japan as relatively free from group influence can be challenged. As discussed below, following World War II successive Japanese governments worked intensively with specific large enterprises in high technology sectors in order to prepare them for global competition (Heidenheimer *et al.*, 1990: 171).

One area where producer interests might be expected to be particularly influential in determining economic policy is that of trade policy: the use of subsidies, tax exemptions, low-interest loans, tariffs and quotas to improve the position of domestic producers. Unlike capital, workers in many trade-exposed industries are relatively immobile, and might be expected to press politicians for protective measures to ensure that levels of domestic production are maintained (Rogowski, 1987). However, different industries in different nations are subject to differing levels of trade protection. The UK cutlery industry, for example, enjoyed an effective tariff rate of 30 per cent throughout much of the 1960s and 1970s, which was far higher than that in Germany and the USA, despite the fact that cutlery was also produced in both those nations. Support for the cutlery industry in the UK was particularly surprising, given the small size of the industry (e.g. compared with British shipbuilding, which had received comparatively little state support when faced with foreign competition), and the relatively invisible and badly organized workforce.

Fiona McGillivray (2004) explains this by demonstrating that the interests of producer groups are important, but their influence is mediated through particular institutional parameters, which differ between nations. British governments were predisposed to aid domestic producers through trade policy in circumstances which might affect their re-election. Industries would enjoy protection, on this analysis, when they were situated in marginal constituencies. The British cutlery industry was concentrated overwhelmingly in Sheffield which, at the height of tariff protection in the 1970s, was home to a number of seats which alternated in political control.

In contrast, the German cutlery industry was based in Solingen, which was not politically a strategically important area in Germany. Unlike the importance of marginality for first-past-the-post systems, in strong-party PR systems, such as that in Germany, the political importance of areas differed according to whether they were strongholds of support for a potential governing party, which could be the main governing party or one of its coalition partners.

Finally, in weak-party majoritarian systems, such as that in the USA, the importance of particular constituencies to powerful office holders helped explain the protection of certain industries through trade policy. Hence, the leather footwear industry enjoyed high levels of protection. It was based in Missouri and Maine, and senators from both those states sat in strategic positions on relevant committees (*ibid.*).

The structural influence of producer interests I: corporatism
One systematic approach to the examination of the influence of interest groups on economic policy is provided by analyses of corporatism. The study of corporatism is at once descriptive (which nations are corporatist), analytical (why certain nations become corporatist, and how corporatism operates), and normative (whether corporatism should be adopted in certain nations). This section considers corporatism as a *descriptive* tool for categorizing nations' economic policy-making structures.

Corporatism was influentially defined by Schmitter (1974: 93–4) as 'a system of interest representation in which the constituent units are organised into a limited number of singular, compulsory, noncompetitive, hierarchically ordered and functionally differentiated categories, recognised or licensed (if not created) by the state and granted a deliberate representational monopoly within their respective categories in exchange for observing certain controls on their selection of leaders and articulation of demands and supports'. An alternative, but similar, definition comes from Grant (1985: 3–4), who describes corporatism as 'a process of interest intermediation which involves the negotiation of policy between state agencies and interest organisations arising from the division of labour in society, where the policy agreements are implemented through the collaboration of the interest organisations and their willingness and ability to secure the compliance of their members'.

Both definitions share three features. First, corporatism involves the stable penetration of the state by organized groups. Unlike pluralist systems, where interest groups may participate in policy-making on a case-by-case basis, with corporatism certain interest groups have a sustained relationship with the state. Second, corporatism involves what is described as 'intermediation' – interest groups represent their members' interests to government, but this is in exchange for observing certain controls on their activities and promoting any collectively-agreed measures such as wage restraints. Finally, the interest groups involved in corporatism are representative of labour (trade unions) and capital (business), rather than other interests.

Nations still arguably falling into the 'corporatist' camp include Germany (at least, in relation to certain industries – such as metalworking), Switzerland, Denmark, Sweden, and, for some, Japan – sometimes qualified as mid-level corporatism (Bruno and Sachs, 1985) or corporatism-without-labour (Wilensky and Turner, 1987). Corporatist arrangements have historically proved particularly important in smaller, trade-exposed nations where it is both relatively easy for 'social partners' (the representatives of capital and labour) to build up professional relationships with each other, and where a distinctive national interest can be identified and promoted through collective action (Katzenstein, 1985). 'Tripartism' – a rather 'weak' form of corporatism involving consultation with interest groups, if not sustained direct influence – arguably obtained in Britain throughout the 1960s and 1970s, before the status of trade unions was reduced by the Thatcher governments (Grant, 2002: 4).

The structural influence of producer interests II: power resources
Rather than focusing on the structures through which 'social partners' are incorporated in decision-making (or not), a different approach stresses the extent to which workers' interests are reflected in governing parties or coalitions. This 'power resources' approach suggests that leftist parties will adopt distinctive approaches to economic policy-making, based on their linkages with the trade union movement. Although accorded less attention in the literature (Allan and Scruggs, 2004), right parties from this perspective would be expected to adopt policies which favour the interests of capital, particularly investment capital. This echoes debates within welfare policy (see Chapter 4), within which theorists such as

Esping-Andersen (1990) have linked patterns of welfare state development with trade union and left party influence. Implicitly, power resource theories suggest there is some type of trade-off between equality and efficiency (Okun, 1975). They suggest that left parties will prioritize reducing unemployment even if this comes at the expense of higher inflation (at least, for the short term), whereas right parties will be significantly more tolerant of unemployment and determined to reduce inflation (Heidenheimer *et al.*, 1990: 168).

The evidence on the influence of different types of partisan control on economic policy-making is mixed. Certainly, until the 1980s, most research suggested that left parties were more likely to prioritize reducing unemployment in government (Korpi, 1983). This did not necessarily result in lower growth rates, however – but sustained growth was most frequently observed in situations where left parties in government rested on strong, encompassing trade union movements. Left parties without such extensive linkages to the workforce were not as successful (Lange and Garrett, 1987; Garrett 1998b; see also Swank, 2002).

It is arguable that the power resources perspective has become less relevant with the advent of 'third way' social democratic parties committed to lowering inflation and focused on the use of active labour market policies (see Chapter 4) rather than Keynesian demand management as a means of reducing unemployment. Furthermore, numerous countries

Figure 3.1   *Trade union density rate, 2002 and 2008*

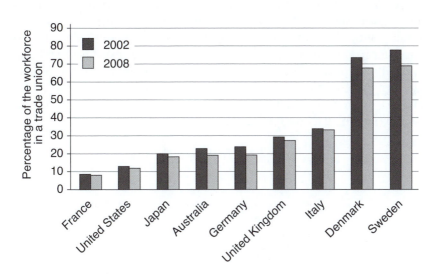

Source: OECD (2011a – StatLink): 162.

subject to extensive right-wing control of government experienced high inflation as well as depressed rates of growth during much of the 1970s and 1980s (including the USA and Britain) (Heidenheimer *et al.*, 1990: 169). Regardless of the influence, or otherwise, of left-party control on economic policy-making, it is generally accepted that the main 'resource' for left party power, the trade union movement, is reducing in power in most nations. Figure 3.1 indicates the fall in trade union membership in selected countries between 2002 and 2008. Chapter 8 considers power resource theory in greater detail with reference to its focus on labour interests.

Politicians' interests and economic policy-making

As mentioned at the start of this section, some analyses have viewed politicians' interests as important shapers of economic policy. One particularly influential approach argues that economic policy-making is dominated by politicians' interests in being re-elected. This will lead them to expand the economy in the run-up to elections, using the methods available to them (lowering taxes; increasing spending), only for the new government that is subsequently elected to have to act to contract the economy to prevent inflation (increasing taxes; reducing spending) (Schumpeter, 1939; Nordhaus, 1975). This approach, known as the 'political business cycle', rests on a number of assumptions: that voters choose who to support on the basis of their economic performance, particularly on the reduction of unemployment; that governments can actually manipulate the economy in this manner; and that politicians are primarily motivated by the desire for re-election when deciding economic policy. Political business cycles will inhibit growth over the longer term as bursts of inflation eventually reduce investment and thus productive capacity, and as the 'stop–go' cycle produces uncertainty (Keech, 1980: 345). This approach assumes that unemployment and inflation are locked in an adversarial relationship, as indicated by the 'Phillips Curve' displayed in Figure 3.2:

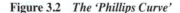

Figure 3.2   *The 'Phillips Curve'*

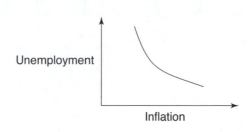

Despite the intuitive attractiveness of this approach, most studies have suggested that whilst some governments may, on occasion, stimulate the economy prior to elections (the US government's tax cuts in 1984 providing a prime example), generally there is no 'systematic tendency' towards this (Heidenheimer *et al.*, 1990: 163). Furthermore, from the 1960s onwards it was evident that inflation could persist alongside low growth and relatively high unemployment – what is described as 'stagflation' – rather than their being always negatively correlated.

Varieties of capitalism

The 'varieties of capitalism' approach to explaining differences in economic policies across countries rejects traditional analyses' focus on interests. It places firms at the centre and suggests nations can be differentiated according to the way in which they deal with coordination challenges for firms. Firms need to coordinate their activities in five spheres: industrial relations, vocational training and education, corporate governance, inter-firm relations and their relations with their individual employees.

The 'coordination problems' that arise in each of these spheres are solved in different ways in the two types of capitalism distinguished by this approach: 'liberal' and 'coordinated' market economies ('LMEs' and 'CMEs', respectively). The manner in which each of the five 'coordination problems' is solved has knock-on effects on the others. Hence, there are 'institutional complementarities' between, for example, the system of worker training (undertaken by firms in CMEs, by workers themselves or government in LMEs), the system of labour relations (the relatively expensive cost of hiring and difficulty of firing in CMEs, easy hiring and firing in LMEs), and the financing systems used in each country ('patient' capital in CMEs, enabling the long-term development of specific industries; 'short-term' financing in LMEs, privileging adaptability).

'Complementarity' refers then, here, to the presence, or efficiency, or one kind of institution increasing the returns from, or efficiency, of one kind of institution (Hall and Soskice, 2001: 17). Examining these coordination problems, and how they were resolved, helps explain policy patterns in a variety of sectors including monetary, social, training and skills, transport, and industrial policy, as well as policies concerning the EU and corporate governance (*ibid.*).

Examples of liberal market economies are the UK and USA. Those countries were, Hall and Soskice argued, characterized by market-driven and competitive inter-firm relations, and relations between management and labour; arms-length relations between business and government; coordination through price signals; competitive labour markets; and short-term share price maximization. Liberal market economies have the benefits of low unemployment and the ability to adjust rapidly to changing global market conditions. Intensifying globalization has led to these nations becoming more competitive and market-oriented – that is, more 'liberal', rather than less.

In contrast, Germany, and to a less extent Japan and Switzerland, are characterized as coordinated (or, sometimes, 'managed') capitalist countries. In these nations, firms often collaborate with each other as well as competing; the state plays an enabling role in relation to business; relations between management and labour are cooperative, within the context of notions of 'industrial citizenship' for workers and frequent power-sharing within firms; labour markets are rigid; and financing is generally long term, with 'patient' capital provided by banks. Benefits arising from these arrangements include the fact that employment is generally highly-skilled, highly-waged and highly productive. Globalization has limited and patchy effects upon these economies; governments and firms push some liberalization of labour-management relations and some coordination between firms broke down, but has not precipitated a wholesale move towards the liberal market model.

The 'varieties of capitalism' approach harks back to previous analyses, such as Albert's distinction between 'Anglo-Saxon' and 'Rhine' models of capitalism. Albert's main exemplar of the Rhine model was Germany, but he argued it also applied to other nations crossed by the River Rhine, such as Switzerland and the Netherlands (and, cheekily, Japan as well, 'with allowances for the inevitable cultural differences'). A separate type of 'Neo-American' or 'Anglo-Saxon' capitalism, found in the UK and, particularly, the USA, was 'based on individual success and short-term financial gain' (Albert: 1991: 19). Albert's approach was explicitly normative, arguing that 'In the last decade or so, it is [the] Rhine model – unheralded, unsung and lacking even nominal identity papers – that has shown itself to be the more efficient of the two [models], as well as the more equitable' (*ibid*. 18–19).

The 'varieties of capitalism' approach has been criticized for a variety of reasons. First, some have argued against the focus of 'varieties of capitalism' theories on the firm as the centre of the analysis. This arguably obscures the importance of organized labour and governments as political actors, not simply resolvers of coordination problems. This is perhaps inappropriate when, in many nations, 'class contestation over the central institutions of capitalist political economies' has been extremely vigorous, with labour movements (or elements of them) playing crucial political roles in shaping institutional conditions in the economy (Howell, 2003: 112).

Second, Howell argues that 'varieties of capitalism' analyses assume that the interests of governments are perfectly aligned with those of business (since governments' role in economic policy is uniquely to resolve coordination problems) (*ibid*.: 110). Yet business may actually push for particular types of policy to be adopted by government (as arguably occurred in the 1970s and 1980s in Britain) (*ibid*: 119). In addition, governments may, driven by ideology, attempt to alter the institutional conditions within the economy and even push it from one type into another, as Howell maintains could be argued for Britain's shift from possessing, and intensifying, many CME features in the 1970s, towards an LME in the 1980s and 1990s (*ibid*: 119). Institutions, on this analysis, can reflect 'asymmetries in power and conflicts of interest' rather than 'just' existing to coordinate different economic activities (Amable, 2005: 19).

Finally, the category of CME appears heavily reliant on one exemplar – Germany, which has been subject to sustained economic policy reforms over the past few decades. As Howell puts it, given reforms through the 1990s and early 2000s, 'It is . . . questionable to what extent Germany can remain the poster child for an alternative to deregulated liberal market economies' (2003: 109). Recent scholaship has, indeed, suggested that the extent to which Germany represents a high-skill 'alternative' to liberal market approaches is progressively diminishing (see Box 3.1).

BOX 3.1   Fleckenstein et al. on the dual transformation of social protection and human capital

Using data on skill endowments in Britain and Germany, Fleckenstein *et al.* take issue with claims that Germany's economy differs qualitatively from Britain's. The 'varieties of capitalism' approach points to Germany's higher reliance on industrial skills and high-technology production as mutually reinforcing elements of its institutional context. The authors argue, however, that 'postindustrial developments in social protection and human capital suggest that Britain and Germany have embarked on a shared path of structural change and corresponding institutional reform' (Fleckenstein *et al.*, 2011: 1642).

First, Fleckenstein *et al.* indicate how the 'returns' to investment in skills have been diminishing over time in Germany. For example, whereas previously there was the expectation that unemployed workers with specific skills would not be expected to seek low-skill work, changes to unemployment entitlements now require them to accept a broader range of jobs. This has occurred at the same time as increasing numbers of women have joined the workforce, supported by increased childcare entitlements.

Simultaneously, the number of people using 'specific skills' in the workforce diminished by almost one quarter in Germany between 1992 and 2007, with only slightly over one fifth of the workforce with specific skills at the time of writing. As a result, the similarities between Britain and Germany are increasing, while the differences are diminishing. Most jobs in both countries now require just 'general skills', although more require 'low-general' skills in the UK than in Germany, where 'high-general skills' are in greater evidence.

The extent of government intervention

One approach which explicitly takes into account the role of government as an autonomous actor comes from Vivien Schmidt (2003). Rather than two varieties of capitalism, she sets out three 'varieties of state'. In addition to 'liberal capitalist' and 'managed capitalist' or 'enabling' states, she distinguishes the category of the *dirigiste* state, which produces 'state' or 'state-enhanced' capitalism. In distinction to Hall and Soskice, she develops her analysis mainly looking at only three nations: Britain (liberal capitalist), Germany (managed capitalist), and France (state-enhanced capitalist), although she does sometimes make reference to other managed capitalist countries, such as the Netherlands and Denmark. Schmidt is keen to 'underline the fact that these [categories of state] are empirical patterns [drawn from the three exemplars] rather than any new, stylized typology' (*ibid*: 527).

In Britain, the 'liberal capitalist' state, business operated at arms-length from government, and the scope of economic policy was restricted to arbitrating amongst economic actors and setting up broad rules of competition, which were often then administered by other, self-governing bodies (as, for example, in the financial sector). With liberalizing reforms introduced from the 1980s onwards, Britain rapidly became even more liberal, often pulling the EU with it.

In contrast, in Germany, the 'managed capitalist' state, governments were more likely to target aid to industry – through, for example, regionally focused loans and subsidies – and the state took a more active role in supporting education, apprenticeships and training. When liberalizing reforms did occur, these were in the 1990s and generally rather limited in scope.

Finally, in France, subject to 'state capitalism', governments played an activist role in planning and industrial policy, and were keen to hold a stake in many parts of the economy. Whilst reforms were undertaken from the 1980s onwards – which, for Schmidt, suggested a move towards a new 'state-enhanced' approach in France – these reforms also had limited impact, because they fitted in with existing patterns of state intervention in the French economy. For example, ownership in many large companies was liberalized through the selling of shares, but in practice many of these remained within the hands of actors closely connected to the state – 'the corporate governance system evolved from a state-centered structure run by a tight elite network, to what looks like a private structure but is run by the same elite as before' (Hancké, 2002: 55).

Schmidt's approach taps into a long tradition in comparative analyses of economic policy which have examined the different policy 'styles' adopted in different countries; in particular, the extent of adoption of activist as against laissez-faire approaches to economic policy. This approach indicated how, in some nations, industrial policy decisions were left to business and the operations of the market; and in others an interventionist industrial policy was adopted, which strategically targeted 'some firms and economic activities but not others through credit regulations, research support, targeted subsidies, and so on' (Heidenheimer *et al.*, 1990: 138).

Shonfield's (1965) analysis of economic policies in Britain and France was, at the time, groundbreaking. For example, it demonstrated that, despite the fact that both countries were liberal democracies, they had demonstrated a 'sustained polarity' in their economic policies. In particular, whilst British decision-makers had been reluctant to intervene directly in markets, in France, governments had been keen to exercise close control over the nation's economic life – including through choosing and buttressing 'national champions' through industrial reorganization, tax breaks and the manipulation of trade barriers (*ibid.*: 71). A similarly activist approach was adopted by successive Japanese governments, which attempted to identify future 'industrial leaders' and manipulated the conditions for competition so that these firms could develop critical mass before attempting to participate in international markets. Policy-makers in both France and Japan developed strong alliances with specific industrialists, nurtured specific firms, and attempted the precise planning of economic development over the long term.

On the contrary, in Britain and the USA policy-makers generally focused on the 'big levers' of macroeconomic policy (Heidenheimer *et al.*, 1990: 154). This was particularly marked in the USA, where interventions such as price and wage controls were generally only invoked in wartime. Although assistance was occasionally made available by US governments for ailing firms (e.g. Lockheed, Chrysler), this was on an *ad hoc* basis, rather than as part of a national plan (Heidenheimer *et al.*, 1990: 155). President Obama's extensive public works plan suggests that this categorization of US economic policy-making may no longer hold; and international trade rules (see p. 67) have restricted the room for governments to promote individual firms. Nonetheless, Schmidt's analysis indicates continuing broad differences between nations in the degree of state intervention in the economy, even if the strategies pursued by nations may have changed over time.

In contrast to 'varieties of capitalism' theories, Schmidt's approach is much more reliant on political factors than on institutional complementarities for explaining developments in economic policy. For example, Schmidt (2003) explicitly accords a causal role to political discourse as a factor shaping institutional change. This also enables her to suggest that reforms will occur in different ways in different sectors, as well as between countries: 'firms in financial services, biotechnology and the "new economy" more generally will increasingly operate along the UK's market-capitalist lines; . . . firms in high-precision engineering and man-ufacturing are likely increasingly to adopt the techniques of Germany's managed capitalism; [and] . . . firms in sectors such as defence, which are influenced by the priorities set by national governments and the EU, or the railroads, which require heavy investments with low rates of return over long periods of time, are likely to follow France's pattern of 'state-enhanced' capitalism' (*ibid.*: 549).

However, it is arguable that firms in all three sectors appear increas-ingly subject to liberalizing pressures, as do all three countries Schmidt examined. A distinctive characteristic of both Schmidt's 'varieties of state' and Hall and Soskice's 'varieties of capitalism' theories appeared to be their claim that liberalization is not an inexorable process across all economies; divergence is as likely as convergence (Berger and Dore, 1996; Schmidt, 2002b). Certainly, there does appear to be some evidence that globalization has not immediately led to convergence in economic policies across countries (Hall and Gingerich, 2004; Rhodes and Thatcher, 2007).

Nonetheless, looking more closely, there does appear to be a bias in favour of development in a liberal direction across all types of political economy, even if changes have been patchy and inconsistent. As Hall and Soskice (2001: 245) put it, 'it is not unreasonable to posit a long-term historical bias leaning in the direction of liberalization'. The coordi-native institutions that characterize CMEs must be painstakingly built up over long periods (Streeck and Yamamura, 2001) and are heavily reliant on trust relationships which can be easily destroyed (Goodin, 2003). LME development is thus more likely than that of CMEs; it is 'easier to make fish soup out of an aquarium than the other way around' (Offe, 2005: 154). Similarly, one might argue that the types of 'underground' state coordination operating in France identified by Schmidt as quali-fying it as a 'state-enhanced' capitalist nation are being undermined by the opening up and internationalization of recruitment to the *grandes écoles* and other traditional elite 'breeding-grounds'.

Some more recent studies have attempted to explain the apparent 'bias' towards liberalization in greater detail. Liberalization has arguably existed '*simultaneously* as a set of "internal" characteristics both of the liberal model and of key multilateral institutions; as an "offshore" threat to, and internal undercurrent within, coordinated capitalist systems; and as the prevailing "rules of the game," structuring relations between national models' (Peck and Theodore, 2007: 755, their emphasis). One approach assumes that the institutional level can, to an extent, be analytically sepa-rated from the production process, and that it can autonomously shape production relations, rather than merely supporting them (Hollingsworth and Boyer, 1997; Coates, 2000; Amable, 2003). This insight has been developed by Streeck and Thelen (2005) in their analysis of liberalization.

They argue that liberalization – for them, the most significant postwar development in economic policy – often occurs within institutions themselves, as part of a gradual process. Again, Streeck and Thelen (*ibid.*) highlight asymmetries between LMEs and CMEs, by arguing that whilst liberalization can occur essentially by setting up appropriate institutional conditions which will then be exploited by competitively-minded actors, more concerted action is required for the production of coordinated or managed capitalist institutions.

The influence of international factors

Perhaps the greatest challenge to theories positing systematic differences between countries' economic policies comes from the influence of international factors. Even by the early 1990s, it was widely acknowledged that advanced capitalist economies needed not only to compete with each other, but also to 'respond to growing pressures from newly industrializing third-world nations where labour is cheap and some developmental shortcuts (for example, copying technologies) are possible' (Heidenheimer *et al.*, 1990: 170).

'Strong' globalization theories have argued that, even aside from these pressures from other nations' productive capacities, the growing number and size of trans-national corporations (TNCs) will lead to a uniform process of economic policy convergence and, ultimately, a 'race to the bottom' in regulatory standards (see Chapter 8). Some more nuanced studies have suggested that international firms will aid the spread of both management and policy practice, which could lead to pressure for increased as well as decreased regulatory standards (Djelic and Quack, 2010). A concrete example comes from Britain's opt-out from the Social Chapter of the Maastricht Treaty. Even though the British government had rejected the provisions of the Social Chapter, many large TNCs, in practice, ended up implementing one key element of the Social Chapter – the introduction of works councils in their British outposts. This was due to the costliness of adopting different approaches to industrial organization in different countries (Callaghan, 2010: 573). The influence of TNCs as facilitators of policy convergence is examined in greater detail in Chapter 8.

Another aspect of internationalization which has been accorded significant attention in the economic policy literature is the influence of international organizations such as the EU, IMF and OECD. These organizations have become increasingly high profile with the advent of the 2008 financial crisis, which indicated the problems associated with focusing purely on nationally-based macroeconomic policies as a means of trying to prevent, and climb out of, recession (Claessens *et al.*, 2010: 286–8).

For its member states, particularly those which are part of the Eurozone, the EU has become an increasingly important decider and shaper of economic policy. The EU, as a whole, is now 'the largest exporter and importer of both goods and services ... and is one of the largest hosts and sources of foreign direct investments' (Dür and Elsig, 2011: 323). It is now the EU, rather than member states, which is mainly responsible for negotiating foreign economic policies (e.g. within the WTO), although this is not the case within the IMF, where individual states still retain control (*ibid.*: 325). Furthermore, the EU has been relatively activist in its foreign economic policy-making, appearing eager to use the WTO's procedures to prevent dumping, for example (*ibid.*: 326–7).

In the realm of domestic economic policies, until 2008 the EU possessed little control over states' fiscal policies. Members of the Eurozone were required to sign up to a Stability and Growth Pact which contained stipulations about deficit levels, but otherwise taxation and spending were the exclusive purview of member states (see Chapter 8). This contrasted with bodies such as the IMF, which imposed strict deflationary measures on Britain in 1976 (Heidenheimer *et al.*, 1990: 142) and, more recently, strict deficit reduction measures on Greece and Ireland in the wake of the 2008 economic crisis. These measures were imposed by the IMF as conditions for aid to finance large deficits. The 2008 economic crisis has led to a renewed focus on fiscal policies in the Eurozone following extensive effective 'debt transfers' to financially stricken nations, and more control will be exerted by the EU over fiscal policies in the future, with sanctions applied for nations that obtain deficit-financing support.

Previous to 2008, however, the EU arguably had a much more significant impact in the realm of industrial policy. One recent example of this is the Lisbon Strategy, subsequently relaunched as the Europe 2020 strategy (Borrás and Radaelli, 2011). The 'Lisbon Strategy' was launched in March 2000 and included a number of measures aimed at improving competitiveness in Europe, with the overall aim of the EU becoming the most 'competitive, sustainable, socially inclusive knowledge-based society' in the world (*ibid.*: 480). These have included, from 2005, the production of economic policy guidelines and targets, their implementation through periodic reform programmes, and performance monitoring (*ibid.*: 465).

The implementation of the Lisbon Strategy has proved difficult, given the essential ambiguity of 'competitiveness' as a policy goal, and the divergence in economic performance across Europe (*ibid.*: 480). This is highlighted in the case of the Services Directive, which was focused on completion of the internal market in services (with a single market having been effectively created for goods, following the abolition of internal tariffs and reforms to state support for domestic industries). The Services Directive, as initially framed, stated that 'service providers offering a temporary service outside their country of origin would be subject only to the national provisions of the member state in which they are established, regardless of where they provide a service' – described as the 'country of origin' principle (Loder, 2011: 572). This would, obviously, have entirely removed states' abilities to impose regulations on foreign service providers – meaning that, for example, their staff would not have been subject to the same rules concerning minimum wages, sickness pay and redundancy as staff employed by domestically-owned businesses. In the event, the 'country of origin' principle was removed by the European Parliament and substituted for the principle of the 'freedom to provide services', which is likely to provide 'host member states with more options for restricting services' (*ibid.*: 576–7).

The power of the EU to control economic policy-making is not, therefore, absolute – but it has been significant. In addition to the direct impact of EU directives, the multi-level political process involved in economic policy discussions within the EU has indirectly impacted on economic policies in a variety of ways. Domestic policy actors' preferences about desirable economic policies are arguably shaped by their activities at an EU-level, thus undermining national specificities. However, the 'disruptive' potential of the EU for different economic policy models is further enhanced by the fact that policies for different areas of the economy – the different 'regulatory subspheres' – are subject to differing governing dynamics within the EU. This means it is difficult for one 'dominant social block' or 'ideological approach' to dominate 'across all the regulatory subspheres of coherent production regimes' (Callaghan, 2010: 565, 570). As a result, 'multilevel governance affects preferences and cleavage patterns in ways that threaten to undermine both liberal and coordinated varieties of capitalism' (*ibid.*: 565).

Comparing economic policies across nations

The use of financial resources

In a sense, all attempts by government to use their control over financial resources could be defined as 'economic policy'. When it comes to activities directly targeted at economic policy goals, however, three main categories of activity can be identified as tools of both macro- and micro-economic policy: the provision of tax-funded services, the targeting and manipulation of taxation rates, and the provision of tax breaks.

The provision of tax-funded services
First, governments use their control over financial resources as a lever in both macroeconomic policy and industrial policy.

Keynesian demand management relied on governments' abilities to stimulate demand through public works programmes and the expansion of state employment. The overall level of spending, and where it is targeted, continues to be viewed as a tool of macroeconomic policy, albeit not always from within a Keynesian paradigm. Fairly obviously, government fiscal priorities continue to have strong effects on the macro-economy, with an extreme example of this coming from the wave of inflation in the USA that followed major spending on the Vietnam War, paid for through increasing budget deficits rather than increased taxes (Heidenheimer *et al.*, 1990: 132). Governments may also explicitly use their spending powers as tools to affect the macroeconomy in times of crisis. An example of this comes from Australia, where the government gave almost everyone, other than the very richest adults, a cheque for AU$9,000 in 2008, to spend as they wished to boost the domestic economy.

Aside from during times of war and economic crisis, however, most governments' approaches to spending are generally relatively stable. A recent in-depth study of government budgeting across developed countries concluded that at 'least until the recent financial crisis, the volatility of budget series declined over time' (Jones *et al.*, 2009: 860), with budgets generally 'display[ing] periods of quiescence interrupted by bursts of frenetic activity' (*ibid.*: 870), with the latter generally promoted by extreme external or internal pressures. Unsurprisingly, given that local governments tend to be unable to borrow funds unless for the purposes of capital investment (unlike national governments), their approaches to fiscal policy vary even less over time (*ibid.*: 863).

One area where, at least until the 1990s, governments differed more substantially in their approach is the use of financial resources in industrial policy. A good example of this is provided by the French government's 'massive program of accelerated investment in nuclear power' in 1974, which provided the basis for that country to become more self-sufficient in energy production (Heidenheimer *et al.*, 1990: 140). As mentioned, theorists such as Shonfield (1965) and Schmidt (2003) have suggested that countries can be distinguished according to the extent to which their governments play an 'activist' role in economic policy, including their use of state subsidies for particular industries and firms. According to this approach, nations such as France and Japan, where governments used their power over financial resources extensively to support particular industries, can be contrasted with more '*laissez-faire*' approaches as adopted in nations such as the UK and USA.

It has sometimes been argued that US governments' consistent financial support for procurement and research and development in defence could be viewed as a form of industrial policy, not least because of the purported knock-on effects of growth in the defence sector for techno-logical innovation (Heidenheimer *et al.*, 1990: 155). This may have only applied up to a certain level of military build-up, however; there is some evidence that 'increased levels of military expenditures dampen invest-ment, which reduces growth'; this is because they can 'crowd out' investment which, in turn, 'may have a dampening effect on growth' (Mintz and Huang, 1991: 741). Defence industries are also heavily reliant on highly-skilled workers and, again, it has been suggested that this has led to shortages of these workers in some nations (see Ram (1995), for a review).

In any case, it is arguable that states' abilities to selectively subsidize particular industries or firms is declining with the growing reach of organizations focused on creating a 'level playing field' for trade. Whilst, in the past, governments in numerous nations stepped in to subsidize ailing industries – such as steel, coal, shipbuilding and vehicle manufac-ture, or emerging industries – such as electronics and aerospace, this type of intervention is increasingly penalized at an international level as unfairly distorting competition (Zahariadis, 2010: 954). For example, state aid to firms to aid them to restructure or prevent bankruptcy is out-lawed by EU treaties, with compliance monitored by the EU Commission. However, in practice, compliance is generally sought through 'political negotiation and persuasion' rather than the imposition of fines. This does not apply, however, to uses of aid to promote regional development or sustainability, which are generally exempted from such rules (*ibid.*: 958).

Aside from direct support for particular industries, governments may indirectly attempt to provide the conditions for economic growth through taxation-funded support for training or industrial infrastructure. The former has been particularly important in nations such as Sweden, where extensive state involvement in active labour market policies (see Chapter 4) was adopted by successive Social Democratic governments as an alternative to state ownership as an economic strategy (Shonfield, 1965: 200–1). Through the provision of training and targeted support for those seeking work, these policies aided the Swedish workforce to respond flexibly and rapidly to new market opportunities. These policies perhaps reached their apogee in Iceland which, until the 2008 economic crisis, regularly recorded extremely high rates of employment with 80 per cent of the population in (legal) work (Deacon, 2008: 315). In addition to investment in the workforce, governments may attempt to invest in trans-port and other infrastructure. The rates of such investment vary signifi-cantly between nations, with countries such as France and Germany consistently promoting transport infrastructure, for example, as a priority for public expenditure, with less emphasis in this area in nations such as Britain and the USA (OECD, 2011a).

Taxation

Taxation offers governments another economic policy lever in addition to their control over public spending, as described in the previous section. As with public spending, policies towards taxation 'are characterized by a complex interaction between revenue-raising functions on the one hand, and other economic and social policy functions on the other' (Heidenheimer *et al.*, 1990: 183). Again, as with public spending, 'sweeping changes' in tax regimes are relatively unusual – aside from when in periods of intense external or internal pressure, such as the Reaganite ideological 'revolution' which proposed significant tax cuts in the USA in the early 1980s (*ibid.*); or, less spectacularly, the temporary reduction in the UK's VAT rate as part of attempts to boost the economy in the wake of the 2008 economic crisis.

As with public spending, the levels of government responsible for taxation differ between countries, with some collecting almost all taxes at a national level, whilst others devolve many tax collecting responsibilities to local governments. In addition, governments' reliance on direct taxes (such as those levied on income, property or corporations) and indirect taxes (such as those levied on consumption, including 'value added' taxes) differs across nations.

One of the most consistent trends across countries has been moves towards an increasing proportion of government revenue coming from consumption taxes. This particularly intensified with the creation of the Common Market, where numerous member states rapidly reduced or eliminated excise taxes, increased the rate of sales taxes, and shifted them towards the 'value added tax' (VAT) model. Member states within the EU were generally faster to introduce VAT than other countries, with the initial member states generally adopting it in 1972, 'whereas the rest of the OECD took almost 15 years more, and the US has yet to introduce it' (Kemmerling, 2010: 1065).

Kemmerling (*ibid.*: 1069) argues in this context that the EU may have served as a 'legitimatory device' for the introduction and/or increase in VAT in member states. 'Universal' consumption taxes such as VAT are generally unpopular as they are regressive, with less well-off people paying proportionally more of their incomes in these taxes than better-off people. However, they have been promoted by organizations such as the OECD, which maintains that they are less likely to distort competition, and less easy to avoid than other forms of taxation. As a result, the OECD has praised nations such as Japan, which is considering increasing its consumption tax rate –the lowest amongst OECD countries at the time of writing (OECD, 2011a).

In contrast with EU nations' early introduction of and increases in VAT, almost all OECD countries paralleled EU nations in reducing excise taxes (Kemmerling, 2010: 1066). At the same time, however, continuing differences exist between nations (including those in the EU) concerning the taxation of specific goods related to environmental and health policy goals – such as fuel, alcohol and cigarettes. Countries, including Australia, have moved to increase and improve taxation on non-renewable energy sources as part of wider tax reforms (OECD, 2011a). Separately, the UK imposed a 'windfall tax' on privatized utility companies in 1997, in order to provide funds for a new welfare-to-work programme and educational infrastructure.

Income tax rates have been argued by some to impact on work incentives, and have been subject to extensive reform in numerous countries. Since the 1980s, in Denmark and the UK the top marginal income tax rate has been lowered and income tax thresholds raised; income tax on overtime has been reduced in Italy; and the lower threshold for income tax has been raised in Sweden (*ibid.*). Arguably the least 'distorting' approach to the taxation of income is the so-called 'flat tax' approach. An attempt to introduce a version of a locally-set flat tax to pay for local services (the 'Community Charge', popularly known as the 'Poll Tax') had to be abandoned in Britain following massive non-payment and civil disobedience. However, nationally-levied 'flat taxes' on income have been implemented in a number of countries, particularly in Eastern Europe and the Baltic and Balkan nations.

Aside from the shape of taxation regimes, one parameter which differs between nations is the degree of compliance. Italy is often isolated as an OECD nation where there is a relatively low level of compliance with taxation. Whilst it raised 'one-off revenue', the Italian government's decision in 2009 and 2010 to offer a partial amnesty for 'funds held abroad . . . gave ambiguous incentives for tax compliance' (*ibid.*).

Tax expenditures

As with tax expenditures in health care (see Chapter 5), governments' tax expenditures in economic policy can sometimes dwarf their use of other types of financial resources. As an example, Figure 3.3 indicates the level of tax subsidies provided by governments in selected countries for research and development activities.

Tax expenditures have been used in a variety of countries to support specific industries. The West German government relied heavily on tax breaks to promote specific industrial sectors as a means of economic recovery following World War II. The tax breaks were concentrated on industries including steel and energy production and mining allotting them 'exceptionally large depreciation allowances' on new investment for tax purposes, effectively significantly reducing their 'profits' for taxation purposes – on the condition that any gains went into investment rather than being passed on to shareholders (Shonfield, 1965: 282). This procedure offered particularly strong incentives for investment in West

Figure 3.3   *Rate of tax subsidies for one dollar of R&D, 2008 and 2004*

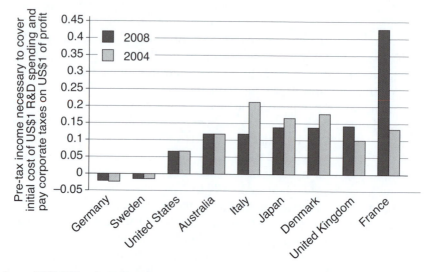

Source: OECD (2011a – StatLink): 177.

Germany because of the otherwise high tax rates prevailing at that time (*ibid.*).

Even countries traditionally viewed as committed to a '*laissez-faire*' approach to economic policy-making have often adopted tax incentives as a lever of economic policy. Tax relief to encourage investment was introduced in Britain as early as 1945, for example (Heidenheimer *et al.*, 1990: 152). The pervasiveness of tax breaks for specific business activities (particularly investment) arguably means that 'mere' comparison of corporate tax rates offers an incomplete picture of the tax burden on business. For example, two of the countries possessing the ostensibly highest corporate tax rates in the late 1980s, Sweden and Germany, also had the most extensive systems for tax deductions (*ibid.*: 193).

In addition to exemptions for the tax paid by businesses, governments may also attempt to induce saving amongst their populations as a method of increasing the availability of investment capital. One particularly extreme example of this comes from Japan's postal savings system, where individuals were incentivized through tax breaks to place funds in the system, which were then available to the state for economic policy purposes. Indeed, at one point, funds within the postal savings system were, according to Heidenheimer *et al.* (*ibid.*: 149), four times the size of the world's largest commercial bank (the Bank of America).

The use of authority

Governments use their powers of authority in a variety of ways in the field of economic policy, by prescribing certain economic activities, regulating which economic activities do occur, imposing restrictions on pay and shaping employment conditions, and controlling the flow of goods, services and workers across their borders.

Prohibition of economic activities

First, in a number of nations, certain activities or goods are excluded by governments from formal economic activity, such that they cannot legally be traded. These encompass a huge range of goods and services including the sale of sexual services (prostitution), certain hallucinogenic and mood-altering drugs, certain types of guns, certain types of potentially vicious dogs, bodily organs, people (e.g. children, 'slaves') and captive peoples' activity ('bonded' or 'slave' labour). Despite this, there are informal markets for most if not all these goods and activities in virtually all nations, including those within the OECD.

Regulation of economic activity

Governments 'have always laid down rules for the conduct of trade, rules that put certain social and political objectives and certain social and political values above the total freedom of the market' (Strange, 1994: 175). Furthermore, the existence of markets themselves arguably rests on the power to enforce contracts, requiring some kind of formal or informal authority which has historically been provided by state actors. Governments regulate economic activity by attempting to shape prices; controlling who can engage in particular types of economic activity, and when; and regulating the size and activities of different companies.

Governments have attempted to control prices for a variety of reasons, to varying degrees of success. The OPEC oil embargos in the 1970s and 1980s offered an example of oil-producing nations restricting supply in order to increase prices and, therefore, state and private revenue in those countries (Heidenheimer *et al.*, 1990: 139). Other nations have attempted to control prices to reduce or contain inflation, as in Holland in the 1950s and 1960s (Shonfield, 1965: 213), although such measures rarely proved sustainable.

Governments may also attempt to restrict which people are able to engage in particular types of economic activity, and when they can do this. An obvious example comes from the age restrictions that apply for holding office within a registered company and for the consumption of alcohol in licensed premises (in countries where alcohol is legal). In addition, particular trades or activities are restricted to specially licensed individuals or companies. This generally applies to restricted goods (e.g. alcohol, poisons, weapons) and activities requiring high levels of expertise (medicine) and/or 'honesty' (e.g. money lending). In nations such as France, Germany and Italy, these 'product market restrictions' can impose high costs for those wishing to enter a particular industry (OECD, 2011a). In many nations, some activities used to be reserved to nationals, but these restrictions have gradually broken down as markets have internationalized. Some additional procedures may nonetheless be applied to foreigners who wish to enter a market. Hence, in Australia, extra screening procedures are required for any foreign investors wishing to invest above AU$231 million in the country (*ibid.*). Specific types of company may also be controlled in their operations by government. Hence, larger retail outlets are subject to specific rules in France (*ibid.*).

Governments can also impose restrictions on when economic activity occurs. This covers the imposition of bans on Sunday trading and other restrictions on opening hours, as apply in Belgium and Luxembourg (*ibid.*), and the imposition of bank holidays. Whilst the latter are generally viewed as providing populations with an enjoyable extra day off work, they have also been used to try to prevent runs on banks. Whilst a seven day-long bank holiday imposed by Roosevelt in 1933 appeared to stem what had been a month-long 'run' on banks and a crisis of economic confidence, attempts by individual states in the weeks before to impose bank holidays had acted to increase, rather than reduce, panic and the rate of withdrawals, perhaps because they were not coordinated with each other (Silber, 2009).

Governments may also attempt to constrain the size of companies through the use of 'antitrust' policy. This was first introduced in the USA by the Sherman Act of 1890, although antitrust actions became less frequent from the 1980s onwards as the influx of Chicago school economists into the administration argued that market concentration in and of itself was less harmful than price-fixing (which they accepted was distorting) (Eisner and Meier, 1990: 274).

Finally, governments may attempt to regulate how certain economic activities are performed, often ostensibly in the interests of the consumer and the promotion of economic competition. There has been an exponential increase in the number of public regulatory bodies over the last thirty years (Levi-Faur and Gilardi, 2004). Two movements have occurred in parallel: a decline in trust in self-regulatory measures, combined with a vogue for 'independent' regulatory agencies at arm's length from government (see Moran, 2007). Despite these trends, substantial differences between nations continue to exist. For example, whereas some nations within Europe have adopted the model of one multi-purpose agency covering the range of financial services (such as the UK's Financial Services Authority, and Germany's BaFin), in other countries regulatory responsibilities concerning financial services are divided between different agencies (as in Italy and Spain) (Perez and Westrup, 2010: 1171).

Regulation of pay and conditions

One of the most significant ways for governments to control pay is to impose a minimum wage. Figure 3.4 provides an indication of the worth of the minimum wage compared with the median wage, and how this changed between 2006 and 2009. It excludes Italy, Sweden, Denmark and Germany which do not have a minimum wage for all sectors, although minimum wages may apply in some sectors. Finally, the minimum wage given for the USA in Figure 3.4 is an average, since different minimum wages apply in different states.

From the 1990s onwards, there has been a trend towards increases being proposed by a combination of 'experts' and representatives of labour and business interests, rather than by governments themselves. This approach has been adopted in France, for example (OECD, 2011a), and has existed in Britain since the introduction of its minimum wage in 1999.

Governments have also, on occasion, attempted to control the growth in wages as a means of reducing wage-push inflation. What was described during that period as 'incomes policy', the imposition of either imposed or negotiated controls on pay, was a relatively constant feature of economic policy-making in Britain from 1960 to 1979 (Grant, 2002: 5). A target for wage level growth also existed in Sweden during the 1960s (Shonfield, 1965: 201).

In contrast, in Holland wage restraint was used not to reduce inflation, but to attempt to make exports more competitive. Hence, wages were

Figure 3.4 *The value of the minimum wage as a percentage of the median wage in selected countries, 2006 and 2009*

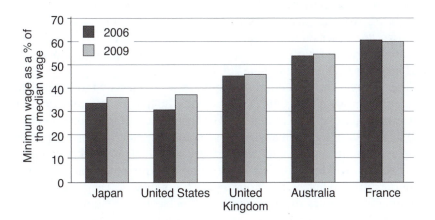

Source: OECD (2011a – StatLink): 154.

Figure 3.5   *Protection for employment in selected countries, 2003 and 2008*

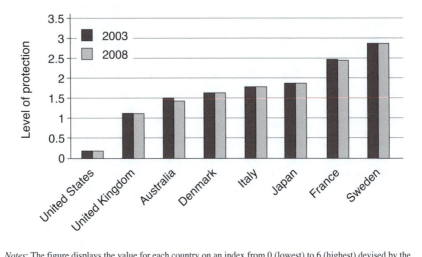

Notes: The figure displays the value for each country on an index from 0 (lowest) to 6 (highest) devised by the OECD. The figure given for France is 2009, rather than 2008.

Source: OECD (2011a – StatLink): 161.

'deliberately' kept 'below the West European standard' as part of an attempt to encourage Dutch industry. By 1963, however, the system had broken down, as numerous Dutch workers were choosing to cross the border into Germany, specifically to earn higher wages (*ibid*.: 212–13).

In addition to pay rates, governments may also attempt to control the conditions of employment: the procedures to be followed when hiring and firing workers, and the provision of holidays, time for caring for children and other entitlements. Figure 3.5 displays results for selected countries of an index of the degree of protection for regular employment, and how this changed during the 2000s.

The degree of protection for employees differs wildly between nations, even within the OECD. Particularly high levels of protection for permanent jobs apply in France, Germany, Italy, Japan and Sweden (OECD, 2011a: 36). In many of these countries, controls for temporary employment are significantly weaker, leading to 'labour market dualism' – a two-tier workforce subject to differing working conditions. In some countries, the number of 'non-regular' workers is very significant, standing at one third of total employees in Japan at the time of writing (OECD, 2011a). Control over pay and conditions for welfare purposes, and the degree to which welfare services and benefits are contingent on employment status, are considered in detail in Chapter 4.

Regulation of cross-border flows

Finally, governments may attempt to control the flow of goods, services and workers across their borders. In the field of goods and services, the general trend across OECD nations has been towards the reduction of barriers to trade. This follows some periods of relatively high trade restrictions, including in nations which might otherwise be viewed as relatively '*laissez-faire*' in their economic policies. The USA, for example, was subject to particularly 'formidable' trade restrictions in the 1930s, which were gradually eased following World War II. Excise duties, import quotas and licences have gradually been dismantled in most nations, sometimes encouraged by international bodies such as the World Trade Organization. Despite this, periodic restrictions have been imposed such as the US 'MultiFibre Agreement', which 'restricted developing country exports of textiles and apparel and generated large quota rents' (Irwin, 2010: 121), and restrictions have also been imposed for health reasons such as the EU ban on beef produced using high levels of hormones.

In addition, governments may increase or reduce access to employment opportunities for foreigners as an explicit part of economic policy. An extreme example of this comes from Switzerland, where the number of immigrant workers increased eight times within one decade, such that 'by the early 1960s one-third of its labour force consist[ed] of foreigners' (Shonfield, 1965: 7). 'Guest worker' programmes have also been introduced, albeit to a lesser extent, in nations including (formally) Germany, with its *Gastarbeiter* programme, and (informally) Britain, with its initial relative openness to immigration from the Commonwealth. However, most OECD countries have seen significant restrictions on immigration for work purposes from the 1980s onwards, with many adopting variants of Australia's 'points-based' immigration system as a means of restricting the entry of foreign workers.

The use of organization

The appropriate organization of the economy, particularly the extent to which economic activity should be planned by governments and the producing organizations owned by them, has long proved highly controversial. In addition to governments' use of planning and public ownership as industrial policy levers, governments have also attempted to control the macroeconomy through creating different types of economic institutions such as exchange rate systems and independent central banks.

Planning

Until the 1970s, one of the key differentiating factors between governments' use of their organizational powers was the extent to which they could create, and impose, economic plans. The best-known, and arguably most successful, approach to economic planning occurred in France. A special Commission, the *Commissariat Général du Plan*, set out targets to improve industrial performance in a variety of sectors, indicating the resources required for these improvements. A variety of business, finance and government actors were involved in the process of creation of the plans (Heidenheimer *et al.*, 1990: 146).

This system of 'indicative' planning was reliant on the French state's close relationship with a 'central core of important enterprises which [were] more responsive to the desires of the state than the ordinary private firm' (Shonfield, 1965: 84). Attempts were made by some nations to adapt the French system to their domestic context, albeit with limited success, as with Britain's creation of a National Economic Development Council in the early 1960s (*ibid.*: 72).

An alternative, significantly more interventionist approach was adopted in Italy and Japan, whereby the state openly and actively identified and supported a small number of protected firms until they achieved monopoly or near-monopoly of the domestic market. Firms such as Fiat, Pirelli and Olivetti were supported in this way in Italy, which gave them the 'technical advantages of scale' in order to be able to compete internationally with the opening up of international markets (*ibid.*: 178).

These approaches to planning appear, however, to have been relatively short-lived. With the increasing scope of trade regulations, interventionist attempts at planning have become less feasible, whilst indicative planning, at least in France, became an 'increasingly meaningless formal exercise offering speculations about the future' (Heidenheimer *et al.*, 1990: 147).

Public ownership

Another previously highly significant attempt by governments to use their powers of organization in the economic policy realm was through public ownership. In some cases, public ownership arose through crisis, as with the nationalization of numerous companies in Italy in 1933 after a banking crisis. This nationalization led to the creation of the gigantic Istituto per la Ricostruzione Industriale (Shonfield, 1965: 179), one of the largest employers in Italy, which brought together numerous firms facing bankruptcy. Although Alitalia was privatized in 2008–9, a significant proportion of industries, including the media, remains either in public hands or the hands of one single private company with significant connections to the state (OECD, 2011a). A further example of crisis nationalization comes from the UK state's takeover in 2008 of the mortgage provider Northern Rock and the partial nationalization of the Royal Bank of Scotland and the HBOS-Lloyds TSB bank.

Fewer nationalizations have occurred since the late 1970s for ideological reasons, although as late as the 1980s, Socialist governments in France took over all of the major banking institutions and a significant proportion of heavy industry, to the extent that the state accounted for 'roughly one-quarter of the workforce' (Heidenheimer *et al.*, 1990: 148). The measures did not last, however, and by the end of the 1980s most of these nationalized assets had been returned to private ownership, albeit with continuing connections to key state actors through concentrated ownership of shares (see p. 60).

Rather than a strict delineation between public and private ownership, however, in many nations the involvement of governments in enterprise has changed rather than disappeared altogether. For example, in the UK context, in many industries 'ownership and financial structures' are neither private nor public but, instead, 'lie between the two', reflecting a complicated 'balance in the allocation of equity risk and incentives' (Helm and Tindall, 2009: 412).

Creation of economic policy institutions

Governments have also created a variety of different organizational forms within their economic policies. One area where organizational forms have differed significantly over time is that of the definition of currency value – how the domestic currency is valued in relation to other currencies. The Bretton Woods system, initiated following World War II and lasting until 1971, pegged different currencies against each other as part of a fixed exchange rate system, albeit with variation of up to 10 per cent (Heidenheimer *et al.*, 1990: 132). The European Monetary System (EMS) was created in 1971 in the wake of Bretton Woods. It was based on a 'notional' currency, the ECU. The EMS collapsed in the early 1990s in the face of extensive currency speculation. The adoption of these types of approaches to currency value required the use of various policy instruments directed at restraining imports and boosting exports. Fixed, or semi-fixed, exchange rate regimes allowed countries to devalue their currencies in order to boost exports, although this tool could only be used very occasionally as it undermined confidence in the currency concerned.

With the creation of the Eurozone, monetary policy control passed to the European Central Bank for member countries, which are no longer able to engage in devaluation as a means of realigning their economy with international markets. Beyond the Eurozone, many other developed and developing countries' governments have been keen to cede control over monetary policy-making to independent, or quasi- independent bodies, particularly independent central banks. At first sight, this appears surprising and to run 'counter to post-war experiences of expansion in state activities and competencies in Western Europe' (Thatcher and Stone Sweet, 2002: 9). In practice, however, the creation of independent central banks provides monetary policy with greater credibility by removing incentives to engage in the political business cycle (see p. 56), since it involves this area of economic policy-making being taken out of the hands of politicians and placed in the hands of supposedly 'neutral' economic experts.

The provision of information

The provision of information and advice to the public
Governments have traditionally intervened in a variety of ways to ensure the provision of information to the public, generally in their role as consumers. Hence, for example, specific accounting standards have been decided on at both domestic and international levels. Accounts produced in line with these standards are then verified by auditors, who are legally required to make public any reservations they may have. Governments, or their agents, have also on occasion required companies to include information about the unpleasant side effects of particular goods (as with cigarettes); the presence of particular chemicals or additives (as with food labelling requirements); and to spell out in 'plain language' the risks of particular products (as with certain particularly expensive and/or risky financial products).

Governments have also, on occasion, attempted to 'educate' the public and producers about appropriate economic activity. Hence, the USA (unsuccessfully) attempted a public relations campaign in the 1970s to 'whip inflation now' to try to 'urge voluntary price restraint' (Heidenheimer *et al.*, 1990: 142). Publicity campaigns may also urge individuals to report non-compliance with minimum wage regulations or other restrictions on pay and conditions by their employer. Finally, in most OECD countries workers are legally obliged to be able to seek out, or to be provided automatically with, information about risks to health and safety in their workplace and how to deal with them.

The production and dissemination of information to inform policy-making
In practice, much of the information required by governments for economic policy-making is obtained from the market itself. In capitalist countries, the price mechanism forms a core source of information for calculating macroeconomic variables such as the rate of inflation in the economy (increases in the price of chosen bundles of goods and services over time), economic growth (the total market value, based on their price, of all goods and services, and how this varies from year to year), and shortages (increases in the price of specific goods or services). Where the price system has been abandoned, as has often occurred in

certain sectors during wartime, and exists in fully-planned economies, governments lack adequate cost information and may find it difficult to take economic policy decisions (Dahl and Lindblom, 1976: 374).

Nonetheless, the provision of policy-related information about the economy has, on occasion, been subject to considerable controversy. This is the case with the calculation of unemployment, with some nations relying on the 'claimant count' (the number of people claiming unemployment benefits or insurance) and others using representative surveys.

In addition, some policy-makers have attempted to shift away from traditional indicators of economic policy impact (such as GDP as a measure of economic growth), towards more sophisticated measures. The United Nation's Human Development Index, first created in 1990, is based on a basket of indicators which considers, as markers of development, life expectancy, living standards and education, as well as economic outputs. During the 2000s, governments (including France and the UK) have started to incorporate happiness indicators into routine data collection by statistical authorities.

The scope of economic policy

Economic policy is by its very nature distributive. This obviously applies where economic policies are targeted at specific sectors or firms, as with industrial policy. However, it has also been argued that macroeconomic policies can have significant redistributive effects. Policies focused on reducing inflation, including the introduction of independent central banks, effectively prioritize the interests of holders of financial assets as against the poor, whose incomes are often protected through indexing (as, for example, with old age pensions in many countries) (McNamara, 2002: 67). Stiglitz *et al.* (2006) concur with this assessment, maintaining that, so long as inflation remains at a low to medium level, without having 'severe effects on the economy', it is 'worse for bondholders than for most other parts of society' and thus 'reduces inequality'.

Other areas of economic policy-making have similarly indirect impacts on different groups. Greater reliance on private pension schemes (see Chapter 4) has resulted in regulatory decisions about financial markets having a significant impact on large sectors of the population. This is because a more significant proportion of households' assets has shifted from 'secure assets' such as bank deposits towards riskier types of investment, through the medium of their pension funds. Indeed, between '1980 and 2000, the total proportion of risk assets rose from 53 to 74 per cent of household savings in Britain, from 33 to 60 per cent in Germany, 30 to 61 per cent in France, [and from] 24 to 75 per cent in

Italy' (Perez and Westrup, 2010: 1180–1). As such, a large proportion of the population in many nations is exposed to the vicissitudes of market events, as has been painfully highlighted by the 2008 financial crisis (*ibid.*: 1181).

Conclusion

Rather than adopting the usual division between macroeconomic, fiscal and industrial policies, this chapter has compared economic policies across nations by considering their reliance on different policy types: the use of financial resources, authority, organization and information. In particular, it considered how government control over financial resources encompasses both wide-ranging and targeted changes to tax and spending policies; how governments can use their authority to prohibit and regulate different types of economic activity, determine rates of pay and working conditions, and control cross-border flows of goods, services, and workers; how their ability to organize diverse economic policy actors has enabled them to set economic plans, to take over specific firms or even industries, and create new economic policy institutions; and how control over, and the ability to produce information has enabled governments to inform both consumers and policy debates.

Although battles over nationalization versus privatization and intervention versus laissez-faire may appear less salient in current times, the chapter has indicated how it is premature to suggest that economic policies are converging in all sectors across all developed capitalist states. As indicated in the first section of this chapter, the direction of travel in many nations' economic policies has been towards liberalization. Nonetheless, this has been implemented in a variety of different ways in different countries, reflecting the continuing importance of distinctive sets of national institutions. Whilst international pressures may be facilitating convergence by, for example, reducing barriers to trade, this has on occasion been slowed, if not reversed, by national-level actors, as with the forced removal of the 'country of origin' principle in the EU's Services Directive (pp. 64–5). This is particularly the case because economic policy is not necessarily 'neutral' but, to refer back to the first lines of this chapter, 'married to politics' – not least because of its direct and indirect redistributional impacts.

Summary

❑ Traditionally, approaches to explain why economic policy differs between nations have pointed to the interests of producers – both business and workers – and how these are translated into policy through political parties and other institutions.

❑ The 'varieties of capitalism' approach focuses attention on the coordination problems faced by firms and how these are resolved differently in liberal as against coordinated market economies. However, this approach has been criticized for failing to accord sufficient importance to political factors, including the role of government.

❑ Liberalization appears to be a core feature of economic policy in all the nations examined here, but its progress has been patchy and inconsistent.

❑ The policy instruments used in economic policy:
   – Governments use the *financial resources* available to them to fund particular industries and firms; provide infrastructure and training; tax undesirable activities; and provide tax breaks for favoured firms, industries and activities.
   – Governments use their *authority* to prohibit and regulate certain types of economic activity; to influence workers' pay and conditions; and to control cross-border flows of goods, services and workers.
   – Governments use their powers of *organization* to plan economic development, directly participate in the economy through publicly owning certain firms or industries, and create economic policy institutions.
   – Governments use their control over *information* to provide information and advice to the public as consumers, and to inform policy debates.

❑ Clearly, some economic policies, like minimum wages, will have a direct impact on individuals' incomes. However, economic policies such as measures countering inflation and regulating financial markets can also have a differential, if less direct, impact on different income groups.

Chapter 4

Welfare Policy

The term 'welfare' has been understood in a variety of different ways. Social security and pensions have often been seen as core areas of welfare provision (Esping-Andersen, 1990). However, 'welfare policy' can also be defined as covering *all* activities in which governments engage to promote the wellbeing of their populations, covering health, housing, nutrition and education, as well as income maintenance (Wilensky, 1975: 1). This chapter concentrates on income maintenance policies such as transfers, but also refers to other areas of welfare policy (including housing and family policy) where relevant. Education and health policy are considered in subsequent chapters.

Governments are often taken to be the originators of welfare policy, given the widespread use of the term 'welfare state'. However, some would argue that the 'welfare state' includes not only the 'public' activities of governments and their agencies, but also the 'private' provision of welfare in the home (Dominelli, 1991). The view that population welfare can be promoted by a variety of actors informs the term 'the social state', which is commonly used in Germany and Italy. Although this chapter primarily focuses on governmental policies in relation to welfare, it also examines government promotion of welfare provision by the private and voluntary sectors, and by families.

It is important to note that, whilst we generally view welfare policy as in some way stemming from a desire to improve citizens' wellbeing, on occasion it may be motivated by different objectives. For example, one of the reasons for the introduction of slum clearance and improved public hygiene in the UK was concern over the poor health of recruits for the Boer War (Williams, 2008: 161), rather than reflecting sympathy towards the poor. Furthermore, whilst welfare policies may be presented by politicians as increasing wellbeing, in practice they may harm some individuals' interests, a matter examined in detail in the last section of this chapter.

Even where welfare policies appear to share similar objectives, a closer look reveals they can differ substantially. 'Social protection', for example, could refer to a 'safety net' designed to stop unemployed individuals and families from falling into destitution but little else, providing them with only a minimal income. Similarly, it could refer to a system of welfare which maintained individuals' and families' incomes if they became unemployed or retired – which for most individuals would mean a relatively good standard of living being provided through welfare, and not merely a bare minimum.

Even within the same country, welfare policies may pursue radically different objectives. To take the example of the UK, national insurance (covering the basic state pension, some unemployment and disability benefits, and health care costs) pools risks across all workers, thus redistributing from low- to high-risk workers. In contrast, social assistance (used to boost individuals' incomes) provides a subsistence income to certain disadvantaged groups through the tax system, thus redistributing mainly from the middle and upper working class to the lower working class. Finally, tax credits, again, use the tax system, but top-up low to middling wages, and cover a very significant number of people – around one third of UK families (calculated from HMRC/National Statistics, 2011 and UK census data).

Despite such internal inconsistencies within welfare states, numerous authors have claimed it is possible to distinguish the different welfare models, regimes or even 'worlds' exhibited by different nations. This chapter critically examines these approaches as background for an exploration of the use of different welfare policy tools by governments. It examines the degree to which welfare policies vary across nations in their use of financial resources, authority, organization, and the provision of information, as well as examining how the scope of policies can differ in terms of their impact on different groups. The chapter touches, *inter alia*, on the role of interests, ideas, institutions and cross-national factors in the production of welfare policy – themes which are developed in significantly greater detail within Chapters 8 to 12.

The context: theories of welfare policy development

Early attempts to explain welfare policy development in different nations generally suggested that this was positively correlated with economic modernization and industrialization (Wilensky, 1975). In the postwar period up to the beginning of the 1980s, it appeared that the share of GDP taken up with growth in social expenditure – at least in some areas, such as unemployment insurance – was increasing over time across Western democracies, and that this process of growth was intensifying. However, rather than different nations 'catching up' with each other, by the late 1970s new patterns were forming as welfare states matured (Alber, 1981).

Rather than relating growth in social expenditure to economic modernization, an alternative approach linked economic openness (the level of trade in relation to the rest of the economy) to expenditure growth.

Cameron's (1978) analysis, for example, suggested that international economic competition was pushing governments (particularly in smaller, more open nations) to protect their domestic populations more actively by expanding the size of the public sector (see also Katzenstein, 1985).

More recent analyses have, on the contrary, argued that economic openness, together with other forces promoting globalization, has led instead to a *reduction* in social protection. This is because governments have been able to promote retrenchment in social expenditure by arguing that high levels of taxation and regulation make their domestic economies less competitive. Mishra (1999), for example, claims that particular international organizations, such as the International Monetary Fund and World Bank, have been very effective at promoting a view of welfare expenditure as crowding-out economic growth.

The view that globalization is likely to lead to lower levels of social protection has been labelled that of a 'race to the bottom'. The concept was initially used in relation to federal systems such as the USA, following the 'Delaware case'. In the mid-1970s, the state of Delaware reduced its requirements for company registration (corporation), in a bid to attract more economic activity. A high percentage of firms then chose to incorporate in Delaware rather than in other states. This example suggested that both sub-national regions and nation states would be increasingly forced to compete against each other to attract business, by progressively lowering social protections and the regulation of economic activity. Despite this, however, there is limited evidence of a 'race to the bottom' (Harrison, 2006). This issue is returned to in Chapter 12, which examines in detail cross-national pressures on policy-making, such as globalization.

For the moment, it should be noted that, whilst there may be common trends across developed nations (broadly towards retrenchment in spending levels), the way in which these changes have been implemented has varied significantly across countries (Daly, 1997). Whilst welfare expenditure growth has certainly slowed in many nations from the 1980s onwards, this has not been the case universally; and, furthermore, has sometimes reflected changes in macroeconomic conditions (e.g. reduced unemployment) rather than policy decisions. Instead, a more differentiated (and potentially confusing) picture has emerged.

Theories of systematic difference across nations

The complex picture indicated above has led to the positing of different 'models', 'regimes' or 'worlds' of welfare provision. The following sections consider the most influential attempts to identify distinctive patterns of welfare state development, as well as critiques of these approaches.

Classifications based on the extent of welfare policy coverage

Wilensky and Lebeaux (1958) provided one of the earliest attempts to distinguish different models of welfare in different nations. They argued that a 'residual' model, such as that in the USA, could be distinguished from an 'institutional' one, such as that in Scandinavia. In 'residual' systems, welfare provision acted as a 'safety net' for the worst-off, those who were unable to benefit from family support or succeed in the marketplace. The 'institutional' model, on the other hand, was far more expansive, and used welfare policy not merely as a safety net but, rather, as part of an overall redistributive strategy.

Richard Titmuss, the social policy theorist, developed this approach and argued that three models could be distinguished (1958; 1974). The first, as with Wilensky and Lebeaux (1958), could be described as 'residual'. This model had originated in the UK with its 'Poor Law' tradition, with the state providing welfare as a last resort for the very worst off. Systems based on this model often drove down take-up of benefits (as they were perceived as stigmatizing), and involved considerable administrative costs (to determine eligibility). In contrast the '*institutional redistributive*' model viewed the provision of welfare not as an exceptional occurrence for the very worst off, but as a resource for the entire population – as with the more comprehensive systems developing in Scandinavia. This approach inevitably imposed costs on virtually the entire population, as tax-payers, to provide the necessary resources required for such an expansive approach.

Titmuss also identified a third model, the '*industrial achievement*' model, in which welfare policies buttressed economic divisions and performance. Hence, individuals' status in the labour market was preserved by welfare policies under this model, with the exception of some 'safety-net'-style provision for those who were not integrated into the labour market (such as the long-term unemployed, or women with caring responsibilities). Titmuss argued that West Germany offered an example of such an approach, which led to stark and entrenched divisions between the low- and better-paid, and between the long-term unemployed and the rest of society.

Another approach to classification – perhaps more common amongst continental scholars (see, e.g., Chassard and Quintin, 1992; Join-Lambert *et al.*, 1994) – distinguished German-style '*Bismarckian*' from British-style '*Beveridgean*' systems. These approaches focused on the extent to which certain groups of people were targeted, or otherwise, by welfare systems – effectively distinguishing occupational insurance-based systems (i.e. Titmuss's 'industrial achievement' model) from welfare systems which did not preserve labour market status differentials in this way.

Whilst Beveridgean systems distribute wealth vertically – that is, down the income distribution (with the rich taxed more than the poorest, and funds from general taxation being used to pay for welfare provision), Bismarckian systems redistribute 'horizontally'. This is because they are based on insurance funds covering particular categories of people with similar incomes, who pool their risks across the group. As a result, inequalities are often intensified by Bismarckian systems, whilst they tend to be reduced within Beveridgean systems (Bonoli, 1997).

Classification based on decommodification

A different, and very influential, attempt to classify nations' welfare regimes came from Gøsta Esping-Andersen (1990; see Abrahamson, 1999, on its use by other authors). He argued that, rather than focusing on the 'construction' of welfare regimes (as with the approaches mentioned above), it was also important to consider 'how these influence employment and general social structure' (Esping-Andersen, 1990: 2). In particular, he argued that consideration should be given as to how welfare policies influenced 'the degree to which individuals, or families, can uphold a socially acceptable standard of living independently of market participation' (*ibid.*: 37) – what Esping-Andersen described as 'decommodification'.

OECD welfare regimes can, Esping-Andersen argued, be clustered according to the level of decommodification they induce, and the type of social stratification they employ. These arose from historical patterns including the nature of class mobilization (the strength of trade unions and left parties, in particular), and the legacies of previous welfare institutions. This approach is often described as concerning 'power resources', and is considered in detail in Chapter 8.

Following this approach, Esping-Andersen distinguished three 'worlds of welfare capitalism': liberal, conservative, and social democratic. '*Liberal*' *regime* types led to low levels of decommodification and redistribution, and were based on a view that individuals and their families should be largely self-reliant. Examples of this kind of regime, Esping-Andersen argued, were provided by the USA, the UK and Australia. In these countries, the state encouraged the market to provide welfare services, both actively (through tax incentives for private schemes, such as private pensions) or passively (through keeping many social benefits to a means-tested, stigmatized, minimum – thus incentivizing participation in the labour market).

'*Conservative*' *regime* types, on the other hand, were based on social insurance and supported 'traditional' family structures. Whilst benefits were often set at a relatively high level, these were related to market position. These systems were therefore only modestly decommodifying, as they maintained status differentials (redistributing income across groups, if not among them). These approaches stressed the role of the family and other non-state institutions (such as trade unions, business associations and religious groups) in providing welfare, as opposed to that of the state. Esping-Andersen (1990) argued that France, the Netherlands, the then West Germany and Italy could be seen as examples of this regime type.

The third and final type of regime identified by Esping-Andersen was the '*social democratic*' system, which led to high levels of decommodification and reduced levels of income stratification across the population, due to significant amounts of redistribution. Within this system, benefits were contingent not on occupational status within the labour market, but guaranteed as a right of citizenship. Examples of 'social democratic' regimes included Sweden, Norway and Denmark. Within these nations, benefits were set at a relatively high level, and services (and public sector employment opportunities) facilitated the employment of women. Such systems rested on a national commitment to ensuring, as near as possible, full employment. However, as van Kersbergen and Manow (2008: 536) point out, even in such universalistic systems the 'better-off and highly-educated people with higher skills and competences are much better capable of taking advantage of universal services (health care, education) than poorer and less educated people'.

Esping-Andersen's approach has informed analyses of other areas beyond income maintenance, such as active labour market policy (Powell and Barrientos, 2004). Nonetheless, Esping-Andersen's analysis has been criticized by some authors. The first set of criticisms focused on his empirical analysis. For example, Scruggs and Allan (2006) attempted to recalculate Esping-Andersen's data, and suggested, following this, that several countries appeared to have been placed into the wrong regime categories, and that the coherence within the clusters of countries was less strong than originally portrayed. Perhaps more substantively, other criticisms have concerned the specific typology used by Esping-Andersen, and its focus on decommodification.

How many worlds of welfare?
Esping-Andersen's typology has been criticized for a perceived inability to deal with specific countries, both within and outside the OECD. One approach, for example, argues that a distinctively '*Catholic*' *type of corporatism* can be identified, applying to nations such as Ireland (McLaughlin, 2001: 226) and to 'Southern' European countries. Such countries generally enjoy minimal state provision coupled with the encouragement of provision through voluntary associations and families (what is often described as the promotion of 'subsidiarity').

Other authors have spoken not of a 'Catholic corporatist' regime but of a '*Latin Rim*' model (Leibfried, 1992), which has only a 'rudimentary' welfare system; or of a '*Southern model*' (Ferrera, 1996; Bonoli, 1997).

Esping-Andersen did not include Spain, Portugal, Greece, or Ireland within his typology; and he classifies Italy within the corporatist (conservative) welfare regime type. It might be argued that such nations do not offer a specific welfare regime 'on their own', but instead constitute 'underdeveloped species of the Continental model' (2002: 145), or underdeveloped hybrids of liberal and conservative regimes (Leibfried, 1993).

However, many Southern European nations do share some specific features, such as fragmented systems of social protection (with some very generous benefit levels, for example, for certain groups of pensioners); institutionalized health care; and particularism and targeting (which can lead to clientelism and, under certain circumstances, corruption (Arts and Gelissen, 2002)). Furthermore, the view that such states are merely 'underdeveloped' versions of other models appears to ignore the persistence of these specific types of welfare state, and their basis in domestic social institutions (Marinakou, 1998).

Esping-Andersen's typology has also been criticized for failing to include a separate category for the '*wage-earner's welfare states*' of Australia and New Zealand. Esping-Andersen argues that Australia offers an example of a liberal welfare regime, a position criticized by Castles and Mitchell (1992), who argue that a separate, 'radical', welfare regime type can be distinguished which applies to Australia, New Zealand and Britain. In Australia and New Zealand, in particular, rather than welfare being pursued primarily through transfers, it was (at least, traditionally) pursued through market-shaping measures such as wage controls, rights for workers, and controlled prices for essentials such as utilities.

One more criticism of Esping-Andersen's approach comes from those who argue that it fails to consider in sufficient detail the impact of welfare policies on caring and family arrangements – a matter which is developed in significantly greater detail in the section on the 'scope' of welfare policy at the end of this chapter.

Moving beyond typologies

It has been argued by some that the 'welfare modelling business' (Abrahamson, 1999) is, in any case, of limited benefit when it comes to comparative public policy analysis. Do welfare regimes as 'ideal types' need to have a basis in reality, or can they be 'merely' conceptual and be used as yardsticks for measuring 'real' welfare states? Assuming that the ideal types are based on empirical data, and do reflect 'reality', the delineation of Esping-Andersen's regimes appears to rest substantially on his interpretation of the (sometimes rather patchy) data (Shalev, 1999).

Furthermore, Kasza (2002: 277) argues that welfare state typologies 'have been of limited or no help in explaining the different patterns of

welfare cutbacks in recent years'. Instead, 'today's policies are the cumulative work of different governments and sometimes different forms of
government, and they represent responses to a variety of historical circumstances' – which cannot be easily assimilated to one particular model
(*ibid.*: 273). He offers the example of Japanese social policy, which was
shaped by a parliamentary then military government, and then by occupying powers, all within just a 25-year period. Because of these different
influences, 'Japan has a public health care system that provides good
service for all, a pension system that provides uneven protection, and an
inadequate system of unemployment benefits' (*ibid.*: 275). Incoherence
can also be produced by policy differences between ministries, policy
learning from other countries, and path dependence from old policies.

Rather than structuring the analysis according to a typology, this
chapter instead examines welfare policies in different nations in terms of
their use of different policy instruments: financial resources, authority,
organization, and the provision of information. It indicates the incredible
variety of ways in which welfare systems are structured and operate in
different countries, thus providing some support to those who would
challenge simple typologies of welfare regimes. However, the chapter
also highlights some of the broad trends which can be discerned amongst
nations.

Comparing welfare policies across nations

The use of financial resources

As indicated, whereas social expenditure levels initially appeared to be
converging over time, from the 1980s onwards a more differentiated
picture emerged. This is clear from Figure 4.1, which represents government spending on transfer payments from the late 1950s onwards. The
spending patterns represented within this figure could lead us to a classification of different groups of nations similar to extant classifications:
such as 'families of nations' (Castles, 1998) or, indeed, 'worlds of
welfare' (Esping-Andersen, 1990). For example, we could distinguish
roughly between a relatively high-spending group comprising the Nordic
countries (Sweden and Denmark); a relatively medium-spending group
(France, Germany and Japan); and a relatively low-spending group (the
USA, Australia, the UK and Italy). However, as indicated below (pp.
91–6), when we look at the detail of spending in different areas, a variety
of different policy approaches can be discerned, which belie simplistic
classification.

Beyond these overall spending levels, however, there is wide variation
in the funds nations devote to specific policy areas. This is clear from an

Figure 4.1 *Social security transfer expenditure from 1958–96*

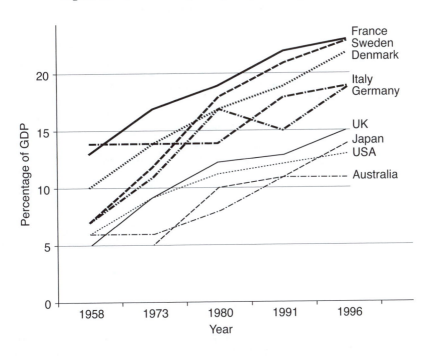

Source: Huber and Stephens (2001) table A3.

examination of income protection measures such as publicly-funded pensions and unemployment benefits.

Publicly-funded pensions

The German Chancellor Otto von Bismarck created what is widely credited as the first modern pension system in 1889. Publicly-funded pensions now constitute the largest single component of government transfers in many nations – amounting to 14 per cent of national income in 2009 in Italy, the highest proportionate spender in the OECD (OECD, 2009a). This highlights the importance of examining discrete policy areas within welfare, as well as welfare expenditure as a whole. Although Italy is a comparatively low spender on welfare policy as a whole, the public contribution to pensions in that nation is substantial.

The provision of public pensions has become a particularly contentious issue in the light of demographic change. Many governments have attempted to reduce eligibility for, and the amount of, public pensions, but reforms have often been hotly contested. Pension systems have

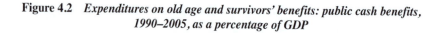

Figure 4.2   *Expenditures on old age and survivors' benefits: public cash benefits, 1990–2005, as a percentage of GDP*

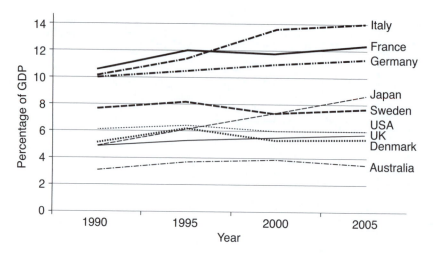

Source: OECD (2010b).

a 'strong built-in inertia', given the numbers of individuals typically involved, and the fact that both current and future pensioners are likely to have particular expectations of their 'due'. Such expectations were in evidence during riots against French government proposals to increase the minimum age at which the full pension was payable from 65 to 67 in October 2010.

Nonetheless, population ageing is placing increasing pressure on existing pension systems. Population ageing is not a uniform phenomenon – countries such as the UK, Sweden and the Netherlands will be less affected than Spain, Italy and Bulgaria, for example (Börsch, 2009: 173). Furthermore, the experience of demographic change in many developed nations is less significant than that in many developing countries. In much of sub-Saharan Africa, reduced life expectancy for the middle-aged due to the AIDS epidemic has led to a 'gap' between the very young and the very old.

Figure 4.3 displays measurements and projections of the proportion of the population in both developed and developing nations falling into older age categories, from 1950 until 2050.

Pensions can be categorized into contributory and non-contributory types. Non-contributory pensions are paid for through the taxation system or other public funds, such as the Norwegian government's Petroleum Fund. They cover all eligible members of the population, regardless of whether or not they have contributed to an insurance

Figure 4.3   *Projections of population ageing in developed and less developed nations*

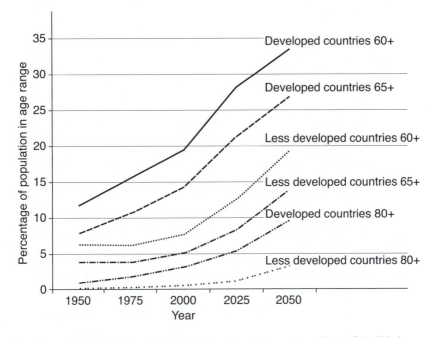

Source: Data are from tables in Population Division, Department of Economic and Social Affairs, United Nations (2002): 50–1.

scheme, for example. As can be seen from Figure 4.2, the publicly-funded contribution to pensions varies significantly even within the OECD and, furthermore, coexists with a variety of other types of pension provision.

Some developed nations rely heavily on non-contributory systems, such as New Zealand, the Netherlands, and Australia. The New Zealand system, for example, pays out 72.5 per cent of the average wage for a married couple, upon passing a residency requirement (Barr, 2009: 221). As another example, the Dutch non-contributory system pays 70 per cent of the net minimum wage – again, depending on residence (*ibid.*). Although traditionally a relatively durable element of welfare states, pensions policies have been subject to reform in a number of nations from the 1980s onwards.

Publicly funded unemployment support
As with publicly-funded pensions, the level of provision of public unemployment support varies widely, from the low levels offered by the USA (with the unemployed receiving one third or less of the income of working people), to the relatively generous support provided by Norway,

BOX 4.1   Kent Weaver's 'chutes and forks' approach to explaining pension reform

Weaver (2010) argues that it is important to acknowledge the potentially negative (as well as the positive) feedbacks from public policies. While pensions systems might create groups of beneficiaries (positive feedback), they can also become increasingly unstable over time by, for example, causing financing problems (negative feedback).

Weaver argues that contributory, occupationally-linked but only moderately status-maintaining pension systems (what he calls 'Bismarckian-lite' systems) and 'mixed regimes' (comprising private, occupational and state pension layers) have proved more durable than 'universal' and 'residual' regimes. Whilst pension regimes generally gravitated towards more universality of provision up to the 1950s and 1960s, since the 1970s most have moved towards 'mixed' or 'Bismarckian-lite' regimes.

This is partly due to the negative feedbacks of different types of regimes, with mixed regimes proving very difficult to shift into other types of provision. As a result, policy stability may 'mean that despite very strong negative feedback effects, there are no plausible regime transition options or that incremental patches are cheap and politically acceptable' (*ibid.*: 158).

for example (where state support makes the unemployed only around one quarter less well-off than those in work).

The general trend in provision of support for the unemployed has been towards more extensive conditions being placed on recipients (as discussed on pp. 100–1) and lower levels of provision. Between the years 2001–7, one third of OECD nations reduced the value of unemployment benefits – as, for example, occurred in Germany with its Hartz IV reforms. In addition, in many nations the proportion of support during unemployment provided by social assistance – often to cover housing and child-related costs – has increased in relation to that provided by national insurance and other forms of unemployment benefit. This has been the case in the UK, for example, where unemployment benefit (Jobseekers' Allowance) has fallen over time, from amounting to 18.7 per cent of average earnings in 1981 to 10.5 per cent in 2007 (McNulty, 2009).

Other publicly funded transfers
In addition to pensions and unemployment insurance, governments can provide a variety of other non-contributory transfers to different population groups.

In some cases, transfers are designed to increase individuals' incomes to a higher level. Such transfers are often 'means-tested', with only

Figure 4.4   *Percentage of average earnings replaced by unemployment transfers*

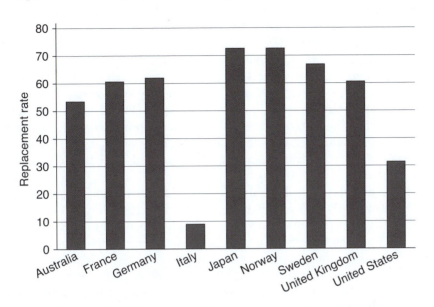

Notes: The bars represent total insurance and social assistance, averaged over different family types, over 60 months in selected nations as at 2008. Data are from the OECD's Work Incentives database, accessed December 2010.

individuals earning below a certain amount becoming eligible. Examples of means-tested benefits for older people include the UK's Minimum Income Guarantee (renamed 'Pension Credit'), available to the poorest British pensioners on top of the basic pension (Walker and Maltby, 2008: 399); and the new Chilean means-tested pension, payable to the least well-off two thirds of pensioners (Barr, 2009: 220).

More generally, 'social assistance' programmes are designed to offer a minimum income to the very worst-off in society. The majority of OECD nations possess such 'last resort' systems, available to those with least resources, with the exception of Greece, Italy and Turkey. Such schemes are often heavily stigmatized, however, leading, alongside other factors, to relatively low take-up.

Special payments may also be available to specific categories of individuals, such as those unable to work through ill-health. An example comes from the Italian invalidity pension which came to absorb an increasing proportion of Italian social spending, given its lax entry requirements and the absence of other types of social assistance (Fargion, 2009: 178).

In addition to transfer payments being used to support individuals' incomes, they may also be provided to help cover the costs of specific activities or disadvantages. In many nations, individuals can apply for public funds to help cover the additional costs of living with a disability (for example, to cover the costs of special equipment). Support may also be provided 'in kind', such as the food stamps programme for those on very low incomes in the USA.

In some cases, public funds are provided automatically to all those who fall into a certain perceived category of need, as is often the case with those who care for children. The majority of nations within the OECD, and many outside it, provide some version of universal child benefit which helps cover the costs of child-rearing. However, in some nations – including the USA, New Zealand, Italy and Canada – transfers to cover the costs of child-rearing are means-tested in relation to parental income.

Governments may also subsidize individuals' housing costs, either through the provision of low-rent, social housing, or through direct (to the individual) or indirect (to the landlord) transfers to cover housing costs. Given the high relative costs of housing, such support has become an increasingly important element of assistance to those on low incomes in many nations, including the UK, Finland, Poland and Greece. This has particularly been the case with extremely high rates of increase in the cost of housing from the mid-1980s up to the financial crisis of the late 2000s. For example, real house prices increased by 90 per cent or more in Australia, Norway and the UK, from 1980 (or the earliest year available) to 2008 (OECD, 2011b: 6).

The extent of subsidy provided varies substantially within nations. This is clear from examining just one aspect of housing – the provision of social housing – within Europe. Whilst social housing amounts to 35 per cent of the overall housing stock in the Netherlands, it accounts for only 4 per cent in Hungary (Whitehead and Scanlon, 2007: 5). The extent to which residents own, rent from public bodies, rent from private bodies, or are housed in other arrangements such as private cooperatives is indicated in Figure 4.5.

The use of tax expenditures and other incentives
Tax expenditures involve governments willingly forgoing revenue by providing exemptions to tax for certain groups, or for certain activities. In some nations, tax expenditures constitute an extremely significant element of welfare policy. In the USA, tax expenditures 'with social welfare objectives' amounted to 'roughly one-third of what the government spent on traditional social programs' in the early 1990s (Howard, 1993: 413). Tax expenditures can be used to try to incentivize a number of behaviours, from encouraging private pension provision to 'making work pay' and encouraging marriage.

Tax expenditures supporting pensions in the USA constituted the 'third largest social program in the American welfare state after Social

Figure 4.5 *The share of different types of housing for six developed nations*

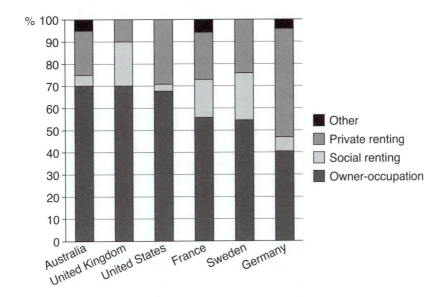

Notes: The data represented in the figure were collected as follows: Sweden, 1997; Australia, 1999; Germany, 2001; UK, 2001–2; and USA and France, 2002.

Source: Data are from Scanlon and Whitehead (2004): table 2.

Security and Medicare' in the early 1990s (*ibid*.). The USA is, however, somewhat of an outlier in this regard. Other OECD nations spend considerably less on supporting private benefits in this way (Hacker, 2002: 16), although the tax incentives for pension provision have grown substantially in nations such as Italy (Adam and Gough, 2008: 122) and Germany (Schmähl, 2007) from the 1990s onwards. Unfortunately, there is little available data on the extent of these arrangements, when compared with that available concerning the extent of 'ordinary' transfers (Hill, 2006: 51; although see Kvist and Sinfield, 1997).

More visibly, a number of governments, particularly in developed nations, have introduced measures through the taxation system, ostensibly to improve the attractiveness of low-paid work and thus increase employment. The case of the US Earned Income Tax Credit was used as an example by many other countries. This tax credit operated like a 'negative income tax', being paid on incomes below a certain amount, provided that this income came from the work of the head of the family. The measure started as 'a little-noticed tax provision in 1975', but was expanded significantly from then onwards (Clarke with Piven, 2009: 40). The US Earned Income Tax Credit is often viewed as the inspiration for the UK 'Working Families Tax Credit', although it is arguable that the latter built on existing UK provisions such as 'Family Credit' (Page and Mark-Lawson, 2007: 57). Similar systems of tax credits or payments to support work operate in Canada and France.

The use of authority

In addition to the use of financial resources, governments can also use their powers of authority to require their populations to adopt certain behaviours. This can involve mandating participation in certain schemes, such as contributory pensions, or the imposition of conditions on obtaining financial resources, as with workfare policies. As well as exercising their authority in relation to their own populations, governments may also attempt to control, or at least shape, the activities of other actors – such as private companies – as part of welfare policy.

Publicly-mandated pension provision
Contributory pension schemes require individuals to put some of their current income towards their retirement, with the collection of funds occurring generally but not exclusively through the payroll (via wages). Nations where such pensions are funded from current contributions, what is known as 'pay-as-you-go' systems, include France, Germany, Italy and Britain (Barr, 2009: 220). These systems effectively involve the creation of a 'social contract between the generations' (Walker and Maltby, 2008: 398). For example, the UK system of National Insurance involves contributions from both employees and employers, which then go to fund current pensioners' pensions ('pay-as-you-go'), Incapacity Benefit (for the long-term ill or disabled), and up to six months of Job Seekers' Allowance (which after six months becomes payable out of general taxation) (Alcock, 2009: 126).

'Funded' systems, in contrast, rest on assets which are built up over time, either by the recipients themselves (as in Singapore which, essentially, has developed a system of individual accounts (Barr, 2009: 200–1), or through a collective trust fund (as with the Canada Pension Plan (*ibid.*)). The Chilean funded pension system has inspired reforms across nations from Latin America (Weyland, 2006) to Central and Eastern Europe (Orenstein, 2008). It is based on 'individual capitalisation accounts', which are privately managed, but are part of a state-supervised scheme (Vial and Melguizo, 2008: 15), based entirely on workers' contributions. This system was, however, augmented in 2008 by a new public pillar of non-contributory pensions to aid those with irregular or non-existent contribution histories (such as women and those who work in the informal economy).

Mandatory pension schemes may be 'defined benefit' – guaranteeing a certain pay-out in the future for current contributors, often based on their overall salary average or final salary. Alternatively these schemes may require a 'defined contribution' from employees, but not guarantee that any level of pay-out would be forthcoming in the future. There has been a general move towards 'defined contribution' schemes across the OECD, although some groups (such as senior executives) appear to have been less significantly affected by this trend than other employees (Waine, 2008).

In nations such as France, Germany and Italy, mandatory pension schemes have traditionally helped perpetuate status differentials from the world of work in individuals' financial status during retirement. This is, however, increasingly being eroded following pension reform. For example, the German pension system, implemented from 1957 in West Germany and now applying across unified Germany, was traditionally designed to differentiate between occupational groups. However, reforms during the 2000s have homogenized the main public pension, with the traditional distinction between blue- and white-collar variants of pension insurance no longer applying (Schmähl, 2007). Similarly, the Italian public pension system has been reformed so that the old earnings-related (status-preserving) system is being removed and replaced with a defined contribution scheme, which is planned to apply from 2013 (Fargion, 2009: 180).

Publicly-mandated unemployment insurance
In many nations, workers are required to contribute to an insurance fund which is then drawn upon to cover any periods when they are out of work. Many of these systems are analogous to pay-as-you-go pension systems – that is, they are paid for by the contributions of current workers (who are required to participate, often above a certain income level), rather than through the deposit and building up of assets by previous workers.

Systems of mandatory unemployment insurance have traditionally reflected each nation's own economy, although a common shift towards more restrictive approaches is increasingly clear. For example, in 1971, the qualifying period for Canada's system of 'Unemployment Insurance' was reduced to as few as 12 weeks, 'depending on the regional unemployment rate', to acknowledge the highly seasonal nature of employment in some parts of Canada, particularly within the fishing industry, for example (Lightman and Riches, 2009: 57–8). However, from the mid-1990s eligibility was 'tightened dramatically' (*ibid.*: 59).

Another type of contributory system involves the provision of occupationally-specific insurance plans, rather than national plans.

Occupationally-based unemployment systems are viewed as an essential component of 'Bismarckian' systems, such as Germany and Austria, and were also a feature of the Italian regime. Replacement rates in these nations are relatively high and were initially related to the claimant's previous salary, although there has been a trend from the 2000s onwards towards reducing the length of time when the income-related component can be claimed, as has occurred in Germany.

A specific variant of occupationally-based systems is the Ghent system, which covers approaches to unemployment insurance which are dependent on union membership. Sweden, Iceland, Finland, Denmark and, to an extent, Belgium, all possess Ghent systems. For example, the Swedish system involves numerous voluntary societies which are managed by the trade unions, and paid for through contributions from trade unions and also from government and employers. Contribution levels are set by the funds concerned, and depend on the perceived likelihood of future unemployment. Ghent systems obviously provide additional incentives for workers to join trade unions. Replacement rates paid by these systems are relatively high and sustained for a comparatively long period compared with other countries.

The imposition of conditions to receive public funds
In addition to the provision of funds being related to claimants' incomes or needs, governments may also exercise their authority to apply conditions which restrict availability to those who behave in a particular manner.

The field of unemployment benefit is particularly notable for the cross-national spread of 'conditionality' of benefits. This draws on the legacy of what are known as Active Labour Market Policies (ALMP – sometimes also known as AMS, referring to the central actor which promoted these policies in Sweden, the *Arbetsmarknadsstyrelsen* or National Labour Market Board). ALMP were initially adopted 'to promote labour-force mobility, education and occupation flexibility' (Salonen, 2009: 134). In this context, ALMP enabled the reconciliation of 'structural economic change with social protection' (Wincott, 2003: 548). Sweden's ALMP have acted as an example for a number of nations, particularly those with strong intermediary institutions (such as trade unions and religious institutions) such as the Netherlands and, to a lesser extent, Germany (*ibid*.: 548–9). ALMP have become increasingly popular, showing a 30 per cent rise on expenditure in this area across EU countries throughout the 1990s (Powell and Barrientos, 2004: 89).

However, in many countries, participation in ALMP – generally involving the acceptance of jobs and/or participation in training – has become a condition for the continued receipt of benefits, as part of what has come to be described as 'workfare'. These approaches often include elements of ALMP – for example, by including job experience projects (as in Australia's 'Work for the Dole' (Stewart, 2009: 92)), a choice between education, subsidized work in the private or voluntary sectors, or placement on an environmental taskforce, as with the British New Deal for Young People (Deacon, 2008: 313).

In many cases, however, ALMP's focus on education and training in order to ready individuals for work has been reduced in workfare pro-grammes to a requirement for recipients of benefits (including, but not restricted to, unemployment benefit) to participate directly in the labour market. Hence, the Australian 'Job Compact' involved the government stating its 'obligation' to provide work for claimants, whilst claimants were obliged to 'accept any reasonable offer or be subject to penalties' (Kennett, 2001: 139).

Workfare schemes are frequently mentioned in studies of policy transfer, and it is notable that many schemes explicitly draw on examples from other countries or, within federal systems, from other states. This was particularly the case with the USA, where states were explicitly encouraged to 'experiment' with different workfare models from Reagan's presidency onwards (Peck, 2001). The 'Wisconsin Works' pro-gramme in the USA was drawn upon not only by other national govern-ments (such as the UK), but also by regional politicians from other countries. For example, Roland Koch, the state premier of Hesse, a German *Land* (region), visited Wisconsin in 2001 and argued for the adoption of this model both within his region and across Germany (Turner, 2011). The process of policy transfer across regions also occurred in Canada, where the states of Alberta and Saskatchewan acted as initial 'experiments' with workfare, which were then drawn on across the country (Lightman and Riches, 2009: 56).

Some would argue, however, that certain 'workfare' schemes are not based on ALMP but, instead, simply constitute limits on benefit avail-ability. An example comes from reforms in the USA to the AFDC pro-gramme (Assistance for Dependent Children). In the late 1990s, President Clinton imposed a two-year limit on receipt of this benefit, beyond which point recipients needed to find a job either in the private sector or within a publicly subsidized, minimum-wage job, alongside a five-year total limit on receipt of this benefit. The Personal Responsibility and Work Opportunity Reconciliation Act, which then reformed AFDC into TANF (Temporary Aid for Needy Families), led to a situation where 'the primary obligation of poor mothers was to find employment (a requirement that distinguishes them from non-poor mothers)' (Clarke with Piven, 2009: 37). TANF did not primarily operate on a 'conditional' basis but, instead, on the basis of a simple cut-off in benefits beyond a certain period. As a result, it is arguable whether it rep-resents ALMP or simply a restriction on benefit availability.

Government control of the private sector

In addition to requiring individuals to participate in certain schemes, and imposing conditions on the receipt of welfare payments, governments can also exercise their authority by regulating the provision of private welfare.

One example of government control of private provision comes from the regulation of private pension providers. Governments often require private pension providers to apply for a licence from the state, either in order to operate (as in Australia and many Latin American nations), or to qualify for tax relief (as in the UK and USA); they may impose capital adequacy or other requirements on private pension fund portfolios (such as limits on holding particularly risky or foreign assets), as in much of Europe, or alternatively, impose certain governance requirements (as in the UK, through Trust Law); or they may ensure that insurance is provided to protect against pension fund insolvency (as in the USA).

Licensing processes – which often, again, enable private providers to qualify for tax exemption – also apply in many countries to other areas of private insurance (such as private unemployment, life or ill-health insurance), as well as to areas of private welfare service provision, such as children's homes and adult social care. Governments may also 'regulate' welfare provision by private providers through contractual mechanisms. This has occurred, for example, in the field of work activation, where in some countries (such as the Netherlands) a private market has been created whereby private providers compete for contracts to provide employment-related services to the unemployed.

The regulation of welfare services by private providers has proved challenging for many nations, particularly when this applies to highly technical areas such as pensions. The introduction of Chilean-style individual accounts, for example, requires 'financial institutions that are effective enough that the added weight of pension business will further strengthen them' – which was not necessarily the case in nations such as the Ukraine and Russia, which were encouraged by the World Bank to adopt such systems (Barr and Diamond, 2009: 23). Reviews of pension regulation have occurred in a number of nations following apparent failures in private pension systems, such as with the Enron pension scheme in the USA, and the UK's private pensions 'misselling' scandal, where over 300 firms were disciplined by the UK's financial services regulator (BBC, 2002; Waine, 2006).

Public authorities in some countries have also attempted to use their authority to regulate the terms of employment as a means of promoting welfare. This is the understanding of 'social policy' embodied in, for example, the EU's 'Social Chapter' (the 'Protocol on Social Policy'), which focuses mainly on the rights of workers (Cochrane *et al.* 2001b: 272), rather than on the direct provision of transfers or welfare services. Both Australia and New Zealand have been described as examples of 'wage-earner welfare states' (Castles, 1985), where welfare goals were pursued through labour market regulation. In each case, federal-level courts made decisions in the first half of the twentieth century which required the payment of minimum wages that could adequately support an average-sized family. This approach stressed the 'industrial citizenship' of the male head-of-household, who possessed substantive individual rights (e.g. to a reasonable level of pay which could support an entire family) and collective rights (e.g. to strike and form a trade union).

Given that 'wage-earner welfare states' rested on providing rights to the male head-of-household, it 'seriously disadvantaged' women workers (Bryson and Verity, 2009: 75; Davey and Grey, 2009: 90). It also rested on tight controls on immigration in order to exclude competition in the labour market, as well as on extensive tariff regimes to reduce foreign competition in trade (Castles, 1988).

From the 1990s onwards, however, the use of nationally-mandated systems to set wages has been abolished in New Zealand, with its Employment Contracts Act enabling localized wage bargaining and 'contractual arrangements between employers and employees' – thus significantly weakening the power of trade unions (Davey and Grey, 2009: 94). A new Employment Relations Act introduced in 2000 attempted to increase the role of trade unions in wage bargaining once more although, by 2005, union coverage had slumped to 22 per cent of the working population (*ibid.*: 96). In Australia, the introduction of much freer trade has been accompanied by a move towards wage- and conditions-bargaining at firm as well as at sector level, thus also reducing trade union power in that nation (Bryson and Verity, 2009: 70).

Finally, in some other nations (such as France) governments have presented reductions in working time as a welfare-related measure, linking this to work–life balance andt also to attempts to increase employment rates (Salonen, 2009: 143). However, the current policy orthodoxy followed by most OECD nations is that 'far from discouraging or redistributing employment, governments need to maximize it' (May, 2006: 109).

The use of organization

It is, obviously, in relation to the delivery of welfare services by public sector organizations that governments primarily exercise their powers of organization. These powers concern the actual provision and delivery of welfare services and transfers to individuals, and also the indirect impact of creating additional employment opportunities through the public sector.

The administration and delivery of welfare
The field of comparative public administration has compared aspects of the organization of public services in specific areas such as housing

(Duclaud-Williams, 1978) and across the state as a whole (Peters, 1988; Farazmand, 2001). The extent to which differences in governing institutions can lead to differences in policy between nations, because of their formal and their informal aspects, is examined in greater detail in Chapter 10.

At this stage, it should be noted that the organizational challenges facing nations differ substantially depending on the welfare policy area concerned, and the nature of the territory and polity. The administration of a pension system, for example, becomes more complex with a rural and/or highly mobile population, and/or with low rates of the population employed in the formal sector. A lack of administrative capacity can open the road to corruption, with, for example, checks on identity being difficult if civil records are of low quality (Barr and Diamond, 2009: 23).

The provision of work-related measures

As mentioned, in addition to engaging in income maintenance programmes involving cash or in-kind transfers, governments can also attempt to sustain individuals' incomes through the direct provision of employment, either explicitly through public works schemes, or implicitly through expanding the size of the public sector.

Perhaps the earliest large-scale example of a public works scheme in a democratic polity was Roosevelt's New Deal programme, which combined reform of welfare benefits with employment creation. Albeit on a smaller scale, some contemporary governments, including in the USA, have attempted to follow this approach once more with the announcement of major public works programmes in the wake of the 2008 financial crisis.

In other nations, governments effectively (if indirectly) boost the employment of certain groups through their incorporation into the public sector. For example, the expansion of the public sector in Scandinavian nations led to a situation where work was virtually guaranteed, particularly for women, as part of a work-based welfare state. Clayton and Pontusson (1998) have argued that reforms during the 1980s and 1990s within welfare states have involved reducing the size of public sector employment – a factor which can be separated from the more traditional role of governments in providing transfer payments, and which is often not picked up when analysts focus merely on levels of welfare expenditure (see also Rose, 1985).

In some other nations, governments have attempted to 'create' jobs by encouraging private sector hiring, rather than directly providing jobs through public works or the public sector. Examples would include the German 'Mini-' and 'Midi-Jobs', introduced in 2003, which exempt employers from social security payments for certain categories of part-time, low-paid employment, and similar approaches in France. However, such programmes may have little impact on the overall level of employment, merely incentivizing employers to take on one particular kind of worker on a short-term contract (i.e. the longer-term unemployed), rather than take on new staff for indeterminate contracts (Garraud, 2000).

The provision of information
Governments' activities here relate both to the direct provision and structuring of information about welfare-related matters, and to shaping public debates around welfare policy.

Governments act in a variety of ways to help overcome information deficiencies and asymmetries which may affect individuals' welfare. Two examples come from the realms of pension provision and the labour market.

First, in systems where a choice of different types of pension are available, individuals are required to make difficult long-term decisions involving complex trade-offs between current and future consumption. Governments may act to structure information and choices about pensions, with a view to improving both individual and overall outcomes. For example, the US 'Thrift Savings Plan', a pensions scheme introduced for federal civil servants in 1986, involves a clearly differentiated, strictly limited number of possible funds for workers to choose from, and a 'good default option' for those workers who do not make a choice of fund in which they wish to be enrolled (Barr, 2009: 214, 219).

Another example that has acted as a 'lesson' for other nations comes from Sweden, which has developed an 'orange envelope' system providing pension contributors with a clear and personalized pension statement, following the introduction of pension reforms (Larsson *et al.*, 2008: 148). However, even this allegedly successful means of communication with the public appears to have limited impact on individuals' awareness of their pension status. Whilst 90 per cent of recipients surveyed claimed they knew they had received the orange envelope, only 'about half' reported 'reading at least some of [its] content' (*ibid.*: 154).

When it comes to the labour market, governments in many nations have long been involved in providing 'labour exchanges' or 'employment agencies' for those seeking work, in addition to private agencies which cover specific occupations (e.g. executives or secretaries). This approach recognizes that individuals may be unable to access sufficient information about employment opportunities using private means alone. In many countries, attempts have been made to increase coordination between the provision of information about job opportunities at employment agencies with 'employment activation' activities and the provision of unemployment benefits (OECD, 2006).

As mentioned, governments may also attempt to structure and influence debates about welfare policy issues in order to legitimate particular, favoured, approaches. This may involve fostering public recognition of a 'crisis' or, less substantively, problems with existing provision, and the need for new policy solutions (Palier, 2007); or may involve propagating a particular (often negative) view of welfare recipients in order to pave the way for reform.

The area of workfare is arguably one where governmental powers of persuasion have been in strongest evidence. In some nations, government pronouncements on welfare recipients have frequently involved pejorative descriptions which concern not only claimants' unemployed status, but also invoke 'moral' concerns – such as marital status. For example, the concept of a 'welfare queen', referred to by a number of political and governmental actors in the USA, arguably contributed to the adoption and intensification of workfare in that country (Hancock, 2004). Indeed, the area of workfare is arguably one where a particular view of welfare policy has become predominant, whereby welfare states combine access to rights with the imposition of responsibilities (Rodgers, 2000: 8).

Governments and occupational and voluntary welfare

The text above has considered the role of governments in providing, encouraging, regulating, or providing information about welfare services and transfers. However, governments may also, through action or inaction, involve private or voluntary sector organizations or bodies in the provision of welfare. Occupational and voluntary systems of welfare are in evidence in many different nations alongside public provision, as part of a 'mixed economy of welfare' (Powell, 2007).

The social policy theorist Richard Titmuss (1958) drew attention to the growing extent of what he described as 'occupational welfare' – the provision by firms of welfare-related services for their employees. Japan has been referred to by many authors as a nation where occupational social security is a particularly significant element of the welfare mix. Hence, Jones (1993: 212) argues that 'for those in mainstream employment [in Japan], especially with a major corporation, quality of career very much spills over into quality of social entitlements', with some companies providing not only pensions, but also insurance to cover health care and unemployment, and housing support. Such benefits are coupled, particularly in large companies, with effective guarantees of 'lifetime employment' (Kennett, 2001: 122).

However, such provisions infrequently apply to part-time and contract employment (often undertaken by women), or to smaller companies (*ibid.*: 123). In any case, many larger companies are also reducing the extent to which they provide 'company-based welfare' (Kono, 2005).

Furthermore, the Japanese state does provide some basic services and transfers, particularly health care and pensions, for all eligible individuals so that those who fall outside employment within certain large corporations have a 'safety net' of coverage on which to rely; one which some would argue is more generous than often supposed, with the exception of protection for the long-term unemployed (Kasza, 2006). As such, it would perhaps be too strong to describe the Japanese welfare state as entirely occupational, although company-based schemes do play a stronger role than in many other nations.

In many countries, governments also encourage non-state bodies (the voluntary and third sectors) to contribute to the provision of welfare. In some, this is due to a tradition of 'subsidiarity', the notion that decision-making and service provision should take place at the lowest level possible – an approach which often grew out of extensive conflict between different social actors (particularly religious ones) and the state. The Netherlands – and, to an extent, Germany – offer examples where the role of voluntary groups is enshrined in legislation. In these nations, non-state bodies – including charities, religious associations and associations of employers and employees – are involved in the provision and, often, the administration of welfare. In other nations, a commitment to subsidiarity is combined with one to liberalism, viewing provision by both the voluntary and private sectors as preferable to state-run services. Such a situation arguably applies in the USA (Ginsburg, 2001) and is increasingly popular amongst other developed nations such as the UK (with the UK coalition government's support for a Big Society where voluntary organizations play a more powerful role).

The scope of welfare policy

Previous sections have considered the policy tools used by governments in welfare policy: the use of financial resources, authority, organization and the provision of information; and governments' relationship with occupational and voluntary sector providers of welfare. This section focuses on the scope of welfare policy rather than its mechanisms; that is, who is affected by welfare policy, and how.

As examined in Chapter 8, a number of theorists have argued that welfare states help to perpetuate the interests of certain groups – be these particular occupations, classes or genders, and that the different ways in which these groups are organized in different nations helps explain different patterns of welfare state development. Welfare states can simultaneously institutionalize and diminish existing social divisions of class, race and gender (Ginsburg, 1992).

Welfare policy and different racial and ethnic groups

Traditionally, welfare policy has been closely related to citizenship. T.H. Marshall (1963) argued that the introduction of welfare states in developed economies had led to the extension of 'social' citizenship, where individuals possessed not only political rights, but also social ones. However, in many cases 'welfare' policies have led to the imposition of particular 'responsibilities' on recipients, or to the stigmatization of certain individuals (as with the sometimes pejorative use of the term 'welfare' in the USA).

Certain groups have also, on occasion, been barred from accessing welfare services. This can arise not only from explicit restrictions on eligibility, but also from the discretionary interpretation of eligibility criteria by public servants, who may, for example, privilege certain racial groups over others – an issue considered in greater detail in Chapter 10. Finally, less than universal coverage may be due to particular conceptions of citizenship and views of who should be enabled to stay on the national territory. For example, the British 1905 Aliens Act barred those who needed access to public funds, or who became homeless within their first 12 months on British territory, from entering and staying in Britain. This policy continues at the time of writing as the 'no recourse to public funds' rule (Williams, 2008: 160). The extent to which individuals can access welfare benefits and services generally depends on a nation's approach towards citizenship, in particular, whether citizenship hinges on descent ('blood'), or place of birth (Roberts and Bolderson, 1999: 205).

Even policies which ostensibly appear to be 'universal' may fail to cover immigrant groups due to requirements for qualifying residency periods. Non-contributory pension systems, for example, frequently require payees to have fulfilled a residency requirement – for example, 50 years between the ages of 15 and 65 in the Netherlands, and 10 years since the age of 20 in New Zealand (with half the years of residence having been spent from the age of 50 upwards).

Welfare policy and gender

In addition, welfare policies frequently have differential impacts on men and women. The gendered nature of welfare states has only started to be seriously researched by social policy theorists since the late 1980s. New research has highlighted the inadequacy of existing approaches in this respect. For example, Esping-Andersen has been criticized by feminist scholars for focusing on decommodification to the neglect of gender issues. This was despite the fact that the 'extent to which the family, and more specifically women, are considered the "natural" providers of welfare varies from country to country' (Kennett, 2001: 5; see also Sainsbury, 1996).

Furthermore, even where welfare policy is ostensibly provided for all members of the population on equal terms, women and men may end up benefitting from it to different degrees. A clear example of this comes from the realm of contributory pensions. In the UK in 2005, 'only about 85 per cent of recent male retirees and 30 per cent of women retirees were entitled to a full basic state pension' (Barr, 2009: 216). The gap arose not only due to the 'welfare arrangement' (the collection of contributions through wages), which disadvantages those who have interrupted employment histories (as do women who have taken time off to care for children), but also due to women's socio-economic status, given that they are generally lower paid and thus less able to make voluntary 'topping-up' National Insurance contributions to shore up their contributions history (Frericks *et al.*, 2009; Bardasi *et al.*, 2010).

As well as status differentials arising from the operation of the labour market, societies are also stratified by gender; this stratification is affected by the welfare policies adopted by governments (Bussemaker and van Kersbergen, 1994). Esping-Andersen acknowledged in later work (1999b) that his initial typology failed to take into account issues such as 'defamilialisation', dependence on the male breadwinner, and the role of social care, when classifying welfare regimes. Rather than the key nexus being that between the state and the market, he acknowledged that families should also be brought into the analysis.

This recognition followed work by other social policy theorists that examined the extent to which 'defamilialisation', 'personal autonomy' or 'insulation from dependence' could occur for women, in addition to 'decommodification' (Langan and Ostner, 1991; O'Connor, 1993; Lister, 1994). Trifiletti (1999) suggested that the level of decommodification produced by welfare regimes roughly correlated with the degree of defamilialization – hence, welfare regimes which incorporated women as workers tended to have high levels of decommodification (such as Sweden), and those regimes which encouraged women not to work, tended to be more commodified (such as the UK).

Lewis (1992) created a 'male breadwinner typology', which identified a '*strong*' *male breadwinner* model (examples of this being the UK and Germany), a '*weak*' *male breadwinner* model (Sweden), and a '*modified*' *male-breadwinner* model (France). Lewis's analysis highlighted that the German and British regimes were predicated on a particular view of the appropriate role of women in home-making which was not picked up in analyses based on decommodification.

Moving beyond the countries examined by Lewis, certain nations' welfare systems, including many in South-East Asia, could appropriately be viewed as primarily based on the 'household economy', whilst others combine occupationally-based welfare with strong family support – such as in Japan where, for example, a relatively high proportion of elderly people live with and are cared for by their children (Kasza, 2006). In China, a quasi-legal foundation has been provided to promote inter-generational solidarity (through families individually pledging to support their elders), and the role of the family in providing welfare is required at a collective level through a legal framework which 'supports the notion of familial obligation and responsibility within the public welfare system' (Kennett, 2001: 122). In a number of nations the role of women supporting the 'care economy' within the home is promoted by government policy, either explicitly (through separate welfare arrangements for men and women, transfers for stay-at-home mothers, or tax breaks for married couples), or implicitly (through welfare arrangements being focused on status within the labour market).

Conclusion

This chapter first examined the numerous attempts which have been made to offer broad-brush accounts of welfare state development, beginning with theories of modernization and, from the 1980s onwards, focusing on the impact of globalization. A number of different typologies have been developed, with one of the most influential being that of Esping-Andersen concerning the degree to which welfare states 'decommodify' workers. However, this approach is subject to a variety of criticisms, due to where and how particular nations are categorized, and also due to the perceived inadequacy of uniquely focusing on decommodification when other factors (such as gender) may also be important when explaining differences between nations' welfare policies.

The chapter has summarized how governments have enacted welfare policies using financial resources (to provide welfare transfers such as pensions and unemployment benefit, and through tax incentives and credits), authority (to mandate participation in certain schemes, impose conditions on the receipt of certain transfers, and regulate the private sector), organization (to administer welfare systems and create jobs), and the provision of information (to help individuals take decisions about welfare matters and to find information about employment opportunities, and to shape political debates about welfare policy). When performing these activities, governments have often supported or otherwise encouraged the activities of non-state providers of welfare, including the private and voluntary sectors, and families. Finally, the chapter highlighted the often uneven scope of welfare policy, which is shaped by notions of citizenship and ethnicity, as well as by gender divisions.

Chapter 5 looks at a policy area which is often closely aligned with welfare policy – health care. Whilst many of the patterns highlighted in this chapter also apply in that arena, there are, if anything, even more significant differences between nations when it comes to the role of private and public providers in health care, and their use of insurance or general taxation-based funding systems.

Summary

❑ Whilst early approaches to welfare policy suggested that both the coverage and generosity of programmes were likely to grow as nations industrialized, the history of welfare states from the 1980s onwards indicates that welfare systems have developed in a variety of distinctive ways in different countries.

❑ Esping-Andersen's 'worlds of welfare' typology of welfare states, based on differentiating social democratic, conservative and liberal models, has dominated analyses for some time. However, it can be criticized for its limited applicability and lack of consideration of gender relations.

❑ The policy instruments used in welfare policy:
- Governments use the *financial resources* available to them to provide income protection measures such as publicly-funded pensions, unemployment and housing support, as well as for tax expenditures and other incentives.
- Governments use their *authority* to require participation in insurance schemes by the population; to impose conditions on the receipt of transfers; and to regulate private providers of welfare, and the terms and conditions of workers.
- Governments use their powers of *organization* to administer and deliver welfare, and to provide work-related measures.
- Governments use their control over *information* to structure their populations' choices around complex issues such as pensions; to overcome information deficiencies, such as may occur in job markets; and to shape debates around welfare reform.

❑ The extent to which welfare services are provided through occupational schemes and the voluntary sector differs between nations.

❑ Although not always made explicit, welfare policies often affect different racial, ethnic and gender groups in very different ways.

Chapter 5

Health Policy

It is difficult to define 'health policy' precisely, not least because of continuing debate over the definition of 'health' itself. The WTO's 1948 definition of health as 'a state of complete physical, mental, and social well-being and not merely the absence of disease or infirmity' would lead to a number of policy areas being brought under the umbrella of health policy (including, e.g., policies on housing, employment, and poverty reduction).

Furthermore, 'health' services have been used in some circumstances to harm individuals, as with enforced sterilization programmes (which in some nations, such as Peru, have continued until relatively recent times: BBC, 2002a), as well as sometimes functioning effectively as an arm of criminal justice policy (as in England following the Mental Health Act 2007, where those with untreatable mental disorders can be detained when viewed as posing a potential risk to the community (Cairney, 2009)).

This chapter will adopt a relatively narrow focus, by examining policies that are at least ostensibly directed at the treatment, management and prevention of illness. These policies cover what is conventionally known as 'primary care' (family doctor services and health education), 'acute' care (mainly in hospitals – delivered to those who are severely unwell – sometimes described as 'secondary care'), and 'chronic' care (provided to those with long-term conditions, covering palliative care, hospices and elements of 'social care').

Health care policy is notoriously complex, with different nations exhibiting a wide variety of approaches concerning the funding and organization of services (Dierkes *et al.*, 1987). To further complicate the picture, individual countries often exhibit considerable variation in service provision across regions, population groups and/or health-related conditions. White (2010: 115), for example, maintains that whilst the 'US not only represents almost as much medical care spending as the rest of the OECD put together, it also includes almost as much internal diversity in health care financing arrangements as could be found by comparing a number of countries'. Nonetheless, a number of attempts have been made to classify nations' health care systems. These are reviewed in the following section – in particular, attempts to base classification on the degree of decommodification that health care systems involve, and the degree to which services are universally provided (the distinction between 'Bismarckian' and 'Beveridgean' systems).

The chapter then turns to considering government use of financial resources (tax-funded health services and tax expenditures); authority (the mandating of health insurance; regulation of providers of health care, and of pay and conditions for health care workers, and control over individuals' health-related behaviour); organization (the administration and delivery of health care, and degree of centralization of health services); and information (the provision of information and advice to the public, and the production and dissemination of information to inform policy-making) in the realm of health care.

The context: theories of health policy development

Numerous approaches have been developed to understand differential patterns of health care system development in different nations. All countries have, however, been subject to certain common pressures in the field of health care. This section details these common pressures as background for the subsequent examination of core approaches to explaining health care system development.

Traditionally, theories of health policy development suggested a certain degree of convergence among health services as they moved from a focus on preventing infectious diseases, and focused more on chronic conditions. Before the 1950s, health care institutions were often largely concerned with quarantining patients (either because of communicable disease, e.g. tuberculosis, or for the incarceration of what were then described as 'lunatics'). In some cases, this role was taken to an extreme; in 1958, no less than 0.7 per cent of the Irish population had been incarcerated in 'lunatic asylums' (Goodwin, 1997: 7).

From the 1950s onwards, however, health care systems in industrialized nations have been reoriented towards providing treatment and management of health conditions, rather than isolation. Communicable disease has by no means been eradicated – a point underlined by global outbreaks of the H5N1 ('avian flu') virus during the 1990s and 2000s. Yet, broadly, health care policies in most industrialized nations have adapted to the fact that 'however unevenly it occurs across and within different societies, the disease burden will increasingly result from pathologies and disabilities that evolve over long periods of time and that are persistent' (Mechanic and Rochefort, 1996: 247).

An additional change in health policy concerns the identity of users of health care systems. Increasingly, health care services in industrialized countries have come to be consumed far more by older rather than young people, with the former being far more likely to suffer from chronic conditions. Blank and Burau (2004: 5) note, for example, that in 'most countries those over 65 account for at least double the expenditures their size alone would indicate, and in most cases at least triple'.

Policies towards health care have also been affected by rapid technological and scientific developments, from the creation of commercially available antibiotics in the 1930s to the development of organ transplantation from the 1950s onwards, and to innovations in gene technology, pharmacology and advanced surgery (including keyhole and foetal surgery).

It should be noted, however, that some authors dispute the significance of technological and scientific developments as a driver for health care policy change. Goodwin (1997: 28–32), for example, highlights continuing debate over the extent to which the development and use of the major tranquillizers impelled shifts away from incarceration to community-based services within mental health. Similarly, the speed with which new technologies are implemented within health care may be affected by the dominance of particular specialisms within medical care. This appears likely to explain why, for example, certain countries of similar levels of development are nonetheless subject to wildly differing rates of surgical interventions. For instance, US surgeons appear to carry out almost twice as many operations per head of population as their Japanese colleagues (Weiser *et al.*, 2008).

Despite this heterogeneity, one clear trend across countries has been the rise in costs of pharmaceuticals (Mossialos *et al.*, 2004): throughout the 1990s, increases in pharmaceutical costs 'greatly exceeded the rate of growth in other types of health expenditures'. Although this growth has reduced and other 'health expenditures have increased more rapidly in recent years', the 'growth in pharmaceutical expenditures continues to exceed the average growth of OECD economies' (OECD, 2008: 10). Increasingly, this has been driven more by so-called 'me too' drugs – variations on existing drugs – than entirely novel therapies (Geyer, 2011). Given the concentrated benefits accruing to the pharmaceutical industry from increased use of new drugs, it has been described as a paradigmatically 'clientelistic', and very well-organized, pressure group (Permanand and Mossialos, 2005).

In addition to new cost pressures from 'producers' of health care, it is arguable that in most nations, societal understandings of health care have changed substantially. Not only have a range of conditions (such as infertility) become subject to 'medicalisation' (Mechanic and Rochefort, 1996: 248), but the 'consumers' of health care have also become less deferent to medical professionals, there having been an explosion in the availability of information about medical conditions and treatments, particularly through the media and internet. This has put particular pressures on medical systems where 'rationing' of services is an explicit or implicit goal of health care policy (Blank and Burau, 2004: 12). It has been argued that such pressures have led to the development of a universal paradigm across most industrialized nations, whereby public financing has been combined with competition as part of attempts to increase quality and reduce expenditure (Chernichovsky, 1995). However, it is arguable that, whilst common pressures may have led to changes in different health care systems, these are likely to reflect domestic factors including the design of decision-making processes and the power of different groups, leading to the uneven adoption of different service structures (Walt, 1994).

The increasing scope of medicine, greater 'consumer knowledge', and the development of new technologies and therapies has been held responsible by some for the sustained increase in medical spending that has been in evidence for most, if not all, industrialised nations from the 1980s onwards (see Figure 5.1) (Callahan, 1998).

Finally, although not as pronounced as in many other policy areas (such as environmental policy), health care has been subject to a certain degree of internationalization. This particularly applies to the health care workforce, which is comparatively highly mobile (see Figure 5.2). In the USA, for example, one in four physicians have trained in another country (Hussey, 2007: 299).

Figure 5.1   *Overall (public and private) expenditure on health, percentage of GDP, 1980–2007*

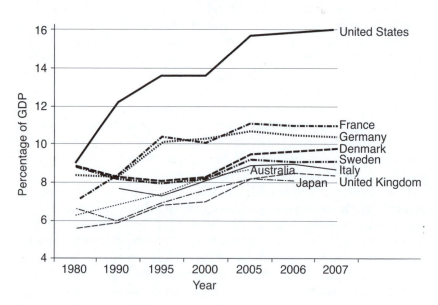

Note: Values are not available for all years for all countries.

Source: OECD (2009b).

Patients are also becoming more mobile, if to a lesser extent. This has been facilitated within Europe by successive rulings by the European Court of Justice (Jarman and Greer, 2010). Whilst the situation has fluctuated over time, the position at the time of writing is that patients are entitled to enjoy treatments available in other EU systems if the treatment concerned is not available within medically justifiable time limits in their home system (Glinos *et al.*, 2010: 105), aside from emergency medical services, which are available freely for European citizens carrying a European Health Insurance Card. Actual flows of patient mobility are still, however, relatively limited within the EU legal framework (Martinsen, 2005: 1046). This is arguably not the case in relation to 'health tourism' more broadly, which is the fastest-growing type of tourism in many countries including Thailand, Malaysia and India. Such tourism involves not only plastic surgery, but also routine and even some highly complex operations (Bookman and Bookman, 2007: 2).

In summary, different authors have pointed to the impact of changes in disease patterns, ageing populations, new science and technology, and changed societal understandings of health care and reductions in deference, as helping explain developments in health policy in different nations. These developments are increasingly shaped by international movements of health care professionals and, particularly from the 1990s onwards, patients.

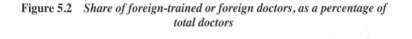

Figure 5.2 *Share of foreign-trained or foreign doctors, as a percentage of total doctors*

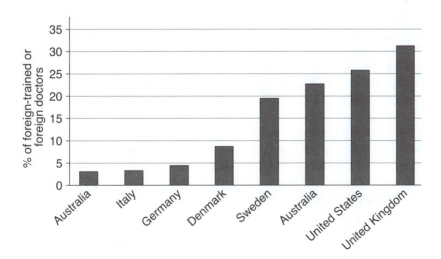

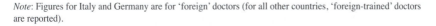

Note: Figures for Italy and Germany are for 'foreign' doctors (for all other countries, 'foreign-trained' doctors are reported).

Source: OECD (2009b).

Theories of systematic difference across nations

Despite these common pressures, health care policies have developed in myriad different ways in different nations. A number of attempts have been made to classify the different types of health care system, and, in some cases, explain why differences might exist between different countries.

The earliest typologies of different health care systems tended to focus on differentiating financing methods and provision levels as a means of categorizing nations (Anderson, 1963). Hence, Terris (1978) distinguished those systems which provided basic facilities through general taxation, from more extensive 'universal' or 'national' health systems, and both from health systems based on insurance. Both Terris's (1978) and Elling's (1994) approaches linked different health care system types to macro-level factors such as economic development and the division of labour.

Other approaches have stressed the influence of institutional and/or cultural factors on producing different types of health care system (Leichter, 1979), or the role of different political party configurations (as with Maioni's (1998) examination of Canada and the USA).

More modern classifications of health care systems have tried to come to terms with the complexity of different systems, often by attempting to delineate the different spectra along which they vary. Powell and Wesson (1999: 12), for example, distinguish eleven 'parameters' of variation. Wendt *et al.* (2009) suggest the existence of three dimensions of difference which could, in theory, result in 27 different combinations – although they acknowledge that some are more likely than others. In practice, however, Freeman and Frisina (2010: 172) suggest that these different categories can generally be boiled down to three or perhaps four: 'a world of so-called national health services, social insurance systems, private insurance systems and (perhaps) "mixed types"' (see also Rothgang *et al.*, 2005).

Classifications based on decommodification
Some authors have adopted Esping-Andersen's (1990) focus on decommodification and stratification, examined in detail in Chapter 4, to categorize health care systems. Bambra, for example, examines 'health decommodification': 'the extent to which an individual's access to health care is dependent upon their market position and the extent to which a country's provision of health is independent from the market' (Esping-Andersen, 2005: 33). She indicates how examining health care services as part of welfare states lends support to the idea that the Scandinavian countries constitute an identifiable, high decommodification group, and that the USA and Australia can be placed in a low decommodification group with

Austria, Belgium, France, Germany, Italy, Japan, the Netherlands and Switzerland in a 'medium' group (*ibid.*: 36). However, she argues that Canada, New Zealand and the UK all exhibit 'high decommodification' health care regimes, despite the fact that they are classified as 'low decommodification' liberal welfare regimes by Esping-Andersen (*ibid.*: 37).

Freeman and Frisina, however, criticize attempts to align studies of health care with Esping-Andersen-style typologies. As discussed in Chapter 4, Esping-Andersen argued that his different worlds of welfare arose out of specific historical legacies and, importantly, the strength of labour movements and parties representing labour movements. However, Freeman and Frisina (2010: 173) argue that the 'universalization of access to health care, at least in Europe, has separated health politics from the politics of organized labor (with the partial exception of organized health labor)'. As a result, they argue, key disputes concerning health care centre not around redistributive issues but, instead, around accounting, accountability, information and technology (*ibid.*).

Goodwin (1997) effectively takes issue with this view in his suggestion that different approaches to mental health can be understood in relation to different approaches to the macroeconomy and, in particular, to different emphases on the desirability or otherwise of commodification. Goodwin delineates three 'worlds' of mental health policy: regimes that are liberal, conservative, or social democratic. He suggests that, in liberal systems such as the UK, shifts towards community-based mental health services signalled a 'recommodification' of patients who were previously 'segregated from the wider processes of a market economy' – that is, who were institutionalized (*ibid.*: 108). In conservative regimes, such as Germany and France, deinstitutionalization only occurred in the mid-1970s, and was not promoted on economic grounds (i.e. not to get patients out of institutions such that they could contribute to the economy) (*ibid.*: 109). Finally, Goodwin (*ibid.*: 110) suggests that in social democratic regimes such as Sweden, deinstitutionalization was promoted on collectivist grounds (to 'normaliz[e] . . . the social conditions of disadvantaged groups').

Classifications based on universality

An alternative approach to the classification of health care systems concerns the extent to which services are provided on a universal basis or otherwise, with different approaches to provision being evident in so-called 'Beveridgean' and 'Bismarckian' systems.

Beveridgean systems include Finland, Sweden, Spain and the UK. Perhaps the earliest example of a collectively-provided, (quasi-) state system was in Sweden, with medical care being provided by the state from the seventeenth century onwards (Blank and Burau, 2004: 44). It was New Zealand, however, which created the first recognizably 'national', universal, health service, in its 1938 Social Security Act (*ibid*.: 24), although as will be discussed, this only covers secondary health care. Beveridgean systems are sometimes known as 'single-payer' systems – given that governments pay for health care services, rather than users, or social or private insurers, doing so (Flood, 2000: 106). In such systems, health care is provided to all on the same basis, regardless of the extent of their contributions through taxation.

Germany was, of course, the first nation to adopt a 'Bismarckian' system, with Chancellor Bismarck introducing a health insurance system in 1873 which created a system of 'social solidarity, freedom of choice for patients and nearly full coverage of services' (Blank and Burau, 2004: 42). Contributions to health insurance depend on economic status (i.e. they are earnings-related). There are some differences in provision for different groups – for example, the health care provision for tenured civil servants (*Beamte*) in Germany differs from that provided to other categories of worker (Leisering, 2009: 157).

However, other differences in provision of health care for different groups have reduced in Germany since the introduction of the insurance system. As a result, Germany's current health care system, 'although formally based on insurance, is strongly egalitarian and near universal' (*ibid*.: 164). It has also been noted that there is considerable diversity even within Bismarckian models (i.e. between Germany and France). Indeed, Steffen (2010: 141) has described Germany's health care system as based on 'renewed social risk management', whilst France exhibits 'liberal universalism'. As a result, the Bismarckian and Beveridgean categories of health care system may be less representative of alternative approaches to provision (i.e. universal versus insurance) than initially was the case.

The preceding discussion has indicated how there is no consensus amongst comparative analysts concerning the appropriate classification of different health care regimes. This behoves a more fine-grained analysis which considers how governments have used their control over financial resources, authority, organization, and information, to pursue health-related policies.

Comparing health care policies across nations

The use of financial resources

Governments have predominantly used their access to financial resources to provide taxation-funded health services. Funding from taxes has been used in some nations to provide, or to subsidize, the use of primary, acute and chronic care services, and for the purchase of medical

Figure 5.3 *Public share of total expenditure on health, split into general government spending and spending through social insurance, 2007*

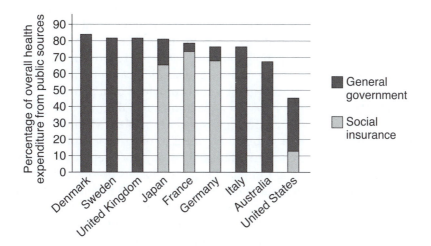

Note: The figure for Japan is for 2006, and that for Australia is for 2006–7.

Source: OECD (2009b).

equipment and drugs. Some governments have also used their ability to control taxation to incentivize individuals to adopt health insurance through tax breaks.

Figure 5.3 indicates how there is a continuum of approaches towards funding health care, from a minimum public contribution (and significant reliance on private provision), through the provision of private, then social, insurance to tax-supported national health systems (Blank and Burau, 2004: 23). Individual states may exhibit a variety of approaches; for example, whilst secondary care may be delivered through general taxation, primary care may be reliant on private payments by users (as is the case in New Zealand) (*ibid*.: 25). Hence, although on paper the New Zealand system appears to be universal, in practice it includes barriers to access to primary health care for poorer people. This can be contrasted with a system ostensibly based on a mixture of public (for the 60 per cent of less well-off people) and private insurance (for the 40 per cent of better off people), as in the Dutch system. In the Netherlands, primary health care is free at the point of use for those who are publicly insured, despite its coexistence with a considerable private insurance market for the better-off (Flood, 2000: 104).

As mentioned, there are some 'single-payer' systems (such as in the UK, New Zealand (for acute services), and Sweden), where governments are the almost exclusive funders of the majority of health services, which are publicly provided through taxation revenue. In addition to these, governments may provide the funds for health care provision, but to largely private or not-for-profit bodies. This is the case in Canada, for example, where provincial governments pay for services, typically using general taxation; these services are then free to citizens at the point of use.

In addition to these systems, governments may fund services for specific categories of the population even when the rest of the health care system is based on private insurance. The Medicaid programme in the USA falls into this category. Medicaid is provided on a non-contributory basis for poorer members of the population, and administered by states. This differs from the confusingly similarly-named Medicare system, which is based on insurance and provided to older people only. In practice, many older people use Medicaid to pay for their Medicare premiums, and older people form the biggest recipients of Medicaid. Not all physicians participate in the Medicaid system, and it is considerably stigmatized (Starr, 1982). Nonetheless, Hacker (2004: 720) describes Medicaid as 'a remarkable oasis of spending and coverage growth [during the 1990s and early 2000s] amid a parched desert of hamstrung antipoverty programmes' in the USA.

For a considerable period, public health spending appeared to be inexorably rising in developed nations. By the period 1980–2000, however, the rate of increase in most nations had slowed. Hacker (*ibid.*: 699) suggests on his own calculations that '[t]wo OECD nations, Sweden and Denmark, actually experienced a decline in health spending as a share of GDP' between 1980 and 2000, whilst Jordan (2011: 125–6) argues that reductions in the public share of health care spending (albeit less statistically significant ones) could also be discerned in Canada, France, Germany and the UK through the 1980s and 1990s, as well as in Sweden and Denmark.

In a number of nations, governments have also used tax expenditures to encourage the adoption of private insurance. These may be offered on a continuing basis; hence, as Hacker notes (2004: 704), tax expenditures in the USA routinely amount to very significant amounts – worth US$188 billion in 2004. Tax incentives were introduced by the Australian government in the late 1990s to try and encourage individuals to take on private coverage. By 2006, 43 per cent of the Australian population had purchased private insurance plans, following the new incentives and also a tax penalty on higher earners who had not taken on private insurance (Bryson and Verity, 2009: 78).

The use of authority

Governments can exercise their authority in a variety of ways in the field of health care policy. In particular, they can mandate their citizens to take on health insurance plans, impose regulations on the providers of health care, exert control over the pay and conditions for health care workers, and attempt to control – or, at least, alter – individuals' behaviour in order to improve their health.

Publicly-mandated health insurance
Publicly-mandated insurance schemes involve governments requiring citizens, and sometimes also employers, to contribute to insurance schemes, often via the payroll. Bismarckian systems such as those in Germany and France are based on this type of insurance, as part of what is often described as 'multi-payer' systems (because of the different insurance organizations involved) (Hacker, 2004: 695).

As with tax-funded services, which may be provided against the background of a system otherwise based on private insurance, governments may mandate individuals to participate in insurance schemes to defray the costs of particular kinds of medical care, if not to cover all medical costs. Hence, as mentioned, the US Medicare scheme for older and disabled citizens is insurance-based, involving compulsory membership, and income-linked contributions.

Government regulation of providers of health care
Clearly, in some nations, most, if not all, health care services are provided through the private sector. Even in ostensibly public systems, however, governments and public actors will need to interact with private actors in order to purchase equipment (e.g. drugs and medical technology) and, increasingly, to provide physical infrastructure (e.g. new hospitals and other facilities), ancillary services (e.g. catering) and even medical services themselves (e.g. the UK's Independent Sector Treatment Centres, used to cut waiting lists by undertaking routine operations such as the removal of cataracts and hip replacements) (Alcock, 2009: 114). In addition, some sectors of the population may also purchase private health insurance on top of their entitlement to tax-funded public services. In the UK, for example, private insurance amounted to 7.9 per cent of overall spending on health in 2005 (World Health Organization, 2008) – a relatively small, if still significant, proportion. Although often subject only to general financial regulations, private insurers may be subject to specialized regulatory regimes, if they cover a large percentage of the population (Jost, 2003).

Although often subject to self-regulation, in some countries the medical professions have been subject to considerable regulation by governments. Hence, Leichter (1979: 103) argues that 'Indian kings, as early as 1500 BC, required all new medical graduates to demonstrate their competence before royal assent to practice was granted'.

Even where medical professionals themselves are subject largely to self-regulation, in many countries the influence of government on otherwise self-regulatory procedures has increased in the face of medical scandals (Moran and Wood, 1993; Kaye, 2006). In addition, the services which health care professionals provide may be regulated by the state. This is the case in relation to the public 'accreditation' of services, as applies in France, for example. Its Agence Nationale d'Accréditation et d'Évaluation de la Santé (ANAES) attempts to assess both public and private hospitals for the quality of care that they provide, using criteria concerning the patient experience, management procedures, and organizational arrangements (Hassenteufel, 2008: 222). Similarly, in Britain, a variety of bodies exist to regulate health care services, including Monitor (which regulates a specific category of semi-autonomous hospitals – Foundation Trusts) and the Care Quality Commission (which is focused on assessing hospitals, care homes and other bodies against specific quality and safety standards).

Governments have also been involved in setting rules concerning the susceptibility of medical practitioners and organizations to legal challenge. There is a considerable degree of diversity between countries, with some adopting 'no-fault' schemes (such as France and New Zealand) – whereby allegations of negligence or malpractice are largely dealt with through specialized bodies, to civil systems – whereby aggrieved patients or their relatives generally use the court system to obtain compensation. The most extreme example of a civil law-based system is arguably the USA, with its relatively high rates of health care-related litigation.

The regulation of pay and conditions

At the heart of all health care policies lies a contradiction between the purchasing and/or regulatory power of governments, and the monopoly power of health care professionals (Immergut, 1992: 35; Giaimo, 2002). Indeed, Moran (1999) argues that what he describes as 'production politics' are essential in explaining the development of the British, German and US health care systems (see also Alford, 1975).

The decision-making role of health care staff tends to be greater in Bismarckian systems, since these often involve health care staff helping to run insurance schemes, alongside insurance funds (Blank and Burau, 2004: 34), and because of the existence of a variety of buyers (governments, insurers, private purchasers, and so on). Tuohy (1999) describes the Canadian Medicare insurance-based system as characterized by 'collegiality' between medical professionals and other actors, reflecting the degree of involvement of medical professionals in decision-making in that system, compared with the UK (marked by hierarchy) and the USA (marked by the operation of the market). It has also been argued that the power of health care professionals over policies increases where the political system is more permeable to medical interests, as occurred in some postcommunist countries (Roberts, 2009) as well as in Western nations (Wilsford, 1991), and was arguably also the case in Japan until the Liberal Party lost power in 1999.

A particularly pertinent case study of conflict between the interests of governments and those of health care professionals comes from the Italian health care system. A National Health Service was established in Italy in 1978. However, whilst funding was collected nationally, decision-making concerning the allocation of resources was devolved to regions and, beneath them, lay management committees. The system did not include any restriction on private practice for public doctors, thus incentivizing high rates of 'moonlighting' and, indirectly, the maintenance of 'public inefficiency' (Fargion, 2009: 177). In the late 1990s, the system was reformed in an attempt to dampen cost pressures. Henceforth, 'medical professionals were required to work full time for the NHS or opt out of the public system' – with an increase in salary for those who stayed with the public system. Some private work was accepted under the new system, but only on top of contracted hours, and with fewer career and economic benefits from so doing (*ibid.*: 181).

Health care professionals have acted collectively to resist NHS-style models being implemented in countries as diverse as Canada (Lightman and Riches, 2009: 56), New Zealand (Davey and Grey, 2009: 90) and the USA (Bjorkman, 1989). Where NHS-style systems have been introduced, these have often involved health care professionals having their independence guaranteed in return for their acceptance (Bryson and Verity, 2009: 77), or being allowed to practice privately as well as publicly – what Nye Bevan, the UK Health Minister in his negotiations in the late 1940s to create the NHS, described as 'stuffing their [consultants'] mouths with gold'.

Certain governments have focused explicitly on reducing the power of health care professionals. Allsop and Saks (2002: 2) argue that this goal motivated successive Thatcher governments to attempt to introduce a 'more competitive internal market based on the purchaser/provider split', but conclude that this 'had limited impact'.

It should be noted, however, that what is perceived as being in the collective interests of doctors differs between different nations. Even within Bismarckian systems, German doctors have concentrated on ensuring collective representation in insurance funds, whilst French doctors have focused on maintaining their ability to set prices for medical services ('tariffs') and the 'free choice' of patients between doctors and medical services more generally (Hassenteufel, 1997). Similarly, whilst Italian psychiatrists may have been influenced by the strong anti-psychiatry and anti-institutional movement within that country, this has not been generalized across Europe and North America (Goodwin, 1997: 38).

Government control over individuals' behaviour
One other use of their authority by governments concerns attempts to change individuals' behaviour in order to promote their health. One of the clearest examples of this comes from the introduction of bans on smoking in public places, which have proliferated from the 1970s onwards (Studlar, 2002, 2004; Marmor and Leiberman, 2004).

Anti-smoking bans have even been introduced in countries with a strong tradition of individualism, such as Italy. Mele and Compagni (2010) explain how the then Italian government was able to appeal to the need for non-smokers to be protected from passive smoking, using that country's constitution and its principle of 'equal duties and equal rights', aided by the prominence of a cancer specialist within government.

The use of organization

Governments have attempted to use their organizational powers in a variety of ways to shape health care service delivery. This has included the use of a variety of administrative instruments and procedures, the introduction of competition between different health care providers, and the centralization or decentralization of service delivery.

Government use of administrative instruments and procedures has often, particularly since the 1980s, focused on controlling the spending decisions taken by medical practitioners. Hence, in France, attempts were made to introduce what were described as 'references médicales opposables' (RMO) in 1993, which specified care pathways and procedures for specific medical complaints. These were introduced in an attempt to steer family doctors away from recommending expensive forms of treatment to their patients. However, they were largely ignored by doctors, who faced limited sanctions if they failed to comply (Hassenteufel, 2008: 91).

In contrast with such approaches, which attempt to reduce costs through trying to influence practitioners' decisions directly, other approaches have attempted to use more indirect methods to reduce costs. In particular, many governments have introduced elements of competition into their health care systems. This approach distinguishes 'purchasers' (insurers, groups of health care providers, or other appointed bodies) from providers (hospitals, clinics, treatment centres), and requires purchasers to 'proactively manage and allocate resources amongst different health care needs', rather than governments attempting to influence this process directly (Flood, 2000: 1).

In both the UK and New Zealand, 'internal market' systems were introduced whereby purchasers were separated from providers within a largely public health care system. The 'internal market' approach in the UK is associated with Professor Alan Enthoven, who proposed its introduction in Britain in the mid-1980s as an attempt to replicate the US 'Health Maintenance Organization' approach, but within a public context (O'Neill, 2000). Although the UK's internal market system was reformed under the New Labour government of 1997–2010, the Conservative/ Liberal Democrat government is currently introducing reforms which would effectively reintroduce, and intensify, the internal market in the NHS. Whereas in Britain the purchasers were based around primary care practitioners (initially, what were described as 'GP fundholders', then 'Primary Care Trusts', and which are likely at the time of writing to soon become 'Clinical Commissioning Groups'), in New Zealand, Regional Health Authorities acted as purchasers (Upton, 1991). In Sweden, experiments have been undertaken with out-patient clinics being given budgets to purchase in-patient care for their patients (Glennester and Matsaganis, 1994). These 'internal market' approaches within public health care systems contrast with 'managed competition' systems, whereby different insurers purchase care (as in the USA and the Netherlands) (*ibid.*: 6).

The evidence on whether these new methods have improved efficiency appears rather mixed. Harrison (2004) argues – on the basis of his examination of marketization in the UK, Sweden and the Netherlands – that, in practice, reforms were 'watered down' as policy-makers were faced with the difficulties of implementing radical change in complex health care systems. Harrison does suggest, however, that the reforms were important in increasing the power of heath care managers in relation to other staff, and by altering opinions about the role of the market and 'business' in health care systems. Greer (2004), however, argues that alternative approaches to administration and delivery were adopted across the UK's component territories: England adopted 'markets', Scotland – professionalism, Wales – localism, and Northern Ireland – permissive managerialism.

Overall, attempts by government to use their powers of organization to control costs have frequently been prone to unintended consequences. For example, targets have often been used in health care to promote efficiency and effectiveness, in both single- and multi-payer systems. However, by focusing organizations on specific outputs, they have sometimes led to a downgrading of other activities, and even to 'gaming', whereby processes are manipulated to hit targets (see Hamblin, 2008; and for an alternative view Box 5.1).

Similarly, from the 1970s onwards, the volume of protocols, standards and guidelines issued within health care has grown substantially across industrialized nations (Berg, 1997). Yet, there is sometimes limited evidence available on the efficacy of these attempts to control health care delivery (Mackintosh and Sandall, 2008). This is particularly problem-

---

BOX 5.1   Kelman and Friedman on the waiting-time target in English hospitals' accident and emergency departments

A four-hour limit on waiting times in accident and emergency ('A and E') depart-ments was one of the more controversial health-related targets introduced by the UK New Labour government. Some had argued that the four-hour target poten-tially compromised patient care, by shifting effort and resources away from other elements of health care (e.g. elective surgery) – so-called 'effort substitution'. In addition, many alleged that hospitals had artificially inflated performance when it was being measured only to let it fall back afterwards, or even that they had manipulated the measurement of waiting times – so-called 'gaming'.

Using data from all 155 hospital 'trusts' in England, Kelman and Friedman (2009) attempted to assess the extent to which effort substitution and gaming had occurred in practice. They found that there was a jump in performance during the first 'sweep' when waiting times were measured. However, they also discovered that much of this increase was sustained over time, such that there was overall a 'dramatic' improvement in waiting time performance from 2003 to 2006.

By combining data on waiting times with other performance data, their analysis also suggested that there was 'no evidence for any of the dysfunctional effects that have been hypothesized in connection with this target' (*ibid.*: 917). This was, they argued, due to a variety of reasons which conspired to prevent dysfunctional outcomes in this specific case. Nonetheless, they acknowledged that, under dif-ferent sets of circumstances, both effort substitution and gaming could occur as a result of target-focused regimes, if these were not designed properly and lacked sufficient institutional support.

---

atic given tendencies towards 'rule-mindedness' (Vaughan, 1999) that can lead to a 'box-ticking' or 'proceduralist' approach to the delivery of care, rather than one that is 'mindful'.

The degree of centralization of health services
Some nations are notable for devolving many decisions concerning health care coverage and organization to regional-level actors. Hence, in Canada, although insurance cover is portable between states, what is available under provincial insurance systems differs from state to state, as do contribution requirements (Lightman and Riches, 2009: 51). Spain's health care system is marked by its system of 'asymettric devolu-tion', whereby traditionally 7 out of its 17 regions enjoyed substantial levels of control over health care policy, with the remaining 10 being allocated more autonomy from 2001 onwards (Mur-Veeman *et al.*, 2008). Indeed, within OECD nations, only Britain and France retain a largely centralized health care system (Freeman and Frisina, 2010: 172–

3). Even in Britain, however, health care policies are starting to vary across the territory, with free prescriptions now available in Scotland and Wales, but not in England.

In decentralized nations, tax revenue to pay for universal systems is often collected regionally, and sometimes combined with funds from national government – as in Italy, Sweden and Spain. Where financing involves central government providing some or all of regions' health care resources, disagreement over funding has often resulted. Hence, in Italy, there were wrangles between the centre and different regions concerning whether the regional tax could be increased to cover increased health expenditures (Fargion, 2009: 184). In Canada, the federal government has used the conditions attached to its joint-funding of health care to try to ensure that often resistant provinces deliver health care which complies with the principles of Canadian Medicare – that is, universally accessible, publicly administered, without being subject to user fees, portable across province boundaries, and comprehensive (Lightman and Riches, 2009: 57).

It has been argued that nations of a more federal nature tend to prevent the development of universal health systems, given the existence in these countries of multiple veto points which can be exploited by those who wish to block change (Immergut, 1992). However, different states can also, on occasion, act as 'policy laboratories' for the creation of new funding systems. Hence, Saskatchewan in Canada pioneered the first medical insurance scheme in North America – an experiment which was then instituted across the country in the late 1960s (Lightman and Riches, 2009: 57).

Aside from policies reflecting formal territorial boundaries, it has also been claimed that considerable policy differences exist informally, even across what are otherwise apparently highly centralized systems. This is reflected in what has been described as the 'postcode lottery', whereby services are available to different degrees in different areas, within otherwise supposedly 'national' health service systems.

The provision of information

Governments use their control over information in a variety of ways in the field of health care policy, both to enable the public to become better informed and advised about health-related issues, but also to shape debate, discussion and, ultimately, policy, in health care.

The provision of information and advice to the public
Governments may attempt to provide information and advice to the public concerning common symptoms and how these could and should be dealt with. In some cases, this may be part of attempts to reduce usage of emergency health care services, as with the UK 'NHS direct' hotline

service (which is, however, being reformed at the time of writing as part of the coalition government's deficit reduction plans).

They may also attempt to provide information to advise the public to avoid unhealthy behaviours and change their lifestyles. This information may be more or less effective. Givel (2007) notes how the provision of visual information on cigarette packets (including pictures of diseases caused by smoking) in nations such as Canada has been linked to higher rates of smoking cessation than in countries such as the USA, where there are no requirements for graphic warnings of this type.

Governments may also attempt to use the provision of information as a tool to protect patients and, in particular to help overcome the asymmetry between them and service providers. As Flood notes (2000: 257), this is underlined in the doctrine of consent, 'which requires the physician or health provider to disclose the risks of treatment that, objectively, a person in the shoes of the patient would want to know'. As another example, during the 2000s the EU mandated that member states must provide information about the quality of care to patients in order to make 'freedom of movement' across the Union a reality and facilitate the 'right to patient mobility' (Jarman and Greer, 2010: 161). The UK offers a particularly clear example of attempts by governments to increase the amount of relevant information available to patients, with a special website ('NHS Choices') providing overall hospital 'scorecards' and 'performance data' on survival rates for particular operations and treated conditions.

Some governments have attempted to codify the rights of users of health care services. Hence, there is a UK charter of patient rights and, in France, a charter for people in hospital ('*Charte de la personne hospitalisée*').

The production and dissemination of information to inform policy-making
Governments can also use their ability to set up information-gathering commissions to improve or change the quality of political debate around an issue. Hence, the Canadian government created a Royal Commission to investigate the future of health care in that country, which arguably consolidated that nation's commitment to a publicly-funded health care system when it reported in 2002 (Lightman and Riches, 2009: 57).

Finally, governments can also use inquiries to gather information about failures in the provision of health care. Inquiries can 'provide impetus for reform or throw fresh light on complex issues' (Stanley and Manthorpe, 2004: 9). They often focus not only on developing an account of why services failed, but are also concerned with informing future policy – what Stanley and Manthorpe describe as their 'Janus' face, looking both backwards and forwards (*ibid*.: 4). Particularly influential inquiries in Britain have included that into the mass-murderer Harold Shipman (Smith, 2005) and negligent and poor-quality practice in children's heart operations at Bristol Royal Infirmary (Kennedy, 2001).

The scope of health policy

A number of studies have indicated the differential impact of health policies on different groups, be these racial and ethnic groups, different
genders, age groups, different socio-economic classes, or those subject to
different health conditions. To an extent, this may reflect the different
rates of consumption of health care services by different groups. Blank
and Burau (2004: 18) suggest that, at any one time, 95 per cent of people
are 'largely healthy' and infrequently consume health care services,
whereas the rest of the population have in the past consumed over half of
the total resources available. However, aside from the degree of illness
experienced by any one group at a particular time, other factors appear to
impact on the extent to which individuals are affected by health care
policy.

In many countries health outcomes and also access to health services
vary across racial and ethnic groups. This applies even within an otherwise relatively homogeneous population. For example, studies in Britain
have indicated that gypsies and travellers face particular problems when
it comes to maintaining and improving health, not least as a result of a
lack of basic amenities such as running water, and low rates of immu-
nization against communicable diseases (Pahl and Vaile, 1988). Different
groups may also be subject to higher rates of diagnosis and/or prevalence
of certain diseases or conditions than the general population (as is the
case with the British and US black population in relation to sickle cell
disease, thalassaemia and schizophrenia) and treatment which may be of
patchy and/or poor quality (Ahmad, 1995; McLean *et al.*, 2003).

In some cases, such problems have led governments to target different
types of health policies at different groups. This is particularly marked in
nations where the health of the indigenous population is substantially
worse than that of the rest of the population, and where traditional health
care services have often been perceived as being of lower quality for (or
even potentially harmful towards) indigenous people, such as in Canada,
Australia and New Zealand. In some cases, the ability to control their own
health care is viewed as an essential element of indigenous people's rights
(Lavoie *et al.*, 2010: 665). In Australia and New Zealand, the provision of
culturally-sensitive, responsive and accountable services to such populations is delivered through contracting mechanisms – differing from the
usual use of contracting, to increase competition and choice (*ibid.*: 669).

There has also been extensive discussion of how health policies
reflect, and affect, the interests of different genders. Women are more
intensive users of health care services, not only because of their greater
longevity, but also during maternity. Overall, women have a slight biological advantage over men. In many industrialized countries, societal
changes have enabled this to be reflected in life expectancy, with women

generally living longer than men. In other countries, however, women's biological advantage may be counterbalanced by societal disadvantages. For example, in India, the overall sex ratio 'fell from 972 women per thousand men in 1901 to 935 per thousand in 1981' (Doyal, 1995: 21). Some aspects of women's health – particularly birth control and fertility – are highly politicized, and the services available differ considerably between nations.

Health policies have also been challenged for their coverage, or otherwise, of health problems affecting older people. An 'inverse care law' has been discerned in relation to dementia, for example – which is an extremely complex condition that is difficult to care for, generally affecting older people, but which is infrequently prioritized in health care policies (Penhale and Manthorpe, 2004: 269). In many countries, health care is informally rationed to the detriment of older people and benefit of younger people (Aaron and Schwartz, 1984).

In addition, numerous studies have indicated the persistence of inequalities in health linked to socio-economic class (DHSS, 1980; Wilkinson, 1996). As noted at the beginning of this chapter, the determinants of health relate to a variety of factors beyond the health care system as well as within it (Frank and Mustard, 1994).

Finally, some have argued that policies in health care tend to privilege the interests of those suffering from certain conditions rather than others. It has been argued, for example, that despite the existence of different systems for the delivery of physical health care, mental health services remain of relatively poor quality in numerous nations (Mechanic and Rochefort, 1996: 262). Nonetheless, Goodwin (1997: 48) argues that insurance-based systems are particularly likely to lead to disjointed approaches to dealing with mental health conditions, 'because claims are made for identifiable mental health problems experienced by individuals . . . [yet, m]ental health problems often do not fit this model'.

Conclusion

Whilst it might be anticipated that virtually all nations would, at least ostensibly, aim at improving the health of their populations, this chapter has indicated the bewildering variety of policy approaches adopted to achieve this aim. Governments not only use their control over financial resources to pay for health care services from taxation, but in some countries forego very extensive amounts of tax in order to incentivize individuals to take on health care insurance policies. Governments invoke their authority in some countries to force citizens to take on health insurance, as well as to regulate health care professionals and providers, and the wages and conditions they provide for staff. Governments also attempt to

Figure 5.4   *Employment in the health and social sector as a share of total civilian employment*

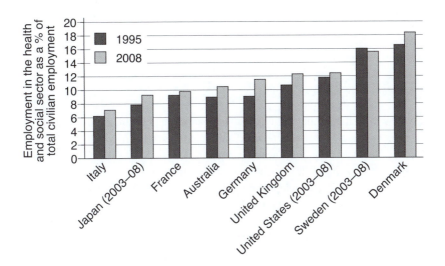

Note: The figure given for France is 2009 rather than 2008.

Source: OECD (2009b).

require individuals to behave in particular ways to promote their health, to varying levels of success. Where health care systems are entirely or partly publicly owned, governments can use their powers of organization to affect the pattern of delivery of health care, which can be nationally, regionally or locally directed. Finally, governments use their control over information to inform the public about health care services and healthy (and unhealthy) behaviour, and to inform policy debates about health.

Rather than governments converging in their approaches over time, the first section of this chapter indicated how countries' health care systems continue to diverge significantly. This is not least because governments generally agree with the goal of promoting population health, but extensive debate continues about the appropriate means by which to achieve this. Current contestation over President Obama's attempted health reforms in the USA indicates how the example of another country's health care system (the UK) can be (mis)used by opponents and proponents of reform. Such debates draw on deep ideological differences over the appropriate role of the state (see Chapter 12). Regardless of the ideology driving health care policies, however, in virtually every nation this sector has become increasingly important. Obviously, health care services are in demand as never before, as Western populations age and the incidence of chronic complaints rises; but, in addition, the proportion of the workforce employed within the health sector is rising in most countries (see Figure 5.4). As such, the sector has become an extremely important element of the economy in many nations.

Summary

- ❏ As with welfare policy, early attempts to understand health policy development suggested services would expand as nations industrialized.
- ❏ As differences in nations' health care systems have persisted over time, analysts have examined the extent to which health care systems fit with other theories of welfare development (such as Esping-Andersen's 'worlds of welfare'), and the degree to which health care services are provided on a universal basis.
- ❏ The policy instruments used in health policy:
  - – Governments use the *financial resources* available to them to pay for health care using taxation and to incentivize spending on health care insurance through tax expenditures.
  - – Governments use their *authority* to require participation in insurance schemes by the population; to regulate health care providers, and the pay and conditions of health care staff; and to attempt to prevent individuals from engaging in unhealthy behaviours.
  - – Governments use their powers of *organization* to administer and deliver health care services, which may be provided on a national, regional or local basis.
  - – Governments use their control over *information* to provide advice to the public about healthy behaviours and health care services, and to inform policy debates concerning health care services and how they should be delivered.
- ❏ Although not always made explicit, health policies often affect different age, gender, racial and ethnic groups in very different ways.

Chapter 6

Education Policy

It is difficult to circumscribe the realm of education policy because opinions differ over the extent to which certain matters *should* be taught or learned, and *how* they should be taught or learned. Education policies themselves 'project definitions of what counts as education' (Ball, 1990: 3), with the religious, work-related, nationalistic and ideological content of education varying across countries.

Despite these differences, in most countries it is possible to discern five broad educational forms corresponding (albeit roughly) to different stages of a learner's life. First, in many developed nations, child and nursery care includes an educational element – what is described as *pre-school education*. This can be provided by the state or by voluntary and private providers, including groups of parents (playgroups) or individuals (childminders) (Hudson and Lidström, 2002b: 43). The provision of *primary* and *secondary education* is generally more uniform in different nations, being provided either publicly or privately, or through a mixture of modes of provision (although 'home schooling', whereby parents educate their own children, is also permitted in some nations). *Tertiary education* includes the provision of further and higher education, which is generally delivered either by public or private colleges and by universities. Finally, *continuing and vocational education and training* is generally provided on a short-course basis, often with the support of an individual's employer (Clarke and Winch, 2007) or trade union (Jarvis, 2007: 187).

This chapter first considers theories which have attempted to explain why, despite pressures towards conformity, differences persist between different nations' education systems, before examining the influence of international factors on educaton policy-making. The chapter then examines government activity in relation to education policy involving the use of financial resources (the provision of tax-funded education, and of tax expenditures to support education), authority (the regulation and control of providers of education, of educational standards and content, and pay and conditions for teachers), organization (governments' administration and delivery of education, including their introduction of competition into educational systems, use of streaming or comprehensivization, and centralization or decentralization of education services), and of information (the provision of information and advice concerning education services, and to guide policy-making). The last section of the chapter considers the scope of education policy and, in particular, the impact of class, gender, race and age on access to education and incorporation into formal education services.

The context: theories of education policy development

Many of the first attempts to compare education policies across countries were allied with attempts to improve educational provision. Hence, in 1817, Jullien de Paris – commonly seen as the founder of comparative education (Bereday, 1964: ix) – set out a list of different 'checkpoints' which could be used to study, assess and, ultimately, improve schools in different national contexts (Crossley, 2007: 259).

Other approaches attempted to generate quantitative generalizations about the preconditions for particular types of educational developments (Sandiford, 1918; Hans, 1949; Holmes, 1965; Noah and Eckstein, 1969; Verner, 1979). Certainly, one of the most significant and uniform developments across nations has been the expansion of tertiary education provision – what has been described as the move from 'elite' to 'mass' and, in some cases, to virtually 'universal' education (Bleiklie *et al.*, 2000: 12; Samoff, 2007: 48). This was often viewed from a functional viewpoint as resulting from the need of newly industrializing nations for trained workers and administrators (King, E., 2007: 28).

Despite this, the format of tertiary education – as well as of preschool, primary, secondary, and continuing and vocational education and training – has continued to differ markedly between nations. Explaining this continuing difference between countries was the focus of studies in the comparative sociology of education, which, to use the title of one of the genre's most influential authors, attempted to uncover the 'social origins of educational systems' (Archer, 1979). This approach acknowledged that, in 'studying foreign systems of education, we should not forget that the things outside the schools matter even more than the things inside the schools' (Sadler, 1979: 49). As such, there was suspicion of approaches which suggested that policy-makers can simply 'pick and choose' amongst different nations' education policies (*ibid.*), preceded by comparative scholars 'capturing' different educational practices and institutions in order to 'display' these at home (King, E., 2007: 24), without situating them in their domestic context.

The tension between the 'universal and the particular' has continued within comparative approaches to education policy – between studies which examine and explain particular developments in a certain nation, and those which examine the impact of broad macro-social processes on different education systems, at a high level of abstraction (Archer, 1981; Parkyn, 2007: 38).

The requirements of the state and education systems

Numerous approaches to comparative education have focused on links between education systems and governments, not only in terms of the content of education, but also its coverage (Green, 1990; 1997).

Traditionally, education in many countries was – at least, initially – the preserve of religious institutions. This was the case in Britain, for example, until 1870, at which point school boards were created to build on churches' educational services in order to ensure a universal primary education service (Hudson and Lidström, 2002b: 28–9).

In many nations, the impetus for expanding state influence in education came from a perceived need for a corps of administrators educated to a high level. This arguably resulted in the Swedish system of gymnasia, created from the seventeenth century onwards (*ibid*.: 28); the traditional Chinese educational system (Gerth and Mills, 1974); and technically-based systems in countries where successful irrigation was both crucial for agricultural production and difficult to manage, as in Babylonia and Egypt. The 'interest' of states in producing a corps of domestic administrators has also been seen as motivating educational policies in the French and British Empires (Cowen, 1996).

However, approaches towards the provision of primary and secondary education differed significantly across countries. Hence, whilst British colonial administration of education was often disrupted by education delivered by missionary groups, the French state often attempted to control Muslim education within its colonies at the same time as introducing secular education services (White, 1996). The relationship between state and religious provision also differed across developed nations, in ways whose legacy is still in evidence today. Hence, for example, in Germany, a number of different types of state school were created as part of attempts to reconcile the interests of the Catholic minority with the (then) Protestant majority (Rothman, 1963: 54). In the Netherlands and Canada, whilst religious schools have remained private and outwith the direct control of government, they are eligible for state funding as if they were part of the public system. This contrasts with the situation in France – where Catholic private schools receive little public funding, and in the USA – where the provision of state funding for Catholic schools was, historically, highly politicized (*ibid*.: 62). In many nations, however, the promotion of religion through religious instruction is undertaken routinely by virtually all schools. This is the case in Spain and Portugal, which have a Catholic majority, and in Britain, which has a Protestant majority.

Perhaps one of the earliest attempts to consider the specific impact of religious as well as class cleavages on education arose from Heidenheimer's (1973; 1981) consideration of why the USA developed a mass education system earlier than many other nations (see also Ringer, 1979) – for example, broadening secondary school education a generation earlier than in Europe. Heidenheimer pointed out that, immediately after the civil war, the USA was only just at the point of trying to introduce compulsory primary education, which had been introduced a century earlier in Prussia, for example. Yet, from the 1890s, a remarkable expansion occurred, such that by 1928 'the proportion of [14–17-year-olds] which was attending general or academic secondary schools full-time was five times higher in the US than in Europe' (Heidenheimer, 1973: 319–20). He suggested that this 'take-off' occurred because the American public school enabled social reforms and the state to 'join forces' in a way which would not have been possible in European nations which were generally characterized by both class and religious cleavages. At the same time, the resources provided per pupil were significantly less within US public schools than European secondary schools (*ibid*.: 320).

Regardless of the issue of the relationship between state and religious provision of primary and secondary education, in most countries, until the 1960s, higher education was provided only to a relatively small sector of the population. Access to university was generally heavily restricted on class grounds, not least because it was generally viewed as enabling access to stable and high-status administrative positions (Mueller, 1984: 2).

As access to secondary education – and, particularly, higher education – expanded in developed nations beyond a small elite, analyses of the relationship between governments and educational policy became more subtle and wide-ranging. It goes without saying that, until the late 1980s, educational provision in many countries was completely controlled by government. This was acknowledged by Kandel (1954), who compared educational policies according to their context within democratic or totalitarian systems.

Thirty years later, however, the theorist Burton Clark argued that the relationship between governments and higher education provision could differ between institutions – even within democratic regimes. Clark (1983) argued that universities are subject to pressures not only from state authority, but also from academic oligarchies and the market. He examined how universities oriented themselves in relation to these three pressures, which ultimately promoted different methods of academic organization, and approaches to access to and the content of higher education. Overall, he suggested that the power of academic oligarchies was being increasingly challenged by outside pressures. Halsey (1992) came to the same conclusion in his analysis of British Higher Education, where he diagnosed a 'decline of donnish dominion'. Students also became an increasingly important political force in some countries, with their degree of activism shaped by the extent to which the university was integrated with the political concerns and goals of the relevant government (Archer, 1972).

The influence of economic factors on education systems

More recently, it has been argued that the relationship between governments and education systems has shifted towards a 'new orthodoxy' (Carter and O'Neill, 1995). This has involved an increasingly strong linkage between educational provision and quality, and national economic development; greater government control over curricula; pressures to reduce costs; and the introduction of 'choice' for parents amongst different types of school, often related to increasing involvement of the voluntary and private sector in education (*ibid.*).

Primary amongst these changes has been a reorientation of education towards the preparation of learners for the job market. Certainly, given technological and economic changes, it is arguable that education, 'together with knowledge development through research', constitutes 'the Western strategy for economic prosperity in a globalized economy, where competition with low wages is out of the question' (Hudson and Lidström, 2002a: 19). Whilst linkages with commerce and industry have long been seen as a goal of education – motivating the creation of 'land-grant colleges' in the USA in the mid-1860s, for example – other goals have previously been privileged, ranging from state-building and nationalistic goals to (for universities) being a producer or custodian of knowledge, and protecting freedom of expression, research and democracy (Bleiklie *et al.*, 2000: 27; see also Ben-David, 1991).

Despite this new alleged 'orthodoxy', the perceived linkage between education and training, and economic development appears to result in different policy responses in different countries. This is clear, for example, from the variety of responses to the economic crisis at the time of writing. Whilst some nations have attempted to increase (relative) funding to education and skills enhancement as a means of exiting the crisis (such as Australia, Canada, Denmark, France, Sweden and the USA), in other nations, education and training budgets have remained static, or have even been reduced following the crisis (such as Japan, Spain and the UK) (see Damme and Karkkainen, 2011).

In contrast with health policy, few attempts have been made to incorporate education systems within welfare state typologies such as those proposed by Esping-Andersen (1990), which focused on decommodification and stratification (see Chapter 4) (although, see also Iversen and Stephens, 2008). Nonetheless, there has been considerable emphasis in recent comparative research on the relationship between vocational education and training, and different economic systems. Kathleen Thelen (2004), for example, has examined vocational training systems in the

USA, Britain, Japan and Germany, and linked the continuation of industrial support for vocational training (e.g., apprenticeships) to the strength of craft unions and viability of manufacturing industry. Others have argued that the contribution of individual firms to workforce training cannot be understood by looking only at the decisions taken by firms themselves; rather, they need to be placed within the context of the overall structure of the political economy. In particular, high levels of investment in worker training may be of doubtful utility for firms in a context of high labour mobility, and/or where the skills required are not, generally, firm-specific (Streeck, 1992).

This insight has motivated much work within the 'varieties of capitalism' literature (see Chapter 3), which separates countries which enjoy coordinated market economies (CMEs) – such as Germany, Japan and Switzerland, from liberal market economies (LMEs) – such as the UK and USA (Hall and Soskice, 2001). In CMEs, firms generally support both their own specific workers and those across their industry in obtaining sector-specific skills. Hence, for example, they are relatively willing to sponsor partnerships, and to engage with local and national government in shaping vocational education systems. In contrast, firms within LMEs are aware that their workforce is relatively mobile – both across firms and, indeed, sectors. As a result, firms are less willing to invest in skill development, which is generally undertaken by workers themselves or through job-based training (*ibid.*; see also Mares, 2003). Two dimensions of differentiation can, thus, be discerned: the willingness of firms to engage in skill formation; and the extent to which the vocational education system trains students about particular jobs/industries, or provides a broader training (the system's 'specificity') (Busemeyer, 2009).

As is discussed in Chapter 3, the 'varieties of capitalism' literature has occasionally been criticized for downgrading the importance of party politics, with its focus on the coordination problems affecting firms (Howell, 2003). A sophisticated attempt to take partisan interests into account comes from Boix (1998), who argues that left parties have privileged expenditure on education and training, often beyond other forms of welfare state investment, since improving this element of the 'supply side' is the only option available in a situation where traditional Keynesian demand-management has become more difficult to achieve given the mobility of taxable resources.

International pressures

Although it is often assumed 'that education is one of the few remaining institutions over which national governments still have effective powers'

(Nóvoa and Yariv-mashal, 2007: 353), and it is certainly the case that 'nation states are still the primary actors in education policy' (Busemeyer and Trampusch, 2010: 9), a number of international pressures are increasingly influencing domestic education systems.

The impact of internationalization is perhaps most keenly felt within the realm of higher education policy. First, increasing numbers of students are choosing to study in countries other than their country of origin. In some countries, such as Australia and the UK, the proportion of foreign or international students amounts to around one fifth of total student enrolments (see Figure 6.1). In many nations, this has been allied with an increasing penetration of English-language teaching within higher education including within countries, such as France, where the domestic language is widely spoken internationally.

Furthermore, there has been a significant expansion in 'distance learning' whereby students can stay at home and yet still obtain a degree from a provider in another country, learning 'at their own pace', rather than having to attend lectures and participate in seminars at specified times. New information technologies are thus facilitating a 'realignment of space and time' (Jarvis, 2007: 188) in relation to both higher, and some further and continuing education services.

Second, higher education policies have been, in many countries, significantly affected by supranational institutions. Perhaps the most successful of these is the so-called 'Bologna process', which *inter alia* promotes the harmonization of degree structures across Europe (but now includes a number of non-EU nations). The Bologna process may, in some countries, have merely served to legitimate reforms which domestic policy-makers would otherwise have found difficult to implement (Witte, 2006; see also Trampusch, 2009). Nonetheless, it has led to significant structural change towards the LMD model ('licence, master, doctorat' in French, or 'undergraduate, masters degree, doctorate' in English) (Neave, 2003).

In addition to the Bologna process (which was initiated by a small number of education ministers, rather than by the EU itself), the EU has also become increasingly involved in shaping higher and further education policies in member states. The EU has long shaped higher education policies through mechanisms including the Erasmus programme and the promotion of lifelong learning (Corbett, 2003; Pépin, 2007). From 2000 onwards, however, its input has been expanded beyond promoting student mobility to include enhancing the impact of higher education in promoting economic effectiveness, initially through the Lisbon Strategy (Walkenhorst, 2008) and, since March 2010, the Europe 2020 programme.

Some other supranational institutions, beyond the EU, have also been viewed as having an actual or potential impact on higher education. These include the General Agreement on Trade in Services (GATS), one

Figure 6.1   *Foreign students as a percentage of all tertiary enrolment*

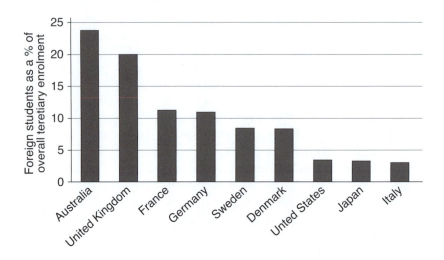

Notes: The US figure is given for 'international students', as information on 'foreign students' is not available. While 'foreign student' generally refers to a student who lacks citizenship in the country where they are undertaking higher education, 'international student' generally refers to a student who has either primarily studied in an other country or, more commonly, is registered as domiciled in another country. Where countries have stringent citizenship regulations, there are likely to be more 'foreign' than 'international' students, since the former category will include those who are domiciled and primarily educated domestically, but who lack domestic citizenship.

Source: OECD (2010c) Indicator C2.

of the agreements overseen by the World Trade Organization. Some have argued that the GATS facilitates the privatization of higher education services (Scherrer, 2005), although debate has raged over the extent to which nations would, in practice, be able to exempt education from coverage by the GATS (Dodds, 2004).

International pressures have also been felt in the realms of primary and secondary education. Policy-makers have been increasingly concerned to 'benchmark' their nation's performance in compulsory education against that of other countries. Benchmarking or measuring programmes have been operated by the OECD, the International Association for the Evaluation of Educational Achievement, and the EU (Nóvoa and Yariv-mashal, 2007: 352). The OECD Programme for International Student Assessment (PISA), established in the late 1990s, has been particularly influential. At the time of writing, PISA had run four times in different countries, assessing the literacy and numeracy skills (and sometimes others) of students around the age of 15 (King, K., 2007; Rizvi and Lingard, 2010). Poor, or mediocre, performance on

PISA indicators motivated extensive reforms in many countries – including Germany and Norway, for example.

In addition, there has been a proliferation of international examination systems, such as the International Baccalaureate (IB), which require the delivery of a specific curriculum across a range of countries (Hayden *et al.*, 2002). Whilst historically offered by private schools catering to the children of expatriates, the IB is now offered by state-run schools in a number of countries, including the UK and USA.

Comparing education policies across nations

The use of financial resources

The level of expenditure on education differs significantly across different nations. Figure 6.2 indicates that, even amongst the developed nations which have formed the focus of our analysis so far, expenditure on primary, secondary and tertiary education varies from below 4 per cent to over 6 per cent of gross domestic product (GDP).

Schools, nurseries, pre-schools, universities and colleges can be funded entirely through taxation (as with UK 'state' schools); through a mixture of taxation, private income and endowments (as with UK universities); or through private income alone (as with for-profit providers,

Figure 6.2 *Expenditure on educational institutions from public and private sources: proportion of GDP in 2007*

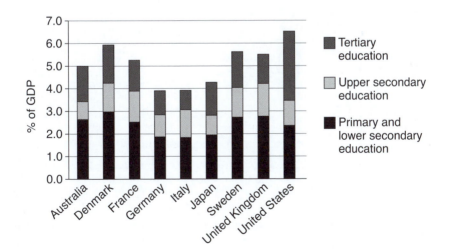

Source: OECD (2010c): table B2.3.

such as many language schools that operate through the summer months in British coastal towns).

There is considerable variation across countries in the extent to which governments partly or wholly fund pre-school, primary, secondary, tertiary, and vocational and continuing education and training. Figure 6.3 indicates the wide range of government contributions to education in different countries, ranging from around one third in the UK, Japan and USA to the vast majority (around or over 90 per cent) in Denmark and Sweden.

The shape of tax funding for education, and how it is delivered by governments, varies significantly across countries. Nonetheless, two parallel trends can be discerned which indicate a shift away from government control over inputs towards attempts by governments to use their powers of funding to shape outputs. First, in numerous countries, governments have moved away from budgets allocated to specific tasks towards 'global' budgets or 'block grants' which give providers much greater financial autonomy (see Hudson and Lidström, 2002b, for one case of this). At the

Figure 6.3   *The share of public investment in education compared with overall (including private) expenditure*

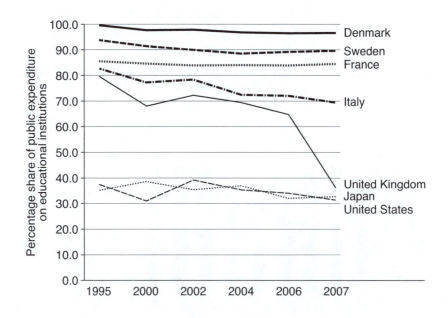

Note: Figures are not included for Germany and Australia, as continuous data are not available for these countries.

Source: OECD (2010c) Indicator B3.

same time, many governments have increasingly imposed conditions on educational providers in exchange for the provision of funding from taxation. This has been extended to higher education in countries including the UK, USA (Neave and Van Vught, 1991b: 243) and France (*ibid.*: 244), as part of attempts to constrain higher education spending.

In addition to direct tax-funded expenditure on education, governments in many nations support their domestic education system through providing tax breaks for educational expenditures. The USA offers a clear example where the revenue foregone by government for educational policy purposes has reached between one third and one half of direct government financial support for education. Figure 6.4 indicates the overall amount of federal contribution to education, split into estimated federal tax expenditures at the bottom and, at the top, total on-budget and off-budget support, and non-federal funds generated by federal legislation.

Figure 6.4 *US education: tax expenditures compared with financing*

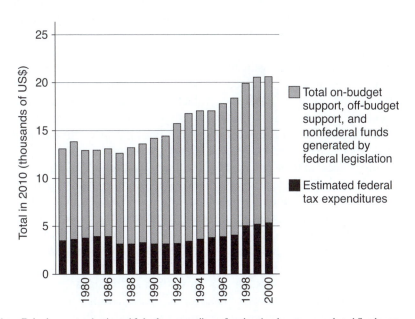

Notes: Federal support and estimated federal tax expenditures for education, by category: selected fiscal years, 1965 through 2010, in constant fiscal year 2010 dollars. The category of federal tax expenditures covers '[l]osses of tax revenue attributable to provisions of the federal income tax laws that allow a special exclusion, exemption, or deduction from gross income or provide a special credit, preferential rate of tax, or a deferral of tax liability affecting individual or corporate income tax liabilities'.

Source: National Center for Education Statistics (undated (a)): table 380.

The use of authority

Governments use their authority in education policy to regulate education providers, educational standards and content, and the pay and conditions of staff within education. Broadly speaking, governments can be seen either as controlling or as supervizing education. France offers an example of the state-control model, whereby the educational system was created largely by the state for purposes of nation-building. Access to, and standards within, primary, secondary and tertiary education, as well as the pay and conditions for staff working within the sector, are all controlled by government. The USA conforms to the state supervizing model. In this case, school and university management have extensive powers to decide on matters such as access, pay and conditions of staff, and standards within their own institution, albeit within certain federal or national guidelines (Clark, 1983; Bray, 2007, 185–6).

Regulation of educational standards through evaluation
As already mentioned, the mix between government-run, independent, and partially-independent (e.g. grant-maintained) educational institutions differs across nations. In addition, in some nations, parents are allowed to educate their own children at home (home-schooling). Governments regulate educational standards within this variety of providers through a range of methods. This section considers attempts by governments, or bodies empowered by them, to evaluate how education is delivered (as opposed to its content, which is considered in the next section). It should be noted, however, that in many cases the evaluation of education is delivered by current or former teachers, lecturers, or other educational professionals themselves who are acting under the authority of the state – that is, professionals themselves may have acted as the major influence on evaluation systems, at least in their practical application (Broadfoot, 2007: 62).

The period from the 1980s onwards has seen, in many nations, an intensification of evaluation of educational providers, which can focus either on the processes operating within schools, or the outcomes of education, or both. Most developed countries now possess some type of systematic system of evaluation, covering primary, secondary, and tertiary education, and increasingly pre-school education also. For many years, the Italian educational system was an outlier, in that it lacked any specific educational evaluator or inspectorate, but a national benchmarking system is under development at the time of writing (Faubert, 2009: 22).

Another developing trend relates to the degree to which evaluations are 'formative' – targeted at improvements in educational processes or outcomes, or 'summative' – designed to measure educational standards. There has been a move in many countries away from formative approaches towards making evaluation more summative (to provide measures of educational quality), as has occurred in Sweden, for example (Hudson and Lidström, 2002b: 46). The move towards a more summative approach designed to increase accountability in education has occurred at different times in different nations. Broadfoot (2007: 58–9) argues, for example, that the shift from the 1980s onwards towards a more competitive ideology – which has underlaid British attempts to increase educational accountability – occurred centuries ago in France, when the education system became virtually entirely subordinated to the state under Napoleon.

Process evaluation tends to focus on specific learning environments (e.g. classrooms, lecture theatres), departmental levels, and/or whole-institution levels (i.e. school or university level). The quality of learning and teaching within these educational environments is examined, as are, sometimes, the linkages between educational providers and other stakeholders beyond their learners (e.g. the parents of school pupils), the local community, and/or local businesses (cf. Faubert, 2009: 8).

The issues to be examined within process evaluations may already be set by government or authorities empowered by them, or may be up to the discretion of the inspector or evaluator. Equally, institutions may be evaluated against their progress towards targets they themselves set, in conjunction with government authorities, as in French evaluations by the Inspecteurs de l'Education Nationale (IEN – National Education Inspectorate), Inspecteurs Pédagogiques Régionaux (IPR – regional educational inspectors) and the Comité National d'Evaluation (CNE – National Evaluation Committee) (Neave and Van Vught, 1991b: 246). (It should, however, be noticed that a more 'summative' approach to educational assessment has recently been adopted in the realm of French higher education with the creation of the *Agence nationale d'évaluation de l'enseignement supérieur et de la recherche* in 2007 (AÉRES: national evaluation agency for higher education and research).) Evaluations may be conducted by a national inspectorate (as with the British Office for Standards in Education – Ofsted), or undertaken on a regional basis, as in Sweden. Process evaluation can focus on the performance of individual teachers or lecturers (as traditionally in France), or on that of whole departments or institutions (as in Sweden), or on both (as in the UK).

An alternative approach attempts to evaluate the outcomes of education rather than educational processes. A key example of this comes from the US 'No Child Left Behind' Act (2001). This Act requires schools to attempt to attain targets for annual progress in test results (Faubert, 2009: 9).

Evaluation has, on occasion, become subject to considerable controversy in different countries when it has been linked to resource allocation or other types of government intervention. For example, the No Child Left Behind Act allows students at a school where one group of students have failed to meet progress targets for two consecutive years to transfer to another school, and requires specific actions to be taken if annual targets are not met during the third consecutive year. Beyond this, some states financially reward or punish schools according to performance during standardized examinations (*ibid*.: 23). These types of systems have been criticized for potentially failing to take into account the varying capacities of different types of child and school.

An extreme example where such differentials were completely ignored comes from the English educational system between 1862 and 1895. During this period, teachers' pay was linked to their pupils' performance during tests. This clearly disadvantaged teachers in industrializing cities, who had to deal with large classes that were poorly attended and whose pupils were undernourished, leading to a number of perverse outcomes (Case *et al.*, 2000).

Governments may also attempt to regulate outcomes through prescribing certain patterns of examinations. This is particularly common in the school system, where harmonized examination systems can facilitate comparison between schools according to pupils' levels of achievement.

The intensity of testing, and the degree to which it is centralized, differs substantially across countries. However, it is possible to discern a trend towards more intense and centralized examination across developed countries.

In this connection, the UK system of pupil testing has been described as one of the most 'ambitious'. Children are tested at the ages of 4–5, 7, 11, 14 and 16. The model of regular, compulsory testing within schools, including primary schools, has been adopted by a number of countries, including those with a less traditionally interventionist approach in education, such as Norway (Helgøy and Homme, 2006: 152). Interestingly, the UK's intensive testing system coexists with a proliferation of different examination boards which control testing at higher levels, predominantly A-level (sat in England by many, but not all, pupils aged 17–18) (Bray, 2007: 182). These often derive from universities such as the Universities of Oxford and Cambridge, or from organizations deriving from technical education providers, such as 'City and Guilds'.

In other countries, there is no formal final examination; instead, students are 'subject to school-based assessment'. In these nations (including Sweden and Turkey), prospective students are required to sit entrance examinations for entry to university (*ibid*.).

Government regulation of educational content

In addition to the regulation of educational processes and outcomes, governments in many countries are also involved in regulating the content of education, generally through specifying a particular national curriculum.

Table 6.1   Is there a mandatory national examination?

	England	Scotland	Denmark	France	Germany	Italy	Japan	Sweden	USA
Home-schooling	No	No	No	No	N/A	N/A	N/A	No	No
Independent private schools	No	No	No	Yes	Yes	Yes	No	N/A	No
Government-dependent private schools	No	Yes	No	Yes	Yes	N/A	N/A	No	N/A
Public schools	No	Yes	Yes	Yes	Yes	No	No	No	No

Notes: Only education at lower secondary level is reported here, and Australia is not included in the statistics. Information for Scotland has been compiled from www.sqa.org.uk and www.educationscotland.gov.uk. In Germany, arrangements are determined by different *Länder*.

Source: Adapted from OECD (2010c) table D5.4.

Table 6.2   Is there a standard or partially standardized curriculum?

	England	Scotland	Denmark	France	Germany	Italy	Japan	Sweden	USA
Home-schooling	No	No	Yes	Yes	N/A	N/A	N/A	Yes	No
Independent private schools	No	No	Yes	Yes	Yes	Yes	Yes	N/A	No
Government-dependent private schools	Yes	Yes	Yes	Yes	Yes	N/A	N/A	Yes	N/A
Public schools	Yes	Yes	Yes	Yes	Yes	Yes	Yes	Yes	No

Notes: Only education at lower secondary level is reported here, and Australia is not included in the statistics. Information for Scotland has been compiled from www.sqa.org.uk and www.educationscotland.gov.uk. In Germany, arrangements are determined by different *Länder*.

Source: Adapted from OECD (2010c) table D5.4.

As is clear from Table 6.2, a number of countries operate either a completely or partially standardized 'national curriculum'. One particularly comprehensive and detailed national curriculum is to be found in England. The English National Curriculum is controlled by an independent authority, the Qualifications and Curriculum Authority (Hudson and Lidström, 2002b: 35). In some countries, national curricula are for guidance only rather than compulsory, although the trend is towards making them compulsory (as occurred, for example, in Norway in the late 1990s (Helgøy and Homme, 2006: 146–7).

Control over curricula becomes particularly contentious concerning subjects such as religious and personal education. Governments might be interested in using educational systems to attempt to shape behaviour in relation to 'risky' areas such as sex, given the relative lack of other public policy instruments in this area (Lewis and Knijn, 2002: 670). However, the manner in which matters such as HIV/AIDS prevention is delivered within schools differs radically between nations. In the UK, for example, governments have required sex education to serve as a tool to strengthen pro-nuclear family attitudes. In contrast, Dutch government policy towards AIDS education has, in the words of one Minister of Public Health, 'always been based on the guiding principle that no value judgement should be expressed about multiple sexual relationships' (*ibid*.: 675).

The relationship between religion and education has also been highly controversial. Some theologians would argue that the two cannot be separated; that, for example, a Catholic education requires not only specific religious education classes, but also a specifically Catholic approach to teaching all subjects (Rothman, 1963: 52).

More broadly, education is often seen as having a wider role in shaping behaviour. As Cowen describes it, states often attempt to use education systems to shape 'the formation of the citizen and the construction of political loyalty and correct modes of civic behaviour'. In some nations, civic or social studies are a common part of the curriculum. In other nations, particular political or moral messages are conveyed through the teaching of national history (Cowen, 1996). Educational systems have also been shown to play a key role in shaping gender roles (Epstein and Johnson, 1998; Middleton, 1998).

The subject of history has proved particularly susceptible to controversy concerning issues such as how colonialism and relations between different ethnic groups should be taught (Foster, 1999). Controversy also remains in many countries concerning national strategies during wartime. Despite the fact that World War II occurred over sixty years ago, it still occasionally excites controversy in Japan, for example, even to the extent of history textbooks' reading of events leading to diplomatic incidents (Shibata, 2010: 171).

The use of organization

The extent to which governments themselves organize education differs between nations: governments may provide 'mass schooling', either through all provision being undertaken by the state (as in the USSR), or by accommodation with religious interests (as in France, Germany and England), or with independent providers (as in the USA, Australia and Canada) (Cowen, 1996). In most industrialized countries, governments require parents to educate their children, although in many they permit parents themselves to teach their children. Hence, in England, Scotland, Denmark, France, Italy, Sweden and the USA, homeschooling is permitted as a legal means of providing compulsory (primary and lower secondary) education, although it is not permitted in Germany and Japan (OECD, 2010c: table D5.9).

Although in many countries university education is provided by a mixture of public and voluntary (charitable) funding, governments may still be able to use their organizational powers to alter the higher education system by, for example, requiring smaller institutions to merge (as occurred in Australia in the 1980s) (Neave and Van Vught, 1991b: 248) or by altering entry conditions for university status (as with the large-scale conversion of polytechnics to universities from the early 1990s onwards in Britain).

There are three basic organizational parameters for educational systems. The first concerns the locus of control over educational institutions – the degree to which educational systems are centralized. The remaining two parameters can apply in either centralized or decentralized systems, and are analytically independent of each other. These concern the degree to which school systems are based on selection or universal access, and the degree of competition between education providers.

The centralization of education services
As Bray (2007: 176) notes, there are different types of (de)centralization. Territorial (de-)centralization refers to the extent to which control over education is exercised at national, regional, local or school level, whereas functional (de)centralization concerns the distribution of power amongst various authorities – for example, ministries of education in relation to voluntary or religious foundations and schools, or semi-independent educational agencies.

The extent of territorial (de)centralization varies widely amongst nations. In federal systems – such as Canada, Australia, Switzerland, Belgium and Germany – state-level governments exercise considerable power over education. Regional-level control over education can result in different educational structures, curricula, and even the language of instruction (as in the Belgian and Canadian cases).

Table 6.3 *Can schools promote religious practice?*

	England	Scotland	Denmark	France	Germany	Italy	Japan	Sweden	USA
Home-schooling	Yes	Yes	Yes	N/A	N/A	N/A	N/A	No	Yes
Independent private schools	Yes	Yes	Yes	Yes	Yes	Yes	Yes	N/A	Yes
Government-dependent private schools	Yes	Yes	Yes	No	Yes	N/A	N/A	No	N/A
Public schools	Yes	Yes	No	No	No	No	No	No	No

Notes: Only education at lower secondary level is reported here, and Australia is not included in the statistics. Information for Scotland has been compiled from www.sqa.org.uk and www.educationscotland.gov.uk. In Germany, arrangements are determined by different *Länder*.

Source: Adapted from OECD (2010c) table D5.4.

Table 6.4 *Must personnel meet employment and certification standards?*

	England	Scotland	Denmark	France	Germany	Italy	Japan	Sweden	USA
Home-schooling	No	No	No	No	Home schooling is not permitted	N/A	Home schooling is not permitted	No	No
Independent private schools	No	Yes	No	No	No	Yes	Yes	N/A	No
Government-dependent private schools	Yes	Yes	No	Yes	Yes	N/A	N/A	Yes	N/A
Public schools	Yes	Yes	Yes	Yes	Yes	Yes	Yes	Yes	Yes

Notes: Only education at lower secondary level is reported here, and Australia is not included in the statistics. Information for Scotland has been compiled from www.sqa.org.uk and www.educationscotland.gov.uk. In Germany, arrangements are determined by different *Länder*.

Source: Adapted from OECD (2010c) table D5.4.

Some countries which are not formally federal are, nonetheless, relatively territorially decentralized. The British system moved from being extremely decentralized, with 2,568 autonomous school boards, to more centralized following the Balfour Act of 1902, which subsumed education under local authorities' control (Heidenheimer, 1973: 327). Despite this, however, there is considerable variation in educational structures across the UK (Raffe *et al.*, 1999: 17–18), as well as different types of examinations in Scotland compared with England. Following the process of devolution in the UK, there are also now different approaches to higher education funding in Scotland and Wales compared with England, with different levels of financial burden being placed on Scottish, Welsh and English students as a result.

In some countries, sub-regional bodies exercise considerable power over education. This is the case in the USA, where school districts are responsible for raising funds for education and controlling expenditure (Bray, 2007: 189). Attempts were made in some states to move powers away from rural school boards, but this met with strong opposition (Heidenheimer, 1973: 327). Heidenheimer argues that this helps explain the remarkably strong growth of secondary education in the USA compared with other countries at similar levels of economic development. He notes that in the USA, the tax-raising powers of school boards, and the fact that they were elected, gave participants an incentive to attempt to increase coverage and to prevent resources for education being diverted to other local priorities. This was not the case in Sweden or Britain, for example, where educational priorities were viewed as in direct competition with other local priorities. Furthermore, Heidenheimer (*ibid.*: 330) suggests that this decentralization has often prevented national- or regional-level pressures for improvement in the US system, since this could be seen as challenging local autonomy.

The degree of functional (de)centralization also varies across nations. It is arguable that, in the UK, functions have become more centralized. Between 1944 and 1988, local education authorities were empowered to administer and interpret broad policies put forward by the Ministry of Education, and generally left much educational decision-making to professionals. The 1988 Education Reform Act removed many powers from local education authorities and placed them within the purview of the Secretary of State for Education (Hudson and Lidström, 2002b: 35).

At the same time, however, both in the UK and in nations such as Australia and New Zealand, many schools have obtained increased powers to control their own budgets and even, in some cases, the terms and conditions of their staff as part of 'school-based management' (Bray, 2007: 187). Table 6.4 details the extent to which staff within schools, and home educators (where relevant) must meet officially defined employment and certification standards. Teachers may be employed by national government (as in France), regional government, or local government (as in Sweden) (Hudson and Lidström, 2002b: 45).

The use of selection
Another way in which governments have historically used their powers of organization within the education system is through setting different access conditions for different types of institution, or educational routes within institutions. This is particularly clear within secondary schooling.

Two contrasting approaches can be clearly identified. The first uses 'streaming by ability' to select students for particular types of school and/or classes within schools. The system which initially characterized British education, and still applies in some areas of England, Scotland, and Wales, and throughout Northern Ireland, coheres with this approach. A special examination (colloquially known as the '11-plus') is taken by all pupils, and used to allocate around 20 per cent of students to grammar schools, whilst the rest attend more vocationally-oriented schools. Although a number of British Labour governments attempted to reform this system, political support for it in many areas has meant that 'strong streaming' still applies in many areas. A similar approach applies in Germany, where some

---

BOX 6.1   Freitag and Schlicht on the foundations of social inequality in German education

Freitag and Schlicht (2009) use Fuzzy Set Qualitative Case Analysis (QCA – see Chapter 14) to provide a political explanation for inequalities in educational outcomes within Germany. They first note that the extent of educational inequality varies radically across *Länder*. In Bavaria, for example, a pupil from the highest socio-economic quartile is over six times more likely to end up at a Gymnasium (equivalent to a 'grammar school') than in Brandenburg (where they are only 2.38 times as likely). To try and explain this, they examine the impact of four features: 'the extent of early childhood education, the development of all-day schools, the degree of tripartition in secondary school [separation into different school types], and the onset of institutional tracking [when students are separated into different schools]' (*ibid.*: 48).

From their analysis, they find that the first factor, the availability of early childhood education, helps explain the degree of social inequality in education. In *Länder* where early childhood education is limited, that is sufficient for there to be a high degree of social inequality; conversely, where there is extensive provision, a low degree of social inequality is observed. In addition, extensive provision of early childhood education combined with a late onset for streaming leads to low levels of social inequality.

Counter-intuitively, their analysis suggests that neither of the last two factors seem to affect the extent of social inequality (neither the extent of tripartition, nor the existence of all-day schools).

Länder also stream students into different types of school. In this case, however, students are generally selected for different schools by their teachers and not only through a universal examination (see Box 6.1).

A contrast to this approach comes from countries such as Sweden, where the system is fully 'comprehensivized' – that is, where all children attend a comprehensive school (including 'free' schools) rather than being split between different types of school (Hudson and Lidström, 2002b: 35). In both selective and comprehensive systems, however, there are often private schools which adopt different approaches towards the selection of their pupils.

Competition between educational providers
One consistent trend across industrialized nations, as evidenced in Table 6.5, has been the introduction of competition and choice within education at primary and secondary levels (Ball, 1998; Whitty *et al.*, 1998) and at tertiary level (Slaughter and Leslie, 1997).

Many of these reforms have followed approaches set out by the so-called 'school effectiveness' movement, which has argued that 'school autonomy and parent-student choice' leads to more effective education than 'direct democratic control' (Chubb and Moe, 1990) – an analysis which has been hotly contested (Gewirtz *et al.*, 1995). Nonetheless, the precise ways in which competition and choice have been introduced, and the timing of their introduction, have varied across nations. For example, in England, marketization arguably dated from 1988, when competitive tendering was introduced for many educational services, and was strengthened by the 1993 Education Act (when 'grant maintained' schools were permitted – that is, schools which opt out of local authority control) (Apple, 2007: 305). This has been consolidated by measures such as the introduction of Education Action Zones, which explicitly involved the private sector as well as voluntary organizations and schools (Hudson and Lidström, 2002b: 42), and the introduction of 'academy' schools, which are relatively autonomous from the state (Ball, 2012). In contrast, despite a new funding system being introduced in Sweden in the late 1980s, which enabled the provision of more independent schools (Hudson and Lidström, 2002b: 52), only 6 per cent of children attended independent schools in 2005. These schools are, however, free of charge for pupils and 'administered through a sort of universal public voucher' (Helgøy and Homme, 2006: 148).

The provision of information

Governments can be involved in providing information for two purposes in the field of education policy. First, they can provide, or ensure the provision of, information and/or advice concerning education to consumers

Table 6.5 *School choice within the public school sector (as at 2008)*

	England	Scotland	Denmark	France	Germany	Italy	Japan	Sweden	USA
Opportunities for school choice among public schools have expanded since 1985	Yes	No	Yes	No	Yes	Yes	No	Yes	Yes
	Yes	No	Yes	Yes	Yes	Yes	No	Yes	Yes
Reforms have reduced restrictions to school choice among existing public schools	Yes	N/A	Yes	N/A	Yes	Yes	N/A	Yes	Yes
	Yes	N/A	Yes	Yes	Yes	Yes	N/A	Yes	Yes
Reforms have included the creation of new autonomous public schools, to offer new options from which parents can choose	Yes	N/A	No	N/A	No	Yes	N/A	No	Yes
	Yes	N/A	No	No	Yes	Yes	N/A	No	Yes
Reforms have permitted greater autonomy for existing public schools, including decisions about enrolment procedures and policies, which can increase school choice	Yes	N/A	Yes	N/A	Yes	Yes	N/A	No	Yes
	Yes	N/A	Yes	No	Yes	Yes	N/A	No	Yes
Reforms have included new funding mechanisms that promote school choice	Yes	N/A	No	N/A	No	Yes	N/A	Yes	Yes
	Yes	N/A	No	No	No	Yes	N/A	Yes	Yes

Notes: Shaded cells refer to primary schooling; white cells refer to lower secondary schooling.

Source: OECD (2010c), table D5.6.

of education or their parents. Second, they can attempt to produce, or to disseminate, information about educational systems in order to improve or shape policy-making on this subject.

In numerous industrialized nations, governments have attempted to increase the dissemination of information concerning school 'quality'. For example, in Britain, following the Education Reform Act of 1988, it became compulsory for schools to produce a prospectus for parents, which included information such as that school's examination results (Hudson and Lidström, 2002b: 50). In England, copies of inspection reports by Ofsted must also be sent to all parents by the school concerned. In many other countries, including Sweden and Denmark, as well as in England, copies of inspection reports are freely available on the inspectorate's website (Faubert, 2009: 24). This has not, however, been a uniform development. For example, in Germany, 'access to school final examination results has been reduced or prohibited' (*ibid.*: 37), and access to results remains contested in Denmark and Poland, for example (*ibid.*).

As mentioned, governments may also attempt to shape education policy through the provision of information. Hence, in numerous countries, changes to education policy at different levels or in relation to different subjects (Samoff, 2007: 50) have followed the creation of government commissions. These have included the Faure deliberations following student unrest in France in 1968, the U68 Commission in Sweden, the 1976 West German *Hochschulrahmengesetz* (Neave and Van Vught, 1991a: xi) and the Dearing Commission and Browne Review on English Higher Education which reported in 1997 and 2010, respectively.

The scope of education policy

The impact of education policies on different sectors of the population has been historically highly uneven.

First, the inclusion and performance of girls and women in education has been steadily expanding in industrialized nations. However, girls and women tend to study different fields than boys and men, with a strong over-representation of men in subjects such as science and technology in most OECD countries (Stromquist, 2007: 163).

Second, numerous studies have indicated how and why middle-class pupils generally fare better out of educational systems than working class students (Bourdieu, 1996). Some have argued that this has intensified with the introduction of more choice-based mechanisms in education, which are often easier for middle-class parents to manipulate (Apple, 2007: 307). Regardless of the degree of choice, however, poorer children generally face greater barriers to learning than other children, which then affects their ability to perform well in examinations. This can result from the expense of 'school-related' factors such as uniform; school lunches; transport and school trips, or other extra-curricular activities, and learning-related factors such as a lack of a quiet space to undertake homework if living in overcrowded conditions; or poor nutrition resulting in problems with concentration when in school (Smith and Noble, 1995).

Third, this is compounded in some nations by the interaction of class with race (*ibid.*). Specific ethnic groups may historically have been disadvantaged by educational systems, such as travellers and gypsies in the UK (Derrington and Kendall, 2004) and black children in the USA, exacerbating the impact of the generally low incomes of these groups (see Arrow *et al.*, 2000, for a review).

The ways in which these factors impact upon children and their future life chances have only been subject to sustained research over the last forty years, which has tended to focus on small-scale sociological studies (Rutter *et al.*, 1979) or, alternatively, large-N statistical surveys (National Center for Education Statistics, undated (b)), rather than adopting a middle-range, comparative method.

Conclusion

The development of education policy was historically tied closely to the needs of the state, both for knowledgeable and capable administrators for domestic and (where relevant) colonial purposes, as well as to inculcate either national allegiance or, in colonies, quiescence amongst the population. More recently, education policy has been seen as essential in the production of growing 'knowledge economies', and policy-makers have been keen to benchmark their educational systems against the performances of other countries.

International pressures might be viewed as presaging convergence amongst educational systems, yet this chapter has indicated the extent of continuing difference between the education policies pursued in different nations. Whilst some state financial contribution is made to education in all developed nations, the extent of that contribution and the proportion of it provided directly from taxation or indirectly from tax expenditures differ across nations. Similarly, although all countries' governments exercise some kind of oversight of educational standards, they differ in the extent to which they use their authority to control educational procedures directly, such as examinations and educational content itself.

Whilst educational systems in some nations are highly decentralized, coming entirely under the jurisdiction of local or regional governments, in others they are entirely, or almost entirely, under the aegis of national government. The solutions employed to apparently technical problems – such as whether division by ability should be employed, and if so, whether by school or by form class – also differ substantially between countries, and have been subject to extensive contestation in some areas (one prominent example being Northern Ireland). Furthermore, whilst in some nations competition between suppliers is encouraged, in others the notion of a 'neighbourhood school' is firmly embedded. Finally, governments have used their ability to produce and disseminate information in a variety of ways in relation to education, be this to support competition, enable international comparison or to inform domestic policy debates.

Summary

❑ Early approaches to education policy attempted to produce typologies of approaches in order to inform policy-makers. Educational sociology rejected these 'pick and mix' approaches, arguing that educational systems could only be understood within their societal context.

❑ The history of education policy in many nations has demonstrated attempts by governments to use education to produce a loyal administrative cadre and citizenry. More recently, analysts have argued that education policies have increasingly become linked to economic policy goals.

❑ The policy instruments used in education policy:
  – Governments use the *financial resources* available to them to provide entirely or mainly tax-funded education, and to incentivize the purchase of private or voluntary education.
  – Governments use their *authority* to regulate educational standards through evaluating education providers, and controlling examinations and educational content.
  – Governments use their powers of *organization* to shape educational systems, particularly the degree to which they are (de)centralized; the extent to which they use selection or 'streaming'; and the degree of competition between different educational providers.
  – Governments use their control over *information* to provide, or require the provision of, data about educational quality to consumers of education or their parents, and to improve or shape educational policy-making.

❑ Children's gender, class, and race have been shown to impact on how they fare within educational systems, in a number of countries and across a range of providers.

Chapter 7

Environmental Policy

Unlike the other areas examined in this book, the environment is a relatively new policy area. Its genesis is generally dated to the late 1960s and early 1970s, the period of 'environmental awakening' in the USA which included the publication of Rachel Carson's book *Silent Spring*, the Love Canal chemical waste pollution crisis, and the first Earth Day (Ervin *et al.*, 2003: 3). Since that period, environmental regulation, and environmental policy more generally, has 'grown from being generally a marginal type of state intervention into an activity which increasingly makes an important impact on people's everyday lives and on the operations of enterprises' (Daugbjerg, 1998: 285).

Environmental policies can be particularly difficult for governments to implement due to the peculiar concentration of costs and benefits that they generally entail. Their costs tend to be visibly concentrated on a small number of producers in heavily-polluting industries. In contrast, their benefits are very widely distributed (for example, to all inhabitants in a particular region who can breathe marginally cleaner air following the introduction of a tax on pollution). Gainers from environmental policy are often ill-defined and badly organized compared with those who are set to lose from it. As such, the environment is often a particularly controversial policy area (Daneke, 1984: 144; Daugbjerg, 1998: 281).

The scope of environmental policy, and how it relates to other policy areas, has changed over time. As well as affecting, in some nations, approaches to economic policy, environmental policy has also become increasingly closely tied to security. For example, the British Cabinet Office in its 2008 National Security Strategy stated that '[c]limate change is potentially the greatest challenge to global stability and security, and therefore to national security' (quoted in Dalby, 2009: 151). Measures which have traditionally been conceptualized as relating to security, such as bans on nuclear weapon testing dating from the early 1960s, could equally be viewed as environmental in their goals and impact (*ibid.*: 37).

Additionally, many of the environmental processes which threaten 'human security' cannot be legislated for on a purely national basis, and viewing environmental change as a threat to conventional notions of national security may be inappropriate. As Dalby (*ibid.*: 3) notes, academic work generally suggests that 'environmental change rarely causes conflict directly', and that viewing 'environmental security' within a state-based framework could exacerbate rather than reduce threats (e.g. by leading to increased concern about military preparedness and border control, rather than focusing on cross-border processes).

Authors such as Jänicke (1990), Mol and Buttel (2002) and Dryzek *et al.* (2003) have argued that states' roles in relation to the environment are one of their core 'metafunctions', alongside economic and social metafunctions (with 'metafunctions' thus called due to their coverage of more than one discrete policy field). Whilst the 'economic metafunction' 'provides the necessary regulatory framework and infrastructure for economic development and growth' and the 'social metafunction' comprises the 'welfare state', the 'ecological metafunction' 'assures the protection of the environment', and covers 'research and education, consumer protection and especially the environmental division of all those policy sectors responsible for environmentally intensive production sectors', as well as 'traditional' areas of environmental policy (e.g. the provision of national parks) (Jänicke, 2006: 88).

Despite the apparently growing scope of environmental policy, contestation continues over its appropriate scope. In some nations, certain types of economic activity are classified as having environmental impacts which are not viewed as appropriate targets for public policy in other countries. Hence, for example, the EU's lengthy dispute with the USA, Canada and Argentina, mediated through the WTO, concerning the strictness with which genetically modified organism (GMO) production should be licensed, and the degree to which GMO foods should be labelled. Another example comes from the Swedish tax on nuclear power, which is described by that nation as a pro-environmental measure (OECD/EEA 2011), despite the fact that in some nations (such as Britain) nuclear power has been promoted as a means of reducing climate change and hence protecting the environment.

A variety of different categories of environmental policy have been identified. For example, policies can be divided into licences for potentially environmentally harmful economic activity; controls over this activity; requirements for 'future cleansing'; and fines or bans following harmful activity (Aguilar Fernández, 1994: 45). More recently, in addition to these traditional 'regulatory' approaches, a number of 'market-based' approaches have been advocated by governments which do not ban or sanction certain activities but, instead, attempt to use reputation or taxes to incentivize pro-environmental behaviour (Steel *et al.*, 2003: 76). The latter category of 'market-based' approaches is often described as comprising 'new' environmental policy instruments ('NEPIs') (Jordan *et al.*, 2003a; 2005).

The context: theories of environmental policy development

Until the early 1960s, in most countries nature was essentially presented as 'unlimited' in its capacity to absorb pollution. This reflected a 'frontier ethic' (Buck, 1998: 11), whereby nature was viewed as an infinitely absorptive wilderness – there was 'space to pollute'. Policy-makers did occasionally react when environmental damage resulted in immediate and visible damage to population health – for example, where high levels of pollution resulted in smog which produced and exacerbated respiratory problems. However, their response was generally to attempt to dilute pollution through 'high-chimney policies', or to shift it away from highly-populated areas using more sensitive planning, rather than to ban or penalize polluting activities (Jänicke, 2006: 86).

The second phase of environmental policy – and the first concerted efforts – focused on reducing pollution and preventing rapid deforestation and other unsustainable destruction of natural resources. These issues could often, if not always, be dealt with on a national basis and without any significant changes being made to nation states' economic policies. During this period, the environment was generally seen as a resource which humans could and should seek to exploit. Science and technology were viewed as means of reconciling population growth with the resource pressures this entailed. This was particularly evident in the so-called 'Green Revolution', which used fertilizers to generate a dramatic increase in agricultural production (Steel *et al.*, 2003: 11).

More recent environmental concerns have challenged this approach. Climate change, ozone depletion, acid rain, and reductions in marine and land biodiversity cannot be dealt with by nation states acting alone (Steel *et al.*, 2003). In addition, some policy actors began to express concerns that economic growth might be limited due to the finite capacities of the environment (Meadows *et al.*, 1972). What Jänicke has described as the 'third stage' of environmental policy – from the 1990s onwards – has focused on bringing 'about a conversion process within the system of production and consumption' which reflects the environmental impact of different types of economic activity (Jänicke, 2006: 86).

Yet, despite this, debate still rages about the validity of so-called 'ecological modernization' policy approaches, which argue that there is no fundamental contradiction between environmental protection and economic growth (Poncelet, 2001: 19). In particular, theories of ecological modernization suggest that: science and technology can help cure and prevent environmental problems, as well as cause them; ecological 'restructuring' and 'reform' can be caused by economic agents as well as by governments and social movements, and can contribute to a more 'bottom-up' approach to environmental governance; social movements are becoming implicated in public and private decision-making around environmental issues; and economic and environmentalist interests and arguments should be viewed as potentially complementary (Mol and Sonnenfeld, 2000). Attempts to integrate environmental with industrial and commercial issues have motivated numerous EU agendas, particularly the Lisbon Agenda (Jänicke, 2007) and the new 'Europe2020' programme (Schiellerup and Atanasiu, 2011).

Nonetheless, some have argued that environmental issues risk being downplayed, in the face of powerful commercial and industrial interests and traditionalist ideas within the EU (Hertin and Berkhout, 2003). More fundamentally, some have disputed the appropriateness of the 'ecological modernization' model, claiming that capitalist development and environmental sustainability are inherently incompatible (Foster, 1992). Others have suggested the need for more research into the conditions under which ecological modernization might be feasible, highlighting the differing cultural attitudes towards environmental protection in different nations (Cohen, 1998).

Some newer approaches to environmental policy also challenge the conceptualization of humans as masters over the environment, suggesting that they should instead be viewed as integral parts of ecologies or ecosystems, rather than totally separate from these (Steel *et al.*, 2003). Whereas a concern for 'wilderness' would argue for measures such as the creation of national parks, for example, a recognition of humans' impact on nature would suggest that trying to preserve 'ecological integrity' is impossible in many areas of the planet. Huge new ecosystems have been created by humans, such as through the creation of massive river damming projects as exist in the Tennessee (USA), Narmada (India) and Yangtze (China) rivers. These projects have resulted in huge 'engineered' ecosystems (Ervin *et al.*, 2003: 13).

Arguably however, there have always been, albeit less dramatic, instances where humans' influence has significantly altered ecosystems. Heather moorland, for example, requires 'a particular grazing and heather management pattern to remain as such', and therefore simply cannot exist without the influence of humans (Hanley and Whitby, 2003: 148). Furthermore, the environmental impact of some societies' activities have indirectly led to increases in their power, and decreases in other societies' power. Hence, Alfred Crosby (1986) has argued that European imperialists' cargo of disease, flora and fauna when colonizing arguably had a more significant impact, over the longer term, than the policies they imposed. The recognition of humans' massive, and now integral, influence on the environment has led some geologists to suggest that a new period has dawned, most appropriately described as the 'Anthropocene' (Crutzen, 2002).

The extent to which human-made approaches can substitute for natural processes has also become more contested. For example, human-engineered attempts to provide levees and other flood control structures for the Mississippi river were shown as inadequate during floods in 1994. These approaches had previously worked well, but the intensity of farming in the surrounding area meant that 'human-made' approaches offered an insufficient 'substitute' for the 'ecological services' traditionally provided by the until-then undeveloped flood plain (Ervin *et al.*, 2003: 11). Similarly, the scale of some natural processes appears so vast that human-made substitutes are difficult to imagine – for example, carbon sequestering 'on the scale of tropical rainforests' (*ibid.*).

Theories of systematic difference across nations

When it comes to the adoption of environmental policies, if not their implementation and outcomes, Liefferink *et al* describe a 'conventional picture of the historical come-and-go of environmental pioneers' which involves 'Japan and the US' setting 'the pace in the 1970s, whilst Germany, together with the Netherlands and the Nordic countries, took over in the 1980s; during the 1990s, in turn, these countries lost terrain to a diffuse group of more specific innovators, including the UK, among others' (Liefferink *et al.*, 2009: 679–80). Two main theories have developed to attempt to explain different approaches to environmental policy between countries: those which focus primarily on economic factors (levels of economic development, or openness), and those based on examining the role of different stakeholders (environmental interest groups and business) in different institutional contexts.

Classifications based on economic factors

The two key approaches linking environmental policy patterns to economic factors focus on levels of economic development and competition, respectively.

The most basic approach to explaining differences in environmental policies between nations suggests that this relies mainly on their levels of economic development. This effectively parallels explanations for welfare development which associate it with industrialization, as set out in Chapter 4 (Wagner's law). However, the 'environmental Kuznets curve' includes the twist that environmental quality is likely to reduce immediately after industrialization, but then to increase steadily as GDP increases and citizens demand policy responds to environmental harm (Ekins, 1997). The curve is named after Simon Kuznets (Kuznets, 1955), who suggested a similar relationship existed between economic development and inequality.

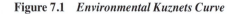

Figure 7.1   *Environmental Kuznets Curve*

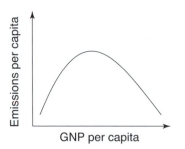

There does appear to be some evidence that 'wealth and post-materi-
alist values' are positively correlated with, for example, nations signing
up to Multilateral Environmental Agreements (Kelemen, 2010: 337;
Börzel, 2002). One of the most comprehensive studies of environmental
policy adoption (if not of implementation and policy outcomes) – that
conducted by Liefferink *et al.* (2009) – suggests that higher levels of
economic development *are* associated with greater levels of environmental policy adoption, and with 'stricter settings' being adopted for specific environmental policies (*ibid.*: 690).

In contrast, approaches considering the role of economic competition
initially suggested that greater levels of trade and economic openness
would lead to reduced, rather than increased, environmental standards.
This approach suggested the likelihood of a 'race to the bottom' in environmental standards. 'Footloose' capital (i.e. business) has an incentive
to threaten governments with relocation to other jurisdictions (and the
reduction in domestic employment this would entail) unless costs of production (including the costs of compliance with environmental measures) are lowered. A 'race to the bottom' occurs when nations then
competitively reduce their environmental protections as part of 'regulatory competition'. Races to the bottom have sometimes been described
as resulting from a 'Delaware effect'. As mentioned in Chapter 4 (p. 85),
the US state of Delaware adopted relatively lax company incorporation
standards and came to capture a large share of company registrations
compared with other states – suggesting that a reduction in standards in
the face of regulatory competition between states had worked for
Delaware. Nonetheless, as discussed in Chapter 12 (pp. 274–5), the evidence for widespread 'races to the bottom' in environmental regulation,
as in welfare provision, is both mixed and disputed.

In any case, pressures towards reduction in environmental protection
from regulatory competition arguably coexist with other confounding
factors, not least 'international regulatory cooperation' (Holzinger and

Knill, 2004: 26). Indeed, regulatory cooperation may occur as a result of fears that competition might develop, with the 'existence of interdependencies or externalities' pushing 'governments to resolve common problems through cooperation within international institutions' (*ibid.*: 28–9). The role of international organizations in environmental policy is considered in greater detail below (pp. 171–3).

Classifications based on political dynamics

The main approach taken to the classification of nations' environmental policy approaches has concerned the relationship that exists between governments and the producers of environmental harm, and the degree to which that relationship is 'legalistic' and 'confrontational', or 'administrative' and 'conciliatory'.

Traditionally, the USA was portrayed as a nation where relations between government and business, at least in the field of environmental policy, were characterized by conflict and legal contestation, whereas the UK exemplified a more conciliatory approach (Vogel, 1986). Specifically, in the USA regulators set ambitious goals, which were often 'technology-forcing' – that is, which required companies to develop new technologies to meet tough standards. This contrasted with UK regulators' more incremental approach. Sanctions for non-compliance in the USA were high, and the process of enforcing compliance was more judicialized and expensive for business than in the UK.

David Vogel linked this to differences in the groups involved in environmental policy-making in the two countries, with more private citizens involved in the US policy process, and more business and expert involvement in the UK. He also argued that, in the USA, environmental regulation was often adopted for 'ulterior motives' (such as the protection of industries in politically significant areas) and, further, that implementation in the USA was significantly patchier and more erratic than in the UK. As a result, although on paper the USA had stricter environmental regulations, in practice, their impact appeared similar to the apparently laxer UK regulations (Vogel, 1986: 146).

The US approach to environmental policy-making was also often compared with that operating in Canada. The US 'penal' model of 'adversarial legalism', 'action-forcing statutes' (such as those contained within the National Environmental Policy Act and Clean Air Act), 'citizen suits, and judicial activism' was contrasted with the Canadian 'compliance' approach characterized by 'voluntary Environmental Assessment Review Process (EARP) "guidelines", administrative standards subject to negotiation of compliance agreements with polluters coupled with a general lack of citizen recourse to overturn administrative decisions' (Howlett, 2000: 305, 311–12, 315). The difference was generally associated with US reliance on 'private attorney-generals' – that is, members of the public, to ensure that the political executive complies with Congressional decisions; and the greater involvement of the judiciary in the policy implementation process. This contrasts with the situation in Canada where, as in the UK, Attorney Generals are accepted as part of a more horizontally integrated (if federal, in the Canadian case) and less judicialized system of government (*ibid*.: 314).

Some analyses in this tradition were highly normative, arguing for example that the USA 'would do well to study the experiences of countries such as . . . Great Britain . . . [and] Canada ... for clues to reducing its combative atmosphere' (Daneke, 1984: 147). Often, the British approach, in particular, was described as 'more effective' than that operating in the USA due to its 'closed system', which allegedly built trust between environmental policy-makers and business (Daneke, 1984: 148). Simultaneously, others viewed Britain as the 'dirty man of Europe' due to its 'dogged determination not to take action in fields with international repercussions, most notably action to reduce emissions of sulphur dioxide' (Weale, 1992: 69).

Certainly, until the early 1980s many policy fields in Britain related to the environment were characterized by relatively closed policy communities, not least agriculture (Marsh and Smith, 2000). However, with the EU increasing its role in this policy area, and growing pressure from actors such as the environmental movement and consumers, the policy community began to expand. Indeed, more recent analyses carried out by David Vogel have argued that the EU's approach to environmental regulation (which determines much of the UK's environmental policy) is significantly more stringent than that within the USA, which is now less legalized and extensive. Vogel highlights, for example, the adoption by the EU, but not the USA, of the Kyoto protocol, and of stricter standards on chemicals in cosmetics, hormones in beef, and GMOs in the EU compared with the USA. He maintains that this has occurred because of institutional factors (specifically, the permeability of EU institutions to influence from environmental interest groups), and what he sees as the greater degree of risk aversion amongst the European public (Vogel, 2003b; 2004).

Similarly, Howlett has argued that the USA and Canadian 'environmental implementation styles' have started to converge (Howlett, 2000: 315–16). This has followed attempts to deregulate in the US environmental policy context, and to involve increasing numbers of stakeholders in the Canadian context. There is also evidence of increased judicialization in Canada, with environmental groups using the courts to impede the construction of dams (Hoberg, 1991: 125). Howlett (2000: 305) suggests convergence has been mutual, with both countries moving towards a 'third, common, style, that associated with the development of self-regulation and voluntary initiatives under the influence of New Public Management ideas and principles'.

One approach to systematize this approach comes from Kelemen and Vogel (2010), described by them as the 'regulatory politics perspective'. This suggests that nations' approaches to environmental policy – particularly that determined at an international level – will reflect the organization of different relevant groups in the polity and their relationship to the political system.

If environmental groups are strong and able to exercise domestic influence on policy, they are likely to argue for the preservation, or even strengthening, of standards at an international level. Similarly, if industry believes it will be unable to block strict standards at home, it will argue for strict standards abroad as well, to preserve a level playing field for competition with foreign firms. This combination of environmentalist and business concerns arguing for international-level regulation has sometimes been described as a 'Baptist-Bootlegger coalition'. Kelemen (2010) applies this approach to the EU, and suggests that it helps explain why this regional body has adopted an increasing leadership role within international environmental policy negotiations.

Kelemen (2000) argues that the greater horizontal and vertical fragmentation of the EU policy-making system (i.e. its separation of powers between the legislature, executive and judiciary, and its federal nature), helps explain why it 'is likely to move down the US path toward detailed, non-discretionary rule making and the use of litigation as a means to secure enforcement' in policy realms including the environment (*ibid.*: 135). For example, in the USA, pro-regulation Congress members were incentivized to develop detailed environmental policies which could then be used by private actors (i.e. citizens' groups) to constrain the executive (*ibid.*: 149). In the EU, whilst it is less easy for citizens' groups to take legal action, Kelemen (*ibid.*: 153–4) argues that the Commission has come to fulfil the role of enforcer; and the role of citizens as private litigants is growing.

The characteristics of the policy network and the opportunity structure for business and environmental interest groups have also been adduced to explain differences in environmental policy approaches amongst otherwise comparatively similar nations, such as Sweden, Denmark and Norway (Daugbjerg and Pedersen, 2004). Some large-N studies have also attempted to assess the impact of different interests on environmental policy-making, within specific institutional contexts. For example, Jacob and Volkery (2006) examined four types of policy towards climate change across thirty countries, and argued that four factors helped explain policy adoption: the degree of neo-corporatism (see Chapter 8), an indicator of governmental effectiveness, the existence of strong environmental interest groups, and the relative balance between 'clean' and 'dirty' industry in the nation concerned. Liefferink *et al.*'s (2009: 692) analysis of the ENVIPOLCON data set (which covers 40 environmental policy areas in 21 European countries plus the USA, Mexico and Japan from 1970–2000) confirms the view that neo-corporatist arrangements can, *inter alia*, lead to higher levels of policy adoption. However, their analysis also questions the conventional view of 'leaders and laggards in environmental policy' – particularly, that Scandinavian countries and Germany were 'leaders' in environmental policy adoption through the 1980s and 1990s. Instead, they suggest that the roles of these countries as environmental 'leaders' generally only 'crystallised' from 1990. As such, they maintain that '[e]nvironmental pioneers, in other words, seem to have 'internal' and 'external' faces which are not necessarily similar' (*ibid.*: 689).

International pressures

Out of the policy areas examined in this text, environmental policy has, at least since the 1960s, perhaps been the most affected by international pressures. This is for a variety of reasons. First, environmental flows generated in one nation have long been able to 'cross borders' and affect other countries. As Hoberg (1991: 108) describes it, for example, the USA has long 'exported' its pollution to Canada through the mechanisms of acid rain and pollution of the Great Lakes.

Second, much environmental protection is now centred on what can be described as 'global commons' – 'Antarctica, the high seas and deep seabed minerals, the atmosphere, and space' (Buck, 1998: 1). These 'global commons' contain so-called 'common pool resources' – resources which are 'managed under a property regime in which a legally defined user pool cannot be efficiently excluded from the resource domain' (*ibid.*: 5). 'Global' commons can be distinguished from 'international' commons, as some states are excluded from property rights in the latter. Hence, for example, the Mediterranean sea and, to a large degree, Antarctica are controlled by regimes operated by a small number of countries which jointly exercise property rights over them (*ibid.*: 6). The definition of 'global' and 'international' commons has changed over time. For example, the Romans declared in the second century that the seas were possessed by all mankind, but by 1269 tolls and other forms of control were being exercised on ships by the Venetian regime (Buck, 1998).

Both global and international commons require nations to cooperate and pool some of their sovereignty with each other, if the so-called 'tragedy of the commons' is to be prevented (Hardin, 1968). This is due to the fact that no one consumer of common pool resources has, in the absence of rules restricting consumption, any incentive to keep their consumption within bounds. For example, no one fisherman will be willing to make a substantial reduction in their catch of fish to prevent an eventual degradation of the fishing stock, if that person knows that other fishermen are unlikely to also reduce their catches. In such contexts, a downward spiral of over-consumption, and eventual exhaustion and extinction, is likely unless institutions can be created which alter individual fishermen's incentives (Ostrom, 1990).

Some attempts have been made at preserving global and international commons, which mainly rest on the agreement of international treaties or, in the EU's case, the specification of binding policies on member states. However, some global commons remain candidates for 'tragedies', not least space, which currently contains tens of thousands of discarded objects, and where attempts at sanctioning transgression have proved problematic. For example, following the crash of a Soviet satellite on Canadian soil, the Canadian regime experienced severe difficulties in obtaining (treaty-assured) damages from the (then) USSR (Buck, 1998: 152).

Treaties

Domestic environmental policies, more than any other area, are bound by a series of international and multilateral treaties, dating from the 1970s onwards. Some are bilateral, such as the Great Lakes Water Quality Agreement between America and Canada, concluded in 1972, which created an international Commission to govern water pollution in the Lakes area (Hoberg, 1991: 115).

Some others began with only a few signatories and later expanded. This was the case with the Montreal Protocol concluded in 1987, pushed forward by the USA and signed by 24 nations and the European Commission – 'the first time the international community had agreed to control a valuable commodity in the present in order to prevent environmental damage in the future' (Buck, 1998: 123). A similar process occurred with air pollution, in a context where other areas (such as security or economic policy) were off-limits for multinational negotiation. The UN Economic Commission for Europe produced a 'Convention on Long-Range Transboundary Air Pollution', which was agreed in 1979. This was then expanded with the conclusion of the Helsinki Protocol in 1985, which prioritized reductions in sulfur dioxide pollution, although some countries which had signed the Convention refused to sign the Protocol, including the UK and USA (Ringquist and Kostadinova, 2005: 89).

Many treaties have been adopted following the holding of large conferences, often under the aegis of the UN. This occurred, for example, with the 1992 'Earth' (or 'Rio') summit, whose formal title was the UN

Conference on Environment and Development (UNCED). This resulted in a range of proclamations, including Conventions on Biological Diversity and Climate Change and two agreements, Agenda 21 and the Rio Declaration (Steel *et al.*, 2003: 5). An alternative approach was in evidence at the 2002 Johannesburg Summit, where the EU worked with around ninety countries to produce a Coalition agreement on renewable energy which did not aim at 'global consensus at any price' but, instead, at innovation and diffusion amongst its signatories only (Jänicke, 2006: 95).

The practical impact of treaties on policy delivery – and, particularly, implementation in different countries – has, nonetheless, been questioned. First, not all treaties involve nations whose behaviour is contributing to the environmental harm they seek to reduce. One prominent example is provided by the Kyoto treaty, which has not been signed by the USA, despite the fact that it produces 'roughly one-quarter of the world's total emissions' (Steel *et al.*, 2003: ix). A more extreme example is provided by the Moon Treaty (1979), which has not been signed by any of the 'major spacefaring nations' (Buck, 1998: 150).

In addition, it is difficult to discern whether signing up to any treaty has a specific impact on policy-making in that nation. Even studies which have compared treaty signing with policy adoption have often failed to take into account the fact that nations do not ratify treaties at random (Ringquist and Kostadinova, 2005: 91). When this is taken into account, treaties' effectiveness can be questioned, as Ringquist and Kostadinova (*ibid.*: 99) suggest for the Helsinki Protocol.

Europeanization

One area where these issues have been studied in exhaustive depth is the EU's environmental policy regime. The EU has, in theory, produced 'total' policy harmonization in some product areas, such as the regulation of car exhaust emissions; 'minimum' harmonization has applied to areas such as air and water quality (Holzinger and Knill, 2004: 34). The EU's 'hierarchical' governance, involving countries being bound by EU rules, now applies to areas as diverse as pollution, biotechnology, climate change and conservation. The EU has also arguably affected environmental policy-making in member nations through 'network governance' – 'softer' forms of communication and information exchange which are not binding (Knill and Tosun, 2009: 875, 877), although 'hierarchical' governance has a far stronger discernible impact (*ibid.*: 889).

Whilst particular nations' policies may have been used as 'blueprints' for EU intervention (as with the EU's clean air legislation, which was strongly affected by German policies in this area) (Aguilar Fernández, 1994: 42), no one country has served as the unique source for EU legislation. Hence, for example, Germany's intention to introduce road user charges was opposed at EU level (Bugdahn, 2005: 184).

The EU's developing policy competence has been paralleled by the increasing influence of environmental interest groups at European level (p. 199). The so-called 'Green 10' comprises large environmental NGOs which frequently combine to mount lobbying campaigns in Brussels.

Comparing environmental policies across nations

The use of financial resources

Governments have used their control over financial resources in environmental policy both negatively and positively; that is, they have taxed or fined certain activities, and financially rewarded others. In addition, on occasion they have directly provided environmental services.

Governments can both tax and/or fine certain activities deemed to be environmentally harmful. Figure 7.2 indicates the percentage of overall tax revenues derived from environmentally-related taxes.

Taxes can be imposed on generally 'harmful' activities by producers (as with the French *Taxe générale sur les activités polluantes*), or by consumers (as with the duties that many countries impose on air passen-

Figure 7.2   *Trends in revenues from environmentally-related taxes, 1995–2004*

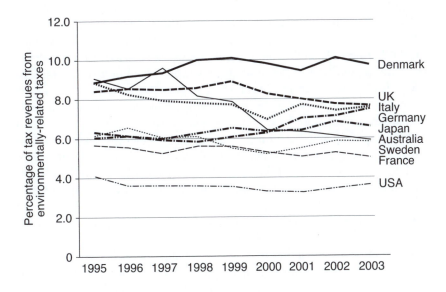

Source: OECD (2007) table 4b.

gers); or on the purchase of certain products related to production or consumption (such as the Italian, Swedish, Norwegian and Danish duties on pesticides; stamp duties imposed on the purchase of motor vehicles, such as in New South Wales, Australia; or the petroleum taxes applied in many different countries). Taxes can also be imposed on the use of generally scarce resources (such as with water pricing) although, as Jänicke (2006: 86) notes, material inputs to production are generally not taxed (aside from mineral oil, which is taxed in some countries).

'Eco-taxes' have been promoted amongst other NEPIs as a means of encouraging more environmentally-friendly behaviour by firms and consumers. Taxation has the benefit of falling outwith the WTO's and EU's jurisdiction, provided the taxes in question do not go against the broad obligations required by each body (Bomberg, 2007: 251). Most 'eco-taxes' attempt to go some way towards the internalizing of negative externalities – that is, they require producers and consumers to take into account the full cost of their activities on the environment, costs which are not reflected in the market price of the activity or good concerned (Daugbjerg and Pedersen, 2004: 219).

At the same time, however, they may be viewed as a source of revenue for promoting environmentally-friendly activity. Hence, Daugbjerg and Pedersen (*ibid.*: 225–6) explain how Swedish governments used revenues from fertilizer and pesticide taxes to pay for 'general environmental' agricultural services, such as research, when they were first introduced, and latterly to help pay for expanded animal manure storage facilities, development projects and land conservation. As such, the tax effectively involved 'redistribution' from all farmers using fertilizers and pesticides to those, especially livestock farmers, who benefited from these environmental services (*ibid.*: 225–6). Alternatively, eco-taxes may offset other taxes such that their effect is broadly revenue-neutral. Hence, for example, the Danish government, when introducing taxes on insecticides, fungicides, herbicides and crop growth-regulating chemicals, stated that the taxes would be offset with a suspension of the federal-level share coming out of the regional land tax (*ibid.*: 225–6).

Eco-taxes may also be subject to significant loopholes. Daugbjerg and Pedersen note that only 64 per cent of Norway's CO_2 emissions were covered by its 'CO_2 tax' (*ibid.*: 228), that a Danish tax on CO_2 was not applied to offshore oil and that special reimbursements were provided in Denmark for particularly energy-intensive industries. Swedish taxes on CO_2 were more encompassing but, even there, metallurgical industries were subject to tax reductions (*ibid.*: 231).

As mentioned, in addition to taxes, charges or fines may also be invoked by governments to dissuade particular environmentally harmful activities and/or to provide revenue for environmentally-friendly purposes. Charges have been imposed on waste water (as in Germany), water pollution (as with Swedish charges for oil spills), the use of particular roads by heavy vehicles (as with German road tolls for this purpose), and on visits to particularly sensitive areas by tourists (as with Australia's charges to visit the Great Barrier Reef) (OECD/EEA, 2011).

Despite the widespread use of financial penalties in many nations for polluting activities, in some nations they remain controversial amongst the general public and politicians. This is particularly the case in the USA, where even revenue-neutral attempts to tax CO_2 emissions have generally proven politically unpalatable. Instead, state and federal governments have generally favoured 'indirect' measures which do not impose, or obscure the imposition of, direct costs on energy consumers (Rabe, 2010).

Equally, governments may use their control of financial resources to reward particular types of environmentally-friendly activity. Hence, the Australian government provides subsidies for the establishment of carbon sink forests; the French government provides a 'bonus' for the purchase of 'green' cars; the Swedish government subsidizes renewable energy plant set-up costs; and the Italian government provides its citizens with a personal income tax allowance to cover public transport costs, and also provides tax credits for biomass heating systems (OECD/EEA 2011).

One well-embedded form of financial reward programme is that of 'agri-environmental schemes'. These involve governments covering the opportunity costs to farmers of the production of environmental benefits, as 'joint products with food and fibre outputs' (Hanley and Whitby, 2003: 145). Various types of agri-environmental scheme exist in countries including Britain, the USA and Denmark, although the activities they target differ from nation to nation. Hence, Hanley and Whitby suggest that British agri-environmental schemes have not focused on non-point pollution, instead privileging wildlife habitat and landscape quality (*ibid*.: 147). As they note, agri-environmental schemes implicitly rest on the assumption that 'farmers/rural land managers have the right to carry out the most profit-maximizing activity on their land, irrespective of the external costs (and benefits) of doing so', and that if 'farming in a more environmentally-sensitive manner imposes costs on farmers, then society must compensate them' (*ibid*.: 151). The Common Agriculture Policy's use of 'set-aside', whereby farmers were paid for leaving land fallow, arguably also falls into the agri-environmental scheme category, although it served the additional purpose of reducing the overproduction of food within the EU. As with Eco-Taxes, the use of subsidies to promote pro-environmental behaviour has also been described as one of the suite of NEPIs (Golub, 1998).

One particularly interesting, and cross-national, example of rewarding environmentally-friendly activity is the provision of compensation to prevent nations from exploiting natural resources due to environmental concerns. The Ecuadorian government was, at the time of writing, attempting to encourage foreign governments and international organizations to provide it with US$3.3 billion over 13 years in exchange for eschewing the US$7.2billion worth of revenue the government would obtain if oil under the Yasuni national park were exploited (Blair, 2011).

Compared with other areas of policy, the extent to which governments directly provide environmental services is limited. This is not least because the environmental harms targeted by public policy are generally created as by-products of economic activity within the private sector. As such, areas of environmental policy such as pollution control could be described as a 'post-welfare state sector of public policy' (Weale, 1992: 7). Nonetheless, governments have engaged in some expenditure for the direct provision of environmental services. Figure 7.3, although reliant on the patchy availability of data, sets out how different countries have used public funds for pollution abatement and control.

Governments may also attempt to support research into environmental change and improvement. Figure 7.4 details public expenditure by dif-

Figure 7.3   *Pollution abatement and control expenditure, 1990–2004*

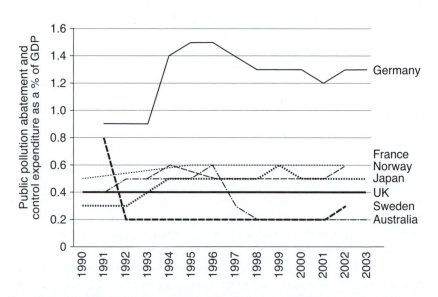

Notes: For Australia, 1991–96 data cover the central and local governments, 1997 data cover only central government, whereas data since 1998 cover only local governments; for Italy, data refer to estimates derived from National accounts, and 1997 data include public specialized producers; and for Sweden, the 1991 data refer to a Secretariat estimate for the whole public sector. Since 1992, data cover general government only for Sweden. Data coverage for the USA and Italy is extremely patchy, so both nations have been excluded from this chart. Note that missing data has been interpolated.

Source: OECD (2007) table 1.

Figure 7.4 *Public R&D budgets for control and care of the environment,
1981–2005, as a percentage of total R&D budget appropriations*

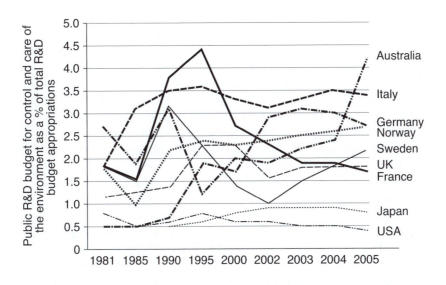

Notes: Statistics for the USA, Japan and Australia cover federal/central government only. For the USA, since 2000, budgets for capital expenditure – 'R&D plant' in national terminology – are included. Data for earlier years relate to budgets for current costs only. Note that missing data has been interpolated.

Source: OECD (2007).

ferent countries on research and development into the control and care of the environment. As with Figure 7.3, the data should be treated with caution as they reflect the variable quality of data collection in this area.

Finally, environmental groups may be provided with public funds to sustain their activities. The EU has been particularly active in this regard, providing, for example, an average of €831,008 per year over the period 2003–7 to the European Environmental Bureau, and also strongly supporting pan-European environmental groups such as the World Wildlife Fund and Friends of the Earth Europe (Mahoney and Beckstrand, 2011: 1351).

❯ The use of authority

Direct use of government authority to reduce the incidence of activities harmful to the environment was initially the most popular type of public action in environmental policy – what Jänicke (2006: 87) describes, along with taxes, as the 'traditional instruments of environmental state intervention'. These approaches are generally described as resting on 'command and control' – 'the exercise of influence by imposing standards backed by criminal sanctions' (Baldwin and Cave, 1999: 35). Within this category, however, a wide range of different approaches to regulation abound, which can be differentiated according to when they occur in the production and consumption process.

First, governments may require the licensing of specific activities before they can commence. This approach is particularly common where plant design can have an environmental impact, and where it would be difficult or impossible to alter design after a facility has been built. This is the case, for example, with foundries and power stations. This approach has sometimes been described as setting 'specification' or 'input' standards, and is ostensibly the most interventionist approach to imposing standards (Ogus, 1994: 151).

Second, attempts may be made to control the environmental impact of economic activity once it has commenced – what can be described as 'process' regulation. This approach includes, for example, the imposition of emission limit values for nitrogen oxides for plants such as power stations and petrol refineries, which the EU (then the EEC) has undertaken since 1988 (Knill and Tosun, 2009: 879). On occasion, such limits may be applied not to individual plants but, rather, to an industrial sector as a whole – hence so-called 'bubble' limits which enable flexibility in the location and timing of harm-producing activities across different firm sites or, indeed, firms in the same district (Daneke, 1984: 143; Sinclair, 1997: 540). This type of limit or licence can be particularly effective where firms are likely to 'strategically subsidiarize' – that is, where there is an incentive for them to 'hive off environmentally sensitive components of their overall operations into independently incorporated subsidiaries with small asset bases, thereby protecting the assets of the parent company from exposure to environmental risk' (Heyes, 1998: 57).

Process-based regulatory intervention can occur either during the production of activities likely to result in environmental harm (e.g. inspecting a factory and penalizing excessive discharges noticed during the inspection), or following detection of harm (e.g. 'tracing back' excessive levels of chemicals in a certain river to a particular factory). Regulation focused on controlling activity once it has commenced is particularly popular where the production of harms can be immediately verified and, indeed, halted. For example, an environmental inspector could be alerted to illegal discharge levels from a factory and immediately halt production at the responsible site – thus immediately remedying the problem (Hutter, 1997: 205). Such approaches may be cheaper as they relate only to actual harm caused rather than potential causes of harm (Ogus, 1994: 166). Approaches based on only penalizing 'real harm' are particularly successful at reducing 'point-source pollution' – pollution whose origin is easy to detect. However, they are less successful at dealing with so-called 'diffuse source pollution', such as 'pesticide run-off from irrigated lands or petroleum products seeping off of parking lots' (Steel *et al.*, 2003: 107–8).

Governments may also attempt to restrict the availability of certain environmentally harmful products. Hence, the Danish government's Pesticide Action Plan, introduced in 1986, removed pesticides deemed unacceptably hazardous, and attempted to halve the use of others (Dubgaard, 2003: 160).

Finally, governments can also control how the legal system deals with the attribution of the costs of environmental harm. The US federal government, for example, created a special liability scheme for oil spills in 1990 which is paid for through a trust fund generated through taxes levied on domestic and imported oil (OECD/EEA, 2011). More broadly, the EU has created an environmental liability scheme to cover all member states, which enables some remediation for environmental damage (European Commission, 2000).

All these types of regulation are subject to two different parameters: the strictness with which they are enforced, and the likelihood of their application. Traditionally, 'compliance'-based approaches, resting on persuasion, have been contrasted with 'deterrence'-based approaches, resting on the threat of prosecution. In practice, however, even in jurisdictions which appear to operate deterrence-based approaches on paper, regulators may be hesitant to impose sanctions, particularly where these require court action (Hutter, 1997: 9). In practice, there is often 'as much art as science in enforcement trade-offs', which have to balance, for example, the punishment of 'infringers' with 'maximizing compliance levels' and the prevention of 'creative compliance' and the production of 'rules that are easily enforced' (Baldwin and Cave, 1999: 117). Therefore, although, in theory 'command and control' regulatory approaches allow firms 'little or no room ... to avoid their regulation obligations' (Sinclair, 1997: 534), in practice, the strictness of application of regulation can differ markedly between nations.

Concerning the second parameter, the likelihood of invocation of regulation, this also differs widely between contexts and countries. First, states differ concerning the extent to which they apply regulation in the face of a possible threat to human health or the environment (the 'precautionary principle') (Majone, 2002). Since the 1990s, the EU has often been seen as following the precautionary principle, which is less frequently invoked in nations such as the USA (Gaskell *et al.*, 1999). States also differ in the balance between 'command and control' regulation undertaken by governments or their authorized agents (such as regulatory agencies) and self-regulation by firms, or associations of firms, themselves. Sinclair has suggested that, in practice, it is most accurate to 'envisage the range of environmental policy instruments as being on a regulatory continuum, with idealized forms of 'pure' self-regulation and 'strict' command and control regulation at opposing ends' (Sinclair, 1997: 532). In practice, most countries fall somewhere in the middle of these two extremes.

The use of organization

There are three areas where governments use their powers of organization in environmental policy. First, they can create agencies, at a national, regional or local level, designed to monitor, regulate or otherwise control environmental harms. Second, they can invoke the market mechanism to attempt to provide new sets of incentives to reduce environmentally harmful activities. Finally, they can conclude voluntary agreements to promote environmental goods.

First, governments can use their powers over organization to create, maintain and control organizations focused on environmental goals. Many nations have created an environmental protection agency (EPA) or similar, which sets environmental standards, enforces these (in combination with other actors), and carries out research and evaluation into relevant areas. The US EPA, created in 1970, is perhaps the best-known, but the Swedish EPA was created three years earlier. EPAs may also exist at a regional level, as with the Australian state of Queensland's EPA, or may exist for different national jurisdictions within the same country, as with the UK's (English and Welsh) Environment Agency and Scottish Environment Protection Agency. A European Environment Agency was introduced in 1989, but its role was initially restricted to information-gathering, rather than inspection and enforcement (Kelemen, 2000: 152).

In addition, governments may create organizations focused on a specific, environmentally sensitive geographical area. Again, some of those in the USA are the best-known, including the San Francisco Bay Conservation and Development Commission and the California Coastal Commissions (Schneider *et al.*, 2003: 154). These organizations may, in some cases, cross state boundaries. This is the case, for example, with the International Commission for the Protection of the River Rhine, covering nine European states, and the International Joint Commission which oversees the Great Lakes Water Quality Agreement between the USA and Canada.

It should be noted that, as with many of the other fields of policy examined in this book, in federal countries such as the USA, Germany and Australia, many environmental policies are delivered at state level, rather than by central government. This can pose challenges for business, which has to deal with different sets of regulations across different jurisdictions (Daneke, 1984: 142). As a result of desires for more coordination between states, in many federal systems including Australia, Canada and the USA, state governments have created intergovernmental bodies which go some way towards coordinating standards (Kelemen, 2000: 146–7).

The extent to which policies are implemented regionally or nationally may fluctuate over time; hence, in the 1980s and 1990s federal governments in Belgium and the USA decentralized responsibility for many environmental policies. This poses problems for attempts to assess the extent of policy adoption across different countries over time, if only the federal level is examined (as, for example, is the case with the ENVIPOLCON data set) (Liefferink *et al.*, 2009: 689–90).

One rather controversial organizational approach by numerous governments has been the development of harm-trading schemes, particularly emissions trading. For some, these systems imply a 'right to pollute' (Bomberg, 2007: 252). Nonetheless, they have become an increasingly popular form of NEPI. Essentially, harm-trading schemes rest on transferable permits. They require the existence of a quantitative environmental performance target which needs to be met by the scheme, generally focused on reduced harm year on year; flexibility for producers in where, and when, to locate polluting or resource extracting activities; enforcement capacity to ensure permits are not being exceeded; and a distinction between responsibility for environmental performance, and the initial allocation of permits (see Godard, 2002: 12).

Trading schemes have existed for some time – from 1980 (the Wisconsin Lower Rox River Trading Scheme) and 1984 (Colorado's tradable phosophorous discharge rights scheme for the Dillion Reservoir) (OECD/EEA 2011). Nonetheless, until the 2000s the most developed, and one of the most contentious, trading schemes was the Southern Californian 'RECLAIM' programme covering Los Angeles – the 'Regional Clean Air Incentives Market', in place since 1993. The first international scheme for emissions trading is the EU-wide Greenhouse Gas Emission Trading Scheme, introduced in 2005. In both cases, over-allocation of emissions permits have led to criticism that the schemes have failed in actively driving down emissions – although proponents have argued that targets are becoming progressively stricter, which will prevent this in the future.

Finally, governments may use their organizational resources to bring different actors together to conclude voluntary environmental agreements.

Agreements can be concluded at regional level, as with the Australian state of Victoria's Sustainability Covenants. Alternatively, they may be concluded at a national level, as with the Italian government's numerous Memorandums of Understanding on environmental issues with actors such as the Italian Mines Association, Pirelli and Fiat (*ibid.*). Such agreements may be focused on meeting specific targets or, alternatively, may have broader and less clear goals which relate more to the method of management of specific resources. For example, US estuaries which have obtained National Estuary Programme status, nominated by their state, are required to put together a Comprehensive Conservation Management Plan, which requires the engagement of governmental, non-governmental and private sector actors, but does not prescribe the exact nature of the plan (Schneider *et al.*, 2003: 145). In this way, different elements of the US government effectively set the parameters for membership in the policy community around such estuaries (*ibid.*: 155).

Voluntary agreements can also be concluded by multinational organizations. One example of this is provided by activities stemming from the EU's Water Framework Directive (2000). This Directive is targeted at 'structuring a collaborative process in which an open-ended notion of good water status is jointly defined and promoted by policy networks' (Lavenex *et al.*, 2009: 826). Crucially, many of these networks cross-national boundaries, being focused around specific rivers, for example. In the EU's case, this has resulted in a number of third countries effectively coming 'under the ambit of the EU's water protection policy, even if such an obligation lacks formal association agreements' (*ibid.*).

Another voluntary approach includes self-certification regimes, such as the EU's Environmental Management and Audit Scheme (Taschner, 1998). This requires companies to report on their environmental performance, and is more rigorous than its non-governmental equivalent, ISO 14001 (see pp. 185–6). Nonetheless, some environmentalists have been critical of management systems, since heavily polluting firms can still comply without reducing their level of emissions. In addition, the data used for audit and reporting are infrequently publicly available, unlike compliance reports for environmental regulators, for example.

The provision of information

Governments can use their control over information both to provide information and advice to the public in order to promote environmentally-friendly behaviour, and to inform environmental policy-making.

One increasingly popular use of information by governments to promote the environment is the mandating of 'eco-labels' on products. Eco-labels 'are logos showing all the effects of the product on the environment, together with its composition'. Eco-labels have been introduced by non-governmental bodies such as the Marine Conservation Council (awarded to sustainable fish products) for some time, as well as being operated by governments in different countries. From 2000, an EU-level eco-label system was introduced, the 'European Flower' label, which in many countries 'exist[s] side by side' with domestic eco-labels (Knill and Tosun, 2009: 879). In theory, eco-labels not only inform consumers' behaviour, but also indirectly impact on producers' behaviour by encouraging them to improve their environmental performance.

As another example of the provision of information influencing behaviour, Hutter (1997) suggests that inspectors may use 'shaming techniques' to enforce compliance with regulation – relying on the reputational effects of poor performance. This involves the provision of information about poor rather than good environmental performance. Badrinath and Bolster (1996) suggest that the bulk of the penalty for firms when prosecuted over environmental misdemeanours comes not from the sanction imposed, but from the damage to a firm's reputation in the marketplace and amongst its employees.

Governments may also attempt the direct education or advising of their populations about environmental issues. One example of this comes from the UK Government's 'Going for Green' Initiative, which was part of a national campaign to promote awareness of sustainable development (Davies, 2002). Less directly, some governments and intergovernmental organizations have promoted freedom of information on environmental issues as part of attempts to increase pressure for environmentally-friendly policy change. This is based on the assumption that members of the public, armed with evidence of environmental harm, would be able to use this to challenge both government and private sector actors to introduce new policy measures.

For example, the Irish 1992 Environmental Protection Act publishes information about issues including pollution and waste management for different plants on its website (Bugdahn, 2005: 187). Similarly, the UK's Environment Agency's website contains extensive information on the environmental performance of different plants, which is provided to it through reporting by the plants concerned, and Environment Agency inspections. The Environment Agency's approach was modelled on that introduced by the English and Welsh Friends of the Earth group, which in the mid-1990s created a searchable website including data on local environmental issues (*ibid.*: 189).

In some cases, this process has been led by subnational-level governments. Hence, in Germany, the *Land* of Lower Saxony took the lead in establishing an 'Environmental Data Catalogue' that was quickly adopted by most other *Länder*. This catalogue enabled interested parties to find where data was available within government on different environmental issues (*ibid.*: 191–2).

An intergovernmental example of this approach comes from the EU's 1990 Access to Information on the Environment (AIE) Directive, which 'forced member states to establish a right to access [environmental] information held by public authorities' concerned with environmental issues; and provided citizens with the right, administratively or legally, to challenge any refusal to provide such information (*ibid.*: 184–5). At the same time, the EU created the European Information and Observation Network, coordinated by the European Environment Agency. The EU's activities in this area have been strengthened by the 'Aarhus Convention' adopted by the United Nations Economic Commission for Europe, which has a wider scope than the AIE Directive (*ibid.*).

Approaches requiring the publication of environmentally-relevant information have been praised as non-interventionist NEPIs although, in practice, information-based tools such as eco-labels are 'relatively soft tools' (Jordan *et al.*, 2003; Bomberg, 2007: 252). They are less successful in contexts where the information involved is detailed or complex, and where it relates to low-probability, high-impact events (which can be overestimated) or to high-probability, low-impact events (which readers are likely to underestimate) (Ogus, 1994: 152).

Governments have used their control over information to aid them in environmental policy-making through the commissioning of research into the state of the environment and policy options which might affect this, and, more systematically, the use of environmental impact assessments (EIAs).

First, governments have attempted to develop a better knowledge of the health of the environment through convening expert panels and commissioning research. The German government, for example, established an Advisory Council on Global Change which, in 2008, reported on Climate Change as a Security Risk (Dalby, 2009: 100). Similarly, the UK government commissioned a review by the economist Sir Nicholas Stern to investigate the financial impact of global warming. The report of the Stern Review of the Economics of Climate Change, released in 2006, emphasized that failing to tackle climate change would ultimately undermine economic growth. Amongst many other claims, it argued that emissions needed to stabilize over the next two decades and then reduce by between 1 per cent and 3 per cent thereafter, which could be achieved by devoting 1 per cent of GDP to reducing carbon emissions. A lack of action on climate change could, under current estimates, cost the world 5 per cent of GDP per year (Stern, 2007). By framing climate change as an economic as well as environmental problem, the Stern Review was highly innovative and influential.

Another influential international example of the provision of information to aid policy-making comes from the UN World Commission on Environment and Development's 1987 report on 'Our Common Future', commonly known as the 'Brundtland report' after the Commission's chair (Dalby, 2009: 21). This report cemented the importance of the then relatively new concept of 'sustainable development' in international – and, indeed, national – environmental policy-making. A more recent example comes from the Intergovernmental Panel on Climate Change (IPCC), which first reported in 1990 (Dalby, 2009: 23–4). The IPCC brings together scientific experts to examine and model the impact of rising carbon emissions and other man-made processes on global warming.

Governments can also encourage the production of information concerning the environmental impact of different policy options. Perhaps the first attempt to systematize this came from the US National Environmental Policy Act (1970), which required that EIAs be conducted of major legislation (Hoberg, 1991: 124). EIAs are now required by both the EU itself (Knill and Tosun, 2009: 879), and, in parallel, by many of its member states.

The voluntary and private sectors and environmental policy

Governments increasingly cooperate with a variety of voluntary and private sector actors in the field of environmental policy. First, governments in many countries effectively 'tolerate' private-sector self-regulation on environmental matters – what has been described as 'regulated self-regulation' (Sinclair, 1997: 535). This covers cases where regulators employ 'the threat of direct regulation explicitly to prod trade and professional associations to prepare self-regulatory standards and procedures as an alternative to government prescription' (Bardach and Kagan, 1982: 220). An example of 'regulated self-regulation' comes from New Zealand, where firms were warned that, if net emissions did not meet a 3 per cent to 4 per cent reduction target by 1997, a carbon tax would be introduced (Gunningham and Rees, 1997: 401).

Such self-regulation covers a bewildering variety of environmental measures – including, for example, voluntary and cooperative agreements, environmental covenants, codes of practice, environmental partnerships, corporate environmental reporting, environmental accounting, environmental self-auditing, and environmental management systems (Sinclair, 1997: 532). In some cases, a variety of self-regulatory measures are combined to form a programme. This is the case with the US chemical industry's Responsible Care programme (*ibid.*: 396). Members of Responsible Care benefit from information shared with other companies about safety and environmental issues in exchange for their compliance.

Environmental management systems constitute a particularly popular type of voluntary scheme. These allow firms to 'self-certify' their environmental performance. The most successful of these is the International Organization for Standardization's ISO 14001 standard, introduced in 1996. This builds on the ISO's original voluntary code for quality management, ISO 9000. The generic environmental standard ISO 14001 can be complemented by a range of additional environmental standards provided by ISO covering issues such as labelling, performance evaluations and lifecycle assessment. In practice, the ISO recommends that firms seek third-party approval of their self-certification (Potoski and Prakash, 2005: 237). Potoski and Prakash have argued that members of ISO 14001 appear to have improved environmental performance beyond that which they would otherwise have achieved had they not been part of the scheme (*ibid.*). They also suggest that environmental management approaches such as ISO 14001 can buttress pressures for 'California effects' (see p. 275) arising from international trade. This is because 'trade can be a vehicle to disseminate ISO 14001 if the key export markets have widely adopted this nongovernmental regulation' (Prakash and Potoski, 2006: 359).

The scope of environmental policy

Authors such as Ulrich Beck (1992) have argued that the macrolevel processes related to current environmental change and crisis can affect all classes of people, unlike the unpleasant side effects of 'traditional' types of industrial activity such as smog, which was generally concentrated in poorer, industrialized areas.

Nonetheless, it appears that certain groups are particularly susceptible to harm caused by environmental change and crisis, in the absence of public policy interventions. As Dalby (2009: 2) suggests, in many cases those who will suffer from macrolevel processes such as climate change are not responsible for them; if 'the poor subsistence farmers of Africa die from drought or flood, or the dwellers on atolls in the Pacific are overwhelmed by rising oceans, clearly they are not responsible for the disruptions and hence their fate'.

Even focusing only on the global North, 'studies have suggested that certain segments of the population face disproportionate exposure to environmental risk' (Ervin *et al.*, 2003: 9). The type of hazards affecting different groups is particularly contingent on their geographical location; those living in rural areas who are unable to protect themselves sufficiently may be over-exposed to chemicals used in agriculture, whilst those living in inner cities face the perils of air pollution and lead paint residues (*ibid.*: 9). The very young and the very old are particularly susceptible to respiratory problems caused by pollution, and the very old were also substantially more at risk during the 2003 French heatwave (Dalby, 2009: 116). The victims of Hurricane Katrina which struck the US city of New Orleans in 2005 were overwhelmingly black, low-income people. As such, 'there is both a geography and a social character to vulnerability' (*ibid.*: 115).

Conclusion

The chapter has examined how environmental policy has developed over time, with moves away from a 'frontier ethos' towards attempts towards reduce environmental impacts, and continuing debate and controversy over the extent to which human-made solutions can hold back permanent environmental degradation. It has indicated the growing importance of international and multinational-level policy-making on the environment. Out of all of the areas of policy examined in this book, environmental policy is undoubtedly transnational in nature.

Indeed, the increasing pace of globalization has caused some to suggest that nation states are becoming increasingly irrelevant as policy actors (Young, 1994) – that the state, just like society, is a 'zombie concept' (Urry, 2003). For others, states are still relevant, albeit in combination with policy networks combining market and civil society actors (Spaargaren *et al.*, 2006: 7), and/or as regulators of mobility and enablers of 'favourable interaction processes and flows', rather than as producers of those flows – as 'gamekeepers' not 'gardeners' (Mol and Spaargaren, 2006: 51).

Normatively, some have argued that state-centric approaches, particularly those that are national-state-centric, may exacerbate environmental problems by assuming that the goals of policy should be national security, rather than accommodation to inevitable ecological change (Dalby, 2009: 4). In this vein, it has been argued that 'conventional', state-based approaches to politics are redundant in the face of policy 'targets' such as the Gulf Stream (*ibid.*: 158; see Latour, 2007).

Despite this, this chapter has indicated continuing differences in approach amongst countries when it comes to the actual delivery of environmental policy, both in terms of participation in international treaties and domestic policy-making. The chapter examined how governments can use their powers over financial resources (to impose financial penalties for environmental harm, rewards for environmentally-friendly behaviour, and for the direct provision of environmental services); their authority (to impose input and process standards, and control consumption and liability); their powers of organization (to create, and operate, environmentally-focused organizations; to centralize or decentralize environmental policy delivery; and to create and run harm-trading arrangements and voluntary agreements); and their informational capacities (to provide information and advice to the public and produce and disseminate information for policy-making purposes). All these activities are delivered in a context where, in many nations, self-regulatory systems focused on environmental issues abound.

Summary

❏ The 'Environmental Kuznets Curve' suggests that environmental performance will improve as nations progressively industrialize, and there is some
evidence of a positive correlation between nations' income levels and higher
levels of economic policy adoption. Evidence is more mixed when it comes
to the existence or otherwise of a 'race-to-the-bottom' in environmental policies as a result of regulatory competition.

❏ Some influential comparative analyses have contrasted 'legalistic' and 'consensual' approaches to environmental policy-making, although which countries fall into which category has arguably differed over time.

❏ Of the policy areas examined in this book, environmental policy is perhaps
the most strongly affected by international pressures, not least due to the
cross-border nature of environmental flows.

❏ The policy instruments used in environmental policy:
  – Governments use the *financial resources* available to impose penalties on
    environmentally harmful activity, and to reward environmentally friendly
    activity; and for the direct provision of environmental services.
  – Governments use their *authority* to impose input and process standards, as
    well as restrictions on consumption of environmentally harmful products
    and on liability for environmental harm. Environmental regulation can be
    imposed with lesser or greater stringency and invoked more or less fre-
    quently.
  – Governments use their powers of *organization* to create and operate envi-
    ronmental organizations, and convene and coordinate voluntary agree-
    ments. Environmental policy-making and delivery can be organized on a
    national, regional or local basis.
  – Governments use their control over *information* in relation to the public to
    promote environmentally-friendly behaviour, and also to inform environ-
    mental policy-making.

❏ Governments increasingly cooperate with a variety of voluntary and private
sector actors in the field of environmental policy.

❏ Whilst some analysts argue the impact of environmental harms, such as pollution, is 'democratic' and can affect everyone, in practice those on lower
incomes in both the global South and in developed nations have borne the
brunt of environmental disasters and policy failures.

Chapter 8

Interests and Public Policy

Ambrose Bierce (1911) famously suggested that 'politics' referred to the 'strife of interests masquerading as a contest of principles'. As this chapter indicates, many authors agree with him, arguing that both politics and policy-making can be assimilated with the pursuit of interest. This is particularly the case for rational choice theorists, Marxists and Elitists, radical feminists, cleavage theorists, theorists of interest groups and of corporatism, and power resource theorists. However, these approaches differ substantially over how interests can be defined, and which group and/or individual interests are perceived as being likely to shape policy. In addition to these approaches, other perspectives on policy-making stress the fact that policies themselves can shape interests, and also that the pursuit of interests can be affected by the institutional and ideational context. A common problem for all of these approaches is the vagueness of the concept of interest itself, considered in detail in the next section.

What are interests?

There is no universally-accepted definition of interests, and interests 'are far from the unproblematic and ever-ready explanatory instruments we assume them to be' (Blyth, 2003: 695). The very concept of interest itself is highly ambiguous. In common parlance, 'interests' are routinely separated from wants, needs, desires and beliefs. However, it is effectively impossible to separate interests from these other concepts when it comes to analysing their role in motivating behaviour (Davidson, 1980; Mercer, 2010). As a result, the distinction between interests and ideational factors (including beliefs) can be difficult to establish in practice, a problem considered in greater detail in Chapter 9.

In addition, approaches to comparative public policy analysis that focus on interests all presume subtly different notions of what interests actually are. For rational choice theorists, interests simply are the preferences which rational actors seek to maximize or, depending on the exact theoretical position taken, optimize. For a rational choice theorist, it makes no sense to separate preferences from action, since individuals (and, for public choice theorists, groups) will always act on the basis of their preferences. Actions are therefore simply 'revealed preferences'.

In contrast, for Marxists, interests are always class-based, and cannot be separated from individuals' class positions. As with rational choice theorists (in this regard, if in few others), Marxists also suggest that individuals will act in accordance with their (class) interests – unless, that is, they are subject to 'false consciousness' which obscures their assessment of where their interests lie. Similarly, for radical feminists, interests are predominantly contingent on gender rather than other factors, with patriarchal – that is, male – interests generally dominating political and social developments. (For socialist feminists, gender-based interests are still, ultimately, contingent on class interests.)

Both cleavage and interest group theorists are agnostic about the ultimate source of interests, with their focus lying instead on how such interests are revealed and put into practice at the political level. For cleavage theorists, differences in interests are revealed through patterns of political behaviour. Interests themselves may, however, stem from a variety of demographic and socioeconomic characteristics, ranging from class to profession, ethnicity, religion and region. For theorists of interest groups, both pluralist and non-pluralist, at least some interests are represented through campaigning groups, charities, business associations and non-governmental organizations which lobby government to adopt policies advocated by their members.

Except for rational choice approaches, all the other approaches to interests to be examined here suffer from the common problem that they posit an actual or potential separation between interests and how interests are revealed during policy-making and policy-implementation. This is problematic since, as will be discussed, it can be very difficult to isolate individuals' or groups' 'real interests' from their presentation of them.

Different interest-based approaches

Rational choice

Essentially, rational choice theory suggests that individual actors will be entirely self-motivated (what is described as 'methodological individualism'), and that they will act to achieve their interests or 'preferences'. Generally, rational choice theorists tend to carry out comparisons across institutions (such as Buchanan's (1954) classic comparison of democratic political systems with markets), rather than across place or time. Two exceptions to this approach come from the Nobel Prize winner Elinor Ostrom's (1990) work on resolving the 'tragedy of the commons', and Mancur Olson's (1982) work on the 'rise and decline of nations'.

Ostrom (1990) compared how 'common pool resources' such as grazing areas, forests, fisheries and water are treated in a number of different national and regional contexts. She was particularly interested in how those who wished to use the resources, 'appropriators', interacted with each other and with the resources themselves, and the extent to which this was governed by collective institutions. Ostrom indicated how it had been possible, in some cases, for appropriators to create institutions which managed access to common pool resources. This was despite the fact that individual appropriators had a short-term interest in over-using the resources concerned (for example, in using more water for irrigation for their individual plot of land than could be sustained over the long-term if all the other appropriators behaved in the same way). Ostrom identified eight 'design principles' which appeared to characterize stable and effective approaches to common pool resource management. Broadly, she argued that localized approaches which balanced the power of different individuals against each other would be more effective than top-down approaches to intervention to protect common pool resources.

More recently, Ostrom (2009: 5) has examined measures to avert the global 'public bad' of looming catastrophic climate change, which is often viewed as a classic collective action dilemma. Ostrom has argued that a 'polycentric' approach is required, with action at small- and medium-sized levels being encouraged, as well as national and international interventions. This is because the 'trust' required to 'overcome social dilemmas' is more likely to inhere in smaller organizations, whereas large organizations may lack the mechanisms, knowledge and legitimacy to enforce change (*ibid.*: 11).

Olson's (1982) work on the rise and decline of nations (nicknamed 'RADON' by the author) has been detailed in Chapter 3 on economic policy. As described in that chapter, Olson pointed out that, despite the existence of many policy areas where individuals had a common interest in policy change, this only occasionally resulted in the creation of an interest group able to lobby on their behalf. As a result, there was a 'collective action problem'. According to Olson's theory, the 'incentive for group action diminishes as group size increases'. This is because not only is it easier to monitor compliance (and thus prevent free riding) within smaller groups, but also larger groups' interests are more likely to be aligned with the interests of society as a whole, rather than being 'sectional' or restricted just to group members (Olson, 1982: 31). The costs of agreeing on actions to be taken also increase as groups become larger and more unwieldy (*ibid.*: 32).

As detailed in Chapter 3, Olson argued that small interest groups were more likely to become embedded in nations which had enjoyed relative stability. Nations which have experienced great disruption – such as revolution or defeat in war – were less likely to be the home of such groups. As a result, Olson claims they will be more efficient. Olson's only caveat is that, in some nations, some organizations are sufficiently encompassing that their members' interests coincide with those of society as a whole. Very large federations of trade unions or of businesses might fall within this category.

Olson used this approach to explain why, at the time of writing, apparently stable countries such as Britain, India, South Africa under apartheid, Australia and New Zealand were growing slowly, whilst postwar Japan and Germany, as well as the 'Asian tigers', were growing rapidly. In stable countries, 'distributional coalitions' – the smaller groups mentioned by Olson – tended to proliferate and achieve privileged positions in policy-making, whilst in unstable countries, the entrenched positions of these groups had been removed during conflict. Although Olson did not apply his approach to issues beyond economic policy, it is also arguably relevant to the development of modern welfare states, with high levels of social dislocation (such as that caused by World War II in the UK, and the Depression in the USA) arguably leading many to argue for substantive policy change (see Barnett, 1986; Piven and Cloward, 1993; Mitchell, 1995).

Olson's theory has, however, come under sustained attack from a variety of quarters. First, Olson suggested that war or revolution was necessary in order to 'sweep away' distributional coalitions, yet the Thatcher government in the UK was highly effective at the democratic removal of the influence of organized interests within decision-making. Second, there are cases where defeated nations failed to prosper economically, such as the American South following the Civil War. Finally, more recent developments have arguably gone against Olson's predictions, a subject returned to in the section on problems with interest-based accounts (p. 210).

Public choice

Another use of rational choice theory comes from its application to bureaucracies and public administration. William Niskanen's (1971) work was particularly influential as a critique of traditional Weberian approaches to bureaucracy. Weber (1947) had suggested that bureaucracy as an organizational form promoted neutrality amongst civil servants and a commitment to the public good. On the contrary, Niskanen argued that civil servants would be more likely to pursue their own sectional interests than the public interest. For Niskanen, rational bureaucrats seek to maximize their budget and the size of their department or bureau, rather than to promote the overall efficiency and effectiveness of the bureaucracy as a whole. Whilst the growth of individual bureaux might be rational for individual civil servants, as a whole it might not reflect the most efficient use of public funds.

Following the publication of Niskanen's work, however, numerous governments across OECD countries began to shift parts of their bureaucracies into new, semi-independent executive agencies, with this process starting in the UK (Pollitt *et al.*, 2001). This appeared to invalidate Niskanen's theory, since civil servants appeared to accept this reduction in the size of their bureaux. Patrick Dunleavy (1991) amended Niskanen's theory to take account of these new developments. He suggested that senior civil servants, at least, were more interested in their overall levels of control over public policy, rather than 'just' the size of their staff and/or budget. For Dunleavy, self-interested civil servants were rational in supporting the creation of executive agencies since this relieved them of the uninteresting minutiae of policy implementation, leaving them more free to concentrate on more satisfying and strategic policy-development work.

Marxist accounts

Whilst rational choice theorists focus on individuals' interest, Marxists focus on collective, class-based interests. For Marxists, governments in capitalist societies will further the class interests of the bourgeoisie, those people who buy labour from the proletariat (the working class), and own physical capital such as machinery. Substantial policy change will then only occur if the relative power resources of different classes change; in particular, if the power of the proletariat is increased through revolution (for Marxist-Leninists, spearheaded by a 'vanguard' party organization). Modern Marxists have argued, therefore, that the 'intervention of the state is always and necessarily partisan' (Miliband, 1977: 91). They argue that, in its current incarnation in democratic nations, the state will focus on securing 'the long-term reproduction of capitalist social relations' (Gough, 1979: 64), particularly the supremacy of the bourgeoisie.

Marxist analyses have been particularly influential in the study of the welfare state. The growth of welfare states might be seen as a counter-example to Marxist analyses, since the provision of (for example) income protection appears to aid working class people, rather than contributing to the power of the bourgeoisie. However, analysts such as Ginsburg (1979) have argued that the ostensible goals of welfare systems, such as income maintenance, are secondary. Instead, social security is focused on maintaining capitalist social relations, including a flexible and disciplined workforce and the patriarchal family unit, and on dampening down dissent. Certainly, particular features of welfare systems actively promote commodification (see Chapter 4) by, for example, maintaining work incentives with low levels of benefits compared to wages. Where welfare systems (such as pensions) are based on a contributory principle, this also acts to maintain women's dependence on men (again, see Chapter 4) (*ibid.*: 80). More recent Marxist analyses (inspired by, but departing from, strict Marxism) have considered the role of welfare systems in maintaining racial as well as class disparities (Ginsburg, 1992).

Elitist theories

An allied approach, which in some cases draws directly on Marxist theory, comes from what has loosely been described as 'elite theory'. This approach suggests that elites will manipulate politics for their own ends, by controlling actors who propagate societal values (such as the media) (Gaventa, 1980), and keeping particular issues off the political agenda (Lukes, 1974). Schneider and Ingram's analysis of policy tools, already considered in Chapter 2, suggests that policy-making elites may buttress the power of the best-off in society through their use of certain instruments. For example, more coercive sanctions, making less use of the provision of information and greater use of emotion and force, appear to be used in relation to certain powerless groups (Schneider and Ingram, 1991: 523).

Feminist theories

A variety of different branches of feminism exist, and controversy rages over their appropriate classification. What is described here as 'feminist theories' refers to frameworks which suggest that the most significant cleavage in modern societies is that between men and women, and that this cleavage at least partly determines policy development. This approach assumes that women can be viewed as having particular interests, even if these might differ between contexts and sometimes be shared with particular groups of men (see Jónasdóttir, 1988, for a discussion).

Analyses which highlight differences in interests between genders have again been particularly influential within studies of the welfare state. Chapter 4 considers various studies which suggest that different countries' welfare states vary enormously in their treatment of women – a factor which was traditionally ignored in studies of welfare regimes. These differences have been tied to varying cultural attitudes towards the family and economy, and women's role within both systems, as well as to the size and strength of feminist movements (see Lewis, 1992).

There are persistent differences in opinion between men and women, many of which apply across countries. Some of these differences have eroded over time. Hence, traditionally, women were more supportive of conservative parties, a trend which has sometimes been linked to women's generally greater levels of religiosity. This has, however, declined over recent decades, with women in many countries becoming more left-wing than men in their voting preferences (Inglehart and Norris, 2000). Women, however, have consistently been less likely to support extreme authoritarianism, and are generally less militaristic (Jelen *et al.*, 1994).

The differences between the genders on these topics can be very significant. A striking example comes from Switzerland, where a referendum in 2011 to restrict civilians' access to arms was defeated, largely on the strength of men's votes. The number of arms circulating within Switzerland has been estimated at two million, one for every four people, lagging only behind the USA and Yemen compared with its population. Whilst a majority of women supported a ban on weapons being kept in the home, most men rejected it, with the difference in opinion between the genders standing at nearly 24 per cent, according to opinion polls (Sage, 2011).

Unfortunately however, few analyses have been carried out into the precise manner in which gender interests feed into policy, aside from those which stress the role of feminist movements in promoting policy change and those which focus on the representational role of women as political leaders (Lovenduski, 2005; see also Box 8.1). Recently, institutionalist analyses have been applied to develop a more sophisticated approach to 'substantive representation' theories, which have long suggested that feminist policies are more likely to be introduced where women are able to capture positions in parliaments and within gender-related units within government. Annesley (2010) notes that 'substantive representation' may fail to result in pro-equality policies if it is not linked to feminists gaining powerful positions in the policy-making system. She explains, through a detailed, process-tracing analysis, how feminists were able to become 'strategic actors' and 'gate openers' during welfare reform in the UK under the New Labour governments. These key actors were not necessarily drawn only from parliament, but also included civil servants and political advisers.

Cleavage theories

Rather than focusing on either class or gender interests as policy determinants, cleavage theories take a broader view of possible divergences in interest (Lipset and Rokkan, 1967; Lijphart, 1984). For these theorists, cleavages can occur along class lines, but can equally be due to differences between regions, religions, professions or ethnicities. For Lipset and Rokkan (1967), a social group can result in a social cleavage if it reflects societal division in some way, is recognized by its members as significant and as worth promoting, and is subject to organized institutional support, such as via a political party. Women, at least when these authors were writing, generally participated as members of these groups,

BOX 8.1   Htun and Weldon's framework for the comparative analysis of gender equality policy

In some states, measures which benefit women as a group (e.g. against violence against women) may be in place in the absence of measures which target gender-based class inequalities (e.g. maternity pay), and vice versa. Furthermore, while some issues are viewed as 'religious' in some countries (e.g. abortion), in others they are not viewed as such.

Htun and Weldon (2010) argue that these differences reflect the extent of control of powerful groups. For example, powerful groups – such as the church or clan elders – can ensure that a certain issue (e.g. female work) is defined as doctrinal (a matter for religious decision) or as non-doctrinal.

Whether or not the advocates of change are able to overcome opposition from powerful groups depends, Htun and Weldon suggest, on four axes of state–society relations: state capacity, policy legacies, international vulnerability, and the degree of democracy.

Their 'framework for the comparative analysis of gender policy' explains how these various features – different issues, actors and the sociopolitical context – combine to explain particular outcomes to struggles around gender equality.

rather than standing apart from them (aside from those within the feminist movement).

Such social cleavages were arguably important in the creation of numerous party systems that still exist at the time of writing. Hence, in the USA, the Democrats and Republicans represented Federalists and Anti-Federalists; in Britain, the Whigs (predecessors of the Liberals) and Tories (predecessors of the Conservatives) represented different attitudes towards religion and monarchy; and in Sweden, the Centre Party focused on rural areas whilst the Social Democrats concentrated on the working class population. More recently, it has been argued that social divisions within the workforce (particularly, between those employed by the private and public sectors) are reflected in differing levels of support for centre-right and left parties, respectively (Dunleavy, 1980; but see Devine, 1996). An increasingly popular position, albeit still highly controversial, views age differences within the population (and particularly older peoples' greater propensity to vote and to organize themselves politically) as explaining why policies favouring pensioners have sometimes been maintained whilst those for younger groups have been reduced (Willetts, 2011; for a counter-argument, see West, 2011b; and for a comparative perspective, see Box 8.2).

When it comes to policy-making, social cleavages have been linked to different policy approaches within a number of fields – with welfare

BOX 8.2 Julia Lynch on age in the welfare state

Using data on social expenditure from a range of nations, Lynch (2006) considers the extent to which different welfare systems favour different age groups, by developing a ratio which measures spending on older people in relation to non-older people. This indicates that the relative amount of spending on older people differs markedly across countries. She then uses a series of detailed case studies to consider why these differences came about.

Lynch argues that universalist (Beveridgean) welfare systems were generally less strongly supportive of older people than occupationally based (Bismarckian) systems (see Chapter 4, for an explanation of these terms). She suggests that governments experienced two 'critical junctures' when they decided whether or not to develop universalist or occupationally-based systems. These occurred at the start of the twentieth century (when welfare states were being created in many nations for the first time), and following World War II (when governments in many nations had the opportunity to undertake radical political change).

Lynch suggests that whether opportunities to shift from occupationally based systems to universalist systems were exploited was dependent on the constellation of political interests at the time. Where politics operated along largely 'clientelistic' lines, with politicians rewarding particular groups of supporters, universalist systems were unlikely to be developed, since they removed some of the levers that politicians could use to create support. Universalist systems were, then, more likely to be developed in political systems which were more reliant on ideology, on 'programmatic appeals', and less on competition between different interest groups. This then locked-in welfare state systems which systematically privileged, or otherwise, the interests of older people in comparison with younger people.

policy, again, providing the clearest examples. Where nations were subject to extensive cleavages (particularly religious ones), as in Germany and the Netherlands, a more differentiated approach to welfare provision generally developed, with non-state actors – particularly churches, but also trade unions – becoming core actors in welfare policy delivery. In more homogeneous nations, such as the UK, universal approaches which treated all groups identically were easier to implement (Bonoli, 1997). At the same time, the legacy of racial oppression in the USA, in particular, arguably supported more residual approaches to welfare (Omi and Winant, 1994; Quadagno, 1994).

Nonetheless, some have argued that political cleavages based on distinctive social groups have become less important over time. Theorists such as Inglehart (1984) and Kitschelt (1994) have argued for a new distinction between postmaterialists (interested in concerns such as freedom of speech and the environment) and materialists (interested in traditional class-based concerns). These distinctions are not easily accommodated within the traditional model of social divisions being based on identifiable social groups.

Interest groups

Another type of analysis focuses specifically on how groups possessing a certain interest influence the policy process. Olson's theory of collective action has already been explained (pp. 51–2). Another approach comes from the theory of 'pluralism'. Whilst for some this theory was normative, arguing that states should be more open to interest group pressure, for authors such as Dahl (1961) and Polsby (1960), pluralism both described policy-making systems and helped explain why they operated in particular ways. For pluralists, as with cleavage theorists, interest groups express societal or ideological divisions. However, for pluralists, no one particular cleavage dominates politics and policy-making. Instead, different interest groups move in and out of the policy process, with their power shifting over time. The state acts as an arbiter between different interest groups, rather than being captured by any one interest. A development of this theory, neo-pluralism, maintained pluralism's emphasis on the state as the arena for competition between interest groups, but suggested that some groups were more powerful than others. For Charles Lindblom (1977), for example, organized business was comparatively more influential than groups representing labour or consumers.

Other approaches at a lower level of abstraction have analysed interest groups with reference to the nature of the interest they promote, and the extent to which they are integrated within governing processes. One form of interest group theory considers the activities and role of interest groups when they are formally institutionalized within policy-making systems. This approach, 'corporatism', is considered in greater detail in the next section. Here, we consider the operation of interest groups which are not formally incorporated within state structures, but which attempt nonetheless to influence public policy-making.

As mentioned, many analyses of interest groups attempt to categorize them according to their function. Hence, Finer (1958) distinguished groups representing the 'narrow' or material interests of their members, from those which were more focused on particular ideas or ideologies (see also Truman, 1951). Hassenteufel sets up a threefold distinction, between 'categorical' groups, which represent the narrow material interests of the group; 'groups of conviction', which represent 'inclusive interests' – that is, interests which other non-group members may share; and 'territorial' groups, which represent regional or otherwise local interests (Hassenteufel, 2008: 174).

Other commonly-used distinctions between different types of interest groups include whether they represent 'single' or multiple interests, whether they represent capital (business associations), labour (trade unions) or specific occupations (professional associations); and the manner in which they represent their members, whether directly (through individualized membership) or indirectly (through other associations, as with peak associations).

A final distinction that is frequently raised is that between so-called 'insider' and 'outsider' groups. The category of 'insider' interest groups includes all those who are involved in consultation/negotiation with government, often before the government's own view has crystallized. In contrast, 'outsider' interest groups are generally excluded from consultation, or involved only in a relatively cosmetic way (Grant, 1989). Maloney *et al.* (1994) argue that 'insider' and 'outsider' status can be ascribed relative to four criteria: access, influence, strategy and the status they are ascribed by politicians and the bureaucracy.

The distinction between these different categories is clear if we consider the example of one interest group whose position has arguably become institutionalized, that of the French campaigning group *Chasse, pêche, nature et traditions* (hunting, fishing, nature and tradition). This group formed its own political party, and has managed to obtain local and European representation (Hassenteufel, 2008: 176). However, despite this institutionalized position, it has largely failed to enjoy independent influence, with many of its more prominent members publicly coming to support the UMP political party.

Which groups enjoy 'insider' as against 'outsider' status differs from country to country. David Vogel's (1986) analysis of environmental policy-making (see Chapter 7 for an extended discussion) suggested that, during the 1970s and 1980s, business groups enjoyed 'insider' status in environmental policy-making in the UK, but not in the USA. In the UK, businesses were actively consulted by government for their input into regulations, unlike environmental activist groups which were not included in the process. Again, as noted in Chapter 7, Vogel (2003b, 2004) has since argued that the role of interest groups has changed with the increasing competence of the EU in the area of environmental policy-making, with environmental campaigning groups becoming far more significant as a policy actor in the European context.

In addition to including specific interest groups within consultation processes, governments may also attempt to boost the role of particular interest groups. A clear example of this, albeit at a multinational level, comes from the European Commission's provision of resources and legitimacy to European-level interest groups ('eurogroups') within the decision-making process (Hassenteufel, 2008: 191).

Yet another approach specifically examines how 'insider' groups relate to each other – the 'policy networks' approach. These analyses stress the interconnections between different interest groups, experts and other actors seeking to influence policy-making. Where policy networks are particularly strongly integrated, they have been described as a 'policy community'. The relationships between members of policy networks are looser and more *ad hoc* than within policy communities (Jordan, 1990).

An application of this approach comes from Daugbjerg and Peterson's analysis of policy-making on green taxation in Sweden, Norway and Denmark. They argue that in Denmark, actors such as agricultural associations and the Ministry of Food, Agriculture and Fisheries are closely integrated and operate effectively as a 'policy community' (Daugbjerg and Peterson, 2004: 233), with a similarly close-knit 'policy community' existing in Norway for 'mainland heavy industry' (*ibid.*: 237). In contrast, a looser 'policy network' exists in Sweden, with consumers' associations involved in the network, as well as traditional actors such as agricultural associations (*ibid.*: 234–5). Daugbjerg and Pedersen then argue that the degree of green taxes reflects the extent of integration of the policy networks in the environmental arena in each country. Hence, the strong policy community around mainland heavy industry (if not around offshore industry) in Norway has helped hold back encompassing and expensive green taxation regimes. The opposite has occurred in the high-taxing Swedish case, where no such policy community has developed. Denmark sits in the middle, with offshore oil being exempt from green taxes, and the revenue from taxes recycled back to industry, which generally does not occur in Sweden (*ibid.*: 231). The authors indicate how well-organized policy communities (such as that in Norway) were able to block policies that went against their interests, even when the government was in favour (*ibid.*: 241).

Corporatism

Theories of corporatism, also detailed in Chapter 3, examine situations where interest groups are not only closely consulted by governments (as policy communities might be), but also have a privileged and *institutionalized* role within decision-making. Corporatism has been advocated by 'an extraordinary variety of theorists, ideologues and activists ... for widely divergent motives, interests and reasons' (Schmitter, 1979: 9). As in Chapter 3, the following text considers corporatism as a means of describing and analysing developments, rather than as a normative model for organizing decision-making.

Early corporatist theories were shaped by knowledge of the mediaeval guilds system, and popular within some religious circles, with their focus on developing societal 'harmony' through each worker and organization having a specific, defined 'place' within the social and political order. As a result, corporatism became popular in a number of Christian Democratic parties, as well as within Fascist and developmentalist movements. Corporatism was a particular characteristic of Italy under Mussolini (Grant, 1985: 5), and Portugal, Spain, Brazil, Peru, Mexico and Greece when under dictatorial rule (Schmitter, 1974: 85). Groups in these 'top-down' corporatist regimes were often almost entirely cosmetic, with the organizations involved only having a 'marginal influence over public policy' (*ibid*.: 124). A more 'bottom-up' form of corporatism characterized nations such as Sweden, Switzerland, the Netherlands, Norway and Denmark (*ibid*.: 104). Here, corporatism coexisted – and, in some cases, still coexists – with a democratic political system. This form of corporatism rests on groups which continue to possess a degree of autonomy from the state, despite their involvement in tripartite policy-making (Grant, 1985: 10).

Some have argued that 'bottom-up' corporatism merely constitutes a particular type of pluralism. Hence, for example, for Atkinson and Coleman (1985), corporatism is 'sponsored pluralism' as opposed to 'pressure pluralism'. Unlike pluralism, however, theories of corporatism captured the process whereby 'what had been merely interest groups crossed the political threshold and became part of the extended state' (Middlemas quoted in Grant, 1985: 1–2). Lindblomian neo-pluralism (p. 198) had recognized the privileged position accorded to certain interests. However, corporatism also indicated that, in many regimes, interest groups not only influenced the state, but the state also influenced them – what is described as 'interest intermediation'. For Crouch (1985), interest intermediation constituted the 'essence' of corporatism since it acknowledged that the groups involved had two functions – representing their members *and* self-regulating in accordance with agreements arrived at with state actors. In contrast, groups within pluralist systems did not need to self-regulate in order to achieve policy influence. Furthermore, whilst pluralism focused on the lobbying activities of all interest groups, corporatism focused on groups representing labour and capital – which, arguably, 'are not simply groups like any others', at least within 'industrial capitalist countries with liberal democratic governments' (Berger quoted in Grant, 1985: 21).

Power resource theories

The relationship between trade unions and left parties
So-called 'power resource theory' also stresses the role of groups which represent particular interests, but focuses uniquely on trade unions and left parties as representative of working people. This approach has already been detailed in relation to analyses of welfare policy. As discussed in Chapter 4, Esping-Andersen is perhaps the most prominent proponent of the notion that strong and organized trade union movements and left parties had a decisive influence on the creation and main-

tenance of welfare states (Esping-Andersen, 1985; but see also Flora and Heidenheimer, 1981; Goodin *et al.*, 1999; Rueda and Pontusson, 2000). With regards to other areas of policy, the strength of the labour movement has been linked to the adoption of specific types of supply-side policies (Garrett and Lange, 1991), and economic policy and performance more generally (Garrett, 1998a; Scruggs and Lange, 2002).

Whilst '[o]rganization in the economic realm is evidenced by labour union strength', it is arguable that in the 'political sphere [it] is evidenced by the strength of left parties in government' (Kelly, 2005: 866). In many nations, left parties grew directly out of the labour movement. Even aside from these, however, in practice many left parties' economic strategies have relied on a close relationship with the labour movement, in order to moderate wage demands to attempt to constrain inflation (Garrett and Lange, 1989: 683; see also Higgins and Apple, 1981). In many nations, social democratic parties also attempted to work with unions in order to dampen down industrial unrest and instability, typified in Sweden's 'Harpsund democracy' (Salonen, 2009: 133).

Do parties matter as representatives of interests?
An extensive literature has developed which tests the influence of left parties on government outputs: it focuses on the question 'Do parties matter?' This literature generally assumes that whilst left parties will tend to promote redistribution, right parties will attempt to inhibit it; and that working class people will vote for left parties at least partly because they favour more egalitarian outcomes than the upper class (Kelly, 2005: 866).

Whilst Stephens found that decommodification was greater in contexts of left-wing government (1979), Huber and Stephens (2001) failed to discover clear correlations between left control of government in the 1980s and 1990s and spending rates. Allan and Scruggs, however, extended analysis to consider the impact of left-wing governments on replacement rates for unemployment benefit, as *compared with* right-wing governments. They found that left-wing control of government tended to be correlated with increases in replacement rates up until the 1980s. From the early 1980s onwards, however, this association broke down. At the same time, right governments became increasingly associated with downward shifts in replacement rates to a greater extent than were left parties (Allan and Scruggs, 2004). This was confirmed by an analysis by Blais *et al.* (1996: 517) which suggested that, all else being equal, 'central government spending increases by 0.4 percentage points ... more when the government is entirely controlled by the left, compared to a government entirely controlled by the right'. Such a difference may appear minimal, but cumulatively would lead to an increase in spending of 5 per cent over ten years.

For Kelly, however, by focusing on transfers such analyses fail to acknowledge the potential impact of governments on the market itself – what he describes as 'market conditioning'. This occurs where 'government action [such as taxation regimes, the introduction of minimum wages, and regional economic programmes] produces economic outcomes different than those which would be produced by market forces in the absence of government action' (Kelly, 2005: 868). Kelly's analysis suggests that shifts in government to the left are correlated with reductions in pre-redistribution inequality, which would be explained by these governments engaging in higher levels of market conditioning.

Revisions to power resource theories
The power resource approach to explaining government outputs has been subject to numerous critiques. First, the political complexion of the party/parties in power is but one of numerous influences on decision-making, with social democratic parties potentially being subject to many constraints including, for example, the nature of their main political competitor (Kitschelt, 2000).

Second, power resource studies generally focus on quantitative outputs, whereas left parties may also have an influence on non-quantitative issues (e.g. abortion, or the degree of selection in schools). Third, and as discussed, the empirical results of these studies generally demonstrate only a weak correlation, rather than causation (von Beyme, 1984).

In addition, in many nations, social expenditure grew and pre-redistribution inequality was reduced during periods where there was no strong left-wing party in place –for example, as in the Netherlands and France (van Kersbergen and Manow, 2008: 529). Some authors suggest that, in these circumstances, Christian Democratic parties sometimes acted as an alternative to social democracy, not least because their policy priorities were often similar to those of Social Democrats in the fields of welfare and the economy, and because they enjoyed support from Catholic-leaning trade unions (van Kersbergen, 1995).

Furthermore, employers – the constituency supposedly represented by right parties – have not always resisted redistributive policies, but sometimes actively *promoted* them. Hence, Mares (2003) argues that firms using highly-skilled workers are likely to support welfare policies which increase differentiation through preserving status, whilst firms using low-skilled labour and/or requiring a flexible labour force are more likely to support universalistic policies which spread the costs of contributions across all workers (see also Swenson, 2002).

More fine-grained approaches which adopt a detailed 'process-tracing' methodology may, therefore, prove more fruitful in explaining the exact mechanisms through which parties influence policy-making.

A recent example comes from Turner's (2011) fine-grained comparison of the impact of switches to Christian Democratic control in four German *Länder*, which suggests that the impact of partisan change was contingent on institutional and cultural constraints. In particular, changes to education and child care policy were undertaken in Western *Länder* which would have been inconceivable in the Eastern *Länder* due to the different political culture and pre-existing delivery systems in both policy areas. Another example comes from the detailed analysis by Kangas *et al.* (2010) of the development and continuation of pension policies in Sweden, Finland and Denmark. They indicate the complex relationship between (parts of) the labour movement and politicians in all three countries. Developments in those countries were broadly consistent with power resource theories, but the influence of the labour movement in particular differed substantially in all three, and was not uniform (with, for example, Dansk Metal's agreement with its employers to create an occupational scheme kick-starting a more differentiated approach to pension provision in Denmark compared with the other countries) (*ibid.*: 271).

Furthermore, the extent to which social democratic parties will focus on securing redistribution across society has been questioned. In some cases, they appear to have focused on providing benefits only to particular, politically-strong groups of workers, rather than all working class people (Rueda, 2005). This has particularly been the case in Latin America, where certain sections of the urban working class were favoured by the Partido Revolucionario Institucional (PRI) in Mexico and the Peronists in Argentina, rather than these parties pushing for policies which would have had wider benefits (Carnes and Mares, 2007: 874–5).

Also, so-called 'political budget cycle' analyses suggest that government spending increases in the run-up to elections, regardless of the political party in power (Franzese, 2002). Some authors have maintained that these cycles apply mainly in newer, rather than older, democracies (see, for example, Persson and Tabellini, 2004). Regardless of their scope, they at least sensitize us to the fact that matters other than ideology and connection to the organized working class may be of importance to left parties – such as electoral considerations.

Finally, it has been noted that the origins of many welfare states lay not in protecting workers but, rather, in other categories of individuals whose interests were not represented by trade unions – such as soldiers, mothers, or families more generally (Skocpol, 1992; Pedersen, 1993).

Policies determining interests

Perhaps the most comprehensive challenge to the 'power resources' perspective, however, comes from Lowi's insight, discussed in Chapter 2 (pp. 39–40), that 'policy shapes politics' – that is, that the types of policies enacted will influence group competition.

Pierson's theory of path dependence offers a systematic consideration of how welfare policies can create new constituencies of recipients, who then act as blocks on attempts at reform (see also Therborn and Roebroek, 1986; Campbell, 2003). He suggested that whilst 'power resource' theories explained how welfare states were first created, once they had been put into place it was the political costs of reform, heightened through the creation of constituencies of beneficiaries, which blocked change, rather than necessarily the actions of left parties or trade unions. Furthermore, Pierson suggested that politicians would try to dodge blame for cutting welfare, completely contrary to their usual attempts to court support from expanding welfare. As a result, he argued, welfare reforms would often be made in an incremental manner, and would be more feasible where blame could be 'hidden' through technical detail and/or complex governing structures.

Certainly, Pierson's 'new politics' has not applied in every instance of welfare state reform, and in many countries, distinctions between left and right parties, and resistance from trade unions, remain determinant (see Kangas *et al.*, 2010, for just such a counter-example). The 'new politics' argument may also be better at explaining developments in some areas (pensions) rather than others (unemployment benefit). Raven *et al.* (2011) argue that this can be explained through the relative age of different elements of the welfare state, with public opinion generally being shaped by existing institutional designs in relation to older policy areas (e.g. pensions), but not new ones (e.g. labour market activation). Nonetheless, their analysis is restricted to only one country, the Netherlands. Jensen (2009) considers a broader range of countries in his assessment of the validity, or otherwise, of the 'new politics' approach to welfare provision (see Box 8.3).

Nonetheless, challenges to the power resource theory have also come from those who have studied the beginnings of welfare states, and their history from reforms in the 1980s onwards. First, in many nations, welfare states were created not due to direct pressure from trade unions and left parties, but as part of attempts to dampen down support for them and 'buy off' potential social democrats, as in both Germany and Britain (Heidenheimer, 1973: 317–18; Flora and Alber, 1981). In other countries, such as Denmark and Sweden, welfare policies were first promoted by parties representing agrarian and middle-class interests, as they were seen as part of a package which would broaden the tax base and promote flexibility, particularly amongst agricultural labour (Baldwin, 1990).

Even more fundamentally, some more recent scholarship has argued that it was policy which first created modern class divisions and linked them to political movements, rather than vice versa.

BOX 8.3   Jensen's assessment of the new politics

Jensen (2009) set out to consider whether Pierson's arguments about a 'new politics' applied. In particular, he focused on Pierson's claims that reforms are likely to be incremental, and that an increased number of veto players will help rather than hinder reform by spreading accountability. Jensen used data from Scruggs (2004), which indicated changes in replacement rates (see Chapter 4) between 1971 and 2002 for 18 Western nations.

Jensen's quantitative analysis suggested that multiple veto players were likely to lead to extended periods of stability, punctuated by periods of rapid change. Nonetheless, it also suggested that stability was more likely in some areas than in others. In particular, it indicated how very large changes had often been made to unemployment insurance replacement rates (with fifty instances where replacement rates were altered by 10 per cent or more). Jensen described how strong 'punctuations' in the policy context could be responsible for these changes, such as the situation preceding the Hartz IV reforms in Germany, involving a high-profile scandal around the presentation of unemployment statistics.

Martin and Swank (2009: 37) argue that 'parties influence[d] the construction of class cleavages', rather than the process occurring only in the other direction. For these authors, parties played a decisive part in determining whether trade unions federated with each other to become powerful peak associations of labour, or were organized along sectoral lines or according to different political persuasions. First, different types of party system promoted different approaches to industrial organization, particularly on the employers' side, which then influenced labour organization. Multiparty systems promoted the creation of strong, widely-focused, encompassing unions and associations, since partisan associations representing specific interests had more of a chance of capturing governing power. In contrast, in dual party systems both capital and labour tended to be spread across the parties and no one party had an incentive to ally itself uniquely with one specific interest.

Hence, during the process of industrialization, in Sweden, Denmark, Norway and the Benelux countries employers quickly developed strong, macrocorporatist representational bodies. The Germanic nations and Italy displayed strong sectoral, but not necessarily cross-sectoral, coordination amongst employers. In contrast, the Anglo-liberal nations, plus Finland and France, exhibited a plethora of employers' associations which only came to be federated into integrated national peak associations following World War II. Martin and Swank argue that these different patterns of interest organization related to the extent of multipartyism within each nation. This was because multiparty systems promote delegation to private interests within corporatist arrangements, since parties representing business would be unlikely to win an overall majority within government, and thus prefer private to public channels for regulating economic issues. In contrast, in dual party systems little policy-making authority will be delegated to business or labour representatives, since the two-party system prioritizes radical changes in policy and, thus, the disruption of consultative arrangements.

A subtly different argument, closely related to the theory of 'varieties of capitalism' (see Chapter 3), comes from Iversen and Soskice (2009). They suggest that both policies and politics – that is, both the level of redistribution, and the nature of the class structure – have developed out of two fundamentally opposed economic structures which solidified in the early twentieth century. These comprise the model of 'locally coordinated economies [which] were coupled with strong guild traditions and heavy investment in cospecific assets', which resulted in greater levels of support for redistribution, and the model of 'market-based economies' which existed alongside 'liberal states and more mobile assets', which reduced support for redistribution (*ibid.*: 438). For these authors, interests were ultimately shaped by history, and particularly the institutional legacy of the path taken by the industrial revolution in different countries.

Problems with interest-based accounts

As indicated by Bierce's mischievous definition of politics referred to at the beginning of this chapter, many people either implicitly or explicitly believe that policy-making is ultimately driven by interests in some way. However, interest-based theories arguably face four challenges. First, it is often unclear exactly how particular goals come to be viewed as being in individuals' or groups' interests. Second, there is a need for clearer specification of how interests directly or indirectly shape policy. Third, there has been comparatively little empirical testing of theories which suggest that interests drive policy-making. Relatedly, despite the frequently wide-ranging claims made about the applicability of interest-based approaches, in practice they have often appeared to have been contradicted by reality.

What is the content of interest?

The first challenge for interest-based accounts concerns the specification of the content of interests. As indicated at the beginning of this chapter, it is often difficult to separate 'interests' from wants, needs, desires and beliefs. Individuals may, for example, believe that a particular policy is in their interests, when it may prove not to be, or vice versa. In countries such as Germany and Belgium, trade unionists often supported universal welfare provision, whilst anti-union politicians supported social insurance. Both groups believed that their preferred system was in their interests. However, as it turned out, so-called Ghent models of social insurance (see Chapter 4) actually consolidated the role of trade unions, rather than diminished them.

It could be argued that both sets of actors were, at that point in time, unable to predict the implications of either system accurately. Even in situations of 'perfect' information, however, it can be difficult to discern what is in individuals' interests. An interesting example comes from the field of income support. It is often suggested that individuals should be incentivized to work and that, therefore, benefits should be kept at a low level. As a result, it could be argued that keeping benefits low will mean that poorer people will do everything they can to find work. However, some would argue that it is equally rational to assume that the poorest people view their situation in terms of (often numerous) problems to be alleviated, rather than money to be made. Becoming marginally less poor by working on low wages, as opposed to not working, would be about as useful as salving one bee sting after being attacked by a swarm (see Karelis, 2007). As another example, rational choice theorists assume that individuals will always be motivated by self-interest. Whilst they may appear to behave in an other-regarding way ('altruistically'), they only ultimately do this because of the psychic benefit they receive from acting in this way (Becker, 1974). Extreme behaviour – such self-immolation to highlight a political cause – brings this assumption into question, even if it occurs only very rarely. To resolve these kinds of problems, interest-based theorists often rely on ideas to explain how interests are given 'content' – but this arguably comes at the price of reducing the theories' simplicity and parsimony.

How are interests translated into policy?

A related problem comes from the issue of how interests are translated into policy. Some of the theories considered above do explicitly attempt to explain how policy-making activity is shaped by interest, but not, perhaps, entirely successfully. For example, for power resource theorists, trade unions and left parties simply represent the interests of working people. As considered above, however, both Christian Democratic parties and business have also appeared at some points in some countries to promote policies similar to those apparently favoured by trade unions and left parties. This suggests that other organizations might promote the interests of working people, even if they do not formally represent them, which rather begs the question of why some groups need not represent the interests of all their members (Christian Democratic parties and business), whilst others are assumed to do this (trade unions and left parties).

Rational choice theorists resolve the issue of the relationship between interests and how they are put into practice in policy by simply identifying actors' behaviour with the revelation of their interests – hence, whatever actors do is simply in their interest. Nonetheless, this does not explain exactly how preferences are translated into action or inaction. A particular preference could be 'revealed' in a variety of policy options, yet no clear guidance is provided by the theory to explain which policies are ultimately chosen and why. Similar criticisms can arguably be applied to claims of Marxist theories that the state will simply act in the interests of the bourgeoisie – especially when governments may appear to act to promote working peoples' interests instead, even if 'only in the short term'.

Lack of empirical testing

Another potential challenge for interest-based theories comes from the fact that they have, on the whole, been subject to more theoretical development than application to real-life cases through empirical research. For example, there are few entirely successful empirical applications of rational choice theory, in contrast with the relative success of more purely theoretical works in this area. Green and Shapiro (1994: 6) maintain that 'the case has yet to be made that these [rational choice] models have advanced our understanding of how politics work in the real world'. Often, rational choice approaches will start with the theory itself, then move into empirical examples which appear to instantiate the theory – merely examining 'positive values on the dependent variable', rather than testing the theory against a range of empirical examples (see Chapter 14, for a discussion of why selection on the dependent variable might be problematic). Green and Shapiro maintain this selective application of the theory is inappropriate.

Again, although the two theories have very different implications, the reductiveness of Marxist theories (assuming interests will always determine policy) has excited similar criticisms as afflict rational choice theory. Marxists often argue, for example, that welfare systems might appear to aid working-class individuals in the short term, but that over the longer term they promote their subjugation to the bourgeoisie. Arguing that a system simply will act in the interests of the bourgeoisie over the longer term, even if it appears not to do so over the short term, is similar to rational choice theorists' claims that certain institutional structures simply are in the interests of actors over the longer term, even if they go against their interests at any particular moment. The problem with this approach is that it is virtually impossible to subject it to empirical testing.

Lack of predictive value

Interest-based theories generally offer wide-ranging explanations for policy development. As a result, many of them are intuitively attractive due to their applicability and relative simplicity. This is notable in relation to, for example, institutionalist analyses (see Chapter 10) which often only apply to particular groups of cases (such as democratic political systems, and not non-democratic ones) during specific time periods (such as the postwar period), and can have limited explanatory purchase.

A by-product of the wide applicability of interest-based theories, however, is the variety of opportunities this throws up for such theories to become disproved by reality, and thus discredited. An example of this comes from Olson's RADON, discussed earlier (pp. 51–2). Many of the economies which RADON identified as fast-growing during the early 1980s became very sluggish during the 1990s and 2000s. In addition, some nations which have been subject to a high degree of institutionalization of interest groups – such as the Netherlands – have prospered economically. Corporatist arrangements have sometimes enabled small countries to coordinate responses to international pressures through, for example, negotiated wage moderation (Hirst and Thompson, 1996: 179). Of course, Olson could respond by claiming that this simply indicates that these groups' interests were aligned with those of the economy as a whole, but this undermines the parsimony of his approach.

Similarly, if from a very different theoretical position, Schmitter argued that corporatist arrangements were functional for the operation of an increasingly complex capitalist economic system, and as a result would become increasingly common. His views on this point are worth quoting in full. He argued that:

> the more the modern state comes to serve as the indispensable and authoritative guarantor of capitalism by expanding its regulative and integrative tasks, the more it finds that it needs the professional expertise, specialised information, prior aggregation of opinion, contractual capability and deferred participatory legitimacy which only singular, hierarchically ordered, consensually led representative monopolies can provide. To obtain these, the state will agree to devolve upon or share with these associations much of its newly acquired decisional authority, subject, as Keynes noted, 'in the last resort to the sovereignty of democracy expressed through Parliament'. (Schmitter, 1974: 110)

However, in the vast majority of nations, the era of 'organized' capitalism has come to an end (Lash and Urry, 1987). In practice, there are few remaining corporatist regimes, beyond a handful of small, trade-intensive nations (and, even within these, the role of tripartite arrangements is diminishing). As Grant (1985: 7) claims, 'the historical verdict on corporatism' could be that 'it is a phenomenon of small countries in prosperous times'. Furthermore, it is arguable that corporatism's effectiveness was heavily dependent on the degree to which the interest groups themselves were truly representative and encompassing of both labour and capital; if not (e.g. as, arguably, in France), corporatist systems provided only a very weak lever for macroeconomic policy-making (Birnbaum, 1982).

The problem of mismatch between interest-based theory and reality is particularly acute for those approaches which have been used not only to describe and analyse reality, but also as normative 'maps'. An obvious example comes from Marxist perspectives when compared with the practice of Marxist-inspired regimes in different countries. Many theorists would argue that no Marxist-inspired party has faithfully followed the theory of Marxism, leading always to a mismatch between theory and practice.

Nonetheless, the practice of Marxist-inspired regimes questions the validity of Marxist predictions about the likely trajectories of both economic and state development. Not only have none of those regimes gone beyond 'actually existing socialism' to the end-point of 'communism', where class relations have been abolished. Many, in addition, have been subject to the very same characteristics that feature in democratic capitalist societies. Hence, in virtually all socialist countries, a new 'class' of party officials, the '*nomenklatura*', were accorded greater material comforts and freedoms than ordinary people (Djilas, 1966). In addition, in many nations, women were required to adopt traditional gender roles by strongly pro-natalist policies, rather than gender difference being obliterated through liberation from market requirements (Hoffman, 2000). Thus, observation of Marxist-inspired regimes has, explicitly or implicitly, undermined the popularity of Marxist theories of policy development.

Conclusion

This chapter has considered the bewildering variety of theoretical approaches which assign either a determining or a predominant role to policy actors' interests. These approaches range from rational choice, with its parsimonious focus on individuals' preference maximization; to Marxists' assumption that political behaviour will embody the interests of the holders of capital; to elitist theorists' views that the holders of power will attempt to retain control through policy-making; to feminists' focus on patriarchy as the source of policy development; and, finally, to cleavage theories' wide-ranging consideration of modern social, economic and geographic difference, and its impact on political opinion.

The chapter also examined approaches to explaining how different groups, representative of certain interests, manage or otherwise influence the policy-making process. It also considered in detail one specific variant of these, so-called 'power resource' theories, which argue that trade unions and left parties will make policy that is in the interests of their members and supporters. However, as was indicated in the chapter, the relationship between policies and interests may not be one-way; policies may themselves shape interest constellations as well as the other way around.

Finally, the chapter considered some commonly-mentioned problems with interest-based accounts: the fact that they generally fail to provide a clear indication of what the content of interests will be, and how exactly they will be translated into policy; the general lack of applied, empirical work focusing on interests as an explanatory variable; and the rather common mismatch between interests-based theories and reality.

Summary

- ❏ A number of analytical approaches suggest that interests are the most influential factor within the policy process, and can explain policy differences between countries: rational choice theory; Marxism; and elitist, feminist and cleavage theories.
- ❏ Pluralism suggests that the policy process provides an arena for contestation between different groups. Typologies of interest groups which separate insider and outsider groups, or policy networks from policy communities, suggest that the influence of different groups will depend on their relationship with government.
- ❏ Corporatism refers to a political system whereby the role of organized labour and business is institutionalized within the policy-making system.
- ❏ 'Power resource' theories suggest that the extent to which public policy will lead to a redistribution of resources is contingent on the power of the organized working class in parliament (through labour-representing parties). Challenges to power resource theories have suggested that policies can determine interests, as well as the other way around.
- ❏ Whilst interest-based accounts have been extremely influential, they can be criticized for often failing to explain the content of interests and the mechanisms whereby interests are translated into policy. In addition, few interest-based theories have been subjected to sustained empirical testing, and many have been seen as lacking in predictive value.

Chapter 9

Ideas and Public Policy

This chapter follows the structure of the previous one by first describing how 'ideas' might be defined, then detailing ideas-based approaches to the comparative analysis of public policy. Some of the ideas-based perspectives described here (such as policy design, policy learning and policy-oriented research) fall within the mainstream of academic and political approaches to policy analysis. Others, particularly postmodernism, are highly controversial. Yet others, such as interpretivism, began at the fringes of policy analysis but have become increasingly common.

The examination of ideas-based approaches is followed by a consideration of attempts to synthesize ideas-based approaches with those drawn from interest- and institution-based perspectives. These syntheses suggest that ideas can be functional to the pursuit of interests and can give content to interests; that institutions can facilitate particular ideas; and that certain groups can be effective in the promotion of specific ideas. The chapter finishes with an examination of why and when ideas change, due to either internal or external pressures.

What are ideas?

As with interests and institutions, 'ideas' have been conceptualized in a variety of ways. A common distinction is made between 'ideology' and 'ideas'. Ideas such as freedom, justice and equality are invoked in most political ideologies, for example, but the importance they are allocated and how they are conceptualized differs radically between, say, communist ideology, fascism, liberalism and social democracy (Freeden, 1998). The same arguably applies in relation to 'national values'; many nations are often described as committed to 'freedom', for example, but that idea can mean something different to each country.

Even the single category of 'ideas', however, covers a wide range of different cognitive attributes. These can be implicitly normative. The idea of 'active ageing', for example, suggests that the elderly should be engaged in activity, rather than slowing down during their 'twilight years', whilst that of 'asset-based welfare' suggests that wealth, as well as income, is important for individuals' wellbeing. Alternatively, ideas may be theoretical, to the extent that they imply specific causal relationships between different factors. For example, the 'ideas' of Keynesianism and monetarism imply different relationships between consumer demand, economic growth and government spending. As another example, New Right approaches to poverty suggest that the key policy priority is the removal of 'benefit traps' and of factors promoting a 'culture of poverty', whereas 'welfarist' approaches suggest that increasing economic opportunities and basic living standards is most important.

Whilst some ideas may be propounded by a variety of different actors, other ideas may act as 'markers' of the personal identity of distinctive groups. An example comes from the 'rainbow' of the gay liberation movement, the design of which specifically assigned different meanings to each of its component colours. Another is provided by the label for the US older peoples' activist group the Grey Panthers, which immediately links their movement to the Black Panthers racial liberation group, at the same time as providing an image of strength and resolution.

Indeed, it is arguable that, often, images can come to symbolize certain ideas, and express them more neatly than would be the case in text. One example of this comes from the appearance of the then Labour Party leader, Michael Foot, at a memorial service for British soldiers in 1981. Foot was wearing an aqua-coloured smart overcoat, which was actually complimented by the then monarch for its appropriateness for the occasion, but black and white pictures of Foot next to other party leaders led to claims that he was wearing a 'donkey jacket'. At that time, donkey jackets were mainly worn only by manual workers. The image conveyed ideas of shabbiness and a lack of respect for convention and traditional British values, which ultimately (if, perhaps, unfairly) significantly harmed Foot and his party in the eyes of the British public.

Ideas-based approaches to explaining public policy

Chapter 8 examined theories including Marxism and radical feminism which suggest that ideas are contingent on class and gender power relations, respectively. Chapter 10 considers sociological institutionalism, which suggests that ideas are at least partly determined by the institutional context of the actors who propound them. In contrast, the approaches examined here reject claims that ideas are entirely determined by contextual features, and suggest that changes in ideas can have independent effects on policy change, which are not reducible to actors' interests or the institutions within which they operate. As such, these theories could be seen as offering an 'optimistic' approach towards human agency suggesting that individuals, acting autonomously, can potentially have a significant impact on public policy-making (Lieberman, 2002).

Policy design, policy-oriented research and policy learning

These three approaches all focus on the role of individual policy-makers and how they take decisions, rather than considering collective processes or trends.

The first approach, already considered in detail in Chapter 2, comes from the field of policy design. This suggests that policy-makers are able to choose, from a toolbox of different instruments, those most suited to deal with any given policy problem. In so doing, they are assumed to act in accordance with their normative evaluation of what policy goals should consist in. As claimed by Bobrow and Dryzek (1987: 19), policy design, 'like any kind of design, involves the pursuit of *valued outcomes* through activities sensitive to the context of time and place' (emphasis added). For authors writing within this perspective, it is assumed that policy-makers can exercise autonomy and genuinely choose which instruments are the most appropriate, in accordance with their ideological goals.

The view that policy-makers can actively exercise choice about which policies to adopt has also informed what is described as 'policy-oriented research', sometimes also described as 'policy analysis'. This approach focuses on the judgements made by decision-makers and the reasons underlying them, as well as the role of information more broadly within the policy-making process, particularly that coming from 'experts' (Vickers, 1965; Jacob and Genard, 2004). In some countries, this approach was particularly salient in attempts to promote 'evidence-based policy-making' within government (for UK examples, see Young *et al.*, 2002; Wilkinson, 2011).

Another approach, considered in detail in Chapter 11, assumes that policy-makers can learn from how policy is delivered and implemented in different contexts. Such 'policy learning' involves governments and, potentially, other related actors learning lessons from other governmental actors, international organizations, think tanks and other related actors, who may be organized into specific 'advocacy coalitions' or 'epistemic communities'. Again, this approach assumes that policy-makers can be persuaded by information about successful, or unsuccessful, policies whether they should adopt such policies in their own jurisdiction, rather than policy-makers' decisions necessarily being determined by contextual factors.

Authors within all three traditions have been relatively willing to intervene in policy debates to promote particular policy approaches, based upon their own analyses. The skills that are viewed as necessary for 'successful' policy design, transfer and analysis are also frequently taught, not only to academic researchers, but additionally to governmental actors such as senior civil servants (see, for example, National School of Government, 2011).

Policy framing

An alternative approach, policy framing, focuses more on collective processes whereby particular meanings are associated with different policy options. This approach starts from the premise that policy-makers cannot, and do not, collect together all potential policy options from those which might conceivably work, and rationally decide between these. Instead, policy-makers use 'frames of meaning' to interpret, condense and simplify the policy context, as well as to help them decide how to intervene in it (Rein and Schon, 1991). In particular, policy-makers are engaged in creating boundaries around, and providing labels for, particular processes and groups, and thus 'making up' the policy world (Considine, 2005: 63). As such, Edelman (1971) has argued that much government activity consists precisely in 'framing', what he describes as 'symbolic action'.

Such framing activity can occur in relation to specific policy targets. An interesting example of this comes from the field of transfers to families, and particularly to single parents, who are overwhelmingly female. Despite these women's family status being identical across different countries, lone motherhood is conceptualized in very different ways by policy-makers in different countries. Whereas lone motherhood is stigmatized in both the UK and USA (and racialized, to a large degree, in the latter) (Hancock, 2004), in other European countries single parents are often considerably better off materially, and have not been singled out as a specific social 'problem' (Lewis, 1999).

Policy-makers may also 'frame' policy problems by adopting differing assessments of the causes of policy problems. Hence, in the UK, those living on very low incomes have been described, in rough chronological order, as poor, socially excluded, then at risk of social exclusion (Dodds, 2009). As a result of the causal relationships posited within each idea, policies have shifted from concentrating on distributional issues (availability of employment and of basic resources) to relational issues (the 'culture' of poverty and/or low social capital) (see Saraceno, 1997).

Finally, policy-makers may also frame the role of government in different ways. Within the Netherlands, for example, individuals' sexual and cultural behaviour is viewed by policy-makers as not amenable to governmental intervention. As a result, decisions on topics such as sex education are largely left up to civil society and schools to resolve. In contrast, in the UK, it is assumed that there are 'causal relationships between law and behaviour', and 'declaratory legislation' is viewed as not just appropriate, but an essential part of the governmental policy-making machinery. As such, policy-makers have frequently intervened in areas such as sex education in order to promote a particular model of the family – the straight, married, two-parent family – rather than alternative models (Lewis and Knijn 2002: 674).

Analysts within this tradition have ascribed the determinants of framing behaviour to policy-makers' own ideologies, to their cultural, historical and social context (May, 1997), and to their links with structural (particularly, class and/or economic) interests (Edelman, 1971).

Research into policy framing has arguably become even more important in the wake of the financial crisis, as debate rages about the causes of the crisis and how it should be dealt with at a policy level. For example, whilst the UK's gross public debt at the time of writing of around 85 per cent of GDP (European Commission, 2011) was described by its government as threatening 'every job and public service in the country' (Osborne, 2010), no such extreme alarm has been sounded by successive waves of Japanese politicians who, in 2010, were faced with a public debt to GDP ratio of nearly 200 per cent (*Global Finance*, 2010). Again, whilst in the UK sales taxes have been raised to 20 per cent with little protest, in Japan suggestions to raise consumption taxes from the current 5 per cent to 10 per cent have provoked controversy.

Similarly, entirely different trajectories appear to have been adopted by countries which have been described as 'surviving' the crisis. Canada's stricter regulation and more conservative banking practices have been described by both academics and policy-makers as partially insulating it from the crisis (Harper, 2009; Brean *et al.*, 2011). In contrast, numerous US commentators have blamed regulation itself as the cause of the crisis (Ely, 2009; Kling, 2010).

Issue attention

One particularly interesting new ideas-based approach, developed out of a large-scale research programme, considers the extent to which political actors devote 'attention' to different issues – what has been described as the 'comparative study of policy dynamics' (Baumgartner *et al.*, 2011). This approach was developed out of smaller-scale studies of US policy agendas, but has now been broadened to consider policy dynamics across a range of nations.

This approach suggests that actors' values concerning different policies – their 'preferences' – can be separated from the extent and type of information available to them when making decisions. Policy-relevant information is provided by, for example, 'media coverage, public discontent, changes in the real world as these are monitored by government officials (such as the unemployment or inflation rates), actions within government as politicians exploit issues for personal or partisan gain, or other factors' (*ibid.*: 953).

At any one stage, a range of issues may be on the policy agenda. Whether or not an issue 'makes it' onto the policy agenda need not (or does not only) reflect its severity, but will reflect the degree of attention being paid to other agenda items at the time. The comparative policy agendas project (see www.comparativeagendas.org) aims to assess how issues 'ebb and flow' on governmental agendas, and how this relates to other contextual factors, including the availability of information, institutions and preferences. The database used by this project contains a staggering 1.5 million reports of comparable events, and is already yielding some very interesting findings (see Box 9.1).

In addition to studies carried out within the comparative agendas project itself, this approach has inspired a number of additional studies which have interrogated certain aspects of issue attention. For example, Darren Halpin (2011) has considered how 'policy bandwagons' arise within one nation – Scotland – over a 25-year period. Halpin considered in detail how 'issue attention' varied between lobbying groups. He concluded that, rather than lobbying reflecting the importance and impact of different issues, it tended to follow a 'bandwagon' effect, whereby 'keystone groups' such as the media, public officials and organized campaigns helped to trigger 'cascades' of attention, which then developed into bandwagons.

BOX 9.1   Jennings et al. on how the core functions of government affect executive agendas

Jennings *et al.* (2001) have used the comparative policy agendas approach to consider a fascinating question: the extent to which 'core' governmental policy areas (such as macroeconomic issues, defence and foreign affairs) 'crowd out' other policy issues and prevent them getting onto governmental agendas.

They coded around 50,000 policy statements, which were drawn from annual executive speeches such as the 'Queen's Speech' in the UK, which sets out the legislative agenda for the year to come. The statements were drawn from a range of nations chosen to reflect different institutional contexts, covering parliamentary systems (Denmark, the Netherlands, Spain, the UK), semi-presidential systems (France) and presidential systems (the USA).

They found that 'core' governmental policy areas did appear to monopolize the agenda, with levels of attention devoted to other policy areas diminishing when government attended to core issues. However, there was no crowding out phenomenon between core issues. That is, when a core issue received attention, this did not diminish the attention paid to other core issues.

These findings led Jennings *et al.* to conclude that '[t]he core functions of government are issues with a pre-eminent status in politics. These main responsibilities of the state are to defend its territory, interact with other states, manage the well-being of its citizens and maintain the state apparatus itself' (*ibid.*: 1022).

Interpretivism

A more radical approach to the role of ideas in policy-making comes from the so-called 'interpretivist turn'. This suggests that the focus of social research should be upon the ideas and understandings held by individuals, as they interact with other individuals and artefacts to produce and shape 'webs of meaning', and how these relate to actions, practices and institutions (Bevir and Rhodes, 2003: 17). These approaches suggest that policy-making and policy-implementation primarily involve symbolic activities as part of a policy 'language' (Yanow, 1996) or 'tradition'.

However, if the subjects of research are assumed to act in accordance with particular interpretations of the world, it would be inconsistent to view researchers as having unmediated access to their research subjects. Researchers should not, therefore, be viewed as having an 'outside' position from which they can objectively interpret the activities of others. Researchers, no less than research subjects, 'cannot be free of [their] own cognitive filters and embedded preferences' (Considine, 2005: 73). Giandomenico Majone (1989) acknowledged this in his description of policy analysis as primarily 'argumentative', claiming that it was impossible to separate values from the process of analysis (see also Roe, 1994; Hajer and Wagenaar, 2003).

The interpretivist approach, therefore, explicitly acknowledges that researchers themselves interpret the world (rather than having some kind of 'direct', unmediated, access to it), just as their subjects do. As a result, for interpretivists, the process of research is one of 'interpreting interpretations' (Bevir and Rhodes, 2005).

For these authors, traditional approaches to explanation which aim at the creation and testing of lawlike generalizations are doomed to failure, since the 'webs of meaning' and 'traditions' interpretivists examine are not reducible to structural contextual factors. Instead, researchers should attempt to 'understand' the meanings behind political behaviour. However, because of their focus on understanding salient traditions or discourses, authors in this tradition generally focus on relatively static meanings, rather than considering situations where ideas change rapidly (see Hay, 2011).

Postmodernist analyses

In contrast, postmodernism stresses the impermanence and ephemerality of policy ideas. It focuses on points of change in traditions – highlighting, for example, the contingency of taken-for-granted scientific, political and economic theories (Latour and Woolgard, 1979; Torfing, 2005) and even social taboos such as incest (Foucault, 1979; although it should be noted that Foucault rejected being labelled as a postmodernist, even if he is frequently classified as such by others). As applied to public policy research, the postmodernist approach stresses the contingency of rationality, interests and causal relationships as various elements of different competing discourses, rather than as possessing any more substantial status (Fischer and Forester, 1993).

Postmodernist theories have also, arguably, been more closely concerned with how ideas 'enact' or create particular objects and practices, than have interpretivists. Hence, for example, Glynos and Howarth (2007) indicate when 'fantasies' about working practices break down, and Mol (2002) considers how different medical 'objects' are 'created' by differing medical practices (for a summary, see West, 2011a).

Attempts to synthesize different approaches

As with approaches to public policy research which privilege interests and institutions as explanatory factors, in addition to theories which reduce all explanation to the role of ideas, others have been developed which combine a focus on ideas with other factors.

Ideas as functional to the pursuit of interests

A number of the interest-based theories examined in Chapter 8 made reference to ideas. This is perhaps most evident in theories of rational choice, and Marxist and radical feminist approaches.

First, ideas have been viewed within some rational choice approaches as mechanisms aiding coordination, particularly during conditions of uncertainty. Thus, Garrett and Weingast (1993: 205) suggest that ideas can play a role 'in coordinating the expectations that are necessary to sustain cooperation among a set of players with divergent preferences'. For example, the legal principles which underlie the single market helped coordinate actors in the absence of perfect information about other market actors' behaviour. Similarly, Goldstein and Keohane (1993) suggest that, where information is limited and the consequences of action unclear, ideas can help provide a 'road map' for policy actors. Hence, when actors find it difficult to plan rationally, ideas can serve to help policy coordination. In addition, they suggest that certain ideas can become 'embedded' in political institutions, through the operation of particular political routines.

For some, however, the use of ideas within rational choice theory undermines its core principle of methodological individualism (see Chapter 8). This is because the ideas referred to above, operating as aids to coordination, need to be held by more than one person in order for them to be functional. By so doing, however, additional considerations are added into the decisional process (namely, ideational ones) beyond the 'mere' pursuit of individual preferences, thus undermining the theory's parsimony (Blyth, 1997). Furthermore, theorists fail to explain why ideas may have causal power at a collective level, but not at the individual level; and vice versa (see Legro, 2000). Second, no clear delineation is provided between ideas and interests. If ideas are ultimately assimilable to interests, it appears difficult to split the two from each other. This highlights a broader problem concerning the status of preferences (interests) within rational choice theory, which has not provided a convincing account of how preferences are generated. Finally, and perhaps most substantially, Blyth (1997) has maintained that ideas are effectively reduced to the status of information for rational choice theorists. This is because they maintain that ideas are only important to the extent that they aid individuals to pursue their interests, and have no independent role to play.

For Marxists – who, again, base their analytical approach on interests – ideas also play a role, this time in furthering the interests of the owners of capital. In particular, the ideologies invoked by governments will implicitly or explicitly privilege the interests of the bourgeosie. This ideology is the 'superstructure' of society, which is contingent on the 'base': the concrete relations of production – that is, the class structure. Members of the working class tend to be persuaded by the prevailing ideology, even though over the longer term it helps maintain their subjugation. This is because, for Marx, they are subject to 'false consciousness'. Gramsci (1971) developed this analysis to argue that bourgeois ideas exerted a 'cultural hegemony' over working-class people.

Radical feminists, in common with some of the postmodernist approaches described above, have drawn attention to the intimate connection between discourse and action. In particular, they have highlighted the 'everyday', and largely ignored, use of gender-specific language, and considered how this reflects unequal relations between the genders (Cameron, 1998). As a result, they have suggested that even some of our most fundamental ideas about the world may be biased towards the interests of one gender over another.

Ideas giving content to interests

For other theorists, ideas are important not just as props to the pursuit of interest, but because they actually give content to interests. Weber, for example, argued that 'material and ideal interests', rather than ideas, 'directly govern men's conduct'. However, he states that 'very frequently the "world images" that have been created by "ideas" have, like switchmen, determined the tracks along which action has been pushed by the dynamic of interest' (Weber, 1946 [1920]: 280). Hence, for Weber, ideas help explain why particular courses of action are taken, when a variety of different approaches would have been consistent with the pursuit of interest. Some authors would go further and suggest that it is virtually impossible to split interests off from the ideas which express them (Muller, 2000).

It is difficult, for example, to specify what someone's interests are, without knowing their beliefs about what is desirable (Wendt, 1999). This is particularly clear under conditions of uncertainty. Cornelia Woll (2008) provides a fascinating example of this in her analysis of an area traditionally viewed as uniquely propelled by interests – trade policy. She indicates how firms may often be unclear on exactly which policy approaches they favour, particularly when the outcomes of different approaches are unclear (e.g. as with economic liberalization in the airline industry). Whilst the strategic environment facing firms is important in affecting their policy priorities, these are also shaped by new beliefs around the importance of different kinds of operations, and firms' own identities.

Another example comes from Sheri Berman's (1998) examination of the role of ideas within social democratic parties. For Berman, party leaders were able, through conveying particular ideas, to change their supporters' beliefs about the content of their interests. An excellent example of this comes from the division in social democratic parties between those committed to (eventual) revolution or to 'reformism'. Where parties adopted a reformist platform, they could engage in the construction of policies to 'tame' and 'stabilize' capitalism. This approach was, however, impossible for social democratic parties which argued that the ultimate goal of policy was to achieve revolution, albeit through democratic means. Parties, in this context, acted as the 'carriers' of ideas, rather than merely representing interests (Berman, 2006).

Jobert and Muller (1987) and Muller (2000) systematically consider the stake of different actors in the creation and maintenance of particular policy ideas. They argue that different 'sectors' of policy-making will be subject to different *référentiels sectoriels* – that is, different sectional paradigms or frameworks. These enable individuals to interpret the policy context ('*décodage*'); provide the various actors involved with an identity; and enable them to explain, justify and legitimate their activities ('*recodage*'). At the same time, however, *référentiels sectoriels* exclude from the policy process those actors who do not share this frame of meaning, preserving the privileged position of those sharing and benefiting from the *référentiel*. As such, they are 'hegemonic' – that is, they are extremely difficult to dislodge, and brook no challenge from other ideological frameworks (Gramsci, 1971).

Another systematic attempt to explain the close interrelationship between ideas and interests comes from Kathleen McNamara's (1998) work on Economic and Monetary Union within the EU. For McNamara, elite interests have been the driving force behind the eurozone, which – at least until the time of writing – has prioritized constraining inflation over other goals, such as increasing employment. However, a variety of different policy approaches (such as the strengthening of independent central banks) would have been consistent with the pursuit of this interest. Instead, as McNamara explains, the neoliberal policy consensus crystallized around the idea of monetary cooperation, with elite interests propelling this specific policy approach over others. The current crisis offers a rich (if highly unfortunate) set of national cases to test approaches such as those of McNamara that were developed to explain arguably less fraught economic decision-making processes.

In particular, there is a need for a greater focus on the formation of elite 'knowledges' across different national and international contexts, directly examining the 'episteme' in epistemic communities and how this is created. Some provocative new research has started to consider this in relation to the financial crisis. Engelen *et al.* (2011), in an analysis of media and political explanations, argue that the crisis is best analysed not as a 'normal accident' (Perrow, 1984), but as an 'elite debacle'. According to their approach, it was elite actors' confidence in their own 'folk knowledge', despite a lack of buttressing evidence, which led to 'hubris' and ultimately to an inability to prevent negative consequences through policy-making. Alasdair Roberts (2010) also detects overconfidence amongst elites as one reason for the crisis, suggesting that this directly related to what he calls a 'naïve institutionalism', which assumed that technocratic rules would be sufficient to avert financial crisis. More empirically-informed research (see Fourcade, 2009, for an example) is required to assess the relative contribution of elite norms to promoting risky practices, in combination with other factors such as pressures towards social conformity.

Institutions facilitating ideas

Some institutionalist scholars have viewed institutions as intimately related to ideas (see Chapter 10). For sociological institutionalists, institutions themselves directly embody particular ideas by promoting particular customs and norms which constitute their 'logic of appropriateness' (March and Olsen, 1984). For rational choice institutionalists, ideas can provide a coordinating function (see Garrett and Weingast, 1993).

It is perhaps within the area of historical or political institutionalism, however, that some of the most sophisticated and empirically-rooted attempts to combine ideas with institutions can be found.

One comes from Peter Hall, whose approach has already been examined in Chapter 3 and and is considered again in Chapter 10. Hall divides orders of policy change and types of policy learning into those affecting the settings of policy instruments (first-order change), the instruments themselves (second-order change), and the goals of policy (third-order change). Hall's (1993: 279) notion of policy paradigm can be assimilated with that of the 'policy frame', since it comprises the 'framework of ideas and standards that specifies not only the goals of policy and the kind of instruments that can be used to attain them, but also the very nature of the problems they are meant to be addressing'. Hall argues that the use of policy paradigms can be compared with that of scientific paradigms, as set out by the author Thomas Kuhn (1970).

For Kuhn, scientific worldviews do not develop through the 'classic' process of falsification as detailed by authors such as Popper (2002). Instead, scientists will generally attempt to fit aberrant observations within a particular paradigm until that paradigm is eventually discredited, a scientific 'revolution' occurs, and a new paradigm comes to shape scientific endeavour.

Hall (1993) argues that policy outcomes which are not in line with policy paradigms will, similarly, be tolerated for a particular amount of time, until the burden of evidence becomes overwhelming and the paradigm is abruptly abandoned, to be substituted by another. In order for such 'third-order' change to occur, Hall suggests it is necessary for dissenting voices to have captured positions of power within institutions, particularly the media and politics.

Hall's analysis thus argues that policy change results from change in ideas, associated with alterations in the political context. This has been subject to criticism from Blyth, who suggests that it is difficult to ascertain the exact influence of ideas within Hall's account. In particular, Blyth argues that, for ideas to play a genuine role in Hall's analysis, they must be responsible for change which would not have occurred if the ideas had not changed – yet, this does not appear to be the case (Blyth, 1997: 236). For Blyth (*ibid*.: 229), this use of ideas is simply an 'ad hoc attempt' to better explain policy change within historical institutionalism (see Chapter 10), a theory generally viewed as better at explaining policy stability.

Another influential approach, which does *explicitly* acknowledge the causal role of ideas, comes from Vivien Schmidt's (2002b; 2009) examination of the role of discourse in policy-making, what she describes as 'discursive institutionalism'. For Schmidt (2002b: 210), discourse is the carrier of ideas, and comprises 'whatever policy actors say to one another and to the public in their efforts to generate and legitimize a policy programme'.

She identifies two 'dimensions' of discourse, ideational and interactive. The 'ideational' function of discourse both elaborates a policy's appropriateness and necessity, and legitimates it by relating it to national values. Hence, the discursive justification for a particular policy would aim at indicating its relevance, applicability, and coherence, but may also appeal to particular ideological commitments such as 'fairness', 'solidarity' or 'freedom'. In practice, however, these different 'ideational' elements of discourse are difficult to separate from each other, since normative prescription (what ought to be) is often difficult to separate from description and analysis (what is) (Schmidt, 2010).

The ideational elements of discourse can be boiled down into politicians' evocative 'soundbites', which attempt to demonstrate both the appropriateness and necessity of a particular policy, and its ideological attractions. A specific example comes from the former British Prime Minister Margaret Thatcher's neoliberal policy discourse. Thatcher combined pronouncements on macroeconomic issues, such as the relative benefits of monetarism when compared with neo-Keynesianism, with stories about the merits of hard work, thrift and family budget-keeping by British housewives (*ibid.*: 215). Another example comes from the British leader Tony Blair's description of social security as a 'hand up not a hand out', conveying both the broad thrust of workfare policy and the idea of mutual responsibility underlying it (see Chapter 4).

The other function of discourse identified by Schmidt is what she describes as its 'interactive' dimension. This covers the coordinating role played by discourse in establishing a shared set of meanings and understandings for policy-makers; essentially, a shared policy language (Schmidt, 2002b: 232). Thus, discourse can be viewed as offering a series of 'recipes for operating in reality' (*ibid.*: 215) which simplify the policy context and provide a model for how its different elements relate to each other. An example of this 'interactive' function of discourse is found, she claims, in the 'social market economy' discourse within Germany. This discourse privileges policy solutions which recognize the role of social partners (trade unions and business), and which tread a 'middle road' between socialism and capitalism. The '*dirigisme*' approach in France also serves an 'interactive' function, privileging state capitalist approaches to economic organization.

For Schmidt, discourse, and the ideas conveyed by it, can independently exercise pressure on policy-makers. It can, for example, 'chart new institutional paths instead of simply following old ones' (*ibid.*: 212), and thus be more than simply 'cheap talk' (*ibid.*: 252) which is assimilable to interests or institutions. However, the extent to which ideas can exert independent influence is, for Schmidt, dependent on the institutional context. Where political power is concentrated in a single actor, such as the centralized UK executive, for example, the most important type of discourse is that comprising the executive's communications with the public. The impact of this discourse can then be gauged in the public response to policy proposals, such as the degree of protests or quiescence, election results, and shifts in public opinion.

In contrast, where power is shared between actors, such as within the German federal context, discourse is less important at a communicative level than a coordinative one. The impact of discourse can then be ascertained in whether policy actors actually agree with each other. This can be uncovered through researching the content of negotiations between different policy actors, and the opinions of policy elites.

Schmidt argues that, where policy-making elites do not use discourse to communicate the justification for reform *and* to coordinate policy change with other actors, policy failure is likely to result. Hence, she argues that economic policy reform in the UK was successful, because a communicative discourse was established early on which conveyed to the public both the necessity and the appropriateness of policy change in relation to national values. In contrast, in France, whose centralized executive required public support for the enactment of reform, the discourse failed to stress the appropriateness of reform in relation to national values, referring only to its necessity, often linking this only to external pressures. As a result, Schmidt argues, it was more difficult for French policy-makers to push through reforming policies in the economic arena.

Again, given the different rhetorics accompanying responses to the financial crisis, there is a need for greater research in this area. One interesting attempt to consider the interaction between institutions and ideas comes from an analysis of the collapse of the US subprime mortgage market. Gieve and Provost (2012) suggest that the lack of coordination between the ideas driving macroeconomic and regulatory policy led to different approaches being adopted by central banks and regulators. Whilst central banks were driven by the perceived need to restrain inflation, regulators attempted to correct the worst market failures, but otherwise to avoid intervention. This, in turn, led to a lack of coordinatory capacity when it was needed most.

Groups promoting ideas

Two other analytical approaches combine an independent role for ideas with an awareness of the institutional and political context: Paul Sabatier's notion of 'policy advocacy coalitions', and Kingdon's 'agenda-setting' theory.

Paul Sabatier's approach to policy-learning is referred to in Chapter 11 on policy transfer. Sabatier (1987) delineates different 'cores' of beliefs, and suggests that the 'near' or 'outer' core consists in commitment to specific policies, whilst the 'deep core' concerns fundamental policy goals which will change far less frequently.

The process of policy-making can then be understood as 'a competition between coalitions of causes, each one being constituted of actors coming from a multitude of institutions (leaders of interest groups, administrative official agencies, legislators, researchers, and journalists) which share a system of beliefs linked to public action and who engage in a concerted effort to translate the elements of their system of beliefs into a public policy' (Sabatier and Schlager, 2000: 227).

Ultimately, Sabatier's approach is pluralist, suggesting that different groups will share differing belief systems, and that the results of competition between them will reflect group dynamics which cannot be entirely reduced to their differing interests (Sabatier, 1993; see also Schlager, 1995).

Kingdon's approach to agenda setting also suggests that different ideas will be promoted by different groups. He argues that for every policy area, a 'policy stream' will exist, comprising the relevant 'policy community' (typically composed of academic experts, policy 'wonks' and civil servants). Groups within the 'policy community' will advocate particular policy proposals, even where there is no 'policy problem' to be solved. Instead, they create a 'policy primeval soup' (Kingdon, 1995: 117) composed of different policy ideas and proposals, as well as different conceptualizations of policy problems. Particular ideas make it onto the agenda when the 'policy stream' overlaps with the 'problem' and 'political' streams. Any idea must, therefore, be able to 'fit' with a policy problem and be politically acceptable and supported, in order to make it on to the agenda. Highly complex ideas, for example, may 'fit' a policy problem perfectly, but will be unlikely to garner political support because they are difficult to communicate to the public. An example of this comes from Bill Clinton's Health Security proposal of 1993, which appeared technically feasible but politically impossible to communicate simply (Béland, 2005: 12). As a result, for Kingdon, the intrinsic features of ideas are important as well as their political and technical context.

When do ideas change?

Although ideas have often, as discussed, been adduced to explain change within institutionalist and interest-based theories, the question remains of how ideas themselves are created and change. This issue has perhaps been given less consideration within the comparative literature, with little detailed research existing into how ideational frameworks change over time.

Nonetheless, two broad approaches can be discerned: one privileging 'external' influences on ideas, the other 'internal'.

First, and as discussed at length in Chapter 11, ideas about policy can be transferred from jurisdiction to jurisdiction by policy entrepreneurs, including representatives of international organizations, experts, and 'exporting' countries' governments. At a deeper level, populations' ideational preferences may be shaped by their foreign origins. Hence, Lightman and Riches (2009: 47) speculate that the Canadian province of Alberta appears to support more market-based approaches to policy-making partly due to the high numbers of US immigrants in that state, whereas neighbouring Saskatchewan, originally settled by Europeans, is more social democratic, whilst Quebec's policy-making indicates the legacies of an initially strong Church influence due to its more religious population.

Ideas within any particular nation can, then, change when new perspectives are adopted from other countries. Ideas may also change in response to external pressures. Such pressures, particularly if they are very intense ('exogenous shocks'), may result in the intensifying or buttressing of existing ideas, just as much as leading to change. For example, military and economic threats from the USA appear, if anything, to have entrenched support for revolutionary nationalism in Cuba, rather than reduced it. Crises may entrench old orthodoxies rather than lead to their being replaced (Legro, 2000: 419).

Legro argues that external pressures will lead to ideational change when collective expectations, generated by collective ideas, are challenged, and when this is coupled with experience of critical events. Such challenges are far more likely to result in ideational change where collective expectations appear negatively contradicted. An example arguably comes from the Great Depression, which appeared to contradict expectations about the outcomes of protectionism. As Legro (2000: 432) puts it, 'losses are much more likely than comparable gains to trigger aggregation processes that lead to change'. Ideas are likely to remain stable in the absence of negative consequences, reflecting the saying 'if it ain't broke, don't fix it', whilst they are likely to change rapidly following failure, due to the widespread impulse to 'do something!'.

As mentioned, another approach suggests that 'internal' influences within a society may impact upon particular ideas. National 'values' have frequently been adduced to explain policy-making in a variety of areas (see Schmidt (2002b), for a discussion). The genesis and modification of these values is, however, perhaps more difficult to explain. One particularly contentious debate comes from the field of ideas about welfare policy, where strong views abound, ranging from the position that the 'welfare state' is the largest 'threat' to national security (for a popular American expression of this view, see Friedman and Friedman, 1984: 73), to the idea that welfare states preserve social solidarity (as applies, arguably, in Scandinavia; see Cox, 2004). One attempt to explain

---

BOX 9.2   Larsen's examination of how welfare regimes influence public support

By combining data from the World Values Survey with that on welfare expenditure and coverage, Larsen (2008) challenges traditional views on the origins of attitudes concerning welfare systems.

Larsen argues that different types of welfare and labour market regimes lead to, and suppress, different attitudes towards welfare. For example, in 'selective' (or 'liberal') welfare regimes (see Chapter 4 for a full description), debate naturally tends to focus on 'deservingness', since it is easy to identify beneficiaries through means-testing, and to contrast what they 'get' with non-recipients' contributions to the costs of welfare. On the contrary, in social democratic regimes, it is difficult to work out exactly how much different individuals 'get' from welfare, given the relative generosity of provision and the lack of means-testing.

Similarly, in liberal regimes, individuals tend to assume that people are responsible for their employment status and pay, due to the lack of centralized bargaining and relative flexibility of the labour market. This is not the case in conservative regimes, where most people recognize the rigidity of the labour market. This leads to differential attitudes about the extent to which the low-paid and unemployed are 'at fault' for their own situation. Despite the fact that, in the USA (a liberal regime) individuals generally have egalitarian attitudes, this does not extend to the very bottom of the income distribution, towards which individuals often have punitive attitudes.

---

the origins of such views towards welfare policy comes from David Goodhardt (2004), who argued that support for encompassing welfare provision was dependent on feelings of social solidarity, which themselves were dependent on cultural homogeneity. As a result, he argued, societies which were highly culturally homogeneous would tend to be more committed to welfare provision than those which were more diverse. There is, however, little empirical evidence correlating cultural diversity with levels of welfare spending (Banting and Kymlicka, 2007). An alternative view (see Box 9.2) suggests that ideas about welfare spending are shaped by the institutional context.

Conclusion

This chapter has briefly examined the rather bewildering sweep of ideas-based approaches to public policy analysis. Whilst policy design, policy learning and policy-oriented research all assume that decision-makers' ideas about policies are the determining factor when explaining policy development, policy framing approaches are more focused on how particular issues are defined as problems, both by society and political leaders, and how these problems can come to be understood in very specific ways. Interpretivism focuses on social definitions of problems as ideational traditions, and examines how these traditions change over time. Postmodernism, with its radical rejection of the notion that context can impact on policy ideas, suggests that such policy ideas will often be ephemeral and highly changeable over time.

As discussed, numerous attempts have been made to synthesize a focus on ideas with concern for other causal factors, such as interests and institutions. For some authors, ideas are functional only to the extent that they support particular interests; for others, the concept of interest is itself meaningless without ideas giving interest its content. Whilst institutions may facilitate the influence of particular policy ideas, authors differ over whether ideas can have any independent explanatory power within institutionalist accounts, or whether their impact will always depend on other factors. Finally, as with institutionalist accounts, ideas-based approaches perhaps suffer from the fact that they explain policy stability better than they explain change. Change in ideas can come from external pressures and, perhaps, internal societal characteristics, although the origins and sources of change in ideas are highly contentious.

Summary

❏ Traditional approaches to the analysis of public policy – such as policy design and policy-oriented research, as well as the field of policy learning – allocate considerable importance to policy ideas.

❏ Studies of policy framing and issue attention focus on how ideas (amongst other factors) determine how particular issues become conceptualized as policy 'problems' or otherwise to differing extents in different nations.

❏ Interpretivism and postmodernism both suggest that ideas uniquely determine policy, but their conception of the permanence of different types of ideas differs.

❏ In practice, rather than focusing uniquely on ideas, many comparative public policy analyses have combined ideas with the study of interests (suggesting that ideas are functional to the pursuit of interests, or that ideas give content to interests); institutions (with institutions promoting particular ideas); and groups (with, again, some groups promoting particular ideas).

❏ A perennial question for comparative public policy analysts who are focused on ideas concerns the situations under which policy-related ideas change or remain stable across different countries.

Chapter 10

Institutions and Public Policies

Institutions form the context for individual political actors' interactions with each other; provide stability for policy-making; and constrain individuals' behaviour (Hassenteufel, 2008: 119). Institutions mediate the impact of other factors such as ideas and interests, provide a 'strategic context in which political actors make their choices', and lead to 'patterns' in public policy-making (Immergut, 1992: 239).

The study of institutions has dominated analyses of public policy, not least since the realm of public policy is generally 'saturated with rules, conventions and norms' (Palier and Surel, 2005: 10). Nonetheless, it is arguable that institutional analysis has become, if anything, even more important since the 1980s. This can be linked both to progress in state-building and democratization, and to the limits of non-institutionalist forms of analysis. First, as the role of states grew through the twentieth century, so did the penetration of institutions into the economy and society. As March and Olsen (1984: 734) put it, 'social, political, and economic institutions have become larger, considerably more complex and resourceful, and prima facie more important to collective life'. In addition, whilst during the first half of the twentieth century many studies focused on the prospects for democratization in different nations, from the 1960s onwards the plethora of democratic structures evident within what is now a large number of democratic countries invites more detailed institutional analysis than simply considering shifts from non-democracy to democracy.

Second, previously influential non-institutionalist approaches to explaining public policy have arguably been found wanting. Marxist approaches which suggested that class interests determined policy appeared undermined by the considerable variety of welfare state forms in countries which shared similar class structures. Similarly, functionalist approaches appeared unable to explain why so many different institutional responses had developed to deal with apparently similar problems in different countries (Skocpol, 1985: 4). Whilst many such theories were relatively one-dimensional, focusing on a single variable to explain policy difference (such as class), institutional analyses were more subtle, focusing instead 'on illuminating how different variables are linked' (Thelen and Steinmo, 1992: 13).

What are institutions?

As might be expected, '[j]ust where to draw the line on what counts as an institution is a matter of some controversy in the literature' (*ibid*.: 2). This is not least because the different institutionalist approaches all emphasize different institutional elements, and offer definitions which are more or less permissive. However, all definitions share some recognition of institutions as stable or regular in some way. Hence, the institutional economist Douglass North (1986: 231) describes institutions as '*regularities* in repetitive interactions . . . customs and rules that provide a set of incentives and disincentives for individuals' (emphasis added). A further definition from the same intellectual lineage suggests, again, that institutions constitute governance *structures*: social arrangements which are designed to minimize transaction costs (Williamson, 1985).

For the rational choice institutionalist William H. Riker (1980), institutions can be defined as 'temporarily *congealed* tastes'. Shepsle (1986: 74), also coming from a rational choice approach, suggests that they constitute 'ex ante agreements about a *structure* of cooperation' that 'economize on transaction costs, reduce opportunism and other forms of agency 'slippage', and thereby enhance the prospects of gains through cooperation' (emphasis added). Hall and Taylor's definition of historical institutionalism also refers to '*structures*' ('the formal or informal procedures, routines, norms and conventions embedded in the organizational structure of the polity or political economy'), whilst their definition of sociological institutionalism consists in *structures* plus ideational *frameworks* – 'not just formal rules, procedures or norms but the symbol systems, cognitive scripts, and moral templates that provide the 'frames of meaning' guiding human action' (Hall and Taylor, 1996: 938, 947). To summarize, definitions of institutions tend to stress their (at least temporarily) constraining, and potentially enabling, nature.

Formal and informal institutions

Most modern definitions also stress the fact that institutions can comprise informal as well as formal elements, thus moving beyond more traditional approaches which focused exclusively on written sets of rules and procedures. Informal rules can, of course, be highly significant. Whilst Britain's constitution is at least partly informal (with only some elements of it being written), certain written constitutions have arguably remained 'paper-based' only, with informal processes preventing their implementation – such as the Japanese constitution, arguably the most liberal in the world, but whose provisions on women's rights have arguably been only partially implemented (Mackie, 1988).

Informal procedures and rules may be extensive in their impact, despite their informality. For example, informal rules were used for the effective rationing of welfare state resources on a racially discriminatory basis during the 1950s and 1960s in Britain (Jacobs, 1985). As another example, it has been claimed that labour markets are effectively 'gendered' institutions (Elson, 1999), given the existence of many (mainly informal) rules and procedures that discriminate against women. At the same time, formal rules designed to aid women in the workplace can, in practice, inhibit their participation (such as bans on night work) (Anker and Hein, 1985; Tzannatos, 1999).

In addition, 'formal' rules may be passed but never implemented. For example, this applied to the Australian National Insurance Act of 1938, which was never enacted, 'ostensibly because of concern about finances that would be needed for the Second World War effort' (Bryson and Verity, 2009: 68). Similarly, despite a joint agreement on health funding having been concluded between the central and regional governments in Italy in 2001, for a number of years ministers consistently failed to identify the part of the VAT take which would be provided to the individual regions, resulting in policy deadlock (Fargion, 2009: 184–5).

Finally, apparently 'formal' institutions may lay dormant for decades before being recaptured by certain groups of actors in subsequent years, a topic considered at greater length in Box 10.2. An interesting example of this comes from New Zealand, where the Treaty of Waitangi was concluded between the British Crown and some Maori tribal chiefs in the mid-1800s, but largely ignored as a legal document until the mid-1980s, when it began to receive recognition as a 'founding document' for New Zealand 'as a bicultural state', and as a basis for transferring assets to the Maori based on historical claims (Davey and Grey, 2009: 88–9).

Institution-based approaches to explaining public policy

Comparative analyses of governing institutions

Institutionalist analyses within the field of public policy have focused on a variety of different institutions. Some focus almost uniquely on formal, overtly 'political', institutions – with Considine (2005), for example, setting out electoral systems, voting systems, election campaigns, executive and legislative institutions, legislative processes and courts and tribunals, bureaucracy, budgets, and interest mediation systems as 'institutions'. Others have stressed 'softer', informal aspects, such as national cultures (Lauth, 2000; Helmke and Levitsky, 2004). Three institutions which have been subject to particularly sustained analysis include the state itself, electural institutions and property institutions.

The state

The core characteristic of the modern democratic state is of course, following Weber (1948a), its ability to use violence legitimately, in addition to its administrative, legal, extractive and coercive capacity. Macro-level theories have characterized the state in different ways, with Marxists arguing it will embody the will of the class holding the means of production, pluralists suggesting it is a 'black box' within which competing interest groups' claims are aggregated and mediated, and functionalists suggesting that it performs those activities necessary to the production and maintenance of order. As mentioned, the perceived explanatory purchase of these theories has diminished, not least due to the variety of state forms arising within democratic capitalist nations. As a result, states have increasingly come to be viewed as institutions 'whose independent efforts may need to be taken more seriously than heretofore in accounting for policy making and social change' (Skocpol, 1985: 21).

A variety of approaches have focused on states as institutions which not only mediate interests, but potentially also impact on policy-making and help explain differences across countries. One such approach is the policy learning perspective, examined in Chapter 11. This suggests that state actors can exercise autonomy and draw on both positive and negative lessons from other jurisdictions, when it comes to the design of new policies (and the reform of old ones). Another state-based approach attempts to identify the 'strength' of states. In political economy, 'strength' has been assessed in relation to states' ability to stimulate and shape economic growth (Dyson and Wilks, 1983), whilst within international relations, states' abilities to shape both economic and societal characteristics have been examined (Krasner, 1978).

In a contrasting approach, Nettl suggests that perceived 'stateness' will depend on how sovereignty is conceptualized in the country concerned. For Nettl (1968), any state's capacity will reside in a variety of factors, including the degree to which power is institutionalized, the extent to which the state is autonomous from private groups, the cultural resonance of the state, and the autonomy of the state at an international level. Hence, for example, for Americans in the USA 'stateness' may reside in the constitution and legal apparatus, whilst for continental Europeans it may be more closely identified with central bureaucratic institutions.

Yet another branch of scholarship examines the process of state-building in different countries – considering, for example, the relationship between state requirements for trained personnel and obedient populations, and the development of national education systems (Green, 1990: 309). One interesting perspective has stressed the contingency of states as territorially bounded, following a careful analysis of the impact of map-making on inter-state relations (see Box 10.1).

BOX 10.1 Branch on mapping the sovereign state

In a fascinating analysis, Branch indicates how the process of map production in late medieval Europe promoted, unwittingly, the current model of the territorially sovereign state. Branch traced the development of maps' treatment of territory, showing how early maps illustrated authority as relating to specific places (e.g. towns, forts and so on) rather than territories. During the time of the production of '*mappa mundi*', for example, a variety of overlapping zones of authority existed, involving 'city-states, monarchies, the papacy, corporate groups, and city-leagues' (Branch, 2011: 9).

Branch indicates how maps were traditionally produced for commercial and decorative purposes, but that contingent aspects of these slowly began to shape powerful actors' conceptions of authority. For example, those buying maps liked them to be in colour, increasing their decorative value – which spurred cartographers on to colour in land masses which 'belonged' to different national groups, before any definitive basis existed for these attributions.

As 'people came to envision the world increasingly in terms of . . . maps, ideas about political authority that were not depicted in them – or that could not be depicted in them – lost their normative basis and were negated and eliminated as acceptable foundations for political authority' (*ibid.*: 15).

Electoral institutions

Another focus for institutionalist analysis has been the interaction between electoral institutions and approaches to policy-making. This matter has already been considered in the discussion of 'policy styles' in Chapter 2. To summarize, this approach suggests that institutional characteristics, in combination with other features, lead actors to tend to rely on particular decision-making routines; these might be, for example, politically polarized and conflictual, or more consensual, reflecting their electoral systems and other political characteristics (see Lijphart, 1984).

For Richardson *et al.* (1982), most nations in Western Europe could be viewed as adopting a relatively consensual, increasingly reactive policy style, independent of the policy sector under examination. In a more fine-grained and recent analysis, Cairney applied this approach to one policy sector, decision-making in mental health, in two institutional contexts, the UK as a whole and Scotland. He suggested that the differing institutional contexts explained the apparently more consensual approach in Scotland compared with the more conflict-ridden approach in the UK, but that whilst some contextual variables produced systematic, long-term differences (such as the smaller size of government), others only had an impact over the short-term (such as during the period at the start of devolution, when actors were keen to ensure that the new institutional context, devolution, 'worked') (Cairney, 2009: 683).

Another attempt to consider the impact of different electoral systems on policy-making comes from Fiona McGillivray's (2004) examination of trade policy. McGillivray's starting point is the 'puzzle' of variation in which industries are protected by different governments, even where the industries concerned are of a similar size and employ similar numbers of people in the countries concerned. She argues that trade policy is shaped heavily by the interests of the workers involved in the industries concerned, but that how it is affected in this way depends on the institutional structure – specifically, on the electoral rule.

McGillivray's example of the British cutlery industry offers a case in point (see Chapter 3). For many years, British cutlery cost one third as much as it would have done without any protection. This contrasted with the situation in both Germany and the USA, where relatively little assistance was provided to this industry. McGillivray argued that the significant support given to the British cutlery industry reflected its electoral significance, which rested on the electoral rule used in the UK. In single-member plurality systems, as in Britain, winning 'marginal' (finely-balanced) seats is essential in order to capture enough representatives to form a government. The cutlery industry covered 'a slew of crucial marginal seats', at least during the 1960s, 1970s and 1980s. Once all seats in Sheffield became 'safe' Labour seats, protection was reduced (the seats later became a mixture of Liberal Democrat and Labour). McGillivray then indicates how different electoral rules, such as Germany's more proportional system and the US's weak party majoritarian system could help explain why specific industries in those nations were subject to significantly higher levels of protection than others.

Property institutions

Another type of institution which has received sustained attention from comparative analysts, particularly from the 2000s onwards, is that of property rights. Acemoglu *et al.* (2001) and Acemoglu and Johnson (2003) have investigated, in detail and over a number of years, the impact of property institutions on political institutions. This has been in order to explain a particular puzzle: why, in comparison with nations with fewer natural resources, nations with significant natural resources are frequently subject to undemocratic rule and remain relatively poor. They explain this by examining differences in the colonial institutions imposed on developing countries by different groups of European colonizers. These colonial institutions were of two types: 'extractive' and 'protective'.

Extractive institutions were in place in the Belgian Congo, in slave plantations in the Caribbean and in forced labour systems in the mines of Central America. These institutions failed to protect the property rights of the local population, who were controlled by a relatively small number of elite actors. For Acemoglu *et al*. (2001), the lack of property rights for the local population led to a situation where political contestation became focused around the extraction of mineral and natural wealth – a pattern which continued in many countries, even following decolonization. For the elites concerned, in many cases their wealth was entirely contingent on their exploitation of the local population – as with, for example, Caribbean plantation owners' dependence on slaves. A different situation existed in colonies where the private property of domestic populations was protected, as in Australia, Canada, Botswana, the USA and New Zealand. In these cases, settler societies' property rights were generally protected (if not, often, those of the indigenous population), and political contestation tended to be structured not just around the extraction of mineral and natural wealth, but also wider questions of identity, ideology and interest.

Acemoglu *et al*.'s approach has been subject to criticism (Olsson, 2004). Some have suggested, for example, that alternative variables can help explain the political instability and lack of democracy within resource-rich regimes, beyond elites' tendencies to focus on extracting resources for themselves. For example, many types of natural resource extraction rely heavily on migrant labour, with these labourers boosting the power of the non-elite, and leading to increased pressures on elites for financial compensation (from resource rents) in lieu of democratization (Bearce and Hutnick, 2011).

Nonetheless, the 'resource curse' argument links property rights to the operation of the state in an innovative and thought-provoking way. Importantly, it indicates that not only the ability to enforce property rights, but also their scope can differ between countries. A particularly interesting modern example of this comes from Singapore, where property rights have been expanded to cover activities which would not be classified as such in other countries. In numerous countries, individuals and companies are required to obtain permits before they can produce pollution, broadcast through the airwaves, or fish endangered species, for example. In Singapore, individuals also need to purchase permission to buy a new car, with the resultant 'Certificate of Entitlement' only obtainable through an auction organized by the government (Howlett and Ramesh, 2003: 99).

Varieties of institutionalist analysis

A variety of analytical approaches have developed to study institutions from the state to electoral and property institutions and beyond. The following sections attempt to separate out these different broad approaches to explaining the impact of institutions on policy-making. It should be borne in mind that many different classifications are used, and that the different approaches can, in many circumstances, be complementary (see Hall and Taylor, 1996). Each of the three most popular institutionalist approaches in comparative public policy – historical, sociological and rational choice institutionalism – acknowledges that the study of institutions often needs to go beyond how they are 'formally' described in written legislation or procedures. At the same time, however, it is arguable that the various institutionalisms are 'united by little but a common skepticism toward atomistic accounts of social processes and a common conviction that institutional arrangements and social processes matter' (Powell and DiMaggio, 1991: 3). Finally, 'discursive institutionalism', which links discourse to institutional structures, has been described as the 'newest "new institutionalism"' (Schmidt, 2008). However, this type of 'institutionalism' was considered in Chapter 9, due to its focus on ideas as a potentially explanatory variable in accounting for policy change, so will not be considered again here.

Historical institutionalism
The core contention of historical institutionalists is that decisions taken at the formation of an institution shape its trajectory in a path dependent way, constraining future policy options. This is because institutions inflate or decrease the financial and political costs, and the perceived feasibility, of different policy options.

For example, institutions can increase or reduce the power resources enjoyed by different groups, either facilitating or hindering their ability to affect decision-making processes. As Genschel (1997: 47) puts it, institutions 'define what actors in certain situations are prohibited to do, and what they are allowed to do. They allocate information, opportunities, and restrictions, and in this way influence the distribution of power and collective problem solving capacity of a society'.

This helps explain why governments have, in some cases, found it very difficult to change policies, particularly in areas involving significant (re)distribution. Pierson (1994) suggests, for example, that policy change, or lack of it, can be explained with reference to the institutionalized pressures facing reform-minded politicians (see Chapter 8). Even in the absence of strong unions and centre-left parties, politicians may hesitate to cut policies which are popular because of the number and political power of their beneficiaries. As a result, Pierson suggests that policy change is most likely to occur when potential opposing coalitions can be reduced in power. This may occur through obfuscation (where changes are too technical and complex for beneficiaries to realize their likely impact); division (where one group of beneficiaries is split off from another, such as young unemployment benefit claimants from older ones, or men from women); or compensation (where new benefits are provided elsewhere for some portion of the beneficiaries) (*ibid.*: 30).

Arguably, the relative success of reform in the field of unemployment benefit (with a transient, difficult to identify and politically weak constituency) compared with relative failure in the field of pensions (with a permanent, easily identifiable and politically strong constituency) appears to confirm Pierson's approach. Nonetheless, it has been subject to criticisms from Ross (2008), who has argued that 'ageing institutions have not strengthened through increasing returns over the past two decades' – not all groups of recipients from welfare policies have necessarily coalesced into the types of politically-organized conservative constituencies that Pierson predicts.

Second, as well as institutions potentially constraining individuals in their pursuit of their own interests, historical institutionalists argue that they can also shape those very interests. This is because institutions establish certain responsibilities and expectations amongst actors. Institutions can therefore be described as both formal and 'relational', since they shape political interactions (Thelen and Steinmo, 1992: 6; see also Box 10.2).

These insights have been applied to a range of different actors, both individual and collective. Within international relations, for example, a historical variant of institutionalism has developed which seeks to explain why countries often appear to persist as members of international organizations, even though at any one time this may not appear to be in their national interest. Even if such countries may feel that participating in the international organization concerned is in their long-term interest, this does not explain why particular institutional designs have been implemented. Within this context, historical approaches have noted the importance of 'sunk costs, vested interests' and the lack of availability of other 'realistic' options, as reasons for the maintenance of existing institutions (Powell and DiMaggio, 1991: 7). Furthermore, such scholars acknowledge that institutions may themselves shape the preferences and power of national actors (see Keohane, 1984), as well as merely constituting venues where these preferences and power resources play out (as suggested by the traditional 'realist' conception).

Beyond the broad emphases of historical institutionalist analyses, different historical institutionalists have prioritized different institutional elements as being more or less important in shaping policy-making. Whilst it is arguable that most historical institutionalists would agree that certain political institutions are likely to exert an influence on public policies – such as the 'rules of electoral competition; structure of party systems; relations among various branches of government; [and] structure and organization of economic actors like trade unions' (Thelen and Steinmo, 1992: 2), there is less agreement about whether other organizations or procedures should be viewed as 'institutional'.

BOX 10.2 Streeck and Thelen on incremental institutional change

An interesting variant of historical institutionalism has focused on institutions' roles as facilitators, as well as brakes, on policy change. Kathleen Thelen, Wolfgang Streeck and others argue that, in practice, policy change often occurs not due to radical institutional change, but to much slower changes which are often impelled by actors within the institutions themselves.

First, 'traditional arrangements' can be 'discredited or pushed to the side in favour of new institutions and associated behavioural logics' – what they describe as 'displacement' (Streek and Thelen, 2005: 20). These new institutions may result from the 'reactivation' or 'rediscovery' of existing, if defunct, historical institutional examples; or, alternatively, from the 'invasion' of institutions from other countries. An example of the former comes from the 'rediscovery' of the Treaty of Waitangi in New Zealand. An example of the latter comes from the intrusion of 'Anglo-Saxon' approaches into the German banking sector, diluting the hold of the 'patient capital' model (Deeg, 2005).

Second, new institutions can be grafted onto old ones such that they undermine them progressively, but without the old institutions being abolished – what is known as 'layering'. The 'classic' example of this comes from recent attempts to increase provision of private pensions, which have often been seen as indirectly undermining older universal systems (Hacker, 2005).

Third, institutions can be 'converted'; that is, they can be captured by new groups of actors, and/or they can be 'redirected to new goals, functions, or purposes' (Streek and Thelen, 2005: 26). Two interesting examples of the latter come from the field of security policy in the UK. First, in 2007 the UK Crown Prosecution Service used Health and Safety legislation to successfully prosecute the London police, following the shooting and killing of an innocent Brazilian man during a bungled anti-terrorist operation. The 1974 health and safety legislation that was used was intended to protect workers from unscrupulous employers, yet it was used – successfully – in relation to a completely different issue. As another example, in 2008 the UK government used its 2001 Anti-Terrorism, Crime and Security Act to freeze the UK-based assets of the Icelandic bank Landsbanki, the parent bank of the bankrupted bank Icesave, which had a number of UK-based investors. The move was intended to lead to UK investors being compensated and not passed over in favour of Landsbanki's domestic investors. Again, while the rules used here were initially intended to counter terrorism and organized crime, their use against a democratic, 'friendly' country was initially unanticipated.

Finally, institutions can, Streeck and Thelen suggest, become 'exhausted', and as a result, slowly lose their viability. This can occur as they gradually become less and less congruent with their changing context. An example comes from the field of German early retirement policies. These were functional in a context of full employment, but with increasing levels of long-term unemployment and the economic dislocation of reunification, these policies came to be used to facilitate restructuring, a short-term fix which, over the long term, potentially reduced funds available for job creation (Trampusch, 2005).

It is arguable, for example, that the class and economic structures could qualify as 'institutions', to the extent that they both constrain and enable individuals' behaviour, and influence their estimation of their own preferences. Nonetheless, neither structure is generally subjected to historical institutionalist analysis. Instead, analysts often examine the effects of more 'meso-level' structures on macro-structures, such as class and the economic system. An example of this comes from Karl Polanyi's work on the 'great transformation' (2001 [1944]) – the creation of a modern, competitive, capitalist economy. Thelen and Steinmo (1992: 11) detail how Polanyi uses case studies of meso-level processes, such as the rise and demise of the Speenhamland system, as a means to explicate the development of modern capitalism. More recently, a similar approach was adopted by Caporaso and Tarrow (2009), who suggest that rather than markets becoming 'disembedded' from national state structures as a result of Europeanization, decisions of the European Court of Justice have led to changes in domestic social and political arrangements, but not their abolition or redundancy.

However, the category of historical institutionalism should not be viewed as homogeneous. Hall and Taylor (1996) distinguish between a 'calculus' and a 'cultural' approach within historical institutionalism. Theorists following the 'calculus' approach would suggest that institutions will affect individual action by altering the expectations an actor has about the actions that others are likely to take in response. This approach to explaining the impact of institutions on individuals' behaviour is very succinct and clear, but perhaps too parsimonious. A more expansive view comes from theorists adopting the 'cultural' approach, who would argue that institutions not only provide strategically useful information (about the likely responses of other actors), but also affect the very identities, self-images and preferences of actors. Of course, this approach, by its very expansiveness, may lack precision, and risks assimilating all influences on behaviour with institutions. A similar criticism has often been made of the second type of institutionalism to be considered here – the 'sociological' variant.

Sociological institutionalism
The sociological institutionalist approach stresses the non-rational and habitual sources of institutional influence. In particular, it argues that actors will often just do what appears 'appropriate' within institutions, rather than necessarily carefully calculating the likely impact of their actions. For example, March and Olsen (1984) separated out the logic of consequence (where individuals decide how to act in accordance with their weighing up of likely outcomes) from the logic of appropriateness (where actors behave in ways perceived to be consistent with the institutions within which they are embedded). For sociological institutionalists,

certain actions are likely to be associated by actors with 'certain situations by rules of appropriateness' (*ibid*.: 741). Individuals will develop an awareness of what is viewed as appropriate through habituation and socialization, learning from others within the institution about appropriate routines of behaviour.

The sociological institutionalist approach is useful for explaining why institutions persist even when they appear to be manifestly inefficient. Actors within those institutions may act in accordance with habit or custom, and shifting away from established routines will come at considerable cognitive cost (Powell and DiMaggio, 1991: 11). This approach can also help to explain why institutional models can differ in their impact from what their designers intended. This is because the intentions of those who create institutions are often ambiguous and part of far wider belief sets that cannot be assimilated easily with the assumptions inherent within rational models of decision-making. Instead, the intentions which motivate institutional design are 'frequently multiple [and] not necessarily consistent', 'often ambiguous', and 'part of a system of values, goals, and attitudes that embeds intention in a structure of other beliefs and aspirations' (March and Olsen, 1989: 65–6).

For sociological institutionalists, symbolism can be as important as rationality, and implicit meanings as important as explicit goals. This approach is part of a broader critique of rationalist models of decision-making, which is also evident in Cohen *et al*.'s (1972) 'garbage can' model of policy-making. According to this model, it is temporal order which determines which policy solutions are put into practice, not how effective they are at dealing with pre-existing problems. Again, within the 'garbage can' model, policies are driven by the logic of appropriateness at the time – not by the 'logic of consequentiality'.

As will be clear, within this sociological variant, institutions are defined far more broadly than simply consisting of formal rules and regulations. As already mentioned, for sociological institutionalists they also comprise 'the symbol systems, cognitive scripts, and moral templates that provide the "frames of meaning" guiding human action' (Hall and Taylor, 1996: 947). A question remains, however, about how persistent such symbols systems, scripts and templates need to be in order for them to become part of institutions, and not merely fleeting routines of thought. How can we decide what is a 'mere convenience', or 'temporary' habit of thought, and what is a 'norm' or 'convention'? Powell and DiMaggio (1991: 9) argue that only those norms which 'take on a rule-like status in social thought and action' should be included – but we can still ask what is 'rule-like' and what is not. The challenge of explaining change within institutionalist analysis is considered in detail in the final section of this chapter.

Rational choice institutionalism

Rational choice institutionalism applies the insights of institutional economics to political questions. As a result, it is necessary, first, to consider the insights derived from institutional economics. Institutional economics in its current most popular form, transaction cost economics, was developed by Oliver Williamson, Douglass North and other economists from initial insights by Ronald Coase (1937, 1960).

For Williamson (1975), one of the most important costs facing firms was that associated with *transactions*. Transaction costs might include, for example, the costs for a company or a consumer of buying a particular product – or, indeed, of selling it. The costs of transactions will increase or decrease according to a number of parameters. These include, first, the frequency of interaction between the different actors involved. More frequent interactions between actors will tend to reduce transaction costs, since relationships will be already developed, and each party will be more attuned to the capacities and requirements of the other. The specificity of what is being bought will add to the gains from frequent interactions, since existing suppliers will be more likely to possess the skills or capital resources required to fulfil requirements. This also, however, increases the potential bargaining power of existing suppliers in relation to buyers. Additionally, sellers will also possess more information about the nature of what they are supplying than buyers will possess, resulting in an asymmetry of information. Due to this asymmetry of information, suppliers may be able to behave opportunistically (e.g. by artificially inflating the cost of what they are supplying).

Williamson argued that institutions were created in situations where they could reduce these costs. The simplest institution, in this connection, is the contract – which reduces some of the transaction costs, and increases certainty between actors. This approach can also be used to explain both 'backward' and 'forward' integration, where the need to reduce transaction costs leads to firms buying out their suppliers or, contrarily, their sellers. In this way, 'hierarchy replaces markets when there are long-term contracts in an uncertain environment and the barriers to entry are reasonably high, because the costs of opportunism are reduced by substituting an authority relationship ('You now work for me') for a contractual one' (Perrow, 1986: 239).

For Douglass North (1990), 'institutions', covering society-wide structures such as property rights and sets of social norms, can be contrasted with 'organizations', the groups of individuals within firms or other organizations whose interactions are shaped by institutions. North accepted that individuals may, in reality, face sets of circumstances different from those assumed by microeconomic models. For example, they may be subject to asymmetries of information and find it difficult to monitor agreements, and thus be faced with considerable transaction costs. North argued that institutions can then help reduce transaction costs and thus increase efficiency.

Despite its simplicity and intuitive attractions, these economic approaches to institutions have been questioned by some, primarily for their allegedly circular nature. Institutional economics suggests that institutions will be created and maintained where they are efficient; that a number of institutions have been created and maintained; and that, therefore, these institutions must be efficient. However, sociological institutionalists such as Powell and DiMaggio (1991: 4) point to the persistence of manifestly inefficient institutions, such as caste systems, and March and Olsen (1989: 169) to delays in introducing metric systems of measurement. Despite the acknowledged inefficiency of imperial systems of measurement (pints, miles, pounds and ounces), and the announcement of a shift to metric measurement by the UK government in the mid-1960s, the UK still uses non-metric measures in some areas. Other allegedly inefficient but persistent systems include the QWERTY keyboard design (Liebowitz and Margolis, 1990). Perrow (1986: 236) thus argues that transaction cost economics merely constitutes an 'efficiency argument for the present state of affairs, as most mainstream economic theories are'.

Furthermore, transaction cost economics have generally been used to explain the creation of coordinating institutions, yet these institutions themselves may entail considerable costs. As Perrow (*ibid.*: 244) notes, '[i]nternal coordinating costs rise when different operations must be combined'. Surveillance costs, for example, do not disappear following forward or backward integration; instead, internal surveillance is required, which can actually be expensive to set in place and operate. Integration can also be a fraught operation, given the different personalities and political factors involved. In conclusion, the transaction costs within hierarchies can be as significant as those within markets (*ibid.*: 245 – which slightly undermines the rationale for integration.

As mentioned, rational choice draws on institutional economics, by viewing institutions in the field of policy-making as solutions to collective action problems. As with institutional economics' prognoses, this approach suggests that collective action problems will arise due to the costs of transactions of 'political exchange' (Powell and Dimaggio, 1991: 5). Such collective action problems occur when a mutually favourable outcome could be provided through joint action, but where the incentives for individuals to shirk are high (Shepsle and Weingast, 1981).

As with institutional economics, rational choice institutionalism can be criticized for its functionalism – that is, for assuming that political institutions exist to solve coordination problems, and thus increase efficiency, when they may not necessarily do so. As with institutional economics, institutions which have supposedly been created to increase efficiency may prove highly inefficient, and it may be easier for actors to work outside rather than within them, in order to achieve their preferences. If this were not the case, then there would never be rapid change in institutions of the type that Wildavsky (1974) describes, when he indicates how certain actors pushed to change the institution of budget-setting in the USA in order to pursue their preferences.

Furthermore, institutions that were purportedly created to deal with a particular coordination problem may have numerous unintended consequences. As Hall and Taylor (1996: 952) argue, 'unintended consequences are ubiquitous in the social world' and, as such, 'one cannot safely deduce origins from consequences'. As already mentioned (see Chapter 8), a good example comes from the history of unemployment insurance systems. Initially, many trade unions pushed for universalist systems when, in practice, these undermined the role of unions over the long term. On the contrary, where insurance systems were put in place – as in Germany, by politicians attempting to stem the power of left-wing movements – these helped, rather than hindered, support for the socialist labour movement by institutionalizing the role of trade unions in welfare provision (van Kersbergen and Manow, 2008: 525; see also Kasza, 2002: 282).

Others have criticized rational choice institutionalists' conception of mechanisms through which interests impact on institutions. The former argue that institutions are created, and operate, to enable actors to fulfil their preferences; hence, actors' preferences are exogeneous to institutions. However, actors' preferences may themselves be shaped by their institutional context – referred to as institutions 'mobilizing bias' (Schattschneider, 1975). Relatedly, institutions may instil habits in actors which have little to do with their preferences. As a result, not only can institutions be viewed as constraints on, or facilitators of, goal-driven behaviour, they can also be seen as inducing habitual behaviour. Hall and Taylor (1996: 951) usefully illustrate this with their discussion of why individuals obey the institution of road safety – in particular, the prohibition of crossing red lights. The vast majority of actors will obey such rules instinctively, even when there is only a very remote chance that their compliance is being monitored. This is difficult to explain using rational choice institutionalism, which would suggest that institutions constrain behaviour only to the extent that this is in actors' own interests.

A final problem arises from what has been described as the 'second-order' difficulty. This suggests that rational choice institutionalists, by arguing that institutions exist to solve collective action problems, simply push explanatory problems back to the time when institutions were created. This is because the very same collective action problems exist in order to create institutions. Often, other factors such as ideas are adduced to help explain the mobilization of individuals to create political institutions but, as Blyth (2003: 696) notes, this opens up 'a Pandora's box of complications' for a theory that is otherwise commendable for its parsimony.

Institutionalist analysis following the financial crisis

To summarize the previous sections, a variety of institutionalist analyses have been developed to consider the impact of formal and informal rules and norms on policy-making and implementation. The plethora of works deriving from these approaches reflect the 'turn' to 'new institutionalist' analyses that characterized much of comparative public policy scholarship in the 1980s and 1990s. Although the 'newness' of the 'new institutionalism' has been disputed (Almond, 1990), the influence of institutionalist analyses on the field of comparative public policy is unquestionable. This appears set to continue, with institutionalist research agendas offering numerous possible avenues for the examination of the financial crisis and the challenges arising from it.

For example, more scholarship is required to help explain how attributes such as 'reputation' (Maor, 2010) and 'legitimacy' are shaped by different national contexts, given that political (electoral) sources of reputation appear to be being downgraded in countries including Greece and Italy, in favour of perceived technical competence and insulation from societal interests.

Is this due to external pressure? Alternatively, have internal pressures also contributed to the change? Some interesting new scholarship has started to consider how internal actors can link with external power coalitions to facilitate change, thus moving beyond traditional distinctions between exogenous and endogenous institutional change (Mahoney and Thelen, 2010). In addition, researchers have begun to explore how actors manipulate developments within international decision-making arena to consolidate or improve their domestic decision-making position (Thatcher, 2007; James, 2010). This literature could usefully be exploited to consider how the financial crisis has been used as an opportunity by groups of domestic actors in some nations, and to consider how they have been able to build coalitions with external actors to alter decision-making structures in their favour.

Institutionalist research is also important at the time of writing, as it may help illuminate some of the limits to collective and coordinated economic decision-making in an increasingly interconnected world. In the wake of the financial crisis, some nations have been able to collaborate on policies which relate uniquely to the operation of government. For example, in December 2011 the European 26 (the EU membership minus the UK) agreed to work towards an intergovernmental treaty including requirements for member states to pass national legislation providing a 'debt brake', limiting the amount of public debt which member states can amass. Democratic governments have, however, proved far less able to coordinate action which affects powerful non-governmental actors. For example, attempts to institute more powerful macro-prudential – or system-wide – regulation have generally broken down.

Some have argued this is due to the inability of governments to overcome powerful vested interests. As such, reformers have been urged to 'think more carefully about political economy issues involved in the implementation of macro-prudential regulation' – that is, about the different economic interests involved (Helleiner, 2011: 570). Again, there is a rich seam of literature in institutionalist research which seeks to explain how collective institutions can be built which spread costs despite the existence of different vested interests, from fields as diverse as welfare (Streeck and Yamamura, 2001) to common pool resource protection (Ostrom, 1990). This could be usefully applied to consider how barriers to collective action might be overcome.

Conclusion

This chapter has provided an overview of the use of institutionalist analyses within comparative public policy. Despite the plethora of definitions available for 'institution', all share the notion that institutions comprise stable structures – either formal and/or informal – that in some way constrain and/or facilitate certain types of behaviour. Institutionalists have been particularly interested in examining the design, operation and impact of different types of states, electoral institutions and property institutions across countries, as well as a wide variety of other institutional forms. The chapter detailed how analysts have generally adopted one of three broad approaches to examining the formation and impact of institutions: historical, sociological or rational choice institutionalism. Historical institutionalism stresses the sunk costs that institutions incur over time, constraining actors' ability to achieve institutional change. In contrast, sociological institutionalists focus on institutions' cultural and symbolic aspects, and how they promote habitual behaviour. Rational choice institutionalists, on the other hand, indicate how institutions can efficiently resolve collective action problems and reduce transaction costs. Institutionalist analyses appear set to continue to dominate the field of comparative public policy, following the financial crisis. New research agendas are considering how institutions provide actors with new opportunities to shape policy, and how collective institutions can be forged in the face of powerful opposing interests.

Summary

❏ Institutions can be conceptualized as formal and informal sets of rules and norms.
❏ Institutionalist comparative public policy has compared the impact of a variety of institutions on policy-making, including different types of state, electoral institutions and property institutions.
❏ There are three main variants of 'new institutionalist' analysis: historical, sociological, and rational choice institutionalism.
❏ Historical institutionalism focuses on how institutions can constrain policy options into the future, through 'path dependence'.
❏ Sociological institutionalism indicates how norms, values and culture have a reflexive relationship with institutions – being both shaped by, and influencing, institutions.
❏ Rational choice institutionalism focuses on institutions' capacity to reduce transaction costs and thus increase efficiency.

Chapter 11

Policy Transfer and Learning

The transfer of public policies from one country or jurisdiction to another has a long lineage. A very early example comes from the sixth century, when representatives of the Japanese court visited China to examine its educational system, apparently resulting in the establishment of the first national Japanese education system (Arnove, 2007: 5). Transfer can also, of course, occur across time, whereby policies which were 'rejected at one period become feasible in another' (King, E., 2007: 24), although this chapter will focus predominantly on transfer between jurisdictions.

Unfortunately, the policy transfer literature is arguably 'overtheorized and underapplied' (Bennet and Howlett, 1992: 288), a feature which is exacerbated by the multiplicity of terms used when discussing policy transfer (policy learning, lesson-drawing, best-practice, and so on). This chapter will examine what 'policy transfer' and, relatedly, 'policy learning' mean; how they relate to other overarching terms, such as 'policy diffusion' and 'convergence'; and how they can be detected. It will then detail problems associated with the attribution of causal connections between apparently similar policies in different countries.

This chapter considers lesson-drawing, best practice and benchmarking as elements of policy learning, and policy learning as analytically separate from policy transfer. Not all policy transfer need involve learning, whilst not all learning need involve policy transfer. This is for three reasons.

First, as will be discussed at length in this chapter, policy transfer can be coercive, involving the imposition of different policy models on governments by other governments or international organizations. As a result, it appears rather strange to describe clearly coerced policy transfer (such as the imposition of the Westminster model on British colonies) as a type of policy 'learning' (as does Rose, 2005). This chapter restricts policy 'learning' to uncoerced adoption (or non-adoption) of policy. At the same time, however, it should be acknowledged that policy learning can be subject to many of the power imbalances that affect coercive policy transfer (Bomberg, 2007: 263). Policy examples tend to be 'taught' by well-resourced actors, and 'learned' by the less powerful – despite the potential for learning in a variety of directions.

Second, policy learning can involve decisions not to adopt particular policies, as well as to adopt them. This is because 'negative lessons' can be discovered through learning, which lead to the abandonment of pre-vious plans (Stone, 2004: 548). It would be difficult to conceive of such 'non-adoption' as a type of 'policy transfer'.

Finally, whilst policy transfer must be undertaken by those who can actually affect and effect policy-making, policy learning can occur amongst those with less decision-making power. As a result, the concept of 'policy transfer' embodies assumptions about the operative agents involved (governments, or bodies empowered by them), which is not the case for 'policy learning' (Stone, 2004).

Both concepts (policy learning and transfer) can be viewed as species of 'diffusion', which encompasses any following of or reaction to another country's policy resulting from coercion, competition, learning or emulation (Simmons *et al.*, 2006; see also Berry and Berry, 1999; Fink, 2011). Diffusion may lead to convergence but, equally, different countries' policies may converge in the absence of cross-national processes (but due to, for example, similar but isolated domestic pres-sures leading to the adoption of similar policy responses). Policy conver-gence can, therefore, constitute the 'end result of a process of policy change over time towards some common point, regardless of the causal processes' (Knill, 2005: 768). Convergence can then be separated into 'weak' convergence, where one country adopts the policy of another country, or 'strong' convergence, when two countries move towards a third policy model (Unger and van Waarden, 1995).

Studies of diffusion tend to focus on adoption patterns across a variety of countries, whilst studies of policy transfer and learning, as we shall see, generally focus on a smaller number of countries and on the process of policy development rather than its effects (Knill, 2005: 766). Hence, for example, studies of diffusion may differentiate between 'early' and 'late' adopters, as with studies of technological diffusion, whereas studies of policy transfer and learning will generally focus more on the meso-level of policy adoption processes.

Why are policies imposed, taught and learned?

Obviously, it only makes sense for policies to be transferred to other jurisdictions, either through coercion or policy learning, if there are similar problems facing policy-makers in different jurisdictions (either political or reputational). As Rose argues, whilst different policies may have different histories, this does not mean they are *sui generis* and cannot be applied elsewhere. Indeed, he argues (Rose, 2005: 18) that '[u]nique programmes are exceptional and often not desired', pointing to the 'hanging chad' problem arising from the American presidential elec-tions of 2000, which resulted only in other governments wanting to learn how to avoid such an outcome in the future, rather than how to copy the new and unique electoral system that the country had instituted for that election.

In practice, few problems occur in one country alone. As is discussed in detail in Chapter 14, comparative analysis can provide a substitute for experimental approaches to policy development, if suitably similar comparators can be found. Comparative analysis can provide policy-makers with alternative policy approaches which may not have been considered domestically, but which may have sound prospects for success in the domestic context. Chapter 1 indicated how analysts from the times of Muhammad As-Saffār and Alexis de Tocqueville have been keen to explore how other nations dealt with problems which were troubling their own nations' polities at the time.

Furthermore, there may be a clear need for policies to be transferred where problems span jurisdictions, and require a coordinated response. As Rose (*ibid.*: 4) argues, many contemporary 'problems of national government are intermestic, combining both international and domestic influences'. This has, clearly, provided much of the rationale for coordinated responses to issues including climate change and international crime.

Policy transfer

Policy transfer studies were originally developed in the USA as a means by which to explain the adoption of policy throughout this federal system (Stone, 2004: 546). Policy transfer can be understood as a process by which 'knowledge about how policies, administrative arrangements, institutions and ideas in one political setting (past or present) is used in the development of policies, administrative arrangements, institutions and ideas in another political setting' (Dolowitz and Marsh, 2000: 5).

There are, broadly, two types of policy transfer: coercive and non-coercive. Coercive transfer refers to the adoption of a particular policy following financial pressure (either the possibility of extra funds, or the threat of removal of funds), or the threat of military, diplomatic or legal action (Rose, 2005: 96). It thus covers the imposition of policies during colonial rule or occupation, as well as situations where democratic nations are required to comply with the rules of institutions of which they are members (such as the EU, European Court of Human Rights, and World Trade Organization – WTO).

Such pressures need not necessarily lead to policy transfer, of course. Strong governments may simply refuse to implement particular policies with which they disagree, with good examples of this coming from France and Germany's evasion of the stipulations of the EU's Stability and Growth Pact (when weaker countries such as Spain had acted to comply with these) (*ibid.*: 97). Weak governments can retain the 'weapons of the weak' (Scott, 1985) – they can simply fail to implement particular policies once monitoring from external forces has ceased (Rose, 2005: 98). In some cases, it may be difficult for governments to resist the imposition of particular policies. An apparent example of this comes from the Structural Adjustment Programmes which were negoti-ated between the World Bank, the IMF and heavily indebted countries during the 1980s and 1990s which faced national default as the only alternative to accepting programmes of widespread policy reform. At the same time, however, the particular policies adopted in each nation appeared to depend both on pressure from international bodies and domestic political considerations – that is, they were shaped, but not entirely determined, by external pressures (Vreeland, 2003).

Non-coercive transfer occurs where policies are introduced which are similar to those in other countries, but without any pressures to do so. This may be because of policy learning (described later in this chapter), but equally it may occur during periods of uncertainty when policy-makers are unsure about the appropriate model to adopt. DiMaggio and Powell (1983) highlighted the importance of uncertainty in their notion of 'mimetic isomorphism', suggesting that policy-makers were, *inter alia*, likely to copy the organizational forms found in other fields where few other guides existed to appropriate policy development and where conditions were highly uncertain. A possible example of this comes from the introduction of New Environmental Policy Instruments, which Jordan *et al*. (2003: 561) suggest have come to be 'fitted fairly randomly into political problems when the opportunities are favourable'. Governments may thus simply 'imitate' the policies of other nations, par-ticularly if those nations are seen as more successful, without this neces-sarily involving 'learning' (see Weyland, 2000). Identifying such non-coercive 'emulation' or 'imitation' can, however, be fraught with methodological difficulties, not least because it assumes a lack of 'perfect rationality' amongst decision-makers (James and Lodge, 2003), which will, for obvious reasons, be difficult to prove.

What is transferred?

A whole variety of features and types of policy can be transferred. These can range from the politics, meanings or ideas surrounding or consti-tuting a particular policy (Levin, 1998) – which could be described as 'soft' transfer, to the 'harder' transfer of particular policy models (Stone, 2004: 558). As studies of EU policy implementation indicate (Knill and Tosun, 2012), the degree to which 'entire' policies are actually trans-ferred can be limited in a context where there is patchy monitoring of implementation and national contexts that vary widely. Indeed, the term 'policy transfer' may be 'misleading' in this regard by suggesting that the process is 'straightforward' (e.g. such as carrying out a money transfer) when, in practice, the process can be highly complex (Page and Mark-Lawson, 2007: 49).

Who transfers?

In its coercive variant, those transferring policy are likely to constitute either other governments (where policies are imposed on conquered governments, or colonies), or international organizations, whose policies may be based on those of one member state but apply to all members. Foreign governments may also, however, be involved in policy transfer during peacetime, albeit only under rather specific conditions. Hence, perhaps the largest 'policy transfer' operation in history occurred with the amalgamation of East Germany (the GDR) with West Germany (the FRG). This necessitated the imposition of 'all FRG legal and social institutions', not to mention political institutions, on the 'eastern part' (Leisering, 2009: 148).

More commonly, particularly in recent years, policy is transferred through international organizations. Jordan *et al.*'s (2003) analysis of the EU suggests that international organizations can play a range of roles in facilitating policy transfer. First, international organizations can, by bringing together member states, 'passively' encourage proximity between different countries' decision-makers and thus encourage policy transfer, without any direct contribution to this from the international organizations themselves. Second, international organizations can actively facilitate policy transfer through creating the conditions 'in which ideas and experience will more quickly diffuse and be transferred across member states', through their 'policy actors and processes'. Third, they may actually harmonize policies across their member states (as with the creation of the Single European Market in the EU). Fourth, international institutions can act entrepreneurially and independently affect member states' policies, leading to convergence. Finally, one way in which international organizations can facilitate policy transfer which is perhaps specific to the EU and other trade-related bodies such as the WTO, concerns their role in promoting 'negative integration', which removes barriers to trade between countries. With the removal of trade barriers, competition between nations is likely to intensify and, with it, the pressures for member states to seek to impose their own domestic regulations on other member states (*ibid.*: 557) through what has been described as 'baptist/bootlegger coalitions' (see Chapter 7).

The mechanisms whereby transnational institutions promote policy transfer and the barriers and facilitators to this are detailed in Chapter 12.

Policy learning

Hall defines the 'social learning' involved when policy-makers learn about policy as a 'deliberate attempt to adjust the goals or techniques of policy in the light of the consequences of past policy and new information so as to better attain the ultimate objects of governance' (Hall, 1993: 278). A less goal-oriented definition comes from Heclo (1974: 306), who defines policy learning as 'a relatively enduring alteration in behaviour that results from experience; usually this alteration is conceptualized as a change in response made in reaction to some perceived stimulus'.

Policy learning assumes that policy-makers will be interested in developments in other countries, as well as past developments in their own nations, as potential examples for emulation (or demonization). Phillips and Ochs identify various stages in policy learning: cross-national attraction (Phillips, 1989; Ochs and Phillips, 2002) instigated by 'impulses' to look abroad including scientific/academic study of foreign examples, popular perceptions of foreign superiority, or politically motivated attempts to manipulate foreign examples; the decision to 'borrow' policy; implementation; and internalization or 'indigenization' (Phillips and Ochs, 2003).

A variety of different 'subspecies' of policy learning can be identified, which may or may not result in the full gamut of activities just delineated (since they may result in decisions not to adopt, as well as to adopt, a particular policy). These subspecies of policy learning include lesson-drawing, best practice and benchmarking.

Varieties of policy learning: lesson-drawing

Richard Rose (1991b, 1993, 2005) has examined the process and practice of lesson-drawing in detail (see also Stone, 1999). For Rose (2005: 3), lesson-drawing enables policy-makers to move beyond trial-and-error based learning developed from their own experience and conjectures about what 'might' happen, towards the direct observation of programmes already in practice in other settings.

Rose (*ibid*.: 80) likens the process of lesson-drawing to reverse engineering, suggesting that policy-makers and analysts first need to create a model of the policy they wish to draw lessons from. For Rose (*ibid*.: 72), any model must identify the relevant laws and regulations, organizations, personnel, and money necessary for a programme to work, the outputs which result from it, the recipients who benefit from these outputs and the overall goal of the programme.

Two qualifications can be made to this approach. First, the rational assumptions underlying the description of lesson-learning provided above – that, for example, it includes a thorough understanding of the various components of any particular policy, its recipients and goals, and so on – may be untenable in all but the most technical and depoliticized of policy-making arenas (Bomberg, 2007: 255). Second, even where policy-makers are able to make close observation of a policy in practice elsewhere to enable the careful construction of a model which they then use to apply the policy to their own country, this model itself is likely to be flawed. This is because it is difficult for observers fully to understand the nature of the processes which they examine – particularly if these are occurring in a different country.

An interesting example demonstrating the impact of constrained information on the success of policy learning comes from the field of the British and US fire services. In 1944, discussions were held between UK and US officials concerning the extent to which the UK's postwar fire service could be improved using ideas from the USA. In the USA at that time there were significantly more fire stations per head than in the UK. The US official leading these discussions attributed this to the differences in humidity in the USA, leading to more fires, and also to the extent of icy and snowy conditions on US roads, making it more difficult for fire services to reach affected homes. The UK official present at these discussions agreed with this assessment. Yet, these discussions made no reference to the fact that in the US there was a considerably greater proportion of wooden dwellings, which considerably heightened the risk of fire. Without this piece of information, both the policy 'teacher' and 'learner' remained ignorant of one of the most significant reasons for higher levels of fire protection in the USA compared with the UK (National Archives, 1944).

Varieties of policy learning: best practice and benchmarking

Best practice and benchmarking depart from lesson-drawing by involving the measurement of different countries' policies against each other (rather than 'merely' dissecting and then copying these policies). In the case of best practice, one specific policy approach is identified, operating in one particular nation, and promoted to others as the most effective. Obviously, this is a highly prescriptive approach to policy learning, resting on the assumption that a specific policy can be isolated and identified as the 'best'. This contrasts with benchmarking, which enables the comparison of different policy approaches with each other, without necessarily normatively labelling any one approach as superior to all others. Some categorization may, however, be involved; by, for example, describing nations as compliant or non-compliant with a particular regime, or as performing well or not so well. As such, governments can engage in benchmarking in order to try and improve their performance not necessarily to the level of the best, but towards a satisfactory level –

what Rose describes as 'satisficing'. As he puts it, 'in order to satisfice, a policy does not have to be a world-beater; it is good enough if its performance is consistent with expectations' (Rose, 2005: 29).

Both best practice and benchmarking are rather 'gentle' methods of policy learning, and may have limited impacts on domestic policy-making. This certainly appears to be the case with the use of both best practice and benchmarking through the EU's 'open method of coordination' (Chalmers and Lodge, 2003). However, if politicized, their impact can be far more significant. As mentioned in Chapter 1, an example of this comes from the Organisation for Economic Co-operation and Development (OECD) PISA studies of educational attainment. Education policy has long been highly politicized in Germany, where different policies towards selection apply in different *Länder*. The results of the 2001 PISA study suggested that, of 'all the nations participating ... Germany had the highest level of correlation between social class and achievement', and an extension to the study to enable comparison between *Länder* suggested considerable variations in educational standards applied across Germany. The PISA study thus intensified 'already polarised' debates about education policy (Turner, 2011: 33).

What is learned?

A general distinction can be made between learning about policy tools, strategies, tactics or 'means', and learning about policy goals or 'ends'. As mentioned in Chapter 9, Peter Hall (1993) suggests that there are three 'orders' of learning. 'First-order learning' involves changes in preferences concerning the 'settings' of existing instruments (e.g. the magnitude of a pension payment) following experience of new approaches. 'Second-order learning' involves reconsideration of the appropriateness of specific instruments (e.g. shifting from favouring a direct pension payment to subsidized meals in day centres as a means of improving the health of poor pensioners). 'Third-order learning' involves altering the perceived goals of policy themselves (e.g. shifting from the promotion of the medicalized 'health' of pensioners towards promoting their independence as individuals). Similarly, for Etheredge and Short (1983: 42) learning enables policy-makers to better differentiate between policy options, organize these options, integrate them and reflect on the principles underlying them.

Paul Sabatier (1987) focuses, not on the distinction between 'means' and 'ends' or 'options' and 'principles' but, instead, between a 'deep core', 'near core' and 'secondary' aspects within policy-makers' belief systems (see Chapter 9). For Sabatier, policy learning involves policy-makers changing their understanding of external circumstances and incorporating this in their belief system, altering the perceived relationships between different elements of their belief systems (e.g. the perceived cause–effect relationship between different concepts), and responding to challenges to their belief systems. As he puts it (*ibid*.: 672), policy-oriented learning consists in 'relatively enduring alterations of thought or behavioural intentions that result from experience and that are concerned with the attainment or revisions of the precepts of one's belief system'.

Certainly, learning can involve the cherry-picking of apparently attractive means to existing 'ends'. An example of this is the introduction of 'proximity talks' to negotiations over Northern Ireland, which enabled simultaneous negotiations to be held in a manner which preserved hostile parties' perceived autonomy. These were introduced to the Northern Ireland context by Dick Spring, who drew on their use in the Dayton peace negotiations over Bosnia (Page and Mark-Lawson, 2007: 58).

However, whilst policy learning may be restricted to one specific process (such as the Northern Irish peace process) it can have a broader impact. Hence, Oliver James suggests that policy learning within the EU has led to substantial change across the UK and Irish core executives, not least in the field of preparations for holding the EU presidency, where UK officials visited Ireland, the Netherlands and Luxembourg to learn from their presidencies, whilst Ireland itself drew lessons from the UK (James, 2010: 826). Another example of learning which has arguably led to considerable institutional change is the creation of elected mayors in local government, a 'fashionable' trend which has spread from the USA to Germany and the UK (Elcock, 2008). This type of learning has been described as 'instrumental', involving learning 'about techniques, policy design, processes or instruments' (Bomberg, 2007).

Policy learning can also occur in a less organized and direct way, through simply demonstrating the feasibility of new policy options. An example comes from the field of private prisons, once deemed an unthinkable policy departure within the UK. However, after extensive publicity was given to the US experience with private prisons, they became a more palatable option for decision-makers (Page and Mark-Lawson, 2007: 58). Whilst New Right policy advocates promoted examples from the USA, the UK (between 1979 and 1997), Canada and New Zealand (Ball, 1998), thinkers on the left have often drawn on the example of the Scandinavian countries, and it was viewed as a possible model for the development of formerly Communist countries (Brown, 2010).

On occasion, this type of policy learning can involve policy-makers revising their opinions about the causal links between different variables. Hence, in relation to criminal justice, a shift from traditional policing methods towards New York-style 'Zero Tolerance' (Jones and Newburn, 2007) arguably involved policy-makers abandoning views that crime resulted from social factors (such as poverty or unemployment) and/or psychological factors (such as those studied in criminal psychology) towards viewing it as, at least partly, a result of environmental factors (a run-down, graffiti-sprayed neighbourhood full of broken windows). Clearly, this type of learning involves the production of new ways of constructing policy problems, as well as, potentially, revision of the goals of policy (Bomberg, 2007: 257).

Less comprehensively, learning can also refer simply to tactics, influencing policy-makers' ability to push through their policy priorities, but not having any impact on the nature of those policies themselves; what Bomberg describes as 'political learning' (Bomberg, 2007).

Who learns?

One of the distinctive traits of the policy learning literature is its acknowledgement that policy-makers can exercise choice over policy-making, thus going against hyperglobalization accounts (see Chapter 12) and Marxist approaches (see Chapter 8) which view state actors as either heavily constrained in their policy-making, or simply a transmission belt for class interests, respectively. Rather than merely functioning as a container for other interests or policy imperatives, a focus on policy learning examines policy-makers as the agents of change and not just carriers of it. Policy learning approaches do not necessarily 'dismiss structural forces but suggest that in varying degrees, states and organizations can mediate these dynamics' (Stone, 2004: 548). As Heclo famously put it, politics 'finds its sources not only in power but also in uncertainty – men collectively wondering what to do'... and as such, policy-making can be viewed as 'a form of collective puzzlement on society's behalf' (Heclo, 1974: 305).

The question of who exactly 'learns', however, reflects continuing disagreements about the primacy or otherwise of the state in the public policy-making process. Bennet and Howlett (1992: 278) note that, depending on one's assessment of the predominance of state actors, learning could be seen as uniquely occurring 'during the intra-governmental stages of the policy cycle', only involving state actors; as occurring within societies, with policy-makers then responding to ideas propounded by actors from outside government; or by a mixture of actors internal and external to government.

Ultimately, where 'learning' occurs is a question which must largely be answered through empirical research. Certain bodies have, nonetheless, been designed specifically to promote learning, whether or not this has been successful. For example, the National School of Government in the UK, originally the Centre for Management and Policy Studies, was explicitly responsible for training UK civil servants in the machinery of government, including drawing on international examples (it now shares this task with other bodies within the Civil Service Learning organization). Trips may also be organized between different political groups or civil services, explicitly to encourage learning. Famous 'trips' of this sort include several from Britain to the USA to examine private prisons, the then Minister Kenneth Baker's trip from Britain to the USA to examine student aid arrangements, and that of Roland Koch, the Premier of Hesse, to Wisconsin to learn from their welfare-to-work package. However, the value of such 'study trips' can be overstated, particularly where they form part of official exchange or diplomatic processes. There can be a strong incentive for hosts to present their approaches in a positive light, and for guests to refrain from hostile questioning (Page and Mark-Lawson, 2007: 54). This may not necessarily be the case, however; one example comes from the 'negative lesson' drawn by the then Munich Mayor, Christian Ude, who visited London to investigate its system of utilities regulation, and decided not to adopt a UK-style approach in his city (*Münchener Merkur*, 2007).

Who teaches?

Bomberg (2007: 250) argues that there has been little research focus on the question of who 'teaches' policy lessons, as opposed to what 'learners' do (generally governments). Broadly, four types of 'teachers' can be identified: governments; entrepreneurs and middlemen; international organizations; and think tanks, who may also form part of 'advocacy coalitions' and/or 'epistemic communities'.

First, local or national governments may promote particular policies to other governments (Wolman and Page, 2002). This may be through civil service or political contacts, or through paying for 'expert advice' to be provided via consultancies. For example, the US Agency for International Development (USAID) has been particularly active in providing funds for consultancies to advise newly democratizing governments in the former Soviet Republics in the field of health care (Mechanic and Rochefort, 1996: 250–1) and in the former Yugoslav republics on regulation issues (Dodds *et al.*, 2011).

Second, policy ideas may also be promoted by what Heclo describes as 'policy middlemen', or policy entrepreneurs. These include international consultants themselves; academics; and professional groups, such as international lawyers or economists. Academics, for example, were responsible for bringing ideas about research-oriented graduate schools from Prussia and other European countries to the USA, which led to the creation of institutions such as Johns Hopkins University (Arnove, 2007: 5). As another example, private consultancies have been at the forefront of providing information about New Environmental Policy Instruments (NEPIs) within the EU (Bomberg, 2007). This category perhaps also covers Hall's 'officially-sanctioned experts'. Such experts may be based in government but, equally, they may come from outside it, from within the 'intellectual enclaves of society' (Hall, 1993: 277).

Third, international organizations can also be responsible for 'teaching' policy lessons. The OECD, for example, enables member nations to benchmark their public spending, policy systems and (to an extent) policy outcomes against those of other nations, and has attempted the explicit encouragement of learning between member nations around new forms of public management and 'good governance'. On occasion, such organizations may explicitly promote one country's policy model as 'best practice', arguably the case with the World Bank's promotion of Chile's pension system (Kasza, 2002: 280). Pressures from bodies which can affect the financial position of countries may, however, be more easily understood within the framework of coercive policy transfer rather than policy learning *per se*.

Fourth, think tanks and policy institutes have often attempted to promote policies drawn from other jurisdictions. Perhaps the first think tank focused on policy issues was the democratic socialist Fabian Society, founded in 1884 in the UK. This was followed by the creation of the Brookings Institution in 1927, the Rand Corporation in 1948 (both intended to be politically neutral), and the American Policy Commission which was created in the 1940s by Harold Lasswell, the founder of public policy studies (Hassenteufel, 2008: 19).

The importance of such bodies varies between countries. In France, there is a preponderance of public research institutes and internal state bodies which act effectively as think tanks, despite their lack of formal independence. In Britain and, particularly, in Germany, think tanks are more closely linked to particular political parties or, at least, political tendencies. The German situation is shaped by party funding rules which promote the creation of research-based organizations associated with each party. This has led to the creation of the renowned Friedrich Ebert and Konrad Adenauer *Stiftungs* (Foundations) allied, respectively, with the Social Democratic and Christian Democratic parties (*ibid.*: 210).

Individual actors from governments, consultancies or professions, international organizations and think tanks can promote policy learning individually or, equally, as part of a network. Two approaches have been put forward to understanding how individuals can 'teach' policy as part of networks.

The first approach, coined by Paul Sabatier, suggests that 'advocacy coalitions' will often form to promote learning. These are similar to 'policy networks' or 'communities' (see Chapter 8) which include people 'from a variety of positions (elected and agency officials, interest group leaders, researchers) who share a particular belief system – i.e. a set of basic values, causal assumptions, and problem perceptions – and who show a non-trivial degree of coordinated activity over time' (Sabatier, 1987: 660). The linkages between these various actors are overseen and managed by 'policy brokers' who try to reduce the extent of political conflict in order to focus energies on promoting a particular policy approach or programme. This approach recognizes that policy learning can be promoted by actors operating outside the state or within it, so long as they are part of the coalition – thus moving beyond a 'methodologically nationalist' approach which is determined to separate influences deriving from within nation state governments from those without them (Stone, 2004: 549).

Another approach, first put forward by Haas (1992), suggests that 'epistemic communities' can be the agents of learning. These bring together experts in a particular policy area, who are able to promote particular policy solutions drawing on their professional experience and knowledge. Haas examined how an epistemic community of scientists and other knowledgeable experts managed to achieve the banning of CFCs through the Montreal Protocol, which has been seen as an example where the scientific community had a significant impact on policy-making. This has, however, been disputed by those who argue that the politics surrounding the Protocol were less about different actors (governments and firms) being persuaded by the scientific evidence put forward by the epistemic community, and more about traditional economic interest. For example, it has been argued that the need to reduce CFCs was only accepted by large firms such as DuPont when they realized that promoting high environmental standards across the board would promote, rather than hinder, their competitive advantage (Drezner, 2001: 72–3).

In addition, Hoberg (1991: 127) has suggested that this kind of 'elite-driven emulation' may only be likely when 'the scope of conflict is relatively narrow'. In other contexts, activists (who may or may not have claims to specialist knowledge) may be key actors in promoting particular policy models from other countries to policy-makers. Hoberg details how activists failed to urge Canadian regulators to adopt American standards in relation to radon and the pesticide dinoseb, resulting in a distinctive Canadian approach being maintained, whereas in other cases they had used the American example to argue successfully for tighter standards (*ibid.*).

What enables learning?

Proximity, power and competition can be seen as core factors in enabling learning.

First, transfer is both more likely to occur, and more likely to be successful, when countries are proximate, either 'geographically, ideologically or culturally' (Stone, 2004: 552). However, what is viewed as proximate 'depends on where you start from' (Rose, 2005: 9).

Geographical proximity may lead to emulation simply due to the availability of a nearby policy comparator. This appears to be the case with Canada and the USA (Hoberg, 1991) for environmental and regulatory policy, as mentioned, with the Canadian–American border being described as 'the world's longest one-way mirror' as well as the 'longest undefended border in the world' (*ibid*.: 127). The interdependence created by such proximity can promote policy learning in a number of ways. One fascinating example comes from the case of Canadian attempts to get the USA to increase its policy efforts against pollution, due to the resultant acid rain from American pollution which was falling on Canadian soil. In the process of negotiating new standards, however, 'Canada learned that some of its air pollution standards were in fact weaker than their American counterparts, jeopardizing its moral high ground in the negotiations' and forcing it to increase its own standards (*ibid*.: 113).

Proximity also, perhaps, has been important in the field of pensions, where India's system of provision was emulated by Malaysia, Singapore, Sri Lanka, Indonesia and Nepal, and Nigeria's by Uganda, Tanzania and Ghana (Kasza, 2002). Perhaps the strongest example from this policy field, however, comes from Latin America, where New Right-inspired Chilean reforms had a significant impact across the region (Weyland, 2005). This can be explained by the 'availability heuristic', whereby it was simply very easy for Chilean consultants to visit Bolivia to advise policy-makers on how to adapt their pension system for Bolivian purposes (*ibid*.).

Nonetheless, geographical proximity may be outweighed by cultural proximity (Knill, 2005: 770), particularly when this is linked to language. This perhaps explains the fact that British governments have historically appeared far less concerned to learn from France, Norway and Ireland (all geographically proximate) compared with the USA (not geographically proximate). The development of UK 'workfare', education, criminal justice, and family and child support policies have all been heavily influenced by the US example (Page and Mark-Lawson, 2007: 47; see Finegold *et al*., 1993, specifically concerning education). Where 'lessons' are drawn from countries that are seen as culturally incompatible, problems can arise. Hence, the Swiss government initially drew on the US example when attempting to reform its educational system, but following domestic protests this led to ministers promoting European, rather than US-style, reforms (Steiner-Khamsi, 2002).

Additionally, it must be remembered that the policy learning process is not an apolitical one, and that what 'is "learned" and what is "remembered" must always be seen in the context of political interests and political power' (Bennett and Howlett, 1992: 291).

Power manifests itself in a variety of ways during policy learning. First, there may be little choice involved in the process of policy learning, if it is difficult to maintain an alternative system to a large or powerful neighbour. As Hoberg (1991: 128) puts it, in 'small countries like Canada regulators are often not so much policy-makers as they are policy-takers', in the face of the 'elephant' – the USA. A rather extreme example of this comes from the realm of drugs policy, where the more liberal approach of some Canadian states, such as British Columbia, has come under heavy attack from US policy-makers (see discussion in Glenny, 2008). The policy learning process may therefore enable more powerful nations to entrench their power, by enabling them to 'export their own policy preferences and styles' (Bomberg, 2007). More positively, nations may be attracted by other nations' 'soft power' into emulating their public policies (Rose, 2005: 52).

However, *in extremis*, the need for policy solutions may effectively reverse power relations. Rose (ibid.: 53) quotes the example of US policy-makers travelling from the 'world's greatest superpower' to India to 'learn lessons from its successful programme of dealing with power blackouts', after the notorious rolling blackouts experienced in America in 2003. Furthermore, even powerful actors may have different 'lessons' to promote, and so end up clashing with each other (Bomberg, 2007).

Finally, emulation may also be spurred by competition between states and, in particular, a desire to 'catch up' with the state being copied (Simmons and Elkins, 2004). An excellent example of this comes from attempts by Americans to learn from the Soviet education system following the 'Sputnik shock' of the 1950s. The wonderfully entitled *What Ivan Knows that Johnny Doesn't* (Trace, 1961, quoted in Phillips and Ochs, 2003) suggested that Soviet technological advance could be linked to its focus on scientific and technological training and education. From the 1980s onwards, attention has shifted to the 'Japanese educational miracle' and how this might be emulated (Arnove, 2007: 5).

Barriers to policy learning

On the other hand, a variety of barriers exist which can prevent policy learning. First, there is the nature of the policy itself. Policies which would involve a high degree of redistribution of resources in order to function properly are seldom transplanted between jurisdictions (Knill, 2005: 770). Similarly, policies which would involve large-scale changes in policy-makers' belief systems are also, *inter alia*, less likely to be transplanted.

Furthermore, policy transfer is unlikely to occur when existing institutional structures militate against this. It would have been unlikely for British policy-makers, for example, to adopt a Scandinavian-style reflation of the economy during the Great Depression, since their experience so far with public projects had been relatively limited compared with their Scandinavian contemporaries, and they lacked the encompassing institutions which would have facilitated this (Weir and Skocpol, 1985). A more recent example comes from the frequent, almost always failed, attempts by British policy-makers from the 1970s onwards to transfer German-style training and educational policies to the British context. Whilst the German case is often portrayed as an example to emulate, whether it is practical for the UK to attempt to conform to German models given the differences in class and educational systems between the two nations is questionable (Phillips and Ochs, 2003). Another example comes from attempts to directly import Western models into post-communist countries, as has occurred in Poland's educational sector (Elsner, 2000).

This has been described as the 'wicked context' problem by Rose (2005: 10), which he suggests is generally a greater barrier to policy learning than financial constraints. He highlights the challenges of finding 'space' for policy lessons to be implemented in 'a field already crowded with existing commitments' (*ibid.*: 103) – given that policy tends to be added to, not removed, by successive governments. This creates a trap for policy transfer, since any policy will only be innovative if it differs from previous policy, yet it must be sufficiently congruent with previous policies to be feasible to implement (*ibid.*: 107).

Another barrier comes from cultural and language differences, which may inhibit the discovery of possible 'lessons' but also lead to the inappropriate transfer of policies. Generally, concepts can be found which can translate 'features of a programme that operates in Dutch or French' into a 'lesson to be applied in an English-speaking land', for example (*ibid.*: 15). However, Chapter 14 considers in detail the multifarious challenges facing such attempts at translation, where functional equivalence of concepts can be difficult to achieve. A lack of a shared language and/or cultural framework can lead to pretended similarities or differences between contexts where none exist.

Finally, it should be noted that learning often requires a significant amount of effort from policy-makers; effort which may be in short supply given other calls for issue attention (see Chapter 9). It is important to remember that policy-makers often fail to learn even from policy failures in their own countries, let alone within other jurisdictions (Blindenbacher and Nashat, 2010).

Partial policy transfer and learning

Policy learning is infrequently 'complete', resulting in the 'perfect' copying of all elements of a policy as operated in one country to another jurisdiction. This is not least because, under democratic conditions, a variety of domestic political, interest and bureaucratic groups will probably be able to alter any proposed policy before it is implemented (Page and Mark-Lawson, 2007: 55). As a result, 'hybrids' are more likely than 'pure' transplants.

'Hybridity' is encouraged by both 'learners' and 'teachers'. 'Learners' may be keen to transfer policies for symbolic or strategic political reasons, rather than because they have improved their understanding of the domestic policy context (Stone, 2004: 549). Only certain aspects of a policy (in particular, those most easily explained, or the most high-profile) may be transferred, missing out, potentially, on some of the conditions necessary for its operation. Learning can therefore be 'shallow' or 'tactical', as well as the 'deeper' approach required for successful policy change (*ibid.*). Sabatier (1987) suggests that learning around 'core' aspects of policy – such as, around the appropriate goals for policy – may be more likely to come from external shocks (such as a new governing party or economic pressures), rather than from policy learning. Hall, however, suggests that 'third-order' learning, learning which involves shifts in policy paradigms, can occur due to the influence of policy entrepreneurs, but suggests that this is facilitated by new policy actors (such as a new party) coming into power (Hall, 1993).

When it comes to 'teaching' policy, teachers may also focus on the more successful or visible aspects of a particular policy, and fail to publicize its more expensive, difficult-to-implement or culturally-specific aspects. The Chilean pension system, for example, was promoted on the basis of its success in increasing returns on investment in a specific time period, but other impacts of the new system were not subject to the same fanfare by its proponents (Weyland, 2005).

Identifying policy transfer and learning

At the beginning of this chapter, it was stated that policy transfer is perhaps 'over-theorized' and 'under-applied'. This is not least because of the methodological challenges involved in identifying when, and to what extent, policy transfer and learning have taken place. As Bennett and Howlett (1992: 290) note in relation to policy learning, there is little empirical work which 'unequivocally demonstrates that X would not have happened had "learning" not taken place'. In practice, it may be simply 'impossible to observe the learning activity in isolation from the change requiring explanation' (*ibid.*). Indeed, it is arguable that many of the processes which might be viewed as indicating 'policy learning' simply indicate policy 'change' when viewed through the 'rational decision-making' framework, and should be investigated within that perspective, rather than as part of a separate mechanism (James and Lodge, 2003).

In addition, it may be difficult to separate policy 'learning' from imitation and/or coercive transfer. Meseguer (2006: 175) bravely attempts to differentiate between each factor as part of a large cross-national analysis of the adoption of marketizing reforms, concluding that '[l]earning in isolation or in combination with the alternative mechanisms of emulation and imposition explains the decision to liberalize trade, to privatize, and to enter into agreements with the IMF', but not decisions to make central banks independent. However, he is only able to measure learning, emulation (imitation) and imposition (coercive transfer) by adopting proxies which he acknowledges could be challenged, since they assume that governments will act rationally on the basis of past experience taking account of all available information, when many other factors (not least, political ones) are likely to be of importance, and when governments may not act 'rationally' in this way.

Furthermore, most cases of learning and transfer will have occurred in the past, rather than the researcher being able to observe them in practice. This results in researchers having to rely on selective accounts which may over- or underplay the extent to which policy-making was influenced by external pressure or policy 'examples'. In addition, if policy transfer or learning has been successful, the policy's foreign origins may be quickly forgotten; it 'then becomes described as no more and no less than "the way we do things here"' (Rose, 2005: 139) and, thus, its origins may be difficult to uncover through research.

Such empirical research as has been conducted suggests that the degree to which policies are transferred or 'learned' wholesale is limited. When it comes to policy learning, although policy-makers may invoke foreign examples, these may be more important at a rhetorical or symbolic level than a practical one (Bennett, 1997). Page and Mark-Lawson (2007) summarize the findings of research into 'zero-tolerance' policing (supposedly imported from the USA into Britain and Australia), 'workfare' (supposedly imported from the USA into Britain), the development of regulatory agencies (a trend which has started in the USA and Britain and been adopted by many countries) and Enterprise Zones (started in Hong Kong, and imported into Britain and then the USA). In each case, what appeared on initial inspection to constitute wholesale policy learning turns out 'on closer inspection' to constitute only very loose and not very detailed emulation, and/or a transfer of attitudes or symbols, rather than exact policies. It appears that policy learning, in particular, may be an effective mechanism for transferring ideas and impetus, as has arguably occurred in the arena of workfare, rather than wholescale transference of policy models (see Deacon, 2000).

Where policies are adopted in new jurisdictions, these will frequently be adapted substantially to suit domestic circumstances, in ways that fundamentally alter the nature of the policy concerned. One example of this cited by Hoberg (1991: 109–10) is the Canadian decision to transfer the US policy of incorporating a charter of rights into the constitution, but then allowing this 'to be overriden by legislatures through the so-called "notwithstanding clause"', thus radically limiting its impact. Another example comes from the UK's adoption of an early intervention programme called the Family Nurse Partnership, allegedly modelled on the US Nurse Family Partnership. The UK version, however, utilized health workers to visit young families precisely because they were viewed as more trustworthy and approachable by young, vulnerable parents than other professionals, such as social workers. This contrasted with the US case where health visitors were apparently used as part of a medicalized approach to poverty and disadvantage. Despite the similar language used to describe each programme, therefore, their overall goals and ethos seemed rather distinct (Dodds, 2009).

Conclusion

This chapter has considered the processes of policy transfer and learning in detail. It has considered why policy-makers might engage in policy learning, and try to transfer their policies to other countries; who is involved in policy transfer and learning; what is transferred and learned; what enables and inhibits policy learning; the results of policy learning; and problems with the identification of policy transfer and learning. It has indicated both the promise and perils of policy transfer and, particularly, learning. Given the complex nature of contemporary policy-making, 'green-field', empty, policy sites, as Rose (2005) describes them, are far less common than crowded and complicated 'brown-field' policy areas, which mean that it is extremely difficult to implement any new policy without amending it to fit local circumstances.

Nonetheless, the chapter has indicated how numerous actors are engaged in attempting to both generate and implement new policy ideas drawn from across the globe. It is becoming increasingly untenable for policy-makers to operate autarkically, eschewing any ideas from outside and following a particular national 'way'. Policy-makers are not only looking to exploit traditional policy 'mines' (such as the USA, for the UK), but also new ones from countries which are adopting innovative approaches to policy problems, including non-democracies (such as China) and rapidly developing countries (such as India). Even in situations of extremely constrained resources, new democracies have frequently adopted highly imaginative solutions to policy problems. The challenges of implementing policies drawn from other countries necessitates, however, a high degree of knowledge and understanding of comparative public policy-making, demonstrating yet again the value of comparative analysis for policy-makers and analysts alike. As Schneider and Ingram (1998: 63) put it, a 'more systematic and self-conscious approach to pinching [policy] including scrutiny of many examples drawn from a variety of settings will improve [policy] design'.

Summary

❑ Different countries can have similar policies imposed on them through policy transfer, or can borrow other countries' policies through policy learning. Similar policies in different nations may not always indicate policy transfer or learning, however, as convergence can occur due to similar pressures independently producing similar policy responses in different countries.

❑ Policies can be transferred either coercively (through force or conditionality), or through mimetism (e.g. where countries tend to copy 'leading' nations when creating new policies within conditions of uncertainty).

❑ Lesson-drawing, best practice and benchmarking all constitute types of policy learning.

❑ Policy-makers can learn about policy means (instruments; instrument settings) and ends (goals). They can also learn 'negatively' from other countries by deciding not to adopt another country's policy approach. 'Learning' often involves the adoption of similar approaches to the presentation of a policy, although the policy that is actually instituted may be very different from its 'parent'.

❑ Policy learning is facilitated by 'learners' and 'teachers' being ideologically, linguistically, culturally and/or geographically proximate; by the perceived 'power' of the 'teacher'; and by policy competition between countries.

❑ Policy learning is inhibited by institutional, cultural and linguistic barriers. It is less likely where adopting the new policy would require significant institutional change or redistribution between different societal groups.

❑ It is difficult for researchers to undertake direct observation of the processes of policy learning and transfer. In practice, policy learning and transfer are often inferred, rather than directly proven. Research suggests that policy transfer and learning infrequently result in the transfer of entire policies, generally being restricted instead to limited adoption of certain policy elements only.

Chapter 12

Policy-Making beyond the Nation State

More intense and extensive cross-national flows of trade, capital, people and information can destabilize policies which were previously implicitly based on assumptions of restricted mobility. Nonetheless, such destabilization does not itself automatically prescribe the nature of the policy models which follow (Blyth, 2002: 35). Indeed, tracing the impact of cross-national pressures on policy-making is a highly complicated task. Broadly, such pressures can exert influence in two directions: by changing the structural incentives for policy-makers, and by promoting or proscribing certain courses of action (Jakobsen, 2010: 895).

The imposition of specific policy models 'from outside' on different nations has been studied in detail by analysts of Europeanization, who have attempted to make explicit the constraints the EU imposes on policy design (Knill and Lehmkuhl, 2002b). Attempts have been made to compare EU member states with non-EU member states, in order to understand the EU's relative influence on policy change, compared with other cross-national pressures (Verdier and Breen, 2001; Schneider and Häge, 2008).

However, the precise contribution of cross-national pressures to policy reform can be difficult to specify. This is not least because some commentators identify both globalization and Europeanization not only with changes in ideology or rhetoric, but also with changes in policies themselves. Hence, for example, Currie's (1998: 1, 5) 'conception of globalisation' 'combines a market ideology with a *corresponding material set of practices drawn from the world of business*', including managerialism, accountability and privatization (emphasis added). Slightly differently, Rodrik (1997: 85) suggests that globalization 'is part of a broader trend that we may call marketization', which he associates with practices including 'receding government, deregulation [and the] shrinking of social obligations'.

This chapter therefore separates out the different elements of cross-national pressures on policy-making, and considers their impacts on policy-making in turn: cross-national flows and the increasing transnationalization of business, international governing institutions and global trends.

Defining globalization and Europeanization

By examining the impact of cross-national flows and the transnationalization of business, international governing institutions and global trends, this chapter considers features traditionally examined within studies of both globalization and Europeanization.

Whilst some theorists have been happy to use the concepts of globalization and internationalization almost interchangeably (see, for example, Moran and Wood, 1996), others have described globalization as a particularly 'intense' form of internationalization (Hirst and Thompson, 1999). For Scholte (2005: 65), 'international' exchanges can occur only 'between country units, whilst "global" transactions occur within a planetary unit'. The elision of internationalization and globalization is, he maintains, normatively objectionable, as this suggests that 'world social relations are – and can only be – organized in terms of country units, state governments, and national communities' (*ibid.*: 56). In a similar but subtly different vein, Scott has noted the 'neo-imperialist' tones of 'internationalism' which can potentially conflict with the 'non-national' processes of globalization (Scott, 1998: 124). On the other hand, some theorists have maintained that globalization *necessarily* leads to an increasing peripheralization of the developing world, its institutions and its languages (Pennycook, 1994) – which was not necessarily a feature of internationalization.

The meaning of Europeanization has also been contested. Europeanization has been variously defined as referring just to the creation of EU-level institutions and networks (Risse *et al.*, 2001), the impact of the EU on member states (Knill and Lehmkuhl, 2002b), or alternatively *both* to member states' implication in policy-making at the EU-level *and* to the imposition of EU policies on them (Bulmer and Burch, 2000). The latter definition takes on board the fact that European Union institutions both reflect and shape member state preferences whilst also imposing upon them specific policy approaches. As with globalization, Europeanization is thus Janus-faced: it impacts upon member states' policy-making and the power and opportunities held by different policy actors, at the same time as member states shape it in multifarious ways.

It is frequently difficult to disaggregate Europeanization from globalization, both practically and theoretically (Buller and Gamble, 2002; Hennis, 2001). This chapter avoids artificial distinctions by treating the European Union as just one, albeit a very important, example of a transnational governing institution. One type of cross-national pressure is not considered here, however: that of bilateral pressures. Policy transfer is the main mechanism through which bilateral pressures are felt, and this has been considered in detail in Chapter 11.

Capital and trade flows

For some commentators, globalization simply *consists in* various flows, which 'move along various global highways' (King, nd.). For the purposes of this brief chapter, these can be delineated as flows of capital and trade, people, and information. Flows which are not *directly* related to human activity are not considered here, although they are of course cross-national, and may have been accelerated by globalization – such as the mobility of invasive species (Perrings *et al.*, 2010). Two of the most significant flows, often seen as constitutive of globalization, are those in capital and in trade.

Cross-national flows in capital have increased substantially over time, particularly in recent years (albeit with a reduction during the recent financial crisis). Figure 12.1 indicates inflows of foreign direct investment to selected economies at two points, between 1995–97 and 2006–08. Whilst inflows have increased across all nations, this has been particularly pronounced in the liberal market economies of the UK and USA. As is discussed below (pp. 274–9), for many authors, the increasing openness of national economies has led to the potential for a 'race to the bottom' in regulatory and welfare standards, as foreign investors and transnational corporations (TNCs) seek to avoid higher tax rates.

There has been a similar increase in the extent of world trade, which has more than tripled following World War II, as measured by the proportion of GDP made up of world exports (Glyn, 2004: 2). This followed

Figure 12.1   *Inflows of foreign direct investment in US dollars (billions)*

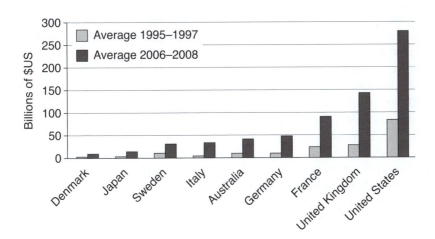

Source: OECD (2010a).

a massive decrease in trade during the periods of World War I and World War II. As a result, some of the increase has simply been 'catch-up' with the previous situation (Maddison, 1991: 326–7). However, for some countries, recent decades have witnessed a huge increase in trade, not least nations such as China, which were previously effectively closed markets.

The highest trading countries are not necessarily either the largest, or the richest. Smaller countries have often proved the most trade-dependent, and have become more so over time. Castles (1998: 38) links this to the fact that 'large-scale exposure to trade is substantially a function of a small population size and, hence, of a restricted domestic market'.

Whilst the direction of global trade flows may not have altered so substantially (even if their magnitude has increased), the contents of those flows has altered over time, moving away from trade in commodities, other raw materials, and fuel, and towards services and manufactured goods (see, for example, Glyn, 2004: 4). Nonetheless, the services sector remains far less exposed to trade than manufacturing, for obvious reasons; some services, whether they be a haircut or a health check, are very difficult and expensive to perform across national borders. Within the field of manufacturing, one of the most significant changes has been towards competition in precisely the same, or very similar, products (Rodrik, 1997), whereas previously advanced manufacturing, in particular, was mainly restricted to the most developed countries, whilst developing nations mainly traded raw materials.

The increasing transnationalization of business

The increased economic power of multinational corporations, and the manner in which this constrains national economies, has also been viewed by some authors as constitutive of globalization (Waters, 1995). Emphasis on the freedom of TNCs to relocate as the key feature of 'globalization' has been described as 'strong' globalization (Yeates, 2001: 9–10). Kenichi Ohmae (1995), for example, has argued that some corporations are genuinely global in scope, with it being unclear whether IBM Japan is either Japanese or American, for example. For Ohmae, the international nature of such companies' operations has significant implications for public policies, not least the fact that they are more potentially mobile than companies based only in one nation.

However, far from such companies being a recent innovation, a number of corporations developed their own operations in foreign countries from the mid-nineteenth century onwards, including the Singer Sewing Machine Company and General Electric. The business models adopted by trans-national corporations (TNCs) vary widely, with some, such as Singer, operating as consolidated companies whilst others, such as Coca-Cola, involve entirely or partly separate franchises for some of their operations (bottling, in Coca-Cola's case).

The extent of transnationalization has, however, undoubtedly increased over the decades. A number of factors have promoted business transnationalization. First, consumers generally choose a product on the basis of its current characteristics, rather than on the basis of where (or how) it was made. As a result, they may be equally willing to buy from a company based in their own nation, or in another country. This approach is bolstered by international trade rules (considered on p. 275), which generally uphold the principle that only the characteristics of the product itself matters, not those of the production process. Second, in order to increase profits, companies have broadly two choices: lower production costs or increase sales. Production costs can be lowered domestically by increasing the efficiency of capital. Once this is exhausted, however, costs can only be further lowered by decreasing the costs of labour – which may be possible by moving to a country where lower wages are paid. The prospect of increasing sales may also promote internationalization, as companies seek out new markets beyond the domestic one. Third, as the economic fortunes of previously 'rival' economies are becoming increasingly intertwined, it becomes less rational for companies to focus on a purely domestic strategy (*ibid.*, 1995).

Nonetheless, there are limits to transnationalization. As Hirst and Thompson (1999: 271) argue, 'there is a vast difference between a strictly globalized economy and a highly inter-nationalized economy in which most companies trade from their bases in distinct national economies'. For example, even following the introduction of the North American Free Trade Agreement (NAFTA) in 1994, companies on either side of the USA–Canada border traded intensively with each other, but they remained distinctive. Furthermore, it is arguable that even 'transnational' companies remain highly embedded in national contexts, albeit a number of national contexts, and reliant on government support in relation to education, training, R&D and provision of infrastructure (Kennett, 2001: 17).

The impact of capital and trade flows and the increasing transnationalization of business

Hyperglobalization theorists suggest that cross-national flows of capital and trade, and the increasing transnationalization of business will lead to reductions in regulatory standards. This is essentially because these processes alter the power relationship between corporations and government, since corporations can easily shift their operations to a new country. If they are able to move quickly to another jurisdiction, then the costs spent voicing their concerns and cooperating with government become comparatively more expensive. As a result, governments will focus not on traditional Western political goals (such as the creation and maintenance of a welfare state) but, instead, on ensuring that they can attract to their territory the most profitable and best-performing companies (which will be able to provide employment to the domestic population over the long term) (Ohmae, 1995).

This claim can be related to Hirschman's book concerning the relative importance of exit, voice and loyalty as different strategies adopted by policy subjects. Hirschman (1970) produced this text after working for the World Bank, where he was concerned to discover why the public railway in Nigeria was so slow and expensive, despite the fact that its popularity was falling rapidly amongst companies and, hence, it was theoretically facing considerable pressures to improve its performance. Hirschman concluded that this was because companies were unable to exercise 'voice', and force change within the public railway company, and as a result, where they could, simply exited the public railway system and used road haulage instead. Only small, less-profitable companies which had little choice but to to use the public railway continued to do so.

The hyperglobalization thesis assumes that, faced with increased mobility of capital and business transnationalization, governments will do the opposite to the unfortunate Nigerian public railway. Rather than being unconcerned about capital and business flight, governments will instead attempt to fit their policies to large investors' and companies' preferences, to try and stave off their 'exit' from the territory – particularly if companies do not possess any especial 'loyalty' to the country concerned.

The impact on regulation

In the regulatory context, it is assumed that this will lead to the dilution of regulatory standards covering matters such as workforce pay and conditions, and environmental standards. This is because, faced with low loyalty companies which can easily exit the national jurisdiction, countries will engage in 'regulatory competition' to lower standards and thus retain, and potentially attract new, business to their territories. This results in a 'race to the bottom'.

The 'race to the bottom' thesis includes a number of assumptions, however. First, it is assumed that governments will respond primarily to the preferences of business and capital, rather than the interests of their constituents or other political actors, such as interest groups. Second, it assumes that the costs imposed by regulation will tend to outweigh any differences in labour productivity across countries (Drezner, 2001: 58). Finally, it also assumes that no state possesses sufficient market size for companies or capital to be committed to maintain a presence, due to the size of that market (*ibid.*). This assumption appears contradicted by examples of 'races to the top' in regulatory standards, such as the Californian state's imposition of extra standards for car emissions. California's example was quickly followed by a number of other states and, indeed, countries (Vogel, 1997). Producers appeared willing to comply in order to access the very large Californian market (Vogel and Kagan, 2004). It is also, arguably, disproved by much empirical evidence, which points to a convergence amongst OECD nations in labour standards, for example, and a 'slow drift' amongst developing countries 'toward the enforcement of core labour standards', a pattern which is replicated in the environmental arena (Drezner, 2001: 69, 75).

Nonetheless, it has been suggested that whilst 'races to the bottom' might be inhibited when consumers and/or governments can easily verify compliance with 'product standards' (i.e. that cars are fitted with catalytic converters), they are more likely in cases where standards concern the process of production rather than the characteristics of the product itself. For example, we might expect emissions standards for steel-producing plants to be reduced as part of a race-to-the-bottom. This is because filters to reduce noxious emissions are expensive, and fitting filters (changing the process) does not affect the final product (steel). Steel made in a factory with high process standards is identical to that made in a factory with low process standards. Compliance with process standards is less visible and generally of less concern to importers and consumers, and thus process standards are more likely to be subject to races to the bottom (Holzinger and Knill, 2004: 32). However, large-N studies have suggested that there is no significant correlation between a nation's openness to trade and its level of environmental policy adoption (Holzinger *et al.*, 2008; Liefferink *et al.*, 2009: 696) – apparently regardless of whether these standards apply to processes or products (Drezner, 2001).

The impact on welfare provision

The 'race to the bottom' thesis in relation to welfare states argues that increased capital mobility, in particular, will undermine the tax base which is used to pay for social programmes, and result in a shift away from the taxation of business and towards the taxation of labour and consumption (Garrett, 1998b). In addition, Rodrik (1997) argues that the transnationalization of business has undermined the basis for social insurance. What he describes as a postwar 'social bargain' has been 'loosened' as companies become more footloose and less reliant on maintaining good relations with their workers. Overall, the 'race to the bottom' thesis argues that welfare states will increasingly converge on a minimalist model due to the pressures of international economic competition (Mishra, 1999). Finally, proponents of this view stress its impact on traditional Keynesian mechanisms of demand management; financial integration encourages the pursuit of fiscal austerity, since expansionary economic policies which might counter unemployment during times of crisis are likely to result in capital flight (Yeates, 1999: 378). This 'race to the bottom' argument has also sometimes been described as the 'efficiency hypothesis' (van Kersbergen and Manow, 2008: 538; see also Busemeyer, 2009).

It has been noted that the proportion of corporation tax in relation to overall tax take had not, at least until the time of the economic crisis, altered significantly within OECD countries. The contribution of corporation tax to public funds has been relatively low for a number of years (an average of only 8 per cent of all tax revenue in OECD countries in 1980, and no less in 2001) (Glyn, 2004: 10). Nonetheless, this does not rule out 'strategic interaction' between nations. This refers to the fact that, when one country reduces its corporation tax rate, others consider doing the same in order to retain their mobile corporate tax base (Devereux *et al.*, 2003). Strategic interaction is most likely to occur in relation to the 'effective marginal' or 'average' tax rate, as opposed to the total amount of tax charged, since it is the former which might shape corporations' decisions about where to locate (Devereux *et al.*, 2003).

Some political economists have developed these insights to suggest that not only will welfare expenditure be *reduced* in the face of international competition, but the *nature* of welfare provision will also be changed in order to promote national competitiveness. Hence, Bob Jessop (2003: 10) has maintained that a 'new state form' has been created, the 'Schumpeterian workfare state', which is focused on strengthening 'as far as possible the structural competitiveness of the national economy by intervening on the supply-side; and ... [subordinating] social policy to the needs of labour market flexibility and/or to the constraints of international competition'. Philip Cerny (2007) has described a 'competition state' as the successor to the traditional welfare state: the 'competition state' prioritizes profitability, enterprise and innovation across the economy, rather than welfare goals.

As with the purported 'race to the bottom' in regulatory standards, however, some analysts challenge the view that increased cross-national flows of capital and transnationalized business will necessarily lead to reductions in welfare protection. The so-called 'compensation thesis' suggests that increased openness may lead to greater, rather than reduced, calls for social protection (Blekesaune and Quadagno, 2003). For example, Katzenstein's (1985) work on some small, trade-reliant

European economies suggested that increased competition could coincide with greater attempts at concertation and encompassing welfare programmes, to facilitate adjustment to rapidly changing external economic circumstances (see also Rieger and Leibfried, 1998; Glatzer and Rueschemeyer, 2005; and Box 12.1). Visser and Hemerijck (1997) suggest largely similar, if 'updated', mechanisms enabled another small, trade-reliant economy (the Netherlands) to adapt to global competition whilst preserving an extensive welfare state.

These accounts suggest that, rather than reducing welfare effort, increased exposure to trade could lead to purposive political action to insulate populations from increased competition (Castles, 1998: 37; see also Cameron, 1978). Indeed, van Kersbergen and Manow (2008: 538) note that, given the 'early pessimistic predictions', it is 'most remarkable' that the welfare state has 'basically survived'.

Other findings suggest different ways in which the 'race to the bottom' hypothesis has not been universally fulfilled. First, companies may not be as mobile as is often assumed. Whilst the benefits of a national business culture and networks may be rather intangible, they

---

BOX 12.1   Walter's micro-level analysis of the compensation thesis

Walter (2010) notes that most analyses of the compensation thesis have rested on correlating the 'macro-level' of overall welfare expenditure with aggregates of trade exposure. She suggests this is problematic, since welfare spending is not only shaped by individuals' feelings of economic insecurity, but also by other factors as well, such as the availability of tax revenue.

Instead, she sets out to uncover the 'micro' foundations of the compensation thesis in one particularly trade-exposed nation – Switzerland. She focuses on the transmission mechanism whereby increasing economic internationalization is hypothesized to increase social risks which then, purportedly, increase individuals' feelings of insecurity, leading them to demand greater levels of social protection and vote for welfare-supporting parties.

She combines a range of data, including from the 2007 World Values Survey, the OECD's Industry Structural Analysis database, and an 'offshorability index'. This enables her to examine the views of what she calls 'globalization losers' – those individuals whose labour market position places them at risk from increased economic internationalization.

The results of her analysis support the compensation hypothesis. Walters finds that, in Switzerland, 'globalisation losers' 'experience high levels of job insecurity'; those whose jobs are insecure 'are more likely to favor an expansion of the welfare state'; and 'holding such a view strongly increases the propensity to vote for the Social Democrats' (*ibid*.: 421).

may still be crucial for the success of different businesses (Hirst and Thompson, 1996). Hence, whilst companies may be 'transnational', they are not 'extraterritorial', and are likely to still possess some 'loyalty' to their home jurisdiction. Second, a range of factors may be of importance to politicians when making policy, not just their ability to retain and attract capital and transnational business to their territory. These factors can include the specific nature of the welfare state in their country, historical and cultural traditions, electoral and party considerations, and strong veto players which can prevent extensive reform (Yeates, 1999: 380).

In practice, rather than supporting unambiguously either the 'race to the bottom' or the 'compensation hypothesis', the interaction between cross-national flows can be highly subtle and is not necessarily linear (see, for example, Iversen and Cusack, 2000). For instance, *resistance* to globalization apparently motivated some politicians and trade unions to support what appeared to be a liberalizing measure in France in the late 1990s, when the creation of large French private pension funds was described as necessary in order to increase the share of domestic investment in French business (Palier, 2007).

More broadly, Rodrik (1998) maintains that it is not the overall extent of openness to trade but, rather, its volatility which not only can lead to higher calls for income protection from citizens, but can also reduce governments' ability to tax some of the most highly mobile actors. Nonetheless, Rodrik includes military expenditure and government capital procurement within his definition of government protective activity, and does not focus solely on welfare state expenditure (Carnes and Mares, 2007: 871).

During the recent financial crisis, capital movements were especially volatile, and pressures on governments to reduce expenditure particularly strong. Unfortunately, insufficient time has passed since the financial collapse in 2008 to assess its impact on welfare provision. Whilst the compensation hypothesis may have been broadly borne out in the immediate aftermath of the crisis, given the Keynesian approach to demand stimulation adopted by many governments, it is unclear whether political support for welfare provision will continue if the crisis continues. Furthermore, the compensation hypothesis appears to be far less predictive within liberal market economies such as the USA and UK, particularly when it comes to income-maintenance programmes (Vis *et al.*, 2011: 340–3).

Others have pointed out that the characteristics of the welfare state in question matter when seeking to understand how it is being affected by globalization. For example, coordinated market economies may be better able to resist competitive pressures, which may actually modestly increase social protection (Swank, 2002). This contrasts with the situation for liberal market economies, where globalization has, Swank (*ibid.*) claims, led to retrenchment. Alternatively, the political right may be more willing to act on their perception of competitive pressures than the political left, who may be more concerned to increase compensation in the face of more mobile capital and transnationalized business (Huber and Stephens, 2001). Finally, regional pressures and characteristics may interact with global pressures, mediating their impact on different nations' welfare states. Whereas increases in economic openness have been associated with declines in social spending in Latin American countries, it has been argued that economic shocks led to greater public spending in many Asian economies (Carnes and Mares, 2007: 872).

Flows of people and information

For Scholte (2005: 59), globalization simply is the spread of transplanetary, or supraterritorial, connections between people. Of course, such connections need not necessarily involve the crossborder movement, or emigration, of people, given that such connections can be constituted 'virtually', or through more fleeting interactions such as business trips or holidays. Nonetheless, perhaps the most significant change in flows of people has occurred in recent years with the development of three broad patterns of human mobility, corresponding to the movements of the so-called 'transnational capitalist class' (TCC) and migrant skilled and unskilled workers.

The term 'transnational capitalist class' has been adopted to cover the group of mobile owners and controllers of TNCs and their local affiliates, bureaucrats and politicians, professionals and consumerist elites (Sklair, 1997; Robinson, 2004). This group of people might be compared with TNCs, since their economic interests have arguably become increasingly global. The TCC can also be seen as relatively culturally homogeneous, having experienced similar patterns of higher education and career, and engaging in similar types of consumption (*ibid.*).

This 'elite' group can be contrasted with another group of people whose mobility is also motivated by economic factors: that of mobile workers. Mobility is particularly pronounced in particular sectors, with migrant health workers counting for one third of international migrants (Yeates, 2010: 424).

Whilst international borders are relatively open to the TCC and mobile workers, this is not the case for often relatively unskilled migrants. The selective application of border control on the basis of individuals' characteristics (wealth or skill set) is a relatively recent phenomenon (previous controls mainly focused predominantly on country of origin). The relative magnitude of immigration of unskilled migrants in relation to

Figure 12.2 *Population inflow (I) and outflow (O)*

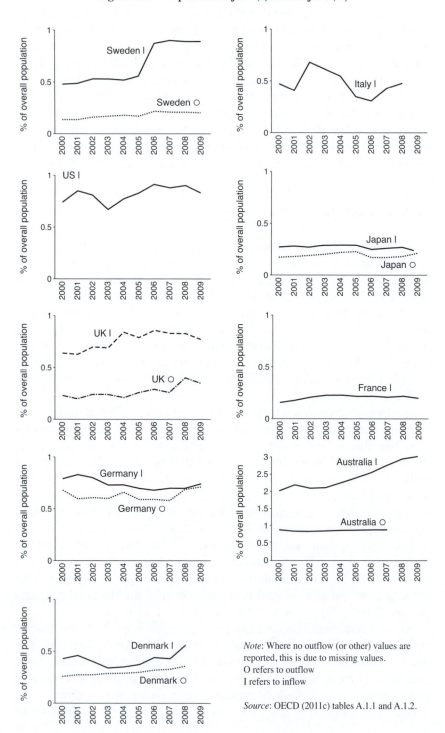

Note: Where no outflow (or other) values are reported, this is due to missing values.
O refers to outflow
I refers to inflow

Source: OECD (2011c) tables A.1.1 and A.1.2.

other migrants has decreased significantly in most developed nations; one need only compare the current US approach to immigration with that which applied in the first years of the twentieth century.

Flows of information have enabled what Giddens (1994: 4) has described as 'action at a distance', which he identifies with 'globalisation'. The greater availability of means of communication and their use to transfer information has led to the creation of a so-called 'global village', whereby 'everything happens to everyone at the same time: everyone knows about, and therefore participates in, everything that is happening the minute it happens' (Carpenter and McLuhan, 1960, p. xi). Whilst terrestrial television was described in the 1960s as leading to this kind of 'shrinking' of world societies, arguably the advent of improved telephony, satellite television and, particularly, the internet has greatly accelerated this process.

Cross-national communication has been seen by some as empowering 'small players' such as non-governmental organizations (NGOs) (Kennett, 2001: 22). The greater availability of communications technology has enabled new forms of political activism which are not solely reliant on the geographical location of individuals' homes or workplaces. Consumer campaigns, in particular, have been successful in pushing for corporate codes of conduct to be adopted in a variety of areas (Yeates, 1999: 387). Greater availability of information across borders has also altered peoples' expectations, by 'spreading information about other peoples' consumption and living standards' (Glyn, 2004: 13).

The greater availability and accessibility of information and other material may also have led to significant changes in social values and meanings (Harvey, 1989b), and even to challenges to traditional 'rationalist' conceptions of knowledge itself. Martin Albrow (1996), in particular, has maintained that globalization has resulted in a decline in the status of 'modern' rationality, in favour of non-rationalist knowledges such as religious revivalism, ecocentrism and postmodernist thought. Whether or not globalization has led to such radical consequences is debatable, but increased global flows of information may have led to the adoption of an increasing reflexive attitude towards gaining and producing knowledge, as intercultural encounters intensify.

Nonetheless, access to such technologies is still heavily concentrated in the global North. It will come as no surprise that the 'typical Internet user worldwide is male, under 35 years old, with a college education and high income, urban based and English speaking' (Kennett, 2001: 24). Furthermore, the 'free availability' of information is potentially being reduced, as some forms of content (such as some academic and teaching materials) are coming under the control of business and for-profit organizations (Morey, 2003: 74; Scholte, 2005: 171).

Figure 12.3　*Increases in internet users, 1996–2009*

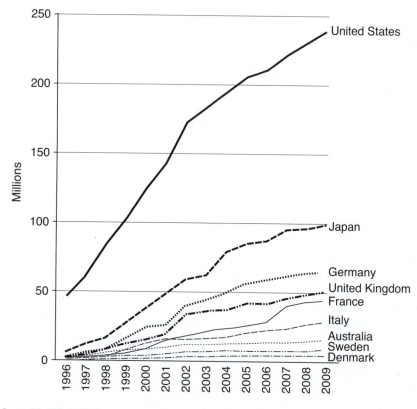

Source: World Bank (2011) .

The impact of flows in people and information

Inequalities in mobility can intensify the impact of the other flows described above (of capital and trade). For example, immobile factors of production, especially immobile labour, are likely to be particularly strongly affected by greater business and capital mobility (Hiscox, 2003). They may also be affected by greater flows of skilled people from other countries, which may help to depress wages for domestic workers (as Yeates (2010: 426) argues in relation to those employed in the caring professions in Western countries).

Equally, previously relatively 'immobile' people, such as women with children in developing countries, may be encouraged by domestic policy-makers to become more mobile. A rather extreme example of this comes from the Philippines, where around one tenth of the population works abroad, and overseas working is actively promoted as a means of economic development (Acacio, 2008). Such movement is, obviously, not without consequences; as Yeates (2010: 427–8) notes, countries 'which have no other (i.e. poorer) countries from which to recruit tend to become reliant on medical charity, with nursing labour often provided by the same countries that have recruited their own nurses'; yet, the value of this aid is significantly less than that arising from nurse migration.

The trajectories of the TCC arguably shape public policies in very different ways. Whilst it is sometimes suggested in political discourse that high tax rates will lead to the richest individuals emigrating, the impact of this is limited. First, aside from a small number of high-profile examples (such as the actor Sean Connery in the UK), the evidence for wide-scale 'rich flight' caused by tax rates is relatively limited. Second, the proportion of tax paid by genuinely mobile high-earners is sufficiently small for it to have a limited impact on, for example, the provision of public services (Glyn, 2004).

Rodrik (1997), however, argues that the impact of internationally mobile groups on policy-making is more subtle. He suggests that increased mobility, particularly of the best-off, will 'loosen ... the civic glue that holds societies together and exacerbat[e] social fragmentation'. This is because these groups have less of a stake in society: they are less willing to exercise voice, because they can easily exit, and are not particularly loyal. In colourful terms, he suggests that this is likely to lead to increasing divisions in society between the winners and losers of globalization; this 'is not a pleasing prospect, even for individuals on the winning side of the divide who have little empathy for the other side. Social disintegration is not a spectator sport – those on the sidelines also get splashed with mud from the field' (*ibid.*: 7).

Whether or not such societal division is explicit or implicit, it is arguable that increasing mobility is leading to a certain homogenization of culture. Social geographers have charted the growth of new, cosmopolitan spaces for consumption, which are easy for members of the TCC to slot into and enjoy, whether they be in Hong Kong, London or New York (Harvey, 1989a).

Cultural homogenization is also, arguably, occurring due to increased availability of information through the mechanisms detailed above. Greater access to information can, however, have a range of impacts on public policy-making. Chapter 11 considers in detail how it can promote policy learning amongst policy-makers. It can also, however, impact upon citizens' attitudes concerning what is and what is not achievable by their governments. A strong example of this comes from the increasing calls for democratization and economic liberalization in the Soviet bloc following relaxations in individual mobility and greater media plurality. Rather than dampen down calls for reform, these changes enabled citizens to compare their living standards with other nations (e.g. West

Germany in the case of the GDR) and to call for further changes. Less dramatically, the availability of comparable data on health spending arguably provided pressure on the New Labour government in the UK to increase expenditure up to the European average (Glyn, 2004: 11).

International governing institutions

International governing institutions come in a variety of shapes and sizes, and perform a dizzying array of tasks in numerous policy areas. They operate at a 'multiplicity of levels and types of governance' (Hirst and Thompson, 1999: 269), with varying relationships to individual nation states. Whilst international governing institutions can be seen as conduits for globalization or regionalization, their very existence could also be construed as pushing globalization and/or regionalization. This is particularly important at the current time, given the lack of any clear hegemonic national power or powers.

International governing institutions can be broadly divided into the categories of regulatory bodies, service-providers and redistributors (see Deacon *et al.*, 1997), as well as on the basis of the extent to which they are supranational or intergovernmental in approach. Over and above the existence of international governing institutions, it is important to note that many charity and campaigning groups have also internationalized, such as Greenpeace and Amnesty International (Bierstecker, 1998).

International institutions can have a variety of impacts on public policies, depending on numerous factors: the clarity and directness of multilateral rules (Schmidt, 2002a), the degree of difficulty of agreeing on common policies (with redistributive policies typically proving more difficult to negotiate cross-nationally), and the nature of the domestic context. As such, whilst international institutions may, broadly, promote policy convergence, the rate and extent of such convergence may be highly variable.

The following sections detail some of the most significant international institutions, before assessing their impact on policy-making.

The European Union

The European Union is the most integrated international governing institution in the world, with its 27 member states cooperating across a range of policy areas, including macroeconomic policy in the case of the 'eurozone' countries.

There are numerous detailed analyses available which examine the mechanisms of the EU and how these impact on policy-making (for a particularly contemporary example, see Buonanno and Nugent, 2012). Rather than attempting a comprehensive analysis (which is not feasible here), this section briefly considers the relationship between the EU's institutions (its Parliament, Councils, the European Council, Commission, and Court of Justice) and member states.

Wallace and Wallace (2000: 38) argue that the EU policy process is a 'moving pendulum' between the 'magnetic field of the domestic arena and the magnetic field of the transnational arena'. Certainly, it is arguable that the methods of policy-making within the EU have changed over time, encompassing (during different periods) the 'Community Method', 'Intensive Transgovernmentalism', 'Supranational decision-making' and 'new modes of governance' (including the Open Method of Coordination) (Buounanno and Nugent, 2012). However, despite this heterogeneity, analysts have been keen to discern whether the EU is 'really' 'supranational' (independent, to an extent, from its member states), or 'intergovernmental' (simply a collection of member states). This moves beyond traditional international relations analyses which view states as, necessarily, fully sovereign (Keohane, 1984).

Perhaps the clearest, and earliest, statement of the supranationalist position came from Ernst Haas (1958), who put forward what has since been described as a 'neofunctionalist' approach. He argued that incremental integration would occur because of pressure from groups pushing from above (the EU) and below (social partners), rather than the impetus for integration coming from different nation states. This pressure would lead to 'functional spillover', as integration in one arena would make it more rational in another. For example, at a political level, if decisions are increasingly taken within the European arena, this will become a self-fulfilling process as political actors (including sub- and supra-member state institutions) will increasingly look to the EU, rather than to domestic institutions, to resolve policy problems. There will also be an 'upgrading of common interests', whereby the process of 'horse-trading' between member states over different policy proposals will lead to the increasing interconnection of different states' policy interests.

A variation on this approach came from Balassa (1962), who also focused on the potential of economic spillover to lead to integration. However, he used this to suggest that integration would occur at different speeds in different areas. For example, it would be necessary for a customs union to have been established before the common market could be fully implemented. Whilst Balassa's model has broadly been predictive of developments in EU integration, the 'logic' of economic determinism has not entirely determined events, with continuing controversy concerning the integration of services markets being a case in point (Buonanno and Nugent, 2012).

Burley and Mattli (1993) broadly supported Haas' approach, but suggested that law has increasingly come to 'mask' politics, rather than economics doing so (see also Alter, 1998). They consider the role of then

European Court of Justice, and argue that it continually justified 'its decisions in light of the common interests of the members as enshrined in both specific and general objectives of the original Rome treaty' (Burley and Mattli, *ibid.*: 68).

Stone Sweet and Sandholtz also put forward a supranationalist argument, but rather than focusing on the interests of economic or legal actors, they suggest that it is the interests of member states themselves which have shaped integration. Whilst transnational activity may drive integration, it cannot explain its timing or form. Instead, this depends on the extent and manner to which member states are incentivized to harmonize their policy positions, which then depends on the costs (or otherwise) of maintaining separate national approaches (Stone Sweet and Sandholtz, 1997: 299). Whilst it is costly to maintain separate trade policies, for example, it is not particularly costly to retain separate security and defence policies (*ibid.*: 309).

Contrarily, intergovernmentalists argue that the interests of member states offer a strong argument for the EU being viewed as fully dependent on member states. For Garrett (1995: 174), for example, if 'member governments have neither changed nor evaded the European legal system, then from a so-called rational government perspective it *must* be the case that the existing legal order furthers the interests of national governments' (emphasis added). Furthermore, member states continue to retain ultimate power over the treaties. Scharpf has nonetheless pointed out that the power which member states can realistically exert through their ability to make treaties is limited. This is because of what he describes as the 'joint decision trap', with all member states having to agree, unanimously, to any change in the treaties (Scharpf, 2005). Hence, treaty revision can be seen as a 'nuclear option', which is 'exceedingly effective, but difficult to use' (Pollak, 1997: 118).

Developments following the 2008 financial crisis suggest that the EU is becoming increasingly intergovernmentalist, with negotiations around debt financing appearing to be dominated by Germany and (to a lesser degree) France, and with supranational institutions such as the Commission playing more of a supporting role. The picture is complicated, however, by the detail of the EU's Fiscal Compact, concluded in March 2012, which requires all nations in the Eurozone to submit their budgets for scrutiny by other members before these are enacted, and which enables the Court of Justice to impose fines on all signatory nations which fail to stick to deficit rules. Only two nations within the EU declined to sign up to the Compact, the UK and the Czech Republic.

For some heavily-indebted nations such as Greece, even the description of the EU as 'intergovernmentalist' may be inappropriate. In these nations, EU pressure on national policy-making systems might more appropriately be viewed as reflecting 'bilateral' policy-making, involving coercive policy transfer (see Chapter 11) from lending to debtor countries. For example, EU finance ministers recently required the leaders of all the Greek political parties to commit to implementing cuts, independent of who was to go on to win Greece's national elections in April 2012, in exchange for continuing financial support. This departs considerably from the 'consensual' approach to policy-making which dominated the EU for its first fifty years of existence.

The United Nations

In comparison to analyses of the EU, scholarly examinations of the United Nations (UN) are generally dominated by approaches from international relations and public law, and often focused on security issues (see Voeten, 2004; Chesterman *et al.*, 2008). This reflects the fact that the UN's peacekeeping budget dwarfs its budget for other areas of activity. As with its examination of the EU, this section cannot attempt to provide a comprehensive picture of the UN's policy-making machinery (see Daws and Weiss, 2008, for an overview). In addition, as this book is focused on core areas of domestic policy-making (economic, welfare, health, education and environmental policy) it would be incongruous to summarize here the UN's conflict brokering and peacekeeping activities (on which, see MacFarlane and Foong-Kong, 2006; Ramcharan, 2008).

Nonetheless, the UN has had a significant, if ambiguous, impact on multiple policy areas. In the area of health, the World Health Organization (WHO) has been important in improving data collection and sharing across countries, and in promoting coordination in relation to infectious disease epidemics and other health threats. One controversial area of the WHO's activities concerns the relationship between health and security. Any use of nuclear and biological weapons would clearly be likely to threaten human security, yet the WHO, as a technical agency, has resisted extensions to its role beyond purely health-related responses to a potential crisis (Burci, 2008).

Other agencies within the UN machinery related to the policy areas considered in this book include the International Atomic Energy Agency (IAEA), International Labour Organization (ILO), United Nations Educational, Scientific and Cultural Organization (Unesco), World Bank and International Monetary Fund (IMF). Treaties under the aegis of the UN have had significant impact in a huge range of areas, from the environment (e.g. the Kyoto Protocol to the UN Framework Convention on Climate Change) to women's rights (the Convention on the Elimination of All Forms of Discrimination against Women – CEDAW).

The World Bank and the International Monetary Fund have often been viewed as agents of coercive policy transfer, with 'structural adjustment' required of countries seeking funds from both for development or debt

---

BOX 12.2   *Simmons and Danner on the conundrum of the International Criminal Court*

Simmons and Danner (2010) note that ostensibly the International Criminal Court (ICC) does not appear to be in any nation state's interest, since it pre-commits powerful political actors to cooperate with criminal prosecutions. Furthermore, from a first glance, there appears to be no clear trend amongst nations signing up to the ICC, with both developed and developing, democratic and non-democratic states signing up (or refusing to sign up, such as the USA, Russia, China and India).

Simmons and Danner argue this can be explained by considering the ICC as a tool for some states to prove 'credible commitment' to ceasing hostilities. As they put it, '[j]oining the ICC is . . . a form of self-binding commitment, in which states attempt to persuade other players – rebels, potentially supportive publics – that the government has voluntarily abandoned the option of engaging in unlimited violence, thus creating incentives for other actors to alter their behavior as well' (*ibid.*: 234).

They test this hypothesis using data on different countries' intensity of conflict, joining behaviour (to the ICC) and extent of the rule of law. Through event history analysis, they consider the sequencing of decisions to join the ICC (or not), and conclude that the 'credible commitment' hypothesis is confirmed. While some Scandinavian nations, for example, might join the ICC for purely humanitarian reasons, nations which are freshly out of, or still experiencing, conflict may well do so for the instrumentalist reason of signalling a credible commitment to abandon violence.

---

payments. Following a revisionist turn, particularly within the World Bank, some of the most radical elements of structural adjustment appear to have been abandoned (see Chapter 13). Nonetheless, the recent debt crisis has involved the IMF as one of a 'troika' (alongside the EU and the European Central Bank) of actors which has imposed swingeing conditions on Greece and Ireland in exchange for offering bail-out funds.

The UN also has an important role as a guardian of numerous conventions on Human Rights, and a legal relationship with the International Criminal Court (ICC). The ICC was developed out of the International Criminal Tribunal for the Former Yugoslavia (ICTY) and the International Criminal Tribunal for Rwanda (ICTR), both of which were developed out of the UN Security Council (see Box 12.2).

The World Trade Organization

The World Trade Organization (WTO) was developed out of the General Agreement on Tariffs and Trade (GATT), with the latter having been formed following World War II to reduce customs tariffs between nations.

The WTO has the goal of facilitating free trade through reducing explicit tariffs and 'non-tariff barriers' to trade (measures which implicitly restrict trade, without this being their stated goal). Its overall architecture is intergovernmental, with a Ministerial Conference meeting every two years to set overall priorities. However, non-majoritarian mechanisms such as Dispute Settlement Panels are in place to guarantee compliance amongst member states with WTO rules. Amendments to WTO rules are agreed during negotiated 'rounds', with recent rounds having included the Uruguay Round (running from 1986–94, and which set up the WTO) and the Doha Development Agenda, begun in 2001.

The WTO's agenda is very wide-ranging, covering trade in manufactures and also in services. Fundamentally, nations are required to treat products from other countries exactly the same as if they were domestically produced (Hoekman, 2002). In theory, nations are able to ignore WTO rules where this is 'necessary to protect human, animal or plant life or health'. However, determining what this exemption means in practice has proven highly controversial. The EU, for example, has consistently argued that the use of artificial beef hormones is potentially injurious to consumers' health, and banned such beef from being sold in Europe. This has been disputed by the USA, which took the EU to the WTO and won its case (including, later, at an appeal by the EU). Similarly, the scope of the WTO has been contested, with some maintaining that particular 'services' are core to the operation of the state and should be operated publicly, rather than constituting 'tradable' commercial operations (Dodds, 2004).

International financial governance: Basel II, the FSB, G7 and G20

There is a wide variety of issue-specific transnational governing institutions, which cannot be examined in detail here. This section considers just one subset of these: those institutions focused on creating standards for the global financial sector. This has involved intergovernmental institutions such as successive Basel Committees and the G7 and G20 groups of countries, which together created bodies eventuating in the Financial Stability Board.

In comparison with other forms of international governance, the development of cross-national banking standards has been relatively recent, with the first Basel Concordat on banking supervision being concluded in 1975. This was followed by the 1988 Basel Accord, concerning capital requirements for banks, and then 'Basel II', concluded in 2004. From the late 1990s, a number of developed nations' governments (primarily from the EU, alongside the USA) began to try to align the Basel developments with discussions in the G7, and created the Financial Stability Forum. This Forum was intended to coordinate the development of international standards across the various interested parties. Core nations within the process then pushed for the resulting standards to be adopted internationally (Helleiner and Pagliari, 2011).

The Financial Stability Board was, then, created after pressures from the broader range of G20 nations to be involved more closely in the process of standard setting and enforcement, and for the IMF and World Bank to be more directly engaged with it. This reflected the growing financial strength of financial institutions in emerging economies, with, for example, the 'three largest banks in the world in 2009 by market capitalization [being] Chinese' (*ibid*.: 176).

As with the EU, the extent to which the new financial arrangements can be viewed as intergovernmental or as supranational is contested. On the one hand, the technical nature of much of their activities means that hitherto their agendas have arguably reflected technocratic and business-led rather than national priorities, and have been driven primarily by international experts rather than politicians (Porter, 2005). On the other hand, the increasingly extensive role of governments and bodies such as the EU in international financial issues has perhaps reduced the power of international experts and business networks (Helleiner and Pagliari, 2011: 184).

The impact of transnational governing institutions

Policy harmonization: upwards or downwards?
All the international organizations described above have some kind of impact, direct or indirect, on the policies enacted by governments. The question immediately arises whether this impact involves levelling spending, the strictness of regulations, and so on upwards (positive integration) or downwards (negative integration). The distinction was coined by Tinbergen (1954), who separated negative integration (removing existing barriers to trade, such as tariffs or regulations), from positive integration (creating new policy measures, which could include regulations such as air quality standards or spending to promote common economic development, such as on research and development). Some have argued strenuously that the institutional design of the EU promotes negative over positive integration (Leibfried, 1991; Scharpf, 1999), a pattern also discerned in relation to other multinational organizations (Mishra, 1999), such as the IMF, World Bank and WTO.

Others suggest, however, that integration via transnational governing institutions can promote positive integration, at least in terms of the shifting upwards of regulatory standards. This is because high-regulating countries have an incentive to impose similar standards on their competitors, so that they are faced with the same costs of regulation and thus do not gain a competitive advantage from laxer standards. Holzinger *et al.* (2011: 29) note that, across the 24 countries they studied which fall within the EU and EFTA (as well as Japan, Mexico and the USA), there was a 'continuous spread of environmental policies across countries', with all the countries studied adopting measures in seven out of the 22 environmental policy measures they examined (*ibid.*: 30). Overall, their analysis confirms that 'convergence is more pronounced for regulatory standards with binding agreements at the international level', but that it has also been occurring within countries and in relation to topic areas that are not covered by such binding agreements (*ibid.*: 33).

In relation to welfare standards, the use of the concept of 'social dumping' enables the upward harmonization of welfare provision to be seen as levelling the playing field for trade. The concept of 'social dumping' suggests that less well-off groups will move to other jurisdictions where they can make use of more generous social security. However, rather than this leading to a race to the bottom, this can promote positive integration, since states concerned to prevent social dumping will argue for all welfare provision to converge with their own. EU measures such as Structural Funds also arguably constitute a redistributive social policy which aims at upwards harmonization of economic activity and employment opportunities (Deacon *et al.*, 1997). Even where redistribution is not involved, however, multinational regulatory mechanisms may promote welfare, if indirectly. A fascinating recent case comes from the field of discrimination in the provision of insurance, which has been challenged through a series of policy initiatives pushed by the Directorate General for Employment within the European Commission (Hartlapp and Rauh, 2011).

Impact on the locus of policy-making power
All the transnational governing institutions described above, barring explicitly judicial bodies such as the ICC, could be viewed as embodying both intergovernmental elements (the EU's European Council and Councils; the WTO's Ministerial Assembly; the UN General Assembly and Security Council) and supranational elements (the EU's Commission and Court of Justice of the European Union; the WTO's Dispute Settlement Panels; the UN's World Bank and the IMF). The question remains as to how, exactly – if at all – domestic preferences are fed into these transnational institutions.

On the one hand, it has been argued that transnational governing institutions find it difficult to impose policy measures without at least some support for these amongst their member states. When it comes to the EU, for example, Schmidt (2002a: 894–5) argues that 'European policies have tended to follow national policy changes as much as lead them, with national policies having shaped those of the EU as often as EU policies have shaped those of its member states'. Similarly, Graziano (2011: 600) suggests that for European pressures to be 'translated into domestic policy change', there is arguably a need for 'support' for change from 'the main domestic institutional and social actors'. Such actors may be non-governmental (e.g. domestic business), member state governments (Fontana, 2011: 656) or political parties, whether in government or opposition (Gwiazda, 2011). Similarly, there is some evidence that dispute resolution panels within the WTO are concerned to exercise 'judicial economy' – that is, to rule that they will not pronounce on non-essential issues raised by litigants – in order to maintain support across the Organization's membership (Busch and Pelc, 2010).

Furthermore, it is arguable that policy adaptation may occur in very different ways in different sectors. Jakobsen (2010) compares the telecommunications and electricity sectors, and suggests that Danish policy-makers were prepared to alter domestic policies more radically in the case of telecommunications because pressures from the EU and globalization were stronger in this regard than they were for the electricity sectors. Whilst international factors may precipitate change, Jakobsen (*ibid.*: 903–4) suggests that they do so 'only to some extent, and unless in very extreme forms, not as the only explanatory factor'.

Indeed, nation states' interactions with many transnational institutions could be viewed as a process of both 'downloading' or receiving policies from these institutions, and of 'uploading' their own domestic policy preferences at an international level (see Bulmer and Burch, 2000, on this process at the EU level). This acknowledges the fact that, as mentioned in Chapter 1, involvement in multinational decision-making can provide domestic policy-makers with opportunities, as well as constraining them. At a rather basic level, domestic policy actors can use international opportunities to capture resources. An extreme example of this comes from the case of the Irish labour market agency, which managed to amass 'up to one third of the EU funding' for domestic purposes during the Delors period (Kirby and Murphy, 2010: 28). Less visibly, but no less importantly, domestic actors can use multinational-level processes to alter domestic policy-making arrangements in their favour (see Lodge, 2002; Radaelli, 2003; James, 2010).

Global trends and their impact

In addition to cross-national flows and international governing institutions, a third pressure on domestic public policy-making can be identified: global trends in ideology and discourse. Some have argued that the frequent conflation of a particular political project with the growth of international trade has confused the meaning of globalization (Gray, 1998: 215; Yeates, 1999: 373). However, for some authors, 'globalisation as political ideology' is rightly one element of globalization, alongside globalization as innovation in the fields of technology and the economy, since all three factors 'drastically reduce the barriers to economic, political, and cultural exchange' (Drezner, 2001: 53).

It is important to focus on ideas, since ultimately it is not (just) the brute 'facts' about cross-national pressures (the extent of cross-national flows, or the legal powers of international organizations) that change public policy, but how these are interpreted by policy-makers. Hence, 'it is the ideas that actors hold about the context in which they find themselves rather than the context itself which informs the way in which actors behave' (Hay and Rosamond, 2002: 148).

Hay and Rosamond (*ibid.*) argue that many policy-makers have relied on a 'hyperglobalisation' thesis, whereby the growing transnationalization of business is viewed as requiring lower levels of regulation and taxation, without necessarily possessing the evidence to prove this thesis. Lacking the evidence is not terminal, since '[p]olicy-makers acting on the basis of assumptions consistent with the hyperglobalisation thesis may well serve, in so doing, to bring about outcomes consistent with that thesis, irrespective of its veracity and, indeed, irrespective of its perceived veracity' (*ibid.*:148).

Hirst and Thompson (1999: 262) make a similar argument, maintaining that the 'rhetoric' of globalization is convenient for both right and

BOX 12.3   Hay and Smith on how policy-makers 'really' understand globalization

Hay and Smith (2010) have attempted the direct investigation of policy-makers' conceptions of globalization and its relationship with views about European integration. The authors attempted this through factor analysis of data comprising an attitudinal survey of 657 civil servants and parliamentarians across the UK and Ireland.

The survey indicated that there were many similarities in the two countries, both between and across parliamentarians and civil servants. Overall, both sets of actors appeared to conceive of globalization and its impacts within a broadly 'neoliberal' framework.

Interestingly, however, the survey did indicate a disparity between these actors' 'private' views of globalization and its implications for policy-making, and how they communicated this publicly. In particular, Hay and Smith suggest that policy-makers may portray globalization as more strongly necessitating particular reforms than they would claim when out of the public eye.

left parties, and that it can become, to a large degree, 'self-fulfilling' by reducing the attractiveness of domestic-level, traditional politics as an arena for socio-economic change. They suggest, however, that domestic politics will tend, instead, to focus upon issues which are seen as amenable to national-level action, such as the 'politics of morality', including issues such as abortion, gay and animal rights, and the environment (*ibid.*: 262).

'Europeanization', it is claimed, has also been used rhetorically to provide justification for particular policies. Indeed, for Lynggaard (2011: 21), it is possible to view both European integration and globalization 'as a set of concepts and conceptions, which makes up a discursive context for domestic decisionmakers, policies and institutions'. Politicians may be able to make strategic use of pressures from Europe in order to strengthen their own position and weaken that of others – for example, to reduce the scope of concertation arrangements and concentrate decision-making within the executive (Fontana, 2011: 666). However, the use of Europe as an 'excuse' for reform may backfire, if this leads to a public perception that reforms are being imposed from outside. Rodrik (1997) argues that this led to strikes in France in 1995, when reforms were presented as uniquely required by the Maastricht criteria, rather than necessary for other, more domestic, reasons.

The influence of ideas and rhetoric about globalization and Europeanization has been traced in detail in a number of studies which have attempted to understand why distinctive, but broadly congruent, reforms have been instituted in different nations, by examining the role of discourse in policy change (see, for example, Schmidt, 2003; and also Box 12.3).

Conclusion

The discussion above has indicated that whilst cross-national pressures have led to considerable policy convergence, these pressures are often expressed primarily through domestic policy structures, and shaped heavily by them. The 'international order is still primarily one of politically constructed nation-states', and indeed, there are many nationalists within existing states who continue to prioritize gaining separate statehood as their policy goal (Kennett, 2001: 38). Very few nation states appear willing to entirely renounce their sovereignty and hand this to other bodies, with perhaps the unique exceptions of Lesotho, home to a popular movement which seeks incorporation into South Africa; and New Zealand, which once considered merger with Australia (Reeves, 1969).

Globalization and other cross-national pressures have not necessarily abolished or wounded the role of the state. Rather, they have altered the 'scale' at which policy is delivered (Jessop, 2000), changing the locus of policy-making but not necessarily radically altering power relationships. At the same time, however, it has become more difficult entirely to separate domestic from cross-national pressures: Galton's problem, referred to in Chapter 14, is still a serious challenge for comparative public policy analysts. Many of the detailed analyses referred to above, however, have illustrated the merits of research which describes and analyses the mechanisms through which cross-national processes lead to policy change, rather than just assuming that they will do so.

Summary

- Cross-national processes can be separated into the impact of cross-national flows, transnational governing institutions, and global trends. These processes are related to developments associated with both 'globalization' and 'regionalization'.
- Cross-national flows include cross-border movements of trade, capital, people and information. There is a large and growing number of transnational governing institutions, from the EU to the IMF, the UN and the WTO. Cross-national trends include the adoption of market-based approaches within the public sector.
- The impact of these cross-national processes is varied and complex. Cross-national processes have sometimes been described as leading to 'races to the bottom' in regulatory and welfare standards, but the evidence for this is mixed.
- Transnational governing institutions can act in an intergovernmental manner (by merely aggregating and promoting the interests of their members) or a supranational manner (by acting independently of their members in at least some policy areas).
- In practice, however, it is arguable that many cross-national governing institutions can be viewed as representing member states' preferences, furthering or hindering their preferences through the imposition of policy, and also shaping those preferences through domestic actors' involvement in international policy-making.

Chapter 13

Comparative Public Policy: A Minority World Pursuit?

It has been argued that '[c]omparative public policy is a young field, even younger than the systematic study of politics in the developing countries of Asia, Africa and Latin America. The hybrid of these two fields – comparative public policy in developing countries – is younger still' (Horowitz, 1989: 197). This chapter considers exactly this 'young field', and how it departs from the approaches to public policy analysis that have been described in previous chapters.

First, it considers the relationship between comparative public policy and the study of development, and explains the use of the term 'Majority World'. The chapter then considers the policy tools adopted by Majority World governments, and how their use of these is affected by more intense external pressures than generally apply in Minority World countries. Following this, the chapter considers how Majority World governments' policy-making processes can be analysed. It details how many of the frameworks previously considered in this book are inappropriate or redundant for the analysis of many Majority World nations. Numerous alternative approaches have been put forward to explain policy-making in these countries, of which developmentalism, stratified development, neoliberalism, dependency theory and area studies are considered here. Finally, the chapter concludes by considering the ambiguous role of Minority World academics and academia in the scholarship and policy-making of the Majority World.

The term 'Majority World' is adopted here to avoid prejudicing claims about the nature of countries falling outside the OECD, which comprised 82 per cent of the world's population at the time of writing. An alternative, frequently used, term is 'developing world', intended to cover all those countries which are not 'developed' – that is, all those which have not 'experienced ... [nor are experiencing] industrialized economic growth' and which have not 'developed extensive state structures to manage and support that growth and to provide (to some extent) for the consequential welfare needs of their citizens' (Alcock and Craig, 2009: 1). The problem with this definition of the 'developing world', however, is that it excludes those countries in the Majority World where government has attempted to direct economic growth and its proceeds towards the welfare of the population, either successfully or unsuccessfully (as with many socialist and developmentalist states). It also suggests that Majority World countries should be primarily defined in relation to what they lack (economic wealth), rather than viewing them as a category worthy of investigation in their own right. Whilst the terms 'global South' and 'global North' are also sometimes used to reflect differentials in economic and political power, in practice these terms are often used as shorthand for whether nations are developing or developed since, geographically, Australia belongs to the global South, whilst Mongolia belongs to the global North, yet they tend to be classified as 'Northern' and 'Southern', respectively.

As used here, the term 'Majority World' brackets together those countries traditionally viewed as the 'third world' (i.e. non-aligned, developing nations) with the communist (and now generally post-communist) nations viewed as the 'second world' (i.e. China and the USSR's component nations), as well as with the 'emerging' nations of Latin America. There is, clearly, a significant difference between the public policies which can be adopted by so-called 'least developed countries' (LDCs) and those nations at the richer end of the scale which nonetheless are not members of the OECD.

At the time of writing, in order to qualify as an LDC a nation has to satisfy the three criteria of having a gross national annual per capita income of under US$750, weak human resources, and economic vulnerability. Furthermore, given that the LDC criteria indicate the presence of 'structural handicaps', no country with a population of over 75 million can be classified as an LDC. This contrasts with the populations of China – 1,343 million; India –1,205 million; Brazil – 205 million; and Russia – 138 million. Amongst these populous 'BRICs' (Brazil, Russia, India and China) there is considerable heterogeneity, with Russia's annual GDP per capita of US$16,700 being substantially more than Brazil's (US$11,600), twice that of China (US$8,400) and over four times that of India (US$3,700) (all at US$ 2011 prices). Despite this, all the BRICs can be clearly delineated from LDCs, with India's per capita GDP, for example, being over ten times higher than that of the Democratic Republic of Congo, and almost five times the LDC threshold (CIA, 2012).

What these Majority World nations do share, however, is their general exclusion from studies of comparative public policy. The two most highly-cited texts on comparative public policy restrict their analyses to Europe and America (Heidenheimer *et al.*, 1983), and a selection of OECD nations Castles (1998). As a result, it is appropriate to consider whether 'Majority World' nations can be analysed using the approaches promoted by traditional analyses of comparative public policy, or whether alternative perspectives are required.

This chapter concentrates on the existing comparative public policy literature, rather than examining work from within development studies (although there is some overlap between these two categories). This is partly for reasons of parsimony, but also because development studies tend to be more focused on 'the immediate need of the developing countries to achieve economic, political and social modernization' (Parkyn, 2007: 39). As such, development studies generally focus on specific features of public policy and their relationship with economic development, rather than isolating separate areas of policy, as within this book.

Development studies also implicitly embody the assumption that social scientific endeavour should be focused on promoting economic growth, and are thus inherently normative in a way that comparative public policy analyses need not be. It is important to note, for example, that 'development' can lead to worsening living standards for the majority of the population, at least in the short term, whilst conditions for a smaller number of people improve (Minns, 2006: 3).

Comparative public policy: excluding the Majority World?

Chapters 3 to 7 considered how Minority World governments used their financial resources, powers of authority, ability to organize service provision and control over information in the fields of economic, welfare, health, education and environmental policy. However, many of the approaches adopted by Minority World governments in these fields are not possible for Majority World governments, for reasons ranging from extreme resource constraints to political and territorial instability. The following sections consider some of the challenges facing Majority World governments in relation to their use of these different categories of policy tools.

A final difference between Minority and Majority World countries concerns the extent and nature of international influence to which they are exposed. Whilst Minority World country governments are heavily affected in their policy choices by multinational pressures, these generally emanate from organizations of which they are members – such as the EU, in the case of European Union countries (see Chapter 12). This is not necessarily the case with Majority World countries, which may also face a higher degree of bilateral pressure from hostile neighbours than do most Minority World countries.

Financial resources

Clearly, Majority World governments are unable to garner the levels of tax revenue from their populations that Minority World governments can, because of relatively low population income and relatively high levels of informal (untaxed) work. The lack of financial resources has, in many cases, resulted in Majority World governments requiring aid from international donors. An interesting new development in this area has already been mentioned in Chapter 7 – the Ecuadorian government's request for funds to cover the costs of not exploiting oil reserves in an area of protected rainforest. This approach, and other incentive and financing mechanisms, may be more realistic than the imposition of new international regulations, given 'strong economic and demographic pressures on environmental resources' in many Majority World countries (O'Connor, 2008: 368).

More broadly, the lesser availability of financial resources for Majority World governments has an obvious impact on the public policies which they can pursue, given their often extremely tight fiscal situation. For example, the generosity of welfare provision in such nations tends to be considerably less than in Minority World countries – at least, for the majority of the population. Whilst many nations have introduced non-contributory public pensions, for example, such as South Africa, these often involve rather small transfers (Barr, 2009). This contrasts strongly with some Minority World nations where the rate of the non-contributory pension can be set relatively high, with an extreme example coming from the Greek public pension before that country's fiscal crisis. In 2009, the Greek public pension exceeded 100 per cent of the average worker's wage (Börsch, 2009: 178) – a level which was arguably unsustainable over the longer run, but utterly inconceivable within the Majority World.

As with the Minority World, the use to which financial resources are put within Majority World countries varies substantially across policy fields including economic, welfare, health, education and environmental policy. Useful reviews of policy-making in these areas are available from the World Bank and the UN's various agencies, such as the World Health Organization and UN Development Programme.

Family policy is one area where some Majority World governments have adopted novel approaches to incentivizing population growth and restraint. Attempts to increase and limit the population through the use of authority are considered in the following section. Here, it should be noted that some Majority World governments have been keen to provide direct financial incentives to increase the population. For example, in Russia, women who give birth to a second child are given a substantial sum to encourage them to increase the size of their family. The fund can be put towards the costs of education, housing or an individual pension account, but only after the child concerned reaches three years of age (Davidova and Manning, 2009: 200). In this way, the funds are provided not (necessarily) to cover the costs of child-rearing, but rather (potentially) for the mother herself to use (on her own pension, for example). This approach continues previous Soviet-era policies to incentivize the production of larger families.

Authority

The extent to which governments can use their powers of authority to shape population behaviour obviously differs between democratic and non-democratic Majority World countries. In all democratic nations, governments possess authority and autonomy over their territory and, in particular, a monopoly of legitimate violence within that territory (Weber, 1918). The legitimacy of the use of violence and of other powers is, of course, disputed within non-democratic nations.

As with Minority World nations, the use of governmental authority in these countries obviously includes the prohibition, prescription and regulation of individual and collective activities across different areas of public policy. Again, as with Minority World nations, certain groups of the population may be singled out within this process as eligible or ineligible for certain activities. In non-democratic nations such as Apartheid South Africa, extensive arrangements were put in place to prevent black South Africans from undertaking activities as diverse as living in white areas, marrying white people, and even using particular bridges, hospitals, schools and buses. To take a different, more current, example, Saudi Arabian women were at the time of writing unable to participate in any way in the political process, including voting and standing for office (although it appears that the franchise may be expanded in 2015) (Hausmann *et al.*, 2010). No laws exist to punish crimes against women, and women are forbidden from driving and from associating with men who are not close relatives. Their dress code is also strictly regulated by the religious police (*Mutawwa*).

Other uses of authority that, on paper, should be applied universally, may often be focused upon specific groups. This highlights the importance of informal institutional elements as considered in Chapter 10. Again, the realm of family policy provides numerous examples of this, particularly from the two most populous nations of the world: India and China. The intensification of Indira Gandhi's family planning policy in India during the late 1970s led to some slum dwellers and villagers being forcibly sterilized before the policy was abandoned in 1977. China's 'one child' policy, introduced in the 1970s and ongoing at the time of writing, has been blamed for increasing gender-selective abortion, with 135 boys born for every 100 girls in 2002 in Hainan province (Gittings, 2002).

Organization

Majority World governments' abilities to use their power of organization vary substantially and are used in very different ways. For example, whilst in many Majority World nations the degree of state ownership is minimal, in others it comprises the use of sovereign wealth funds (as in the Middle East), the use of state-owned trading companies (as by the Chinese government), and direct public ownership (as in countries such as India and Brazil).

One feature of many Majority World countries which applies to a far less significant degree in the Minority World is the supplementation of formal organizational systems with informal ones. This is clear, for example, in the use of 'informal payments' – sometimes also called 'under-the-counter' payments – in fields from health care to immigration. Nonetheless, the incidence of informal payments varies substantially, with, for example, only 3 per cent of patients reporting having paid them to health care professionals in Peru, whereas 96 per cent report having done so in Pakistan (Lewis, 2007). However, the generally illegal nature of informal payments means that reported figures should be treated with caution.

Another challenge for many Majority World countries is their sometimes limited administrative capacity, given financial, geographical and practical constraints. The Chinese pension system, for example, suffers from both vertical (between different levels of administration) and horizontal (across administrative unit borders) fragmentation. Whilst local administration might be advisable in such a context, the 'extremely large migration movements' in China – 'an estimated 115 million migrant workers in 2006 – limit the capacity of the system to deal effectively with this problem' (Salditt *et al.*, 2008: 66).

Another example comes from the field of education, where government abilities to regulate private providers of primary, secondary and tertiary education is often limited. Ronald Dore famously used an interest-based argument (see Chapter 8) to explain the particular pressures facing late-industrializing countries in the field of education. As the demand for high-skilled labour increases rapidly in these nations, 'the more widely education certificates are used for occupational selection; the faster the rate of qualification inflation and the more examination-oriented schooling becomes at the expense of genuine education' (Dore, 1976: 72).

Use of information

The extent to which Majority World governments can use information to change population behaviour is, obviously, reliant on the same factors that affect their ability to use organization – affordability, practicality and the degree of remoteness (or otherwise) of their populations.

When it comes to the provision of information and advice to citizens, certain tools adopted by many Minority World governments are effectively redundant in many Majority World countries. Only one out of every one hundred people in the world own a computer (100 People, undated), clearly restricting the utility of internet-based information in many countries. The growth of mobile telephony has been far more significant, with half of the world's population owning a mobile by 2007. Mobile phones have been used to deliver information to remote groups of villagers, to improve disaster response, and to facilitate election monitoring. At the same time, however, governments have been able to use mobile phone networks – as well as internet services – to block communications and/or identify possible opponents during times of extensive civil unrest (as during the Arab Spring of 2010–11), or on an ongoing basis (as in China) (see Institute of Development Studies, 2007).

Government use of information to inform public policy-making depends on the effectiveness of both their administrative apparatus and other organizations (such as academic institutions and statistical institutes). However, in many Majority World countries, pressures on data-gathering organizations, both practical and political, have reduced the reliability and validity of the information they produce. For example, statistics in many countries within the former Yugoslavia ceased to be collected during its civil wars. In any case, both before and during the Yugoslav wars, statistics were routinely manipulated for political reasons.

In such circumstances, both domestic actors (think tanks, private companies and NGOs) and international actors (NGOs, international organizations and consultants) now provide many of the studies used by governments when planning policy. The particular role of academics as consultants in Majority World countries is considered again in the conclusion to this chapter.

Pressures beyond the nation state

As just indicated, the way in which Majority World governments can use financial resources, their authority, powers of organization and control over information differs in many ways from Minority World governments. In addition to this, external pressures on policy-making are often far more intense in Majority World countries. In these nations, whilst public policy-making is certainly affected by the global and regional flows detailed in Chapter 12, it is also impacted by bilateral and multinational pressures, as well. Dependency theory, considered in greater detail below, argues that all public policy in Majority World countries is determined by their subordinate position in the world economy. However, it is not necessary to adopt that rather extreme position to acknowledge that many Majority World countries are subject to extensive external pressures which can have a profound effect on public policy.

First, many Majority World nations, due to their lack of financial resources, are heavily dependent on bilateral and multinational aid. This aid often comes with conditions attached. These need not always be heeded, as can be seen in Ghana and Kenya where higher education fees were heavily contested, despite international pressure for them to be introduced (Samoff, 2007: 59). Furthermore, some bilateral donors (particularly China) are willing to fund aid and provide low-cost credit, with far fewer conditions than 'traditional' donors such as the USA and EU. Nonetheless, governments in Majority World countries have historically been subject to strong external pressures from bodies of which they are not necessarily members, such as the IMF and EU. They thus have to negotiate at an international level whilst simultaneously (in the case of democratic regimes) persuading their populations of the suitability of new policies.

These different kinds of external pressure mean that analytical approaches adopted to explain policy-making in the Minority World may be less than helpful in explaining developments in the Majority World. For example, it has been argued that politicians will adopt independent regulatory agencies when they have been persuaded of the merits of a commitment to economic efficiency, rather than just trying to distribute

BOX 13.1   The regulatory state in Kosovo

Kosovo, formerly part of Yugoslavia, is perhaps the most contentious and high-profile contemporary contested state, as well as being the second-newest proclaimed state, following South Sudan's declaration of independence on 9 July 2011. Along with Jelena Obradovic-Wochnik and Ahmed Badran (Dodds *et al.*, 2011), I have researched the developing regulatory state in Kosovo in the field of energy, through documentary analysis of institutional reports, legislation, and press reports, corroborated by informal discussions with key actors.

Kosovo demonstrates many of the accoutrements of regulatory states, to the extent that it has witnessed a proliferation of non-majoritarian institutions. However, the reasons behind the creation and development of the Kosovan regulatory state depart significantly from those posited by 'mainstream' regulatory state theories.

First, within Kosovo, the most significant change in the nature of the state has not been from a Keynesian to a regulatory state, but from a Socialist to an ethnicized, semi-Socialist confederation, then towards an incipient independent, but still ethnically contested, polity. Within this context, the authority of the state itself is highly contested, let alone the nature of its activities.

Second, the Kosovan energy regulatory space reveals the importance of non-domestic pressures, but not in the way conceived by regulatory state models, which focused on globalization and Europeanization. Kosovo's energy sector is powerfully shaped by its attempts to accede to the European Union, but also by bilateral relationships with donor countries, and by continuing conflict with its neighbour Serbia.

resources to supporters (Lodge and Stirton, 2006; see Chapter 2). Yet, in many developing nations, independent regulatory agencies are simply imposed by external actors. In these circumstances, the claim that governments have voluntarily bound themselves not to interfere – that they have 'credibly committed' to support independent regulatory arrangements – is not tenable (Badran, 2010; see also Box 13.1).

It should be noted that many Majority World countries are also subject to territorial conflict, in a manner which has not affected any Minority World countries for decades (with the exception of civil conflicts in Northern Ireland, the Basque region and Israel). The existence of conflict – particularly over natural resources – can, obviously, have a significant impact on public policy-making. For example, Wood and Gough suggest that nations subject to conflict can be described as 'insecurity regimes'. Here, nascent or previous 'welfare regimes' have been destroyed or attenuated because external pressures prevent internal social support from developing, leading to an exclusive reliance on family- and locality-based provision. Wood and Gough (2006) suggest this regime applies in much of sub-Saharan Africa. Indeed, the very nature of government sovereignty is challenged in many Majority World countries. The most extreme version of this occurs in contested states such as Abkhazia, Kosovo, Nagorno-Karabakh, Somaliland, South Ossetia, Transnistria and the Turkish Republic of Northern Cyprus, where statehood applies in a '*de facto*' and temporary manner, and is 'internationally disputed' (Geldenhuys, 2009: 7; see also Lynch, 2004).

Majority World analytical approaches

Approaches to explaining public policies in the Minority World have been viewed as inappropriate for the Majority World for three reasons. First, some of the concepts they rely on simply do not make sense in the context of many countries within the developing world.

For example, Walker and Wong (1996) have argued that the concept of the 'welfare state' implicitly or explicitly embodies the view that such a state must be capitalist as well as democratic. As a result, the term 'welfare state' excludes those nations which lack 'one or both of the supposed core institutions' of the welfare state: 'a capitalist economy and a western parliamentary democracy' (*ibid.*: 69). Indeed, Gough *et al.* (2004) suggest that it is often more appropriate to speak of different 'meta-welfare regimes' in relation to developing countries, than to describe these as 'welfare states'.

To take another example, claims that nations are increasingly adopting regulatory approaches to public policy-making, and thus becoming 'regulatory states' (see Chapter 2), are disputed by some scholars of developing countries. They have argued that, *inter alia*, increased regulation can occur without any regulatory state necessarily being created – since such regulation is simply imposed on top of state-owned utilities (rather than the privatized ones envisaged by the model) (Phillips, 2006).

Second, many of the theoretical tenets within public policy analyses of the Minority World are shown as redundant, or even contradicted, when those theories are applied to Majority World countries. For example, it is difficult to apply traditional models of capitalist variation to Latin American countries, since 'these countries change their versions of capitalism more frequently, and more radically, than European countries do', contradicting claims that economic policy models will tend to change only slowly (see Chapter 3) (Sheahan, 2002: 25). Overall, the 'structural characteristics' of Majority World countries 'still differ greatly from those of the industrialized countries', meaning that 'even formally similar models cannot be expected to have consistently similar consequences' (*ibid.*: 26).

Finally, it also does not appear to be the case that Majority World countries are all converging towards Minority World policy paradigms, as might have been predicted by so-called 'modernization' theories. These argued that existing analytical frameworks covering OECD countries would increasingly become applicable to the Majority World because the latter would gradually reform their policies to conform with those operating within the Minority World (Rostow, 1960; Apter, 1965). There were two variants of this approach. The first suggested that nations would have to go through a number of different stages of development in order to industrialize and become integrated in the world capitalist economy. This approach suggested that public policy developments in Majority World countries would slowly converge over time, both amongst the category of Majority World countries but also in relation to Minority World countries. The other branch of modernization theory agreed with the first to the extent that Majority World countries would eventually converge towards Minority World policy paradigms, but suggested that they would do so in very different ways, given that their starting positions were marked by 'extreme divergence' (Rudra, 2007: 378).

Neither branch of modernization theory appears confirmed by empirical developments. Whilst some Majority World nations may be adopting certain policy approaches from Minority World countries, increasing divergence is also evident in some areas. The growing influence of China on sub-Saharan Africa (Rotberger, 2008) and the diverse trajectories of authoritarian regimes (Levitsky and Way, 2010) suggest that a uniform shift towards democratic capitalism may be unlikely.

The sections that follow therefore consider novel approaches which have been developed to explain public policy developments in Majority

World countries: developmentalism, extractive strategies, neoliberalism and dependency theory. It should be noted, however, that all these approaches have, at times, been used both to describe and analyse public policy developments, and to advocate particular approaches to public policy-making. For example, developmentalism is lauded by those who favour extensive state involvement in the economy, whereas neoliberalism is proposed by those who want to see a reduction in government 'interference' in the economy.

Developmentalism

One approach which has been specifically developed to explain public policy-making in many Majority World countries is what could be described as 'developmentalism'. This approach focuses on the challenges faced by nations which are industrializing 'late'. These countries are likely to adopt specific patterns of public policies depending on how late they are in industrializing compared with other countries. For example, if they are industrializing very late, they will be likely to: grow economically very quickly; have governments which focus more on large-scale production – and, particularly, producer goods – and less on agriculture; have more pressure put on the consumption levels of the domestic population; and have a greater part played by the state and/or domestic banks (Gerschenkron, 1962).

These requirements place particular pressure on the state to overcome domestic pressures to retain the *status quo* (particularly, domestic consumption levels). As Minns (2006) argues, in order to be able to act against the interests of existing groups, the state needs more than an ability to repress opponents, since this need not necessarily facilitate industrialization. Instead, rapid industrialization also rests on the 'historically determined structural abilities of the state and its connections with the broader society' (*ibid.*: 27).

The state's ability to act *autonomously* from societal forces has been seen as essential in explaining its success, or otherwise, in promoting industrialization (Trimberger, 1978; Weiss and Hobson, 1995). State autonomy can enable governments to push forward industrializing policies which go against the interests of powerful groups. However, it can equally facilitate extractive approaches to politics whereby politicians concentrate not on industrialization but, rather, on acquiring rent from exploiting natural resources (see the next section and Chapter 8).

Minns's description of how states acquire autonomy is rather similar to Mancur Olson's 'RADON' (see Chapters 3 and 8), but Minns restricts his analysis to the ruling classes rather than looking at all groups in society. Hence, he indicates that some sort of 'cataclysmic disruption of the ruling class of the old society' was necessary in Mexico, South Korea and Taiwan to prepare the ground for the rapid industrialization that all three experienced up until the 1980s (Minns, 2006: 233). However, this rapid industrialization eventually reduced the autonomy of the state, since it created a more powerful private capital sector and middle and working classes (*ibid.*: 1). After being forced to accommodate at least some of these groups' demands, each state lost its ability to 'lead' a 'miracle' economy' (*ibid.*: 1).

Nita Rudra's (2007) examination of welfare states in the Majority World separates developmentalist approaches, with extensive state autonomy (described as 'productive' welfare states), from those focused on maintaining the status of specific groups (described as 'protective' welfare states) (*ibid.*: 379). She considers five dimensions of activity undertaken by developing nations: the extent of public employment; the level of expenditure on social transfers (pensions, unemployment benefit, family allowances and so on); housing subsidies; protections in the labour market; and investment in further and higher education (*ibid.*: 387).

Productive welfare states – such as Chile, Colombia, Greece, Malaysia, and Singapore – promote the market dependence of citizens and prioritize their commodification. Hence, the focus of policy is not on decommodification (as with welfare states in the Minority World – see Chapter 4) but, instead, on commodification – to ensure that the population is dependent on the formal labour market, rather than able to rely on other sources of income (e.g. from informal labour or from the state). For many of these nations, the issue for governments is not how to improve the condition of the working class, but how to promote the growth of such a class, through industrialization. Status equalization is thus less important, for many such countries, than 'catching up' economically (*ibid.*: 382; see also Holliday, 2005).

This approach approximates to many analyses of the 'developmentalist' model applied to East Asian countries. Studies of the welfare state in these nations have often claimed, for example, that systems of social provision have been specifically designed to promote economic development (see Goodman *et al.*, 1998; Jones, 1990). These approaches to welfare can be differentiated from those in many countries in South Asia, for example, where the state's role in welfare provision is minimal, and communities and families are the locus for the vast bulk of provision – what could be described as 'informal security regimes' (Wood and Gough, 2006).

Stratified development

Yet another approach focuses on the abilities of state actors to extract economic resources. This concerns both the extraction of rent from eco-

---

BOX 13.2   Segura-Ubriego's assessment of Latin American welfare states

Alex Segura-Ubriego (2007) combined a variety of different methodologies – Qualitative Comparative Analysis (QCA – see Chapter 14), time-series cross-sectional data, and case studies – to investigate the development of welfare systems in Latin America.

His analysis enabled a close consideration of the role of factors including democracy and left-labour power on whether encompassing systems of welfare were created or otherwise. Interestingly, Segura-Ubriego suggests that, in Latin America, higher levels of trade were likely to reduce welfare effort. This runs contrary to those studies of Western welfare states which have viewed welfare as compensation for the instability caused by trade, with smaller, more trade-dependent nations generally developing more generous welfare states (see Chapter 4).

The explanation for this lies in the fact that many Latin American countries initially used import-substituting industrialization (ISI) as a means of economic development. This resulted in relatively rapid levels of incorporation of workers into the formal economy, who were then able to provide revenue to pay for welfare. Where ISI was dismantled swiftly in order to increase trade, as in Chile and Peru, the number of workers in the 'informal' sector ballooned, thus reducing the proportional tax base. Where trade was liberalized more gradually, as in Costa Rica, it was easier for the government to compensate those affected by the resultant economic dislocation.

---

nomic activity by government elites, and the preservation of elite groups' status through welfare arrangements. Rent extraction has already been considered in the discussion in Chapter 10 of the role of property institutions in facilitating or hindering corrupt political activity. Literature on the so-called 'resource curse' suggests that the high levels of natural resources available in many Majority World nations may promote economic and political instability, as the legacy of extractive colonialist institutions combines in a toxic mix with the ambitions of corrupt politicians (see Chapter 10; see also Sachs and Warner, 2001; Humphreys *et al.*, 2007).

In addition to enabling the direct extraction of resources by certain groups, states may also promote differential development through the operation of iniquitous welfare regimes and labour market regulations which protect the status of elite social groups. Rudra (2007) argues, for instance, that in addition to *the productive welfare state* category described above, another, *protective* welfare state category exists, which is evident in nations such as Bolivia, Egypt, Iran, India and Turkey. The latter insulate certain groups from the rigours of the market ('decommodifying' them), even although other groups have not yet become participants within the formal economy. These protective welfare states cover only small numbers of people in high-status positions (such as the civil service and military).

Rudra's analysis of this type of welfare state echoes Pierson's claims about the path dependence of Minority World welfare states (see Chapters 4 and 8): once distributional coalitions have been created (e.g. civil servants and the military), they have a 'vested interest in maintaining existing institutions and reinforcing them' (*ibid.*: 391). This approach to welfare provision is perhaps particularly clear in pensions policy. For example, there is a separate pension fund in China for 'civil servants, military officers and employees of public institutions' which is unfunded – that is, paid for out of general government revenue, rather than being based on the insurance principle (Salditt *et al.*, 2008: 48). Such unfunded, generous schemes for certain categories of civil servants or public sector employees have also been a feature in Mexico, where they were viewed as shoring up support amongst civil servants for the PRI party (Marier, 2008: 419), which held a continuous monopoly of power in Mexico for over seventy years.

Filgueira and Filgueira's (2002) category of 'stratified universalism' shares many characteristics with Rudra's 'protective' category, but they note that in some countries (such as Argentina, during the 1970s) social protection covered a large, rather than small, proportion of the population. Nonetheless, just like 'protective' regimes, countries within this category totally failed to cover those who were not incorporated into the formal economy – such as rural workers, the self-employed, those working informally and the long-term unemployed (*ibid.*: 135). As with protective welfare states, groups which received benefits through these systems were generally very politically active in attempting to preserve their protected status (*ibid.*: 138; but see also Box 13.2).

Filgueira and Filgueira (*ibid.*: 139) also argue that an 'exclusionary' welfare regime type can be identified, which involves rather extreme attempts not just to preserve, but also to enhance the status of particular groups. This regime type is a kind of 'protective' regime 'plus', with a tiny elite group benefiting from high levels of state support whilst the rest of the population is very poor. Examples of this type of 'predatory' state included Central American states such as Guatemala and Honduras.

Neoliberalism

The neoliberal approach to public policy is at least partly based on a critique of differential development. This approach identifies government intervention as the main brake on economic development, and advocates a reduction in state involvement and a greater role for markets in allocating resources (Minns, 2006: 3), such that individuals become more responsible for economic failure (Harvey, 2006). Neoliberal approaches go further than traditional liberalism and 'mixed' liberalism (Sheahan, 2002: 28–9), both of which accept that some – indeed, occasionally, significant – government intervention may be necessary. Instead, neoliberal approaches argue that state intervention will generally distort markets and thus hinder economic development. When used to guide policy-making, neoliberalism led to the adoption of three types of reforms: macroeconomic stabilization, trade liberalization and structural change (Sachs, 1994).

The neoliberal approach to economic development has been highly controversial – not least because, of all the approaches considered here, it has been the most closely associated with external pressures on domestic policy-making. Indeed, for some, this approach can be codified as the 'Washington Consensus' (Williamson, 1990). It is strongly associated with economists who have trained at some, mainly North American, neoclassical economics departments with a reputation for propagating neoliberal ideas (Chwieroth, 2007). Indeed, the group of economists associated with rapid neoliberal reforms in Chile were known as the (University of) 'Chicago boys' (Huneeus, 2000).

From the mid-2000s onwards, many previously strong advocates of neoliberalism have toned down their rejection of state support, in the face of increasing pressure on family incomes in countries subject to extreme 'structural adjustment' such as Tanzania (Rodrik, 2006; see also De Vogli and Birbeck, 2005).

Dependency theory

Another approach to explaining public policy developments in the Majority World, which was particularly popular in the 1960s to 1980s, is that of 'dependency theory'. This argued that external, rather than internal, developments were the key explanatory variables for policy development in non-communist Majority World countries. According to this analysis, countries in the Majority World were largely unable to industrialize due to their dependency relationship with the Minority World. Where there was evidence of industrialization in Majority World countries, this was generally controlled by Minority World companies (Cardoso, 1973; Wallerstein, 1974).

As with neoliberalism, 'dependency theory' was normative as well as descriptive and analytical in its approach (Smith, 1979). Empirical developments – not least the growth of the Chinese and Indian economies, and their extension into new areas of manufacturing and service provision – might appear to contradict dependency theory, or at least its less sophisticated variants. More recent developments of dependency theory from the 1980s onwards within what has been described as 'world systems theory' suggest that the meanings of 'autonomy' and 'dependency' need to be reassessed in the face of new production and trade patterns by, for example, taking account of the increasing importance of knowledge and technology (Castells and Laserna, 1989).

Area studies

Aside from within the theoretical areas mentioned above, much work on public policies in the Majority World has taken place within what could loosely be described as 'area studies'. Universities in Minority World countries have developed departments or research groups covering the Middle East, Africa, Asia, and Latin and Central America. Previously, many universities included Soviet Studies departments (now described as 'Slavonic and East European', 'Europe-Asia' or 'Eurasian' Studies). This is in addition to schools and departments of 'development', 'international development' and (if now less commonly) 'third world studies'.

Whilst European and American studies departments have also been created in many Minority World universities, these are less frequently classified under the 'area studies' rubric. Academic endeavour within Minority World universities and beyond often follows the same demarcations, with high-ranking journals devoted to studying policy developments (as well as literature, history and other subjects) within these different 'areas'.

The area studies approach to researching public policy is generally based upon a deep knowledge of the area concerned and countries within it. Although it has been subject to criticism, particularly from more quantitatively-minded political scientists (Bates, 1997), it arguably enables a more nuanced and detailed understanding of policy developments to be provided, which is necessary before generalizations can be established (see Chapter 14, for further discussion of these issues).

Yet, regardless of the relative merits of area-based approaches, common criticisms have been levelled against many of the country groupings that are most frequently adopted. The ambiguous nature of the term 'developing world' has already been considered. The phrase 'the third world' has also been subject to criticism for its homogenizing implications. Whilst 'third world' countries have all been subject to colonial rule, the ways in which that rule operated and the legacy it left differed substantially between countries (Kennett, 2001: 93, 100). Similarly, whilst formerly socialist regimes have been left with a '"service heavy, transfer light" welfare system' (Kovács, 2002: 183), this has been reformed in very different ways in, for example, Albania, Russia, Kyrgyzstan and Slovakia. Overall, the 'new governments of Eastern Europe and the former Soviet Union' have adopted diverse approaches to social policy (Deacon *et al.*, 1992: 1) and many other policy areas, even if these have been shaped by their past as socialist regimes. Again, some have questioned the utility of bracketing together East Asian countries (such as Singapore, Japan, South Korea and Taiwan) as falling under a specific welfare state model, given their diverse characteristics (Kwon, 1997; 1998).

Conclusion

This chapter has departed from the rest of this book by considering public policy-making in the Majority World. It first considered the relationship between development studies and comparative public policy, before examining how Majority World governments deploy their powers over financial resources, authority, organization and information, often in very different ways from Minority World governments. The chapter also detailed how many of the theoretical assumptions and analytical frameworks applied to the Minority World were untenable in the Majority World context. It then examined alternative approaches which have been advocated for the analysis of public policy in Majority World countries: developmentalism, stratified development, neoliberalism, dependency theory and area studies. Overall, the chapter has indicated the striking plurality across the Majority World of both public policy approaches and the theories used to analyse them.

This suggests that the study of Majority World countries is, and should be, extremely rewarding for scholars of comparative public policy. Yet, generally, in 'the modern era, with few exceptions, the direction of influence is from European core to southern periphery. Institutional arrangements, disciplinary definitions and hierarchies, legitimizing publications, and instructional authority reside in that core, which periodically incorporates students and professors from the periphery, of whom many never return home' (Samoff, 2007: 49).

Furthermore, it is arguable that the status of comparative public policy analysts in many parts of the Majority World has been reduced because they have often allowed their work to be used to promote particular policy approaches (indeed, sometimes they have actively encouraged this). Clearly, this need not be a problem if their analysis leads to positive outcomes, but for many it is associated with attempts to force 'Eurocentric paradigms' and 'policy solutions' onto countries where their explanatory power is limited (Kennett, 2001: 114). For example, policy constructs such as the 'regulatory state model' have arguably been imposed on numerous Majority World countries with insufficient consideration of the domestic context (Phillips, 2006).

This is, perhaps, exacerbated by the widespread activity of Minority World academics working as consultants in Majority World countries.

Again, in many circumstances this may be a positive, rather than negative, development. However, it helps promote the view that Majority World countries' policies are of no interest in and of themselves as research subjects. The author has been surprised, for example, that other academics often assume her work in certain Majority World countries 'had to' result from consultancy – since otherwise, why would she have been interested in public policy-making in the Majority World? Rather than policy transfer being necessarily unidirectional from the Minority World to the Majority World, lesson-learning could and should usefully apply in both directions.

Summary

❑ Scholarly works in the field of comparative public policy generally focus on a small group of Minority World nations, or on those nations that are members of the OECD, rather than including or focusing on the Majority World.

❑ The availability of financial resources, extent of authority and organization, and access to information of Majority World governments is generally more constrained than for Minority World governments. At the same time, the tasks to which policy instruments are put by Majority World governments can differ markedly from Minority World governments. Majority World governments, for example, often have a stronger focus on family policy and shaping population numbers than do Minority World governments.

❑ Government use of policy instruments in the Majority World may be heavily affected by external pressures, including but not restricted to those related to globalization. Majority World nations are especially vulnerable to conflict with neighbouring countries, but are also often affected by unequal relationships with donor countries and international organizations.

❑ Public policies within Majority World countries have been analysed using theoretical perspectives including developmentalism, stratified development, neoliberalism, and dependency theory, as well as within the field of 'area studies'.

❑ Public policy scholars from Minority World countries have often been implicitly, or explicitly, engaged in justifying particular policy approaches in Majority World countries, and as a result may understandably be viewed with suspicion in some quarters.

Chapter 14

Doing Comparative Public Policy

Comparative public policy research has enormous promise for improving our understanding – not only of policy-making and implementation in other countries, but also of domestic public policy. However, as with many research strategies, comparative public policy research requires scholars to give careful consideration to a number of difficult choices, and to face up to a range of challenges which threaten the validity and reliability of findings. How this can be done is the focus of this chapter. Hence, whilst preceding chapters focused on the *findings* of comparative public policy research, this chapter examines its *process*.

As discussed previously (pp. 8–10), some authors have suggested that comparative research is methodologically identical to other forms of research (Smelser, 1976). This is trivially the case if one assumes that all research is comparative. This text, however, argues that comparative public policy research *can* be distinguished from other forms of research, not necessarily because of its content (the study of policy processes, outputs and outcomes), but because of the characteristics of the comparative approach itself.

This is evident, first, from the particular *choices* that comparativists need to make when designing any research project. This chapter considers how different cases are selected for investigation, and how conclusions are drawn from such research. In so doing, it examines different approaches to comparative research and how they relate to each other. The comparative research strategies examined here include the 'method of agreement' (or 'most different systems analysis'), the 'method of difference' (or 'most similar systems analysis'), combinatorial analysis, and case studies using process tracing.

The distinctiveness of comparative research is also evident when we examine the challenges for comparative research, particularly in assigning causality, which comparative researchers have dealt with in a variety of highly innovative ways. This chapter therefore accords with Øyen's assessment that 'true' comparativists need to be aware of the specific challenges facing comparative research (quoted in May, 2003: 207). The chapter considers in detail the three core problems facing comparative public policy analysis: the 'Galton problem', the problem of 'selection on the dependent variable', and the 'problem of equivalence'. Each problem is explained fully, before some responses (if not solutions) are indicated.

Finally, comparative public policy research involves the navigating of a number of practicalities which, whilst similar to those arising from any research project, can be exacerbated by the fact that the research has to be carried out in more than one research site. The practical issues that can arise when carrying out comparative research can include issues with organizing an appropriate research team and with finding collaborators, locating equivalent data, and obtaining resources. The final section indicates how, for many researchers, comparative work involves greater compromises in methods than other types of research (Hantrais, 1995), due to its more intensive resource requirements.

Choices in comparative research

In theory 'there are no limits to comparison', if comparison is understood simply as requiring the presence of common attributes between units (Caramani, 2009: 29). The essence of comparison is, of course, relatively simple; the examination of the same phenomenon in different situations, or of different phenomena in similar situations. This, of course, leads to greater insights than can be derived from individual case studies (Przeworski and Teune 1970: 31–46). In practice, however, researchers must consider carefully which units they wish to compare, and why.

Which units should be compared?

As Bollen *et al.* (1993) note, 'not all authors explain why particular cases were chosen for analysis', often appearing to view the choice of cases as self-evident. Further probing often leads to a range of reasons being adduced for case selection, including 'familiarity with certain cases, similarity along one or more dimensions, heterogeneity, particular values of the dependent variable, data availability, or some combination of these' (*ibid.*: 330–1).

Hakim (2002: 202) focuses particularly on three methods for case selection. First, countries may be chosen because they are viewed as 'substantively interesting in their own right'. In these cases, it is some particular aspect of policy-making or policy-implementation within the countries concerned that is seen as interesting and appropriate for analysis, rather than this aspect being seen as, in some way, especially typical or especially untypical of a larger class of instances.

Second, cases may be selected to indicate the validity of a theory, or to test its hypotheses. In these circumstances, aspects of the cases are examined in relation to a wider class of instances, and cases are chosen because they relate specifically to the theory being examined. Theories illustrated or tested in this way can focus on the macro-, meso-, or micro-level, and can have generalizable ambitions (i.e. their authors may claim that they can explain developments in many different countries), or may be focused on explaining developments in just one country or case.

Finally, Hakim suggests that, in practice, many studies are 'opportunistic'. This occurs where researchers make use of their own geographical position and access to policy developments in a specific context, where they have access to data concerning policies for a specific set of countries, or where they are able to communicate with research subjects and gatekeepers to data, because of their linguistic abilities.

Examples of the first type of opportunistic study come from studies which explicitly or implicitly compare developments in the researcher's domicile country with another country. In many cases, the 'other' country may be the country of origin of the researcher concerned. A clear example of the second type of opportunistic study comes from the widespread reliance of comparative policy scholars on data from the OECD (with examples including this book, as well as, e.g., Castles, 1998) and the EU (see chapters in Featherstone and Radaelli (2003) and Haverland (2005), for a critique). The third type of study covers 'Anglophone' studies comparing Australia, the USA, Canada and Britain, or a subset of these (O'Connor *et al.*, 1999; Hoberg, 1991), and 'Francophone' studies comparing France, Belgium, Luxembourg and Quebec (Canada), or a subset of these (Monière, 1999; Faniel, 2004; Dister and Moreau, 2006).

How much comparison?

This book has adopted an expansive definition of comparative research, which includes 'any research which either explicitly or implicitly contrasts policy processes, outputs or outcomes from one or more units'. This approach includes all cross-national research as 'comparative', including work based on secondary analysis of studies carried out previously.

This has been contested by some scholars, who suggest that simply including data from more than one setting does not lead to genuine comparison (Pickvance, 1986). Certainly, merely listing different countries' attributes and the differences between them, or providing a series of case studies of different cases with no attempt to explain why they differ, hardly qualifies as comparative *analysis*.

Such approaches may, nonetheless, be adopted where researchers are faced with limited availability of comparative data, where there are clear linguistic and/or cultural differences between the countries concerned, or where coordination between the different members of a cross-national research team is weak, and no common approach to analysis has been identified (see the last section of this chapter: pp. 339–40). In such circumstances, 'social scientific teeth are gritted' in order to get on with the task of comparison, but 'the legacy of ... fears' about comparability 'survives and is reflected in collections of case studies of individual countries in which little attempt is made to explain how they link together, or even why they have been put together, except in the most general terms' (Cochrane *et al.*, 2001a: 8). Studies carried out in this way might be more appropriately described as 'area studies' (Bereday, 1964: 6), rather than comparative public policy research.

Nonetheless, for comparative research it is not necessary, for example, to ensure that exactly the same research design is used across the two or more cases concerned. Instead, it is possible to carry out systematic cross-national research using secondary sources, provided that the same phenomenon is focused on in the cases of interest (Wilensky and Turner 1987: 382). Only a small proportion of work carried out at, for example, European level is 'strictly comparative at the design and data collection stages' (Hantrais, 1995). This obviously causes problems in relation to data availability and commensurability. However, it need not be terminal for the validity and reliability of findings, provided that any general conclusions are clearly evidenced and, where necessary, qualified; and that the authors are crystal clear about the national specificities of the data sources used.

How do we draw conclusions from comparison?

Whilst comparative public policy research may sometimes merely involve description of the differences between countries, generally it also attempts some kind of explanation for the existence of differences or similarities across countries. Przeworski (1987: 35) has identified this 'explanatory' mission as at the core of comparison, stating '[t]he general purpose of crossnational research is to understand which characteristics of the particular cultures, societies, economies or political systems affect patterns of behaviour within them'.

This understanding of why differences and similarities arise and persist can be developed in a variety of ways. The four core approaches to developing understanding constitute the methods of agreement and of difference, as identified by John Stuart Mill (and contemporarily sometimes referred to as 'most different systems analysis' and 'most similar systems analysis', respectively), combinatorial analysis, and process tracing. The rest of this section examines each approach in turn, before considering the extent to which these approaches can support each other.

The method of agreement

Mill's discussion of comparative research is arguably the first systematic attempt to explain the process of comparison. Mill suggested that there were, broadly, two feasible approaches to comparison: the methods of agreement and of difference. The method of agreement proceeds by elimination. In summary, it explains some common outcome by discovering the causal circumstances in common across cases.

As an example of this approach, one could consider the causes of high levels of violent crime in different countries. Four alternative hypotheses have been put forward in the literature, which variously maintain that high levels of violent crime result from a high number of one-parent families, the lack of gun-control laws, unemployment, and comparatively short prison sentences (Kellerman *et al.*, 1993; Raphael and Winter-Ebmer, 1999; Hopkins, 2002; O'Neill, 2002).

The method of agreement would involve the researcher examining different countries with high rates of violent crime, and adducing the extent to which these four factors were present. In a two-country study (countries A and B), if both nations experienced a high rate of violent crime, and only three out of the four factors present in A were present in B, the fourth factor (say, comparatively short prison sentences) could be eliminated from the analysis as it could not have been a causal factor in country B. This approach can practically be described as involving the study of 'most different systems with similar outcomes' (De Meur and Berg-Schlosser, 1994).

There are, obviously, a number of limitations to this approach. First, it does not reveal any necessary link between cause and effect. Even if, out of five countries, all five had both high rates of violent crime and high rates of one-parent families and no gun-control laws, this does not mean that both these factors necessarily caused the high violent crime rates. It could be that one of the factors (high rates of one-parent families, or no gun-control laws) simply occurs alongside the other, without playing any causal role. This is problematic, since there is often a high degree of 'collinearity' between potentially causally potent variables. That is, scores on some variables which have been used to try to explain high rates of violent crime (e.g. high rates of one-parent families) often co-exist with other variables which have also been viewed as leading to this outcome (e.g. high rates of unemployment). It is, therefore, difficult to find cases where only one of the factors concerned is present (i.e. high rates of one-parent families, or high rates of unemployment, but not both or neither).

In addition, 'multiple causation' may occur, where different factors cause the outcome observed in different contexts. For example, in country A, a rich country with low rates of unemployment, the reason for high rates of violent crime may be the lack of stringent prison sentences to act as a disincentive. In country B, individuals may be culturally less motivated by future-related concerns such as the length of prison sentences if they are caught engaging in violent crime. In contrast, however, in country B, unemployment rates are high, and membership of a gang (which engages in violent crime) is one of very few routes out of poverty in that country. In this case, the method of agreement would maintain that neither stringent prison sentences nor unemployment were causes of violent crime, since they were not present in both countries examined. Yet, comparatively lax prison sentences were a causal factor in country A, and unemployment was a causal factor in country B.

Mill maintained that the only way to be sure that a causal effect has been established is to recreate it experimentally – which brings us to the 'method of difference'.

The method of difference

The method of difference involves cases being compared which differ in only one causal condition: the variable whose impact is being examined. As a result, this is generally viewed as an experimental approach. As Parsons (1949: 743) puts it, experiments are 'nothing but the comparative method where the cases to be compared are produced ... under controlled conditions'.

Fairly obviously, it is extremely difficult to conduct experiments in social science, particularly cross-nationally – as, indeed, acknowledged by Mill himself. In practice, authors have adopted a range of approaches which approximate to the method of difference although without requiring the intervention of an experiment. For example, Theda Skocpol (1979), in her study of social revolutions, maintained that she effectively used the method of difference by comparing cases over time. So, for example, Russia in 1905 was very similar to Russia in 1917, but revolution occurred in 1917 and not 1905. Hence, the researcher can and should attempt to isolate what was different between 1905 and 1917. However, this approach is not without its problems either; an obvious key difference between the country during the two years cited was that 1917 Russia had already experienced 1905 Russia, whereas 1905 Russia had not.

Another approach is what has been described as the method of 'controlled comparisons', 'most similar systems' design or alternatively the 'comparable-case strategy' (Przeworski and Teune, 1970; Lijphart, 1975). This approach acknowledges that any two, or more, cases that are investigated in comparison will be different in a variety of ways, but uses case selection to try and minimize the number of differences between the cases being compared. This enables a closer focus on the cluster of potential independent variables producing variation in the phenomenon of interest (the dependent variable).

One ambitious project in this tradition attempted to identify 'most similar systems with different outcomes' using a very wide variety of societal, political and economic data – 61 indicators in total – to operationalize the independent variables (De Meur and Berg-Schlosser, 1994).

Finland and Estonia were isolated as two particularly close cases, which differed only in 14 out of the 61 variables. Despite their similarities, however, 'outcomes' differed – Finland remained a democracy whilst Estonia's political system collapsed. De Meur and Berg-Schlosser suggest this is due to differing political cultures between the two systems.

In practice, however, the search for '"the" single decisive similarity or difference' is an extremely challenging 'research strategy'. This is because '[s]ocial reality is [generally] too complex for there to be a single cause of a given phenomenon that social scientists would be interested in' (Caramani, 2009: 49).

The two methods (agreement and difference) should not be seen as dichotomous. This is because, first, scholars often use a combination of both approaches. Hence, Skocpol (1979), for example, used both the method of difference (as indicated above) and the method of agreement, in combination, in order to eliminate particular factors as potential causes of social revolutions. Second, Mill himself did not suggest that researchers had to choose between the approaches. He merely argued that his exposition of the two approaches could offer a guide for those engaging in comparative research – they constituted tools for researchers to use, rather than hard-and-fast technologies.

Both the method of agreement and the method of difference rest on the 'prior formulation of hypotheses' – 'statements about circumstances researchers assume as relevant in explaining the observed event' (Caramani, 2009: 54). The two other approaches to comparison which are detailed in the remainder of this section do not require the prior formulation of hypotheses about causal relationships.

Combinatorial analysis

An alternative approach to comparative analysis can be described as 'combinatorial analysis'. This category adopts so-called 'Boolean analysis', and has been developed by Charles Ragin into 'Qualitative Comparative Analysis (QCA)' and 'Fuzzy Set QCA'. These approaches attempt to identify the necessary and sufficient variables underlying particular political or policy outcomes.

'Boolean analysis' refers to the system of logical notation developed by George Boole, which codified logical relationships. It involves examining the relationship between different dichotomous variables – that is, variables which can only either be present (coded as 1) or not present (coded as 0). These relationships are simplified as falling into three categories, represented by the 'Boolean operators' 'and', 'or' and 'not'. Boolean analysis then rests on the assigning of values to different variables, and examination of which relationships between independent variables explain a particular value on the dependent variable. In particular, it involves considering whether the relationship between independent variables is additive ('and'), alternative ('or'), or negative ('not').

An example of this comes from Wickham-Crowley's (1992) examination of why peasants support, or fail to support, guerilla movements, using twenty cases drawn from Latin America. He identifies values for four independent variables – agrarian structure, agrarian disruption, rebellious cultures, and peasant linkages, and for the dependent variable of support for guerillas. Through examining how these variables interrelate in contexts where there is support amongst peasants for guerillas, he identifies a set of sufficient conditions involving a combination of the variables involved, which helps explain this outcome.

Core to this approach is the acceptance that variables may combine in order to produce a particular outcome, rather than assuming that only one variable is essential for a particular outcome to occur – what has been described as a 'combinatorial logic' (Ragin, 1987: 15). The fact that Boolean analysis rests on dichotomous variables also enables the manipulation of a large number of variables using computer packages. Charles Ragin developed just such an approach with his 'Qualitative Comparative Analysis' package. The Boolean variant of QCA has sometimes been described as 'crisp set' QCA.

The technical capacity of computer packages does not absolve researchers from having to decide which cases should be included. It can still be difficult to decide between including a particular case as negative, or as irrelevant. One approach to this issue involves what has been described as the 'possibility principle'. Mahoney and Goertz (2004: 655) argue that 'the assumption that all cases are relevant leads the researcher to waste time and resources by analyzing a huge number of cases that do not teach us anything because the outcome of interest was obviously impossible'. Their 'possibility principle' suggests, therefore, that only cases where the outcome to be explained could possibly have occurred, should be included within the set of negative cases.

The need to classify variables in a dichotomous way can also cause problems for researchers when distinctions are less than clear-cut; or when researchers wish to focus on frequencies, rather than simply presence or absence. Charles Ragin and collaborators have adapted their Boolean approach to also take such frequencies into account, in what they have described as 'Fuzzy Set/QCA' analysis. 'Fuzzy Set/QCA' involves researchers assessing the degree to which a particular case falls into a certain category. For example, researchers might classify certain countries according to the degree to which they possessed the characteristics of a federal nation, with countries such as Germany and Switzerland given values of '1', countries such as France given the value '0', and nations with limited devolution of power to certain regions, such as Spain and Britain, given the value '0.5'. This approach enables researchers' knowledge about specific cases to be explicitly incorporated into the assigning of values for the analysis (Caramani, 2009: 76–7). Both 'crisp set' and 'fuzzy set' QCA have been applied to a variety of policy areas (see Rihoux and Grimm, 2006a, and www.compasss.org).

Process tracing

Combinatorial analysis attempts to discover how independent variables interact with each other to produce particular outcomes on the dependent variable. Like the methods of agreement and difference, combinatorial analysis is based on examining a range of different cases, and attempting to discover causal relationships by creating generalizations which apply across this range.

An alternative approach to comparative research is provided by what can be described as 'process tracing' (George and McKeown, 1985). Rather than looking at the extent to which (particular combinations of) independent variables coexist with certain values on the dependent variable, this approach attempts direct examination of the causal process linking independent to dependent variables – possibly via intervening and/or confounding variables. Often, this method of research does not explicitly use the language of 'variables', focusing instead on tracing general causal processes within a small number of cases (in its comparative variant – more generally, this method is often used to examine just one case). An example of this comes yet again from Skocpol's analysis of social revolutions. In all the cases she examines, an ideologically-motivated vanguard movement was in evidence. Hence, it might be assumed that this movement was significant in fomenting revolutionary change. However, through piecing together the history of revolutions in the cases examined, Skocpol (1979: 170–1) indicates how such movements only participated very late in the process, rather than catalyzing or sparking it (see also Mahoney, 2000).

This focus on the process of change has been viewed by some as revealing causal *mechanisms* as opposed to causal *effects* (George and Bennett, 2005). Causal mechanisms 'tell us how things happen: how actors relate, how individuals come to believe what they do or what they draw from past experiences, how policies and institutions endure or change, how outcomes that are inefficient become hard to reverse, and so on' (Falleti and Lynch, 2009). Falleti and Lynch point out that, whilst some causal mechanisms may be very general (e.g. 'rationality'), others may be contextually highly specific (e.g. 'the circular flow of power that is hypothesized to operate in Leninist regimes'). Hence, they argue that it is necessary to consider the interaction between mechanisms and context in order to understand why particular outcomes occur.

Nonetheless, some are sceptical about the possibilities of genuinely 'uncovering' causal mechanisms. In practice, 'mechanisms' are often simply tightly-coupled 'covariations' between different variables, not least because covariations are relatively easy to prove and test, whereas mechanisms are not. As a result, some have argued that mechanisms are simply 'things that we speculate might be true but cannot prove in a definitive fashion' (Gerring, 2010).

Bringing approaches together

In addition to the four methods identified above (the methods of agreement and difference, combinatorial analysis and process tracing), Dogan (2002) has identified no less than eight other research strategies, adding 'comparison by ideal types and by empirical typologies', 'binary comparison', 'conceptual homogenization of a heterogeneous domain', 'cross-national comparison of intra-national diversities', 'longitudinal, diachronic and asynchronic comparisons', 'comparison of causal relationships staggered over time', 'comparing ecological environments' and 'comparing mini-states and mega-cities (in comparisons of political systems)'. 'Deviant case analysis' could also appropriately be described as a type of comparative research (Caramani, 2009: 87), given that it is necessary already to have an understanding of 'normality' (i.e. of other cases) before 'deviancy' can be identified.

Regardless of which and how many approaches to social research we identify as 'truly' meriting the 'comparative' label, the differences between different approaches must not be overestimated. It has already been stressed that many scholars are keen to combine different approaches, rather than viewing them as mutually exclusive. Eclecticism in methods is becoming more and more popular as the limitations of individual approaches become evident. Increasingly, scholars are being urged to combine approaches which might otherwise have been viewed as incompatible, or, at least, as focusing on different levels of analysis. Hence, for example, Rihoux and Grimm (2006b: 292) have questioned how combinatorial analyses could better incorporate an understanding of time, perhaps through incorporating process tracing or other related approaches. Furthermore, some have questioned whether the purportedly 'straightforward', 'stepwise' approaches to comparative analysis advocated in methods texts, stressing relationships between distinct variables, accurately reflect the actual practice of comparative scholarship. In reality, it is arguable that inference (which underlies all comparative research) is 'a gradual and cumulative process of elimination, falsification, discovery, and corroboration'. Indeed, 'social science research rarely can avoid a stepwise, Sherlock Holmesian style of inference' (Levi-Faur, 2006: 60). As such, it could be argued that comparative analysis is often a good deal messier, more intuitive and 'hit-and-miss' than is frequently suggested by the (*post hoc*) justificatory descriptions of research approaches provided within journal articles.

Challenges for comparative public policy research

Regardless of the research approach adopted, a number of perennial problems afflict comparative research. This is because all comparative research necessarily involves the researcher in deciding upon which cases should be investigated – and which should not. As already mentioned, for some, this may be a pragmatic choice, reflecting cultural or linguistic familiarity, or access to research sites. Even in these cases, however, scholars are usually required to provide some justification for the choice of sites which goes beyond 'just' the perceived intrinsic interest of the case – which is the motivator for most work in the field of area studies. The importance of this choice is even greater where scholars attempt to provide generalizable conclusions following comparative analysis of a limited number of cases.

Four problems have been adduced as potentially affecting the validity of comparative research. The first, the so-called Galton problem, highlights the growing influence of transnational factors on domestic policy-making. If transnational factors have extensive causal potency (as examined in Chapters 11 and 12), then these might 'trump' any domestic factors that could be uncovered by comparative researchers. The second problem, that of 'equivalence', highlights the impact of linguistic and cultural heterogeneity on researchers' ability to identify genuinely analogous factors across more than one context. The third problem concerns the impact of time on case characteristics; this is particularly problematic for 'lone' researchers, who may be required to conduct their fieldwork in different settings over long periods of time. The final problem is restricted to researchers adopting the methods of agreement or difference. This problem concerns researchers' propensities to select cases on the dependent variable – for example, to choose to research countries on the basis of whether they do, or do not, have high levels of gun crime. Selecting cases on this basis arguably leads to various forms of distortion arising from selection bias.

The Galton problem: the influence of transnational factors

The Galton problem, as already mentioned, highlights the interdependencies between different societies and polities. It effectively brings into question the appropriateness of using individual nation-states – or, indeed, regions, or any other geographically-defined units – as the building-blocks for analysis within comparative studies.

We can rather crudely illustrate the Galton problem by considering the field of comparative environmental policy. As is indicated in Chapter 7, most industrialized nations have adopted increasingly stringent forms of environmental regulation. A researcher who ignored international influences might assume that these more stringent regulations had come about in numerous different countries as a result of domestic factors, such as the increasing strength of environmental movements, or following domestic environmental scandals. They might argue, indeed, that such factors, from being virtually non-existent thirty years ago, had assumed increasing importance within Eastern European and Balkan countries – and that this explained their adoption of increasingly stringent regulations, similar to those in Western European countries.

Of course, any researcher with knowledge of environmental policy would counter these claims, pointing out that these countries must make moves towards increasing their levels of environmental regulation, if they are to have any prospect of joining the EU – a stated policy goal across Eastern Europe and the Balkans. In addition, the transnational nature of pollution and climate change has arguably had at least as much influence on international policy-making in this area as have domestic green movements. Ignoring the interdependencies between countries, and the factors affecting their policy responses, can therefore lead to inaccurate conclusions.

Of course, such problems of international interdependence are hardly new. The Galton problem itself was identified by Francis Galton in the early nineteenth century, in his criticism of a wide-ranging comparative analysis in anthropology which failed to note the interdependencies between the different factors described as explaining certain societal developments (Goldthorpe, 1997). Claims of national specificity have always been suspect. Bereday (1964: 6) put this succinctly in his claim that to 'say, as some Americans do, that one is 'one hundred percent American' is to refer to oneself, as the anthropologist Ralph Linton has pointed out, in an Indo-European language, in figures invented by the Arabs, in a decimal system inherited by the Romans, and by the name of the Italian oceanographer Amerigo Vespucci'. However, it is arguable that the Galton problem has still not been solved and, if anything, has intensified, given the ever-increasing extent of cultural diffusion, and intensity of impact from international organizations (Goldthorpe, 1997).

A number of solutions have been proposed to the Galton problem. First, we may feel as researchers that we should 'capitulate' in the face of Galton's problem, accept that the 'world is a single case', and focus purely on 'enclaves of "uniqueness" resisting globalization' (Caramani, 2009: 23).

Alternatively, we can attempt to put the Galton problem in context, by recognizing that diffusion exists, but attempting to incorporate this into comparative analyses, rather than assuming it renders them defunct. For example, some researchers have attempted to incorporate diffusion as a potential independent variable, by assuming that geographical proximity will correlate with the likelihood of diffusion – so that similarities between peoples living nearby each other are assumed more likely to reflect diffusion than if the similarities existed between more widely separated peoples (Naroll, 1965). Of course, such approaches fail to reflect the fact that linguistic or cultural proximity may be important, as well as geographical nearness. An alternative approach would recognize that 'semidiffusion' can be separated from 'hyperdiffusion', with 'some societies [being] more immune than others to external influences (because of selective adoption, cultural resistance, nonpreparation to innovation)', and with differences between policy sectors, such that diffusion appears to affect some policy areas (such as monetary policy) and not others (cultural policies) (see Caramani, 2009: 23).

An alternative solution would come from the process tracing approach, whereby researchers attempt the direct identification of causal mechanisms, rather than inferring them from the apparent interrelationships amongst causal outcomes. This approach should, ideally, be able to identify where international factors pushed change, as well as where change was induced by domestic factors. From the opposite end of the methodological spectrum, researchers could also attempt to tease out the influence of diffusion by developing large-N time-series analyses, which might be able to reveal 'statistical dependence between cases' (*ibid.*: 23).

A rather knottier variant of the Galton problem comes from the political philosopher, Alisdair Macintyre. Macintyre's focus is not on the ubiquity of transnational influences on policy and society but, rather, the ubiquity of human psychological traits. Macintyre amusingly indicates his concerns about contemporary comparative research with an imaginary tale:

> There was once a man who aspired to be the author of the general theory of holes. When asked 'What kind of hole – holes dug by children in the sand for amusement, holes dug by gardeners to plant lettuce seedlings, tank traps, holes made by roadmakers?' he would reply indignantly that he wished for a general theory that would explain all of these. He rejected *ab initio* the – as he saw it – pathetically common-sense view that of the digging of different kinds of holes there are quite different kinds of explanations to be given; why then he would ask do we have the concept of a hole? Lacking the explanations to which he originally aspired, he then fell to discovering statistically significant correlations; he found for example that there is a correlation between the aggregate hole-digging achievement of a society as measured, or at least one day to be measured, by econometric techniques, and its degree of technological

development. The United States surpasses both Paraguay and Upper
Volta in hole-digging. He also discovered that war accelerates hole-
digging; there are more holes in Vietnam than there were. These observations, he would always insist, were neutral and value-free. This man's
achievement has passed totally unnoticed except by me. Had he however
turned his talents to political science, had he concerned himself not with
holes, but with modernization, urbanization or violence, I find it difficult
to believe that he might not have achieved high office in the APSA
[American Political Science Association]. (Macintyre, 1984: 260)

Macintyre's parody highlights what he sees as a core problem for comparative research; the fact that 'the provision of an environment sufficiently different to make the search for counter-examples interesting will
normally be the provision of an environment where we cannot hope or
expect to find examples of the original phenomenon and therefore cannot
hope to find counter-examples'. Where social researchers *can* find sets of
circumstances that are comparable, these generally result, for Macintyre
(1984: 268), in research that produces fairly boring findings. As he puts
it, 'either ... generalizations about institutions will necessarily lack the
kind of confirmation they require or they will be consequences of true
generalizations about human rationality and not part of a specifically
political science'. An example of this might come from comparative
political science's study of electoral systems. First-past-the-post (or
'single member plurality', to describe them most accurately) electoral
systems can be viewed as one of the independent variables which lead to
countries developing a party system which is binary; that is, which is
dominated by two large parties (the dependent variable). This finding,
however, would be fairly uninteresting to Macintyre, because it is fairly
obvious – it merely reflects the fact that voters (as with all human
beings) tend to have transitive preferences; that is, they will tend to vote
tactically for a party which may not be their first preference, but which
they prefer to their least best preference (if that party is likely to win).

It might be assumed that Macintyre's argument would lead us to a
fairly nihilistic position, where all findings from comparative research
were either trivially true (as deriving from basic human psychology), or
on ridiculously shaky ground (due to the incommensurability of the different cases examined). However, Macintyre does offer an upbeat assessment for the prospects of what he describes as 'comparative history' –
which can indicate necessary conditions for the occurrence of specific
outcomes, even if it cannot uncover sufficient conditions.

In addition, it could be argued that Macintyre sets up a very feeble
straw man as the target for his arguments, perhaps due to the less developed state of statistical methods when he was writing. In practice, more
thoughtful quantitative analysis will aim not to produce spurious correla-

tions, but to test the influence of a variety of different variables, *qua* individual variables, in sum with other variables, and in various combinations (as with regression analysis and QCA).

Nonetheless, his arguments might, helpfully, lead us to consider not only whether research findings are valid and/or reliable, but also whether they really tell us anything *important* – whether findings possess any relevance outside academia and its often relatively small circles of topic enthusiasts.

The problem of equivalence

The problem of 'equivalence' concerns the reliability of indicators used to operationalize a concept in different national – or, indeed, regional – contexts. It stems from the fact that, even where similar phenomena are examined in different contexts, these phenomena will not be identical – just from the fact that they are, indeed, situated in different settings. The challenge for social researchers is to ensure that any differences between the phenomena being compared are restricted to 'intrinsic, non-relational properties irrelevant to the goal of our research' (van Deth, 1998: 4). 'Equivalence' thus refers to the degree to which variables, or conceptualizations, show 'validity in terms of each social system and reliability across social systems' (Przeworski and Teune, 1970: 107).

It is arguable that the problem of equivalence has intensified over time. Whilst statistical methods have improved (see below, p. 334), researchers' ability to operationalize concepts appropriately is arguably still limited. Mair argues that an example of this comes from studies which attribute public policy outcomes to the control of government by left or right parties. One very popular work which is frequently referred to as indicating the extent of governmental control by left/right parties – that of Castles and Mair (1984) – may have many good points, but ultimately was based on the assessment of a group of experts, rather than any more robust measurement.

Mair (1996: 327) suggests that the analysis of the relationship between variables in comparative social research is often assumed to be more important, or interesting, than the quality and reliability of the variables themselves. Van Deth (1998: 2) suggests this may be related to the fact that solving what he calls 'identity-equivalence' problems requires quantitative researchers to reach over into qualitative research – a move which they may not find very attractive.

The problem of equivalence is, of course, intensified by language and cultural differences. Concepts and the words used to describe them can mean a bewildering variety of different things in different nations. This is particularly problematic in attitudinal research: partly because, as Hakim notes, such research is already highly dependent on subtle factors such as the wording of questions; and partly also because 'there are few or no other datasources to use as checks on validity' – it is very difficult to find out what someone 'thinks' without asking them directly (it cannot necessarily be inferred, for example, from what they do, as many obstructions and other intervening factors may be in place).

Westle (1998) provides a concrete example of this, using her research into attitudes of tolerance across different countries. As she suggests, virtually everyone views themselves as tolerant, so asking whether people view themselves as such is fairly meaningless. Tolerance, therefore, 'has to show itself not in abstract but in concrete terms', where specific intolerant attitudes can be revealed (*ibid.*: 23). Westle concluded that tolerance was an inherently multidimensional concept, since the categories of 'disliked persons' vary so significantly across settings. This was separate from the broader question about the impact of 'general psychological and social characteristics' which might affect levels of tolerance more generally (*ibid*: 58).

Other extreme examples of dissonance arise in situations where a particular ideational concept simply does not exist in one of the settings being investigated. Hence, for example, there is no word for the Judaeo-Christian-Muslim form of God in Japanese (Hakim, 2002: 207), or for the English notion of loyalty in Turkish, or for Trust, in Hindi (Elder, 1976: 223) – and numerous other examples abound. A lack of linguistic equivalence is significant not only because it prevents communication, but also because it often reflects conceptual differences which are closely linked to wider conceptual frameworks, and which may have deep roots in different societies' ideological and institutional legacies (Hantrais, 1995), as well as in their underlying values (Hantrais and Mangen, 1996a: 7; Jowell, 1998: 170).

Indeed, some languages are seen as particularly appropriate for discussing different topics or within particular situations, due not least to their varying conceptual resources. French, for example, is often described as an appropriate language for diplomacy, as it allows for greater precision than English (hence what is described as *'foison-nement'*, where English text translated into French is generally around one tenth longer than French text translated into English). The relative lack of precision of English may also have its uses, however, in situations where more open-ended responses may be required.

The problem of equivalence does not only affect comparisons between countries. It can also arise during research in countries which are highly linguistically and/or culturally diverse (such as India, Nigeria, and even the USA), and even in otherwise relatively linguistically homogeneous societies such as the UK, but where different groups (young people, prisoners, tramps, lawyers and many others) have been shown in research to have developed their own distinctive vocabulary. As Jowell (1998: 169) puts it, 'no nation is homogeneous with respect to vocabulary, modes of expression, levels of education, and so on'.

How to get around the problem of equivalence

Van Deth (1998: 2) argues that 'the number of proposals to deal with' the equivalence problem 'are rather limited', not least due to the empirical and logical complexity of the problem itself. This may well be the case, but nonetheless a good deal of (sometimes rather technical and complex) thought has been given to the issue by a small number of comparative researchers. They have identified a number of more or less successful approaches to try to deal with the problem of equivalence.

First, researchers may simply be open about potential linguistic and/or conceptual differences that might have affected their findings. Hence, Aulich *et al.* (2010) are concerned to point out in their study of public sector agencies that the notion of an 'agency' in Hong Kong differs substantially from that in their other cases; and that the notion of a 'public organisation' in Italy also differed from their other cases (*ibid.*: 219). This was perhaps due to the fact that the project involved research teams from 11 distinct countries working together – which undoubtedly resulted in excellent in-country, in-depth knowledge, but may have compromised comparability (a factor considered in detail in the section on the practicalities of comparative research, pp. 339–42).

As an alternative, attempts to achieve equivalence may simply be abandoned, with researchers focusing on viewing developments from 'the inside' of the different cases involved. However, this approach 'excludes, by definition, the search for causal explanations which may provide for generalizations across societies' (May, 2003: 213). Furthermore, if one is only able to question a society/polity from within its ranks, one may miss the taken-for-granted elements which could be picked up on by an outside observer, and perhaps wrongly assume a congruence of belief and/or practice which is not the case.

Another approach which tries to square 'external' and 'internal' perspectives involves 'back translation' of research instruments such as questionnaires and interview schedules. This requires the initial translation of a particular concept from language A to language B by a native speaker of B then being translated from B to A by a native speaker of A, with the two translations then being compared and an optimal 'joint' approach developed. Similarly, pictures and prompts can be included within research instruments to clarify their meaning for different linguistic groups (Elder, 1976: 223).

The kind of literal exactness, or linguistic equivalence that results from back translation should ensure validity *within* languages. However, it does not necessarily ensure validity across languages (Iyengar, 1993) – that is, across the various different cases within the comparative research project at hand. Even where 'literal exactness' is achieved, this 'may not be enough' when 'conceptual equivalence' is required to ensure the validity of comparative research. As Elder puts it, if 'country A's youth rebel by cutting their hair short, whilst country B's youth rebel by wearing their hair long, questions about adolescents, hair, and rebellion will have to be worded differently in the two countries to provide conceptual – rather than literal – equivalence' (Elder, 1976: 223). Furthermore, where different sets of operationalizations for certain concepts are developed for the different sites within a comparative research project, this can lead to problems later on, when findings need to be analysed systematically in an integrated manner, in order to produce a synthesis (Kennett, 2001: 45).

Conceptual equivalence

Initially, conceptual equivalence of the operationalization of variables was often taken for granted in large-scale comparative analyses. In more recent years, greater attention to the power of culture and the 'interpretative turn' in social research has led to a greater awareness of potential problems due to the incommensurability of conceptualizations (Hantrais, 1995). There is now far more careful consideration of the way in which concepts are operationalized for different cases – that is, about the extent to which the variables chosen truly represent the underlying factors in which researchers are interested.

One attempt to ensure conceptual equivalence is to ensure that the concepts being examined are sufficiently general, or abstract, that it will be possible to find appropriate conceptualizations to provide variables across all the different cases being compared. This approach suggests that the concepts to be used in comparative analysis must be 'sufficiently abstract to travel across national boundaries' (Rose, 1991a: 447).

Caramani (2009) discusses how to undertake this move, which he calls 'climbing the ladder of abstraction'. He invites the reader to imagine empirical concepts as occupying places along an imaginary scale, which depends on the relationship between the concept's 'intension' and 'extension'. 'Intension', or 'connotation', refers to 'the set of attributes, properties, or characteristics of a concept or category'. The 'intension' of any particular concept is therefore the 'class of properties that determine the 'things' to which the concept applies' – not the concepts themselves, but their properties. In contrast, the 'extension', or 'denotation', of a concept refers to the actual 'set of objects, phenomena, events, or entities to which the concept . . . refers'. When climbing the 'ladder of abstraction', researchers actively select concepts with a greater 'extension' and lesser 'intension' (*ibid.*: 33).

As a result, researchers need to seek out conceptualizations which are equivalent, but not identical. Focusing on higher levels of abstraction enables researchers to take into account local circumstances and conceptual frameworks when constructing research instruments. Consequently, research instruments and indicators can vary substantially between cases, provided they are still focused ultimately on illuminating the concept at hand (see Przeworski and Teune, 1966).

This approach, nonetheless, has its risks. The first concerns where we should stop climbing the 'ladder of abstraction'. If we go too far up the ladder, we risk 'stretching' concepts so far that they become meaningless (Sartori, 1970).

One rejoinder to this risk is to ensure that, if the characteristics of a concept cannot be precisely defined in a positive way, the concept can at least be separated from others. According to this approach, it must be possible at least to 'state clearly what the concept is not', even if it is difficult to state precisely what it is (due to its level of abstraction) (Caramani, 2009: 35). Another, alternative, approach can be described as that of 'family resemblance'. This approach involves constructing ideal types (such as democracy, or political authority) at a conceptual level, which are then applied to empirical reality, rather than attempting to specify concepts directly on the basis of empirical analysis. As a result, 'the attribute assumes a "varying geometry" across cases'. The thresholds for the identification of concepts are thus lowered, since any ideal type has a number of characteristics which can be measured and more or less mapped onto different empirical exemplifications (*ibid.*: 35).

An alternative approach focuses on the patterns of relationships amongst conceptualizations, or variables, rather than the characteristics of the conceptualization or variable at hand (see Almond and Verba, 1963: 70). This approach focuses on 'analysing the structure among similar stimuli or items in various settings' (van Deth, 1998: 10) in order to aim at 'internal consistency'. Van Deth refers here to Inglehart's analysis of postmaterialist values across developed countries. He points out that Inglehart does not directly compare 'levels' of postmaterialism across countries but, instead, focuses on 'comparisons within given samples' (van Deth, 1998: 10).

Standardization
The issue of equivalence has been a particular challenge for quantitative analysis, especially the cross-national comparison of social, economic and political statistics. Various types of criteria are used in different countries for reporting statistics. It is obvious that this is problematic, since 'small changes in definition can have large analytic implications' (Mechanic and Rochefort, 1996: 252). For Desrosières (1996), such problems arise, at least partly, because statistical systems represent a compromise between two opposing logics: that of science, which in theory is international, and

that of the state concerned, which will have its own political goals. Certain types of statistics may become highly politicized. This was particularly the case in the 1980s in the UK, for example, where statistical definitions of 'unemployment' were altered on a number of occasions as the number of people out of work appeared stubbornly high, going against the then government's rhetoric that its policies would increase growth and, therefore, employment (Cochrane *et al.*, 2001a: 9).

Rather than attempting, on an *ad hoc* basis, to achieve functional equivalence, many quantitative researchers have tried to work together explicitly to develop agreed-upon definitions for certain concepts or (in particular) statistical items, even if these do not cohere perfectly with domestic understandings. For example, in comparative education 'scholars continue to worry about the reliability of international education statistics' given the different approaches taken in different countries to categorize certain items of educational expenditure. However, concerted action to bring together statisticians and official data collecting agencies by international organizations (particularly the OECD, World Bank and UNESCO, and the International Data Forum) 'has significantly improved the availability of cross-sectional and time-series data on education outcomes and inputs' (Busemeyer and Trampusch, 2010: 417; see also Alcock and Craig, 2009: 7, concerning more general public policy indicators).

The UN has been particularly active in contributing to the harmonization of statistical categories across nations (Dogan and Pelassy, 1990), not least due to the activities of its Statistical Commission, which has published guidelines on procedures and standards to be followed. At a European level, the European Community Household Panel survey was explicitly created as one single survey of 60,000 households across Europe, which would result in comparable data (Kennett, 2001: 55), whilst the Luxembourg Income Study, covering around 25 members of the OECD, has attempted to collate and improve the quality of statistical data on household incomes for over 25 years (*ibid.*: 59).

However, even where harmonized methodological and definitional guidelines have been agreed upon by the different statistics agencies involved, the quality of the resultant data will still reflect the 'quality of national data collation systems and . . . the cooperation [or otherwise] of national statistical institutions with international statistical bodies' (*ibid.*: 59).

This is, obviously, complicated where disputes exist over the appropriate unit of analysis, as with contested governing jurisdictions (Hantrais, 1995). A particularly extreme example of this comes from the contested state of Kosovo, recognized by a majority, but not all, members of the UN. Whilst a census was recently carried out by the Kosovan Census Bureau and Office of Statistics, many Serbian minority people refused to participate, resulting in the census effectively not being carried out in the North of the country (where many, if not all, of the Serbian population lives).

Finally, although harmonization may result in an internally coherent dataset, this can increase, rather than reduce, issues with data comparability across surveys. As an example, Eurostat's surveys exclude people who live in 'live in "non-private" households (hostels, hotels, hospitals) and homeless people' – often described as up to 3 per cent of the population in other surveys. In addition, Eurostat's measure of economic activity differs from that of national governments. This can make it difficult to compare Eurostat data with data from domestic surveys (Kennett, 2001: 57). The differences between surveys may be highly significant; as Kennett points out, in 'the case of Ireland, an additional 36,000 women and 17,000 men are defined as economically active using the ILO definition compared with the PES (Principal Economic Status) method' (*ibid.*).

Time and comparison

Yet another problem of equivalence stems not from differences across geographical or linguistic units, but from differences over time. Mair (1996: 324) notes that cross-national institutional analysis is particularly prone to problems with time equivalence, since institutions can change so rapidly. This can be compounded by the fact that statistical conventions may also alter considerably over time, even within the same data series (Hantrais and Mangen, 1996b: 9).

One way of avoiding this problem is explicitly to incorporate time as a differentiating factor, and to compare different time-periods within countries, rather than merely comparing countries. An example of this comes from Lijphart's (1994) cross-national analysis of political systems. He includes six French cases, comprising the six different electoral systems which France has used since World War II, alongside the other 64 cases he examines.

Indeed, some of the most interesting approaches to comparative research have adopted an explicit awareness of time into their approaches. One particularly innovative approach (at the time) came from Evans and Williams' (1979) comparison of different British family types and the impact of social policy upon them. The authors effectively adopted a type of 'ideal type' strategy, by identifying three different types of family, one middle-income (the Meades), one higher-income (the Moores) and one lower-income (the Lowes), all defined in relation to the average incomes at that time. Successive iterations of their approach have considered how the different 'families' were affected by the different policy regimes (in relation to income support, pensions and housing costs) in operation at different times.

Of course, as with the approach mentioned above, trend and longitudinal analyses are specifically interested in time as a dimension of variation, with different time periods being treated as functionally equivalent to different geographical units (such as countries, or regions) (Bartolini, 1993). These 'diachronic' approaches, where the values 'of cross-sectional, functional or individual cases are measured for different points in time or for different periods', can be explicitly contrasted with 'synchronic' approaches, where the values of 'cross-sectional, functional or individual cases are measured for only one point in time or for one period' (Caramani, 2009: 17).

Although, by making timing explicit, diachronic analyses avoid some of the problems identified with synchronic analyses, they may also be subject to 'historical multicollinearity'. This arises where variables concern broad societal, economic or political trends (e.g. industrialization, or democratization) that 'tend to vary in parallel over time' (*ibid.*: 18). It is important for researchers to recognize the possibility that such independent variables, examined over time, may therefore be associated *with each other*, as well as with the dependent variable.

In conclusion, the problem of equivalence has many facets, and a variety of methods have been articulated to attempt to neutralize it. Here, Hantrais's (1995) injunction appears apposite: 'Whatever the method adopted, the researcher needs to remain alert to the dangers of cultural interference, to ensure that discrepancies are not forgotten or ignored and to be wary of using what may be a sampling bias as an explanatory factor. In interpreting the results, wherever possible, findings should be examined in relation to their wider societal context and with regard to the limitations of the original research parameters'.

Selection on the dependent variable

As discussed above, the problem of equivalence concerns the commensurability of variables across cases – whether they are valid; that is, measure the same concept across cases. The problem of 'selection on the dependent variable' also concerns validity but, this time, of the conclusions drawn from comparative analyses.

This problem was first detailed by King *et al.* (1994), who criticize the readiness of many comparative researchers to 'truncate the dependent variable' – that is, to focus only on extreme values of the variable in question. The tendency can lead, they maintain, to systematic and potentially devastating mistakes in attributing causal relationships amongst variables. Returning to the example of explaining high levels of gun crime can help us illustrate this problem. The researcher, in this case, is interested in what causes high levels of gun crime – a high number of one-parent families, the lack of gun-control laws, unemployment, and/or comparatively short prison sentences. In many cases, researchers would focus on those nations which have comparatively high levels of gun crime, and then use the method of agreement to identify the cause of this. Let's say, all the countries chosen for investigation share high levels of unemployment and comparatively short prison sentences, as well as having high levels of gun crime. The researcher would therefore likely conclude that high levels of unemployment and comparatively short prison sentences *lead* to high levels of gun crime.

The problem with this strategy is fairly obvious, but infrequently acknowledged. The researcher has focused only on those countries with high levels of gun crime. She or he has not examined those nations which have comparatively short prison sentences and/or high levels of unemployment, but which *may not* have high levels of gun crime.

It is not the case that restricting the selection of cases to be examined in this way will always lead to bias. By chance, the cases chosen might display the causal relationship clearly – and a process tracing approach could further evidence it. However, this would be only by chance – the researcher would never know if counter-examples could be found which displayed the same values on the independent variables concerned (e.g. high levels of unemployment, and comparatively short prison sentences), but did not share the same value on the dependent variable (the level of gun crime).

The problem of selection on the dependent variable essentially relates to what Lijphart (1971: 685) has described as the 'principal problem' facing 'the comparative method' – 'many variables, small number of cases'. Two main responses have been articulated to the problem of selection on the dependent variable: increasing the number of cases examined, and engaging in within-case analysis.

King *et al.*'s answer to this problem is to advocate that a full range of cases should be examined, which includes cases which have low as well as high values on the dependent variable concerned. They thus advocate an 'extensive' research design, with 'many cases and few variables', as opposed to an 'intensive' one which would focus on many variables but only in a few cases (Caramani, 2009: 17). Arguably, many researchers have accepted that truncation on the dependent variable can cause problems – and have thus covered a wide range of countries in their analyses (see, for example, Castles, 1998; Swank, 2002), albeit generally only developed countries falling within the OECD (a tendency examined in detail in Chapter 13).

Nonetheless, simply expanding the number of cases to be examined beyond those with extreme values on the dependent variable runs the risk of introducing 'causal heterogeneity' (Collier *et al.*, 2004: 88). As the number of cases expands, more and more possible independent variables are potentially introduced into the analysis, which can require increasingly complex research designs to uncover underlying causal mechanisms.

More radically, it can be argued that *any* approach to case selection potentially risks bias. Caramani argues, for example, that choosing all the members of any international organization, whilst resulting in a large number of cases (34 for the OECD, 27 for the EU, at the time of writing), does not necessarily get over problems of bias. This is because all the cases share at least one similarity – they all chose to become members of the organization concerned. The cases are thus, to an extent, '"self-selected" by their choice to join the organization' (Caramani, 2009: 21). Even choosing the full set of countries – that is, all countries that exist (leaving aside any problems with national recognition!) – would not provide the researcher with the entire set of *theoretically possible* conjunctions of variables. As Caramani puts it, the 'set of real-world cases is biased as a result of "natural" or "historical" contingency, meaning that the pool of cases has been biased by social processes'. This is underlined by the fact that many phenomena which would appear to have been theoretically or practically possible have not occurred. For example, amongst 'advanced industrial economies' there is no case of a 'Protestant country that experienced late democratization' – but this does not mean that such a country could not have existed (*ibid*.: 20–1). Following this line of argument, the problem of selection on the dependent variable could be seen as just a subset of the wider problem of screening out irrelevant variables when carrying out comparative research.

An alternative approach to dealing with the problem of 'selecting on the dependent variable', which does not involve attempting to expand the number of cases, comes from attempts to analyse causal processes *within* cases – the 'process tracing' method referred to above (pp. 323–4). This contrasts with approaches which focus on the relationship between causal *effects* across cases (Collier *et al*., 2004: 92–3). As already described, process tracing examines evidence in detail about the causal mechanisms that appear to have produced a specific causal outcome.

In practice, it has been contended that the 'problem' of selection on the dependent variable is less serious than might initially be assumed. Collier *et al*. (*ibid*.), for example, maintain that the problem relies on the 'mistaken conviction that quantitative and qualitative research employ the same sources of inferential leverage. In fact, they often employ different sources of leverage, and consequently selection bias is not always a problem in qualitative research' (*ibid*.: 101). This returns us to Levi-Faur's (2006) contention, referred to above (p. 324), that inference is 'a gradual and cumulative process of elimination, falsification, discovery, and corroboration' (*ibid*.: 60).

Many studies could provide examples of the gradual and cumulative nature of comparative social research. One interesting example comes from Limerick's (2009) comparative examination of the performance of Aboriginal Councils in Queensland. Initially, two case studies were chosen in order to identify the factors which led to high performance – one high performing council, and one low performing (as assessed by 'annual audits of council finances along with expert opinions of government officers'). A third case study was chosen later, which 'exhibited many of the contextual factors that had emerged as apparently important to the high performance' of the high performing council, yet which nonetheless was not performing at a high level (*ibid.*: 416). Limerick's research indicates how, in practice, comparative researchers are often aware of the problem of selection on the dependent variable and develop strategies to try (at least partially) to deal with it, even if these are not explicitly put forward as responding to King *et al.*'s (1994) original criticisms of small-N approaches to comparison.

The practicalities of comparative research

The most carefully constructed and methodologically sophisticated comparative research projects can still sometimes fail if the practicalities of comparative research are not given the consideration they merit. As Elder (1976: 223) puts it, the 'most carefully translated research instruments will be of little use if a researcher is unable to obtain cooperation from respondents in the field'. Such cooperation will often rest on respondents' assessment of the degree of involvement of local actors, how the research is explained, who is actually carrying out the research on the ground, and how those researchers conduct themselves.

In addition to ensuring the cooperation of potential research subjects, large-scale projects also require cooperation across the project team. The challenge of achieving linguistic or functional equivalence has already been mentioned. Beyond this issue, however, other logistical challenges may often arise. Researchers in different countries may have different attitudes towards different types of methods and their combination; they may have different views concerning the appropriate ways to sample, or of what constitutes an 'acceptable' response rate; and they may have different views about who can appropriately be involved as a researcher and who cannot (see Jowell, 1998). These differences can arise even 'within a single discipline', let alone within explicitly interdisciplinary projects (Hantrais, 1995).

These differing views may, or may not, reflect the situation facing researchers in different countries, where it may be more or less appropriate to use different methods. A fascinating example of this, albeit not from an explicitly comparative text, comes from Young's (2000) study of sworn virgins in (mainly) rural Albania – women who had adopted the male gender within an extremely patriarchal society, often following the murder of all other adult men in the family. Young explains how it would have been impossible to conduct a controlled, tape-recorded interview just with the sworn virgins themselves without causing great offence, not to mention confusion. Instead, her 'conversations' occurred in ways which fitted in with the collective, strictly hierarchical family structures of Northern rural Albania, and were interspersed with the rituals of its demanding approach to hospitality to strangers (i.e. to Young herself).

Kennett (2001: 44) describes a general concern about the 'methods employed and the conceptualisation of issues' within comparative research as one of 'appropriateness'. Unlike concerns over reliability and validity, which relate to the use of specific research methods in relation to specific topics, 'appropriateness' concerns the acceptability of the overall project in the different national contexts where it is undertaken.

Aside from these concerns about research design and methods, comparative research also requires careful consideration of the resources available, both human and financial. By its very nature, considering more than one setting, comparative research is often considerably more expensive than single-case research. It can also be difficult to interest nationally-based funders in a specific research project which crosses borders. This is not only because funding bodies in different countries may have different agendas (Hantrais, 1995), but also because their natural instinct may be to pass any responsibility for funding such projects either onto the other countries involved, or onto multinational bodies. Whilst numerous international sources of funding exist for comparative public policy research, competition for these funds can be fierce, and criteria may reflect an amalgam of different member countries' research priorities, rather than a coherent research vision.

The human resources required for comparative research can also be extensive. However, these largely depend on the ambitiousness or otherwise of the project concerned. In this connection, Hakim (2002: 203–4) identifies four different types of research teams which can be used to carry out comparative research.

The first type, the 'safari', involves a lone researcher visiting the countries they are interested in, and travelling to them to collect data (from documents, observations, interviews, surveys, or other methods). This type is obviously heavily dependent on the time available to the lone researcher, and can (as already mentioned) pose problems for the comparability of data gathered, since the lone researcher will often have to carry out the different stages of data collection spread over an extended period – perhaps 12 months, or considerably longer.

Despite these difficulties, the 'safari' is often the most common method adopted for comparative research. Whilst the 'safari' model provides the lone researcher with great individual autonomy and control over their research project, it also imposes considerable logistical challenges. This is particularly the case for those with children, where long periods away from home may be difficult to negotiate with family members and to organize logistically. Whilst some parents are able to take their children with them to the field, this can cause problems of its own; yet, not all parents may be able to leave their children with a partner or family member back in their home country.

Many female researchers, in particular, abandon 'safari'-style research after having children (Tripp, 2002). As a result, Tripp (*ibid.*: 810) argues that 'funding agencies, tenure review committees, grant proposal reviewers, and individuals administering fellowship programmes would do well to consider some of the particular hardships women with children face if women are going to contribute equally to our understanding of the world'.

A second type of research team is the 'star-led team'. According to this organizational pattern, one researcher in a particular country defines a project and then other researchers in different countries, either explicitly or implicitly directed by the 'star', carry out the research in their own country. A good example of this, as mentioned by Hakim, is Inglehart's world values surveys.

A third type of research team is the 'duo'. As the name suggests, this involves two academics based in different countries, who often already know each other, carrying out research on a specific topic.

A final type of research team is what has been described as the 'democratic' team. This involves researchers in different nations collaborating to produce a piece of research, with all contributing academics playing a role in the organization of the project. The management of the 'democratic' team is perhaps one of the most testing areas of comparative research, particularly for those researchers whose skills are academic rather than managerial. The construction of the 'democratic' team first requires identifying appropriate and reliable collaborators – which can be a difficult task for new researchers, in particular, who may lack existing links with researchers in other countries. As a result, 'stabs in the dark' are sometimes taken which can result in 'depressingly uneven' contributions to joint research projects (Hantrais and Mangen, 1996b: 10–11). In addition, the choice of partner may reflect 'political' rather than 'scientific' factors, such as perceptions that funders would be more likely to support research which involved researchers from a specific country or region (Hantrais, 1995).

However, it is important not to over-exaggerate the logistical challenges facing comparative research conducted within democratic teams. Not only can the gains from this type of research be extremely impressive, but the problems which afflict it can affect any research which involves individuals from different institutional backgrounds and organizational cultures (Hakim, 2002: 207).

The problem of incommensurability of data has already been referred to in discussions about conceptual equivalence. In addition to this, however, there can also be a lack of specific types of data in different countries, which renders comparison extremely difficult without the researcher(s) themselves generating new data (Hantrais, 1995). Extreme examples of this are provided by countries which have recently gone through profound social and political change. From an initially low-quality base, statistics on basic issues – such as the size of the population in different regions and the usage of electricity in different areas – have simply not existed from the mid-1990s onwards in many parts of the former Yugoslavia. Not only was accurate record-keeping ignored during the civil war which wracked the region but, in addition, what statistics were produced were generally explicitly designed for political (often, ethnic) reasons. In areas such as Kosovo, it would make little sense to attempt to carry out quantitative analysis, since the quality and availability of socioeconomic statistics is so poor. This prevents any coherent comparative statistical analysis across the region, not to mention involving other countries situated beyond it.

Conclusion

Whilst Chapter 1 detailed the advantages of adopting comparison as a research strategy, this chapter has tried to highlight the potential pitfalls of this approach. Every comparative researcher is, first, faced with the question of what to compare, and then with how to undertake their comparison. Numerous answers abound to these two questions, but none are completely watertight, and all have attracted criticism over the years. Nonetheless, numerous studies have faced up explicitly to the challenges of validity, reliability and appropriateness that are inherent within comparative public policy research, and produced extremely interesting findings in the process.

A particularly interesting modern development is the willingness of comparative researchers to combine different approaches to research (quantitative and qualitative; the methods of difference and of agreement; combinatorial analysis and process tracing) in order to obtain a sophisticated understanding of their research topics across a variety of cases. Rather than viewing these methodological challenges as reasons not to engage in comparative research, the lively debates they have engendered indicate the reflexivity of practitioners of comparative public policy, and their willingness to question accepted research traditions and practices.

Summary

❏ Comparative researchers face a number of choices: which units to compare, how to compare them, and how to draw conclusions from this comparison.

❏ A variety of research designs are available to researchers seeking to explain similarity or difference between the units they are comparing. These approaches include the methods of agreement and of difference, combinatorial analysis, and process tracing.

❏ As indicated in Chapter 1, comparative research can produce rich and compelling findings, but it is also subject to challenges which are arguably more acute than those faced by other fields of enquiry. In particular, comparative analysts need to beware of the Galton problem, and the problems of equivalence and of selection on the dependent variable. Although various solutions have been put forward to all these problems, they have their own advantages and disadvantages.

❏ Comparative public policy research can also involve considerable logistical challenges depending on the nature of the research team and policy area being studied.

❏ Numerous innovative approaches have been developed within the field of comparative public policy which explicitly face up to its methodological and practical challenges. Increasingly, researchers are combining different methods in order to obtain richer, more robust findings.

References

Aaron, H.J. and Schwartz, W.B. (1984) *The Painful Prescription* (Washington, DC: Brookings Institution).

Abrahamson, P. (1999) 'The Welfare Modelling Business', *Social Policy and Administration*, 33(4): 394–415.

Acacio, K. (2008) 'Managing Labor Migration: Philippine State Policy and International Migration Flows, 1969–2000', *Asian and Pacific Migration Journal*, 17: 103–132.

Acemoglu, D. and Johnson, S. (2003) 'Unbundling Institutions', NBER Working Paper 9934.

Acemoglu, D., Johnson, S. and Robinson, J.A. (2001) 'The Colonial Origins of Comparative Development: An Empirical Investigation', *American Economic Review*, 91(5): 1369–401.

Adam, R. and Gough, O. (2008) 'Pension Reforms and Saving for Retirement: Comparing the United Kingdom and Italy', *Policy Studies*, 29(2): 119–35.

Aguilar Fernández, S. (1994) 'Convergence in Environmental Policy? The Resilience of National Institutional Designs in Spain and Germany', *Journal of Public Policy*, 14(1): 39–56.

Ahmad, W.I.U. (1995) 'Review Article: "Race" and Health', *Sociology of Health and Illness*, 17(3): 418–29.

Alber, J. (1981) 'Government Responses to the Challenge of Unemployment: The Development of Unemployment Insurance in Western Europe', in P. Flora and A.J. Heidenheimer (eds), *The Development of Welfare States in Europe and America* (London: Transaction Books).

Albert, M. (1991) *Capitalisme contre capitalisme* (Paris: Éditions du Seuil).

Albrow, M. (1996) *The Global Age: State and Society Beyond Modernity* (Cambridge: Polity Press).

Alcock, P. (2009) 'The United Kingdom: Constructing a Third Way?', in P. Alcock and G. Craig (eds), *International Social Policy: Welfare Regimes in the Developed World*, 2nd edn (Basingstoke: Palgrave Macmillan): ch. 6: 109–29.

Alcock, P. and Craig, G. (2009) 'The International Context', in P. Alcock and G. Craig (eds), *International Social Policy: Welfare Regimes in the Developed World*, 2nd edn (Basingstoke: Palgrave Macmillan): 1–24.

Alford, R.R. (1975) *Health Care Politics: Ideological and Interest Group Barriers to Reform* (Chicago, IL: University of Chicago Press).

Allan, J.P and Scruggs, L. (2004) 'Political Partisanship and Welfare State Reform in Advanced Industrial Societies', *American Journal of Political Science*, 48(3): 496–512.

Allsop, J. and Saks, M. (2002) 'Introduction', in J. Allsop and M. Saks (eds), *Regulating the Health Professions* (London: Sage).

Almond, G. (1988) 'Separate Tables: Schools and Sects in Political Science', *Political Science and Politics*, 21(4): 828–42.

Almond, G.A. (1990) *A Discipline Divided: Schools and Sects in Political Science* (Newbury Park, CA: Sage).

Almond, G.A. and Verba, S. (1963) *The Civic Culture: Political Attitudes and Democracy in Five Nations* (London: Sage).

Alter, K.J. (1998) 'Who Are the "Masters of the Treaty"?: European Governments and the European Court of Justice', *International Organization*, 52(1): 121–47.

Amable, B. (2003) *The Diversity of Modern Capitalism* (Oxford: Oxford University Press).

Amable, B. (2005) *Les cinq capitalisms: diversité des systèmes économiques et sociaux dans la mondialisation* (Paris: Seuil).

Amin, A. (1997) 'Placing Globalization', *Theory, Culture and Society*, 14(2): 123–37.

Anderson, C.W. (1977) *Statecraft: An Introduction to Political Choice and Judgement* (New York: John Wiley & Sons).

Anderson, O.W. (1963) 'Medical Care: Its Social and Organizational Aspects. Health Services Systems in the United States and Other Countries', *New England Journal of Medicine*, 269: 839–843.

Anker, R. and Hein, C. (1985) 'Why Third World Urban Employers Usually Prefer Men', *International Labour Review*, 124(1): 73–90.

Annesley, C. (2010) 'Gender, Politics and Policy Change: The Case of Welfare Reform Under New Labour', *Government and Opposition*, 45(1): 50–72.

Aoki, M. (1988) *Information, Incentives and Bargaining in the Japanese Economy* (Cambridge: Cambridge University Press).

Apple, M. (2007) 'Comparing Neo-Liberal Projects and Inequality in Education', in M. Crossley, P. Broadfoot and M. Schweisfurth (eds), *Changing Educational Contexts, Issues and Identities, 40 Years of Comparative Education* (London: Routledge): 300–18.

Apter, D.E. (1965) *The Politics of Modernisation* (Chicago, IL: University of Chicago Press).

Archer, M.S. (ed.) (1972) *Students, University and Society: A Comparative Sociological Review* (London: Heinemann Educational Books).

Archer, M.S. (1979) *Social Origins of Educational Systems* (London: Sage).

Archer, M.S. (1981) 'On Predicting the Behaviour of the Educational System', Extended Review, *British Journal of Sociology of Education*, 2: 211–19.

Ariely, D. (2008) *Predictably Irrational: The Hidden Forces That Shape Our Decisions* (New York: Harper Collins).

Aristotle (350BC) 'Politics: A Treatise on Government'.

Arnove, R. (2007) 'Introduction: Reframing Comparative Education: The Dialectic of the Global and the Local', in R.F. Arnove and C.A. Torres (eds), *Comparative Education: The Dialectic of the Global and the Local*, 3rd edn (Lanham, MD: Rowman & Littlefield) 1–20.

Arrow, K., Bowles, S. and Durlauf, S. (eds) (2000) *Meritocracy and Economic Inequality* (Princeton, NJ: Princeton University Press).

Arthur, W.B. (1994) *Increasing Returns and Path Dependence in the Economy* (Ann Arbor, MI: University of Michigan Press).

Arts, W.A. and Gelissen, J. (2002) 'Three Worlds of Welfare Capitalism or More? A State-of-the-Art Report, *Journal of European Social Policy*, 12: 137–58.

Atkinson, M.M. and Coleman, W.D. (1985) 'Corporatism and Industrial Policy', in A. Cawson (ed.), *Organized Interests and the State: Studies in Meso-Corporatism* (London: Sage): 22–44.

Atkinson, M.M. and Coleman, W.D. (1989) 'Strong States and Weak States: Sectoral Policy Networks in Advanced Capitalist Economies', *British Journal of Political Science*, 19: 47–67.

Aulich, C., Batainah, H., Wettenhall, R. (2010) 'Autonomy and Control in Australian Agencies: Data and Preliminary Findings from a Cross-National Empirical Study', *Australian Journal of Public Administration*, 69(2): 214–28.

Bachrach, P. and Baratz, M.S. (1962) 'Two Faces of Power', *American Political Science Review*, 56(4): 947–52.

Badran, A. (2010) 'Steering the Regulatory State: The Rationale behind the Creation and Diffusion of Independent Regulatory Agencies in Liberalized Utility Sectors in the Developing Countries: Initial Thoughts and Reflections on the Egyptian Case', *Paper presented to ECPR Standing Group on Regulatory Governance Conference*, Dublin.

Badrinath, S.G. and Bolster, Paul J. (1996) 'The Role of Market Forces in EPA Enforcement Activity', *Journal of Regulatory Economics*, 10: 165–81.

Baggot, R. and Harrison, L. (1986) 'The Politics of Self-Regulation', *Policy and Politics*, 14(2): 143–59.

Balassa, B. (1962) *The Theory of Economic Integration* (London: Allen & Unwin).

Baldwin P. (1990) *The Politics of Social Solidarity: Class Bases of the European Welfare State, 1975–1975* (Cambridge: Cambridge University Press).

Baldwin, R. and Cave, M. (1999) *Understanding Regulation* (Oxford: Oxford University Press).

Ball, S.J. (1990) *Politics and Policy Making in Education: Explorations in Policy Sociology, Volume 1* (London: Routledge).

Ball, S.J. (1998) 'Big Policies/Small World: An Introduction to International Perspectives in Education Policy', *Comparative Education*, 34(2): 119–30.

Ball, S.J. (2012) 'The Reluctant State and the Beginning of the End of State Education', *Journal of Educational Administration and History*, 44(2): 89–103.

Bambra, C. (2005) 'Worlds of Welfare and the Health Care Discrepancy', *Social Policy and Society*, 4(1): 31–41.

Banting, K. and Kymlicka, W. (2007) *Multiculturalism and the Welfare State* (Oxford: Oxford University Press).

Bardach, E. (1980) 'Implementation Studies and the Study of Implements', 1980 Annual Meeting of APSA.

Bardach, E. and Kagan, R. (1982) *Going by the Book: The Problem of Regulatory Unreasonableness* (Philadelphia, PA: Temple University Press).

Bardasi, E. and Jenkins, S.P. (2010) 'The Gender Gap in Private Pensions', *Bulletin of Economic Research*, 62(4): 343–63.

Barnett, C. (1986) *The Audit of War: The Illusion and Reality of Britain as a Great Nation* (London: Macmillan).

Barr, N. (2009) 'International Trends in Pension Provision', *Accounting and Business Research*, 39(3), International Accounting Policy Forum: 211–25.

Barr, N. and Diamond, P. (2009) 'Reforming Pensions: Principles, Analytical Errors and Policy Directions', *International Social Security Review*, 62(2): 5–29.

Bartlett, D., Corrigan, P., Dibben, P., Franklin, S., Joyce, P., McNulty, T. and Rose, A. (1999) 'Preparing for Best Value', *Local Government Studies*, 25(2): 102–18.

Bartolini, S. (1993) 'On Time and Comparative Research', *Journal of Theoretical Politics*, 5: 131–67.

Bates, R.H. (1997) 'Area Studies and the Discipline: A Useful Controversy?', *Political Science and Politics*, 30(2): 166–70.

Baumgartner, F.R. and Jones, B.D. (1993) *Agendas and Instability in American Politics* (Chicago, IL: University of Chicago Press).

Baumgartner, F.R., Jones, B.D. and Wilkerson, J. (2011) 'Comparative Studies of Policy Dynamics', *Comparative Political Studies*, 44(8): 947–72.

BBC (2002a) 'Mass Sterilisation Scandal Shocks Peru', BBC News, 24 July.

BBC (2002b) 'Pensions Scandal costs £11.8 billion', BBC News, 27 June, available at http://newsimg.bbc.co.uk/1/hi/business/2070271.stm, accessed 27 November 2010.

Bearce, D.H. and Hutnick, J.A.L. (2011) 'Toward an Alternative Explanation for the Resource Curse: Natural Resources, Immigration, and Democratization', *Comparative Political Studies*, 44(6): 689–718.

Beck, U. (1992) *Risk Society: Towards a New Modernity* (London: Sage).

Becker, G. (1974) 'A Theory of Social Interactions', *Journal of Political Economy*, 82(6): 1063–93.

Becker, H. (1967) 'Whose Side Are We On?', *Social Problems*, 14: 239–47.

Béland, D. (2005) 'Ideas and Social Policy: An Institutionalist Perspective', *Social Policy and Administration*, 39(1): 1–18.

Bemelmans-Videc, M.-L. (1998) 'Introduction: Policy Instrument Choice and Evaluation', in M.-L. Bemelmans-Videc, R.C. Rist and E. Vedung (eds), *Carrots, Sticks and Sermons: Policy Instruments and Their Evaluation* (New Brunswick and London: Transaction Publishers): 1–20.

Ben-David, J. (1991) *Scientific Growth. Essays on the Social Organization and Ethos of Science* (Berkeley, LA: University of California Pressarva).

Bennett, C.J. (1997) 'Understanding Ripple Effects: The Cross-National Adoption of Policy Instruments for Bureaucratic Accountability', *Governance*, 10(3): 213–33.

Bennett, C.J. and Howlett, M. (1992) 'The Lessons of Learning: Reconciling Theories of Policy Learning and Policy Change', *Policy Sciences*, 25: 275–94.

Bennett, J. (2010) *Vibrant Matter: A Political Ecology of Things* (Durham, NC and London: Duke University Press).

Bereday, G.Z.F. (1964) *Comparative Method in Education* (New York: Holt, Rinehart & Winston, Inc).

Berg, M. (1997) 'Problems and Promises of the Protocol', *Social Science and Medicine*, 44: 1081–8.

Berger, S. and Dore, R. (eds) (1996) *National Diversity and Global Capitalism* (Ithaca, NY: Cornell University Press).

Berman, S. (1998) *The Social Democratic Moment: Ideas and Politics in the Making of Interwar Europe* (Princeton, NJ: Princeton University Press).

Berman, S. (2006) *The Primacy of Politics: Social Democracy and the Making of Europe's Twentieth Century* (Cambridge: Cambridge University Press).

Berry, F.S. and Berry, W.D. (1999) 'Innovation and Diffusion Models in Policy Research', in P.A. Sabatier (ed.), *Theories of the Policy Process* (Boulder, CO: Westview Press).

Bevir, M. and Rhodes, R.A.W. (2003) *Interpreting British Governance* (London: Routledge).

Bezes, P. (2007) 'The Hidden Politics of Administrative Reform: Cutting French Civil Service Wages with a Low-Profile Instrument', *Governance*, 20(1): 23–56.

Bierce, A. (1911) *The Devil's Dictionary* (New York: Oxford University Press).

Biersteker, T.J. (1998) 'Globalization and the Modes of Operation of Major Institutional Actors', *Oxford Development Studies*, 26(1): 15–32.

Birnbaum, P. (1982) *L'impossible corporatisme,* in *La Logique de l'Etat* (Paris: Fayard) 79–111.

Birnbaum, P. (1988) *States and Collective Action: The European Experience* (Cambridge: Cambridge University Press).

Bjorkman, J.W. (1989) 'Politicizing Medicine and Medicalizing Politics: Physician Power in the US', in G. Freddi and J.W. Bjorkman (eds), *Controlling Medical Professionals* (London: Sage).

Blair, D. (2011) 'Ecuador's Novel Plan to Save Rainforest', *Financial Times*, 3 January.

Blais, A., Blake, D. and Dion, S. (1996) 'Do Parties Make A Difference? A Reappraisal', *American Journal of Political Science*, 40(2): 514–20.

Blank, R.H. and Burau, V. (2004) *Comparative Health Policy* (Basingstoke: Palgrave Macmillan).

Bleiklie, I., Høstaker, R. and Vabø, A. (2000) *Policy and Practice in Higher Education: Reforming Norwegian Universities* (London: Jessica Kingsley).

Blekesaune, M. and Quadagno, J. (2003) 'Public Attitudes toward Welfare State Policies: A Comparative Analysis of 24 Nations', *European Sociological Review*, 19(5): 415–27.

Blindenbacher, R. and Nashat, B. (2010) *The Black Box of Governmental Learning: The Learning Spiral – A Concept to Organize Learning in Governments* (Washington, DC: World Bank).

Blyth, M. (1997) '"Any More Bright Ideas?" The Ideational Turn of Comparative Political Economy', *Comparative Politics*, 29(2): 229–50.

Blyth, M. (2002) *Great Transformations: Economic Ideas and Institutional Change in the Twentieth Century* (Cambridge: Cambridge University Press).

Blyth, M. (2003) 'Structures Do Not Come with an Instruction Sheet: Interests, Ideas and Progress in Political Science', *Perspectives on Politics*, I: 695–706.

Bobrow, D. and Dryzek, J. (1987) *Policy Analysis by Design* (Pittsburgh, PA: University of Pittsburgh Press).

Boix, C. (1998) *Political Parties, Growth and Equality: Conservative and Social Democratic Economic Strategies in the World Economy* (Cambridge: Cambridge University Press).

Bollen, K.A., Entwistle, B. and Alderson, A.S. (1993) 'Macrocomparative Research Methods', *Annual Review of Sociology*, 19: 321–51.

Bomberg, E. (2007) 'Policy Learning in an Enlarged European Union: Environmental NGOs and New Policy Instruments', *Journal of European Public Policy*, 14(2): 248–68.

Bonoli, G. (1997) 'Classifying Welfare States: A Two-Dimension Approach', *Journal of Social Policy*, 26(3): 351–72.

Bonoli, G. (2000) *The Politics of Pension Reform: Institutions and Policy Change in Western Europe* (Cambridge: Cambridge University Press).

Bookman, M.Z. and Bookman, K.R. (2007) *Medical Tourism in Developing Countries* (Basingstoke: Palgrave Macmillan).

Borrás, S. and Radaelli, C.M. (2011) 'The Politics of Governance Architectures: Creation, Change and Effects of the EU Lisbon Strategy', *Journal of European Public Policy*, 18(4): 463–84.

Börsch, A. (2009) 'Many Roads to Rome: Varieties of Funded Pensions in Europe and Asia', *Pensions*, 14: 172–80.

Börzel, T.A. (2002) 'Pace-Setting, Foot-Dragging, and Fence-Sitting: Member State Response to Europeanization', *Journal of Common Market Studies*, 40(2): 193–214.

Bourdieu, P. (1996) *The State Nobility: Elite Schools in the Field of Power* (Cambridge: Polity).

Bovaird, A.G. and Löffler, E. (eds) (2003) *Public Management and Governance* (London: Routledge).

Bovens, M., 't Hart, P., Peters, B.G., Alboek, E., Busch, A., Dudley, G., Moran, M. and Richardson, J. (2001a) 'Patterns of Governance: Sectoral and National Comparisons', in M. Bovens, P. 't Hart and B.G. Peters (ed.), *Success and Failure in Public Governance: A Comparative Analysis* (Cheltenham: Edward Elgar): 593–640.

Bovens, M. 't Hart, P. and Peters, B.G. (2001b) 'The State of Governance in Six European States', in M. Bovens, P. 't Hart and B.G. Peters (ed.), *Success and Failure in Public Governance: A Comparative Analysis* (Cheltenham: Edward Elgar): 641–62

Bradshaw, Y. and Wallace, M. (1991) 'Informing Generality and Explaining Uniqueness: The Place of Case Studies in Comparative Research', *International Journal of Comparative Sociology*, 32(1/2): 154–71.

Branch, J. (2011) 'Mapping the Sovereign State: Technology, Authority, and Systemic Change', *International Organization*, 65: 1–36.

Braun, D. (1999) Interests or Ideas? 'An Overview of Ideational Concepts in Public Policy Research', in D. Braun and A Busch (eds), *Public Policy and Political Ideas* (Cheltenham: Edward Elgar): 11–29.

Bray, M. (2007) 'Control of Education: Issues and Tensions in Centralization and Decentralization', in R.F. Arnove and C.A. Torres, *Comparative Education: The Dialectic of the Global and the Local*, 3rd edn (Lanham, MD: Rowman & Littlefield): 175–98.

Bray, M., Adamson, B. and Mason, M. (2007) *Comparative Education Research: Approaches and Methods* (Hong Kong: Springer/Comparative Education Research Centre, University of Hong Kong).

Brean, D.J.S., Kryanowski, L. and Roberts, G.S. (2011) 'Canada and the United States: Different Roots, Different Routes to Financial Sector Regulation', *Business History*, 53(2): 249–69.

Bressers, H., O'Toole, L.J. and Richardson, J. (eds) (1995) *Networks for Water Policy* (London: Frank Cass).

Broadfoot, P. (2007) 'Changing Patterns of Educational Accountability in England and France', in M. Crossley, P. Broadfoot and M. Schweisfurth (eds), *Changing Educational Contexts, Issues and Identities, 40 Years of Comparative Education* (London: Routledge): 55–73.

Browers, M. (2003) 'The Reconciliation of Political Theory and Comparative Politics', in J.S. Holmes (ed.), *New Approaches to Comparative Politics: Insights from Political Theory* (Oxford: Lexington Books): 7–22.

Brown, A. (2010) *The Rise and Fall of Communism* (London: Vintage).

Bruno, M. and Sachs, J.D. (1985) *Economics of Worldwide Stagflation* (Cambridge, MA: Harvard University Press).

Bryson, L. and Verity, F. (2009) 'Australia: From Wage-Earners to Neo-Liberal Welfare State', in P. Alcock and G. Craig (eds), *International Social Policy: Welfare Regimes in the Developed World*, 2nd edn (Basingstoke: Palgrave Macmillan).

Buchanan, J.M. (1954) 'Individual Choice in Voting and the Market', *Journal of Political Economy*, 62(4): 334–43.

Buck, S.J. (1998) *The Global Commons: An Introduction* (London: Earthscan Publications).

Bugdahn, S. (2005) 'Of Europeanization and Domestication: The Implementation of the Environmental Information Directive in Ireland, Great Britain and Germany', *Journal of European Public Policy*, 12(1): 177–99.

Buller, J. and Gamble, A. (2002) 'Conceptualising Europeanisation', *Public Policy and Administration*, Special Issue: *Understanding the Europeanisation of Public Policy*, 17(2): 4–24.

Bulmer, S. and Burch, M. (2000) 'The Europeanisation of British Central Government', in R.A.W. Rhodes (ed.), *Transforming British Government Volume 1 – Changing Institutions* (London: Macmillan): 46–62.

Bulmer, S. and Burch, M. (2001) 'The Europeanisation of Central Government: The UK and Germany in Historical Institutionalist Perspective', in G. Schneider and M. Aspinwall (eds), *The Rules of Integration: Institutionalist Approaches to the Study of Europe* (Manchester: Manchester University Press): 73–96.

Buonanno, L. and Nugent, N. (2012) *Policies and Policy Processes of the European Union* (Basingstoke: Palgrave Macmillan).

Burci, G.L. (2008) 'Health and Infectious Disease', in S. Daws and T.G. Weiss (eds), *The Oxford Handbook on the United Nations* (Oxford: Oxford University Press): 582–91

Burley, A.-M. and Mattli, W. (1993) 'Europe before the Court: A Political Theory of Legal Integration', *International Organization*, 47(1): 41–76.

Busch, M.L. and Pelc, K.J. (2010) 'The Politics of Judicial Economy at the World Trade Organization', *International Organization*, 64: 257–79.

Busemeyer, M.R. (2009) 'Asset Specificity, Institutional Complementarities and the Variety of Skill Regimes in Coordinated Market Economies', *Socio-Economic Review*, 7: 375–406.

Busemeyer, M.R. (2009) 'From Myth to Reality: Globalisation and Public Spending in OECD Countries Revisited', *European Journal of Political Research*, 48(4): 455–82.

Busemeyer, M.R. and Trampusch, C. (2010) 'Review Article: Comparative Political Science and the Study of Education', *British Journal of Political Science*, 41(2): 1–31.

Bussemaker, J. and van Kersbergen, K. (1994) 'Gender and Welfare States; Some Theoretical Reflections', in D. Sainsbury (ed.), *Gendering Welfare States* (London: Sage): 8–25.

Cairney, P. (2009) 'The "British Policy Style" and Mental Health: Beyond the Headlines', *Journal of Social Policy*, 38(4): 671–88.

Callaghan, H. (2010) 'Beyond Methodological Nationalism: How Multilevel Governance Affects the Clash of Capitalisms', *Journal of European Public Policy*: 564–80.

Callahan, D. (1998) *False Hopes: Overcoming the Obstacles to a Sustainable, Affordable Medicine* (New Brunswick, NJ: Rutgers University Press).

Cameron, D. (1998) *The Feminist Critique of Language*, 2nd edn (London: Routledge).

Cameron, D.R. (1978) 'Expansion of the Public Economy: Comparative Analysis', *American Political Science Review*, 72(4): 1243–61.

Campbell, A.L. (2003) *How Policies Make Citizens: Senior Political Activism and the American Welfare State* (Princeton, NJ: Princeton University Press).

Caporaso, J.A. (1997) 'Does the European Union Represent an n of 1?', *ECSA Review*, X(3): 1–5.

Caporaso, J.A. and Tarrow, S. (2009) 'Polanyi in Brussels: Supranational Institutions and the Transnational Embedding of Markets', *International Organization*, 63(4): 593–620.

Caramani, D. (2009) *Introduction to the Comparative Method with Boolean Algebra* (London: Sage).

Cardoso, F.H. (1973) 'Associated-Dependent Development: Theoretical and Practical Implications', in Alfred Stepan (ed.), *Authoritarian Brazil: Origins, Policies and Future* (New Haven, CT: Yale University Press).

Carnes, M.E. and Mares, I. (2007) 'The Welfare State in Global Perspective', in C. Boix and S.C. Stokes (eds), *The Oxford Handbook of Comparative Politics* (Oxford: Oxford University Press): 868–85.

Carpenter, E. and McLuhan, M. (eds) (1960) *Explorations in Communication* (Boston, MA: Beacon Press).

Carson, R. (1962) *Silent Spring* (London: Penguin).

Carter, D.S.G. and O'Neill, M.H. (1995) *International Perspectives on Educational Reform and Policy Implementation* (Brighton: Falmer).

Case, P., Case, S. and Catling, S. (2000) 'Please Show You're Working: A Critical Assessment of the Impact of OFSTED Inspection on Primary Teachers', *British Journal of Sociology of Education*, 21(4): 605–21.

Castells, M. and Laserna, R. (1989) 'The New Dependency: Technological Change and Socioeconomic Restructuring in Latin America', *Sociological Forum*, 4(4): Special Issue: *Comparative National Development: Theory and Facts for the 1990s*: 535–60.

Castles, F.G. (1985) *The Working Class and Welfare: Reflections on the Political Development of the Welfare State in Australia and New Zealand, 1890–1980* (Wellington: Allen & Unwin)

Castles, F.G. (1988) *Australian Public Policy and Economic Vulnerability* (Sydney: Allen & Unwin).

Castles, F.G. (ed.) (1993) *Families of Nations: Patterns of Public Policy in Western Democracies* (Aldershot: Dartmouth).

Castles, F.G. (1998) *Comparative Public Policy: Patterns of Post-War Transformation* (Cheltenham: Edward Elgar).

Castles, F. and Mair, P. (1984) 'Left-Right Political Scales: Some "Expert" Judgments', *European Journal of Political Research*, 12: 73–88.

Castles, F. and Mitchell, D. (1992) 'Identifying Welfare State Regimes: The Links between Politics, Instruments and Outcomes', *Governance*, 5(1): 1–26.

Cerny, P.G. (2007) 'Paradoxes of the Competition State: The Dynamics of Political Globalization', *Government and Opposition*, 32(2): 251–74.

Chakrabortty, A. (2010) 'Cameron's Hijacking of Nudge Theory is a Classic Example of How Big Ideas Get Corrupted', *The Guardian*, 7 December.

Chalmers, D. and Lodge, M. (2003) 'The Open Method of Co-Ordination and the European Welfare State', CARR Discussion Papers, DP 11, Centre for Analysis of Risk and Regulation, London School of Economics and Political Science.

Channac, F. (2006) 'Vers une politique publique internationale des migrations? Réseaux politiques et processus de transfert de modèles', *Revue Française de Sciences Politiques*, 56(3): 393–408.

Chassard, Y. and Quintin, O. (1992) 'Social Protection in the European Community: Towards a Convergence of Policies', in *Fifty Years After Beveridge, Volume 2* (York: University of York): 103–10.

Chernichovsky, D. (1995) 'Health System Reforms in Industrialized Democracies: An Emerging Paradigm', *Milbank Quarterly*, 73(3): 339–72.

Chesterman, S., Malone, D.M. and Franck, T.M. (2008) *The Law and Practice of the United Nations* (Oxford: Oxford University Press).

Chubb, J.E. and Moe, T.M. (1990) *Politics, Markets and America's Schools* (Washington, DC: Brookings Institution).

Chwieroth, J. (2007) 'Neoliberal Economists and Capital Account Liberalization in Emerging Markets', *International Organization*, 61(2): 443–63.

CIA (2012) *The World Factbook*, available at www.cia.gov/library/publications/the-world-factbook, accessed May 2012.

Claessens, S., Dell'Ariccia, G., Igan, D. and Laeven, L. (2010) 'Global Linkages and Global Policies: Cross-Country Experiences and Policy Implications from the Global Financial Crisis', *Economic Policy*: 269–93.

Clark, B. (1983) *The HE System: Academic Organization in Cross-National Perspective* (Berkeley, CA: University of California Press).

Clarke, J. with Piven, F.F. (2009) 'An American Welfare State?', in P. Alcock and G. Craig (eds), *International Social Policy: Welfare Regimes in the Developed World*, 2nd edn (Basingstoke: Palgrave Macmillan): 25–44.

Clarke, L. and Winch, C. (eds) (2007) *Vocational Training: International Approaches, Developments and Systems* (London: Routledge).

Clasen, J. (ed.) (1999) *Comparative Social Policy: Concepts, Theories and Methods* (Oxford: Blackwell).

Clayton, R. and Pontusson, J. (1998) 'Welfare-State Retrenchment Revisited: Entitlement Cuts,

Public Sector Restructuring, and Inegalitarian Trends in Advanced Capitalist Societies', *World Politics*, 51(1): 67–98.

Coase, R.H. (1937) 'The Nature of the Firm', *Economica*, 4(16): 386–405.

Coase, R.H. (1960) 'The Problem of Social Cost', *Journal of Law and Economics*, 3: 1–44.

Coates, D. (2000) *Models of Capitalism: Growth and Stagnation in the Modern Era* (Cambridge: Polity Press).

Cochrane, A., Clarke, J. and Gewirtz, S. (2001a) 'Introduction', in A. Cochrane, J. Clarke and S. Gewirtz (eds), *Comparing Welfare States*, 2nd edn (London: Sage/Open University Press): 2–27.

Cochrane, A., Clarke, J. and Gewirtz, S. (2001b) 'Looking for a European Welfare State', in A. Cochrane, J. Clarke and S. Gewirtz (eds), *Comparing Welfare States*, 2nd edn (London: Sage/Open University Press): 261–90.

Coen, D. and Roberts, A. (2012) 'Introduction to Special Issue: *A New Age of Uncertainty*', *Governance: An International Journal of Policy, Administration, and Institutions*, 25(1): 5–9.

Cohen, M. (1998) 'Science and the Environment: Assessing Cultural Capacity for Ecological Modernization', *Public Understanding of Science*, 7: 149–67.

Cohen, M., March, J.G. and Olsen, J.P. (1972) 'A Garbage Can Model of Organizational Choice', *Administrative Science Quarterly*, 17: 1–25.

Collier, D. and Mahoney, J. (1993) 'Conceptual Stretching Revisited: Alternative Views of Categories in Comparative Analysis', *American Political Science Review*, 64: 1033–53.

Collier, D., Mahoney, J., and Seawright, J. (2004) 'Claiming Too Much: Warnings about Selection Bias', in D. Collier and H.E. Brady, *Rethinking Social Inquiry: Diverse Tools, Shared Standards* (Lanham, MD: Rowman & Littlefield).

Considine, M. (2005) *Making Public Policy: Authority, Organization and Values* (Cambridge: Polity).

Corbett, A. (2003) 'Ideas, Institutions and Policy Entrepreneurs: Towards a New History of Higher Education in the European Community', *European Journal of Education*, 38(3): 315–30.

Cornia, G.A., Van der Hoeven, R. and Mkandawira, T. (eds) (1992) *Africa's Recovery in the 1990s: From Stagnation and Adjustment to Human Development* (London: Macmillan).

Cowen, R. (1996) 'Last Past the Post, Comparative Education, Modernity and Perhaps Post-Modernity', *Comparative Education*, 32(2):151–70.

Cox, J.R.W., Mann, L. and Samson, D. (1997) 'Benchmarking as a Mixed Metaphor: Disentangling Assumptions of Competition and Collaboration', *Journal of Management Studies*, 34(2): 285–314.

Cox, R. (2004) 'The Path-Dependency of an Idea: Why Scandinavian Welfare States Remain Distinct', *Social Policy and Administration*, 38(2): 204–19.

Crosby, A. (1986) *Ecological Imperialism: The Biological Expansion of Europe, 900–1900* (Cambridge: Cambridge University Press).

Crossley, M. (2007) 'Bridging Cultures and Traditions in the Reconceptualisation of Comparative and International Education', in M. Crossley, P. Broadfoot and M. Schweisfurth (eds), *Changing Educational Contexts, Issues and Identities: 40 Years of Comparative Education* (London: Routledge): 255–72.

Crouch, C. (1985) 'Conditions for Trade Union Wage Restraint', in L.N. Lindberg and C.S. Maier (eds), *The Politics of Inflation and Economic Stagnation* (Washington, DC: Brookings Institution).

Crutzen, P. (2002) 'Geology of Mankind', *Nature*, 415: 23.

Curran, G. and Hollander, R. (2010) 'A Tale of Two Pulp Mills: Realising Ecologically Sustainable Development in Australia', *Australian Journal of Public Administration*, 67(4): 483–97.

Currie, J. (1998) 'Introduction', in: J. Currie and J. Newson (eds), *Universities and Globalization: Critical Perspectives* (London: Sage): 1–10.

Cusack, T., Iversen, T. and Soskice, D. (2007) 'Economic Interests and the Origins of Electoral Institutions', *American Political Science Review*, 101: 373–91.

Cushman, R. (1941) *The Independent Regulatory Commissions* (New York: Oxford University Press).

Dahl, R. (1961) *Who Governs?* (New Haven, CT: Yale University Press).

Dahl, R. (1971) *Polyarchy: Participation and Opposition* (New Haven, CT: Yale University Press).

Dahl, R.A. and Lindblom, C.E. (1976) *Politics, Economics and Welfare: Planning and Politico-Economic Systems Resolved Into Basic Social Processes* (Chicago, IL: University of Chicago Press).

Dahrendorf, R. (1999) 'The Third Way and Liberty. An Authoritarian Streak in Europe's New Center', *Foreign Affairs*, 78(5): 13–17.

Dalby, S. (2009) *Security and Environmental Change* (Cambridge: Polity).

Daly, M. (1997) 'Welfare States under Pressure: Cash Benefits in European Welfare States over the Last Ten Years', *Journal of European Social Policy*, 7(2): 129–46.

Damme, D. V. and K. Karkkainen (2011) 'OECD Education Today Crisis Survey 2010: The Impact of the Economic Recession and Fiscal Crisis on Education in OECD Countries', *OECD Education Working Papers*, No. 56, OECD Publishing.

Daneke, G. (1984) 'Whither Environmental Regulation', *Journal of Public Policy*, 4(2): 139–51.

Darnall, N., Potoski, M. and Prakash, A. (2009) 'Sponsorship Matters: Assessing Business Participation in Government- and Industry-Sponsored Voluntary Environmental Programs', *Journal of Public Administration Research and Theory*, 20: 283–307.

Daugbjerg, C. (1998) 'Linking Policy Networks and Environmental Policies: Nitrate Policy Making in Denmark and Sweden 1970–1995', *Public Administration*, 76: 275–294.

Daugbjerg, C. and Pedersen, A.B. (2004) 'New Policy Ideas and Old Policy Networks: Implementing Green Taxation in Scandinavia', *Journal of Public Policy*, 24(2): 219–49.

Davey, J. and Grey, S. (2009) 'New Zealand: from Early Innovation to Humanizing the Market', in P. Alcock and G. Craig (eds), *International Social Policy: Welfare Regimes in the Developed World*, 2nd edn (Basingstoke: Palgrave Macmillan): 88–108.

Davidova, N. and Manning, N. (2009) 'Russia: State Socialism to Marketized Welfare', in Alcock, P. and Craig, G. (eds), *International Social Policy: Welfare Regimes in the Developed World*, 2nd edn (Basingstoke: Palgrave Macmillan): 190–209.

Davidson, D. (1980) *Essays on Actions and Events* (Oxford: Clarendon Press).

Davies, A. R. (2002) 'Power, Politics and Networks: Shaping Partnerships for Sustainable Communities', *Area*, 34(2): 190–203.

Daws, S. and Weiss, T.G. (eds) (2008) *The Oxford Handbook on the United Nations* (Oxford: Oxford University Press).

De Meur, G. and Berg-Schlosser, D. (1994) 'Comparing Political Systems: Establishing Similarities and Dissimilarities', *European Journal of Political Research*, 26: 193–219.

De Vogli, R. and Birbeck, G.L. (2005) 'Potential Impact of Adjustment Policies on Vulnerability of Women and Children to HIV/AIDS in Sub-Saharan Africa', *Journal of Health, Population and Nutrition*, 23(2): 105–20.

de Vroom, B. (2001) 'The Dutch Reaction to Contaminated Blood: An Example of Cooperative Governance', in M. Bovens, P. 't Hart and B.G. Peters (eds), *Success and Failure in Public Governance: A Comparative Analysis* (Cheltenham: Edward Elgar): 508–32.

Deacon, A. (1993) 'Developments in East European Social Policy', in C. Jones (ed.), *New Perspectives on the Welfare State in Europe* (London: Routledge).

Deacon, A. (2008) 'Employment', in P. Alcock, M. May and K. Rowlingson (eds), *The Student's Companion to Social Policy* (Oxford: Blackwell): 311–17

Deacon, A., Castle-Kanerova, M., Manning, N. *et al.* (1992) *The New Eastern Europe: Social Policy Past, Present and Future* (London: Sage).

Deacon, B. (2000) 'Learning from the USA? The Influence of American Ideas on New Labour Thinking on Welfare Reform', *Policy and Politics*, 28(1): 5–18.

Deacon, B., Hulse, M. and Stubbs, P. (1997) *Global Social Policy: International Organisations and the Future of Welfare* (London: Sage).

Deeg, R. (2005) 'Change from Within: German and Italian Finance in the 1990s', in W. Streeck and K. Thelen, *Beyond Continuity: Institutional Change in Advance Political Economies* (Oxford: Oxford University Press): 169–202.

Derrington, C. and Kendall, S. (2004) *Gypsy Traveller Students in Secondary Schools: Culture, Identity and Achievement* (Stoke-on-Trent: Trentham Books).

Desrosières, A. (1996) 'Statistical Traditions: An Obstacle to International Comparisons?', in L. Hantrais and S Mangen (eds), *Cross-National Research Methods in the Social Sciences* (London: Pinter): 17–27.

Devereux, M., Lockwood, B. and Redoano, M. (2003) 'Capital Account Liberalization and Corporate Taxes', IMF Working Paper No. 03/180, September.

Devine, F. (1996) 'The "New Structuralism": Class Politics and Class Analysis', in N. Kirk, *Social Class and Marxism: Defences and Challenges* (London: Scolar Press): 15–57.

DHSS (1980) *Inequalities in Health: Report of a Research Working Group* (London: DHSS).

Dierkes, M., Weiler, H.N. and Berthoin Antal, A. (eds) (1987) *Comparative Policy Research: Learning from Experience* (Aldershot: Gower/New York: St. Martin's Press).

DiMaggio, P.J. and Powell, W.W. (1983) 'The Iron Cage Revisited: Institutional Isomorphism and Collective Rationality in Organizational Fields', *American Sociological Review*, 48(2): 147–60.

Dister, A. and Moreau, M.-L. (2006) 'Dis-moi comment tu féminises, je te dirai pour qui tu votes. Les dénominations des candidates dans les élections européennes de 1989 et de 2004 en Belgique et en France', *Langage et société*, 115(1): 5–45.

Djelic, M.-L. and Quack, S. (eds) (2010) *Transnational Communities: Shaping Global Governance* (Cambridge: Cambridge University Press).

Djilas, M. (1966) *The New Class: An Analysis of the Communist System* (London: Unwin Books).

Dodds, A. (2004) 'The Politicisation of Trade in Health and Education Services: Black and White Divisions over a "Grey" Area', *Scottish Affairs*, 46: 56–75.

Dodds, A. (2009) 'Families "At Risk" and the Family Nurse Partnership: The Intrusion of Risk into Social Exclusion Policy', *Journal of Social Policy*, 38(3): 499–514.

Dodds, A. (2011) 'Logics, Thresholds, Strategic Power, and the Promotion of Liberalisation by Governments: A Case Study from British Higher Education, Public Policy and Administration', Online first version of article, Public Policy and Administration 0952076711407954, first published on 4 August, 2011 as doi:10.1177/0952076711407954.

Dodds, A., Obradovic-Wochnik, J. and Badran, A. (2011) 'Regulation in a Contested State: Energy Sector Regulation in Kosovo', Paper presented at Structure and Organization of Government Workshop on 'The Future of the Regulatory State: Adaptation, Transformation, or Demise?' (Oslo: BIS Business School).

Doern, G.B. and Wilson, V.S. (1974) *Issues in Canadian Public Policy* (Toronto: Macmillan).

Dogan, M. (2002) 'Strategies in Comparative Sociology', *Comparative Sociology*, 1(1): 63–92.

Dogan, M. and Pelassy, D. (1990) *How to Compare Nations: Strategies in Comparative Politics* (New York: Chatham).

Dolowitz, D.P. and Marsh, D. (2000) 'Learning from Abroad: The Role of Policy Transfer in Contemporary Policy-Making', *Governance*, 13(1): 5–24.

Dominelli, L. (1991) *Women across Continents: Feminist Comparative Social Policy* (Hemel Hempstead: Harvester Wheatsheaf).

Dore, R. (1976) *The Diploma Disease: Education, Qualification and Development* (London: George Allen & Unwin).

Doyal, L. (1995) *What Makes Women Sick: Gender and the Political Economy of Health* (London: Palgrave Macmillan).

Drezner, D.W. (2001) 'Globalization and Policy Convergence', *International Studies Review*, 3(1): 53–78.

Dryzek, J., Downes, D., Hunold, C. and Schlosberg, D. (2003) *Green States and Social Movements: Environmentalism in the United States, United Kingdom, Germany, and Norway* (Oxford: Oxford University Press).

Dubgaard, A. (2003) 'The Danish Pesticide Programme: Success or Failure depending on Indicator Choice', in D.E. Ervin, J.R. Kahn and M.L. Livingston (eds), *Does Environmental Policy Work? The Theory and Practice of Outcomes Assessment* (Cheltenham: Edward Elgar): 169–89.

Duclaud-Williams, R.H. (1978) *The Politics of Housing in Britain and France* (London: Heinemann).

Dunleavy, P. (1980) 'The Political Implications of Sectoral Cleavages and the Growth of State Employment, Parts I and II', *Political Studies*, 2: 364–83 and 527–49.

Dunleavy, P. (1991) *Democracy, Bureaucracy and Public Choice* (London: Harvester Wheatsheaf).

Dür, A. and Elsig, M. (2011) 'Principals, Agents, and the European Union's Foreign Economic Policies', *Journal of European Public Policy*, 18(3): 323–38.

Dyson, K and Wilks, S (eds) (1983) *Industrial Crisis: A Comparative Study of the State and Industry* (Oxford: Basil Blackwell).

Ebbinghaus, B. (1998) 'Europe through the Looking-Glass: Comparative and Multi-Level Perspectives', *Acta Sociologica*, 41(4): 301–13.

Edelman, M. (1964) *The Symbolic Uses of Politics* (Urbana, IL: Illinois University Press).

Edelman, M. (1971) *Politics as Symbolic Action: Mass Arousal and Quiescence* (New York: Academic Press).

Eisner, M.A. and Meier, K.J. (1990) 'Presidential Control versus Bureaucratic Power: Explaining the Reagan Revolution in Antitrust', *American Journal of Political Science*, 34(1): 269–87.

Ekins, P. (1997) 'The Kuznets Curve for the Environment and Economic Growth: Examining the Evidence', *Environment and Planning*, A 29(5): 805–30.

Elcock, H. (2008) 'Elected Mayors: Lesson Drawing from Four Countries', *Public Administration*, 86(3): 795–811.

Elder, J.W. (1976) 'Comparative Cross-National Methodology', *Annual Review of Sociology*, 2: 209–30.

Elling, R. H. (1994) 'Theory and Method for the Cross-National Study of Health Systems', *International Journal of Health Services*, 24(2): 285–309.

Elmore, R.F. (1987) 'Instruments and Strategy in Public Policy', *Policy Studies Review*, 7(1): 174–86.

Elsner, D. (2000) 'Reflections on Megatrends in Education from a Polish Perspective', in T.M. Mehrbratu, M. Crossley and D. Johnson (eds), *Globalisation, Educational Transformation and Societies in Transition* (Oxford: Symposium Books).

Elson, D. (1999) 'Labor Markets as Gendered Institutions: Equality, Efficiency and Empowerment Issues', *World Development*, 27(3): 611–27.

Ely, B. (2009) 'Bad Rules Produce Bad Outcomes: Underlying Public-Policy Causes of the US Financial Crisis', *Cato Journal*, 29(1): 93–114.

Engelen, E., Irtuk, I., Froud, J., Johal, S., Leaver, A. and Williams, K. (2011) *After the Great Complacence: Financial Crisis and the Politics of Reform* (Oxford: Oxford University Press).

Epstein, D. and Johnson, R. (1998) *Schooling Sexualities* (Philadelphia, PA: Open University Press).

Ervin, D.E., Kahn, J.R. and Livingston, M.L. (2003) 'Introduction', in D.E. Ervin, J.R. Kahn and M.L. Livingston (eds), *Does Environmental Policy Work? The Theory and Practice of Outcomes Assessment* (Cheltenham: Edward Elgar): 3–22.

Esping-Andersen G. (1985) *Politics against Markets: The Social Democratic Road to Power* (Princeton, NJ: Princeton University Press).

Esping-Andersen, G. (1990) *The Three Worlds of Welfare Capitalism* (Cambridge: Polity Press).

Esping-Andersen, G. (1999a) *Recasting Welfare Regimes for a Postindustrial Era* (Oxford: Oxford University Press).

Esping-Andersen, G. (1999b) *Social Foundations of Postindustrial Economies* (Oxford: Oxford University Press).

Etheredge, L. (1981) 'Government Learning: An Overview', in S.L.Long (ed.), *The Handbook of Political Behaviour, Volume 2* (New York: Pergamon).

Etheredge, L.M. and Short, J. (1983) 'Thinking about Government Learning', *Journal of Management Studies*, 20: 41–58.

Etzioni, A. (1961) *A Comparative Analysis of Complex Organizations: On Power, Involvement, And Their Correlates* (New York: Free Press).

European Commission (2000) 'White Paper on Environmental Liability', COM (2000) 66 Final.

European Commission (2011) 'European Economic Forecast', Autumn (Brussels: European Commission).

Evans, M. and Williams, L. (2009 [1979]) *A Generation of Change, A Lifetime of Difference? Social Policy in Britain since 1979* (Bristol: Policy Press).

Falleti, T.G. and Lynch, J.F. (2009) 'Context and Causal Mechanisms in Political Analysis', *Comparative Political Studies*, 42(9): 1143–66.

Faniel, J. (2004) 'Chômeurs en Belgique et en France: des mobilisations différentes', *Revue internationale de politique comparé*, 11(4): 493–506.

Farazmand, A. (ed.) (2001) *Handbook of Comparative and Development Public Administration* (New York: Marcel Dekker Inc.).

Fargion, V. (2009) 'Italy: Still a Pension State?', in P. Alcock and G. Craig (eds), *International Social Policy: Welfare Regimes in the Developed World*, 2nd edn (Basingstoke: Palgrave Macmillan): 171–89.

Faubert, V. (2009) 'School Evaluation: Current Practices in OECD Countries and a Literature Review', OECD Education Working Paper, No. 42, OECD Publishing.

Featherstone, K. and Radaelli, C.M. (eds) (2003) *The Politics of Europeanization* (Oxford: Oxford University Press).

Feldman, E. (1978) 'Review: Comparative Public Policy: Field or Method?', *Comparative Politics*, 10(2): 287–305.

Ferrera (1996) 'The "Southern" Model of Welfare in Social Europe', *Journal of European Social Policy*, 6(1): 17–37.

Filgueira, C.H. and Filgueira, F. (2002) 'Models of Welfare and Models of Capitalism: The Limits of Transferability', in E. Huber (ed.), *Models of Capitalism: Lessons for Latin America* (Pennsylvania, PA: Pennsylvania State University Press): 127–58.

Finegold, D., McFarland, L. and Richardson, W. (eds) (1993) *Something Borrowed, Something Blue? A Study of the Thatcher Government's Appropriation of American Education and Training Policy* (Oxford: Symposium Books).

Finer, S. (1958) 'Interest Groups and the Political Process in Great Britain', in H. Ehrman, *Interest Groups in Four Continents* (Pittsburgh, PA: University of Pittsburgh Press): 117–44.

Finer, S.E. (1970) *Comparative Government: An Introduction to the Study of Politics* (Harmondsworth: Penguin).

Fink. S. (2011) 'A Contagious Concept: Explaining the Spread of Privatization in the Telecommunications Sector', *Governance: An International Journal of Policy, Administration, and Institutions*, 24(1): 111–39.

Fischer, F. (2003) *Reframing Public Policy. Discursive Politics and Deliberative Practices* (Oxford and New York: Oxford University Press).

Fischer, F. and Forester, J. (eds) (1993) *The Argumentative Turn in Policy Analysis* (London: UCL Press).

Fleckenstein, T., Saunders, A. and Seeleib-Kaiser, M. (2011) 'The Dual Transformation of Social Protection and Human Capital: Comparing Britain and Germany', *Comparative Political Studies*, 44(12): 1622–50.

Flood, C.M. (2000) *International Health Care Reform: A Legal, Economic and Political Analysis* (London: Routledge).

Flora P. and Alber, J. (1981) 'Modernisation, Democratization, and the Development of Welfare States in Western Europe', in P. Flora and A.J. Heidenheimer (eds), *The Development of Welfare States in Europe and America* (New Brunswick, NJ and London: Transaction Books): 37–80.

Flora, P. and Heidenheimer, A. (eds) (1981) 'The Development of Welfare States in Europe and America' (London: Transaction Books).

Fontana, M.-C. (2011) 'Europeanization and Domestic Policy Concertation: How Actors Use Europe to Modify Domestic Patterns of Policy-Making', *Journal of European Public Policy*, 18(5): 654–71.

Forrest, J.B. (1994) 'Weak States in Post-Colonial Africa and Mediaeval Europe', in M. Dogan and A. Kazancigil (eds), *Comparing Nations* (Oxford, Blackwell): 260–96.

Foster, J.B. (1992) 'The Absolute General Law of Environmental Degradation under Capitalism', *Capitalism Nature Socialism*, 2(3): 77–82.

Foster, S. (1999) 'The Struggle for American Identity: Treatment of Ethnic Groups in United States History Textbooks', *History of Education*, 28(3): 251–78.

Foucault, M. (1979) *The History of Sexuality* (London: Allen Lane).

Fourcade, M. (2009) *Economists and Societies: Discipline and Profession in the United States, Britain, and France, 1890s to 1990s* (Princeton, NJ: Princeton University Press).

Frank, J.W. and Mustard, J.F. (1994) 'The Determinants of Health from a Historical Perspective', *Daedalus: Health and Wealth*, 123(4): 1–19.

Franzese, R. (2002) *Macroeconomic Policies of Developed Democracies* (Cambridge: Cambridge University Press).

Freeden, M. (1998) *Ideologies: A Conceptual Approach* (Oxford: Oxford University Press).

Freeman, G.P. (1985) 'National Styles and Policy Sectors: Explaining Structured Variation', *Journal of Public Policy*, 5(4): 467–96.

Freeman, R. and Frisina, L. (2010) 'Health Care Systems and the Problem of Classification', *Journal of Comparative Policy Analysis: Research and Practice*, 12(1): 163–78.

Freitag, M. and Schlicht, R. (2009) 'Educational Federalism in Germany: Foundations of Social Inequality in Education', *Governance: An International Journal of Policy, Administration, and Institutions*, 22(1): 47–72.

Frericks, P., Knijn, T. and Maier, R. (2009) 'Pension Reforms, Working Patterns and Gender Pension Gaps in Europe', *Gender, Work and Organization*, 16(6): 710–30.

Friedman, M. and Friedman, R. (1984) *The Tyranny of the Status Quo* (San Diego, CA: Harcourt Brace Jovanovich).

Garraud, P. (2000) *Le chômage et l'action publique. Le 'bricolage institutionnalisé'* (Paris: l'Harmattan).

Garrett, G. (1995) 'The Politics of Legal Integration in the European Union', *International Organization*, 49(1): 171–81.

Garrett, G. (1998a) *Partisan Politics in the Global Economy* (New York: Cambridge University Press).

Garrett, G. (1998b) 'Shrinking States? Globalization and National Autonomy in the OECD', *Oxford Development Studies*, 26(1): 71–98.

Garrett, G. and Lange, P. (1989) 'Government Partisanship and Economic Performance', *Journal of Politics*, 51: 676–93.

Garrett, G. and P. Lange (1991) 'Political Responses to Interdependence: What's 'Left' for the Left?', *International Organization*, 45: 539–64.

Garrett, G. and Weingast, B. (1993) 'Ideas, Interests and Institutions: Constructing the European Union's Internal Market', in J. Goldstein and R. Keohane (eds), *Ideas and Foreign Policy: Beliefs, Institutions and Political Change* (Ithaca: Cornell University Press).

Gaskell, G., Bauer, M., Durant, J., Allum, N. (1999) 'Worlds Apart? The Reception of Genetically Modified Foods in Europe and the U.S.', *Science*, 285(5426): 384–87, available at www.sciencemag.org/cgi/reprint/285/5426/384.pdf

Gaventa, J. (1980) *Power and Powerlessness: Rebellion in an Appalachian Valley* (Oxford: Clarendon Press).

Geldenhuys, D. (2009) *Contested States in World Politics* (Basingstoke: Palgrave Macmillan).

Gellert, C. (1999) 'Introduction: The Changing Conditions of Teaching and Learning in European Higher Education', in C. Gellert (ed.), *Innovation and Adaptation in Higher Education: The*

Changing Conditions of Advanced Teaching and Learning in Europe (London: Jessica Kingsley): 9–30.

Genschel, P. (1997) 'The Dynamics of Inertia: Institutional Persistence and Change in Telecommunications and Health Care', *Governance*, 10(1): 43–66.

George, A.L. and Bennett, A. (2005) *Case Studies and Theory Development in the Social Sciences* (Cambridge, MA and London: MIT Press).

George, A.L. and McKeown, T.J. (1985) 'Case Studies and Theories of Organizational Decision Making', *Advances in Information Processing in Organizations*, 2: 21–58.

Gerring, J. (2010) 'Causal Mechanisms: Yes, But …', *Comparative Political Studies*, 43(11): 1499–526.

Gerschenkron, A. (1962) *Economic Backwardness in Historical Perspective: A Book of Essays* (Cambridge, MA: Belknap Press of Harvard University Press).

Gerth, H.H. and Mills, C.W. (1974) *From Max Weber: Essays in Sociology* (New York: Oxford University Press).

Gewirtz, S., Ball, S.J. and Bowe, R. (1995) *Markets, Choice and Equity in Education* (Buckingham: Open University Press).

Geyer, R. (2011) 'The Politics of EU Health Policy and the Case of Direct-to-Consumer Advertising for Prescription Drugs', *British Journal of Politics & International Relations*, 13: 586–602.

Giaimo, S. (2002) *Markets and Medicine: The Politics of Health Care Reform in Britain, Germany, and the United States* (Ann Arbor, MI: University of Michigan Press).

Giddens, A. (1994) *Beyond Left and Right: The Future of Radical Politics* (Cambridge: Polity).

Gieve, J. and Provost, C. (2012) 'Ideas and Coordination in Policymaking: The Financial Crisis of 2007–2009', *Governance: An International Journal of Policy, Administration, and Institutions*, 25(1): 61–77.

Ginsburg, N. (1979) *Class, Capital and Social Policy* (London: Macmillan).

Ginsburg, N. (1992) *Divisions of Welfare: A Critical Introduction to Comparative Social Policy* (London: Sage).

Ginsburg, N. (2001) 'Sweden: The Social Democratic Case', in A. Cochrane, J. Clarke and S. Gewirtz (eds), *Comparing Welfare States*, 2nd edn (London: Sage/Open University Press): 195–222

Gittings, J. (2002) 'Growing Sex Imbalance Shocks China', *The Guardian*, 13 May.

Givel, M. (2007) 'A Comparison of the Impact of U.S. and Canadian Cigarette Pack Warning Label Requirements on Tobacco Industry Profitability and the Public Health', *Health Policy*, 83(2–3): 343–52.

Glatzer, M. and Rueschemeyer, D. (eds) (2005) *Globalization and the Future of the Welfare State* (Pittsburgh, PA: University of Pittsburgh Press).

Glennester, H. and Matsaganis, M. (1994) 'The English and Swedish Health Care Reforms', *International Journal of Health Services*, 24(2): 231–51.

Glenny, M. (2008) *McMafia: A Journey Through the Global Criminal Underworld* (New York: Alfred Knopf).

Glinos, I.A., Baeten, R. and Maarse, H. (2010) 'Purchasing Health Services Abroad: Practices of Cross-Border Contracting and Patient Mobility in Six European Countries', *Health Policy*, 95(2–3): 103–112.

Global Finance (2010) 'Public Debt by Country' (Source: OECD Data), available at www.gfmag.com/tools/global-database/economic-data/10394-public-debt-by-country.html, accessed December 2011.

Glyn, A. (2004) 'The Assessment: How Far Has Globalization Gone?', *Oxford Review of Economic Policy*, 20: 1.

Glynos, J. (2001) 'The Grip of Ideology', *Journal of Political Ideologies*, 6(2): 191–214.

Glynos, J. and Howarth, D. (2007) *Logics of Critical Explanation in Social and Political Theory* (London: Routledge).

Godard, O. (2002) 'Domestic Tradable Permits: Summary of Lessons Learned', in OECD, *Implementing Domestic Tradeable Permits: Recent Developments and Future Challenges* (Paris: OECD): 10–25.

Goldstein, J. and Keohane, R. (eds) (1993) *Ideas and Foreign Policy: Beliefs, Institutions and Political Change* (Ithaca, NY: Cornell University Press).

Goldthorpe, J.H. (1997) 'Current Issues in Comparative Macrosociology: A Debate on Methodological Issues', *Comparative Social Research*, 16: 1–26.

Golub, J. (1998) 'New Instruments for Environmental Policy in the EU. Introduction and Overview', in J. Golub ed., *New Instruments for Environmental Policy in the EU* (London: Routledge, 1–29.

Goodhardt, D. (2004) 'Too Diverse?', *Prospect Magazine*, 95(2004): 49–56.

Goodin, R.E. (2003) 'Choose Your Capitalism', *Comparative European Politics*, 1: 203–13.

Goodin, R.E., Headey, B., Muffels, R., Dirven, H.-J. (1999) *The Real Worlds of Welfare Capitalism* (Cambridge: Cambridge University Press).

Goodin, R.E., Rein, M. and Moran, M. (2008) 'The Public and its Policies', *Oxford Handbook of Public Policy* (Oxford: Oxford University Press): 3–35.

Goodman, R., White, G. and Kwon, H. (eds) (1998) *The East Asian Welfare Model: Welfare Orientalism and the State* (London: Routledge).

Goodwin, S. (1997) *Comparative Mental Health Policy: From Institutional to Community Care* (London: Sage).

Gormley, W.T. (1989) *Taming the Bureaucracy: Muscles, Prayers, and Other Strategies* (Princeton, NJ: Princeton University Press).

Gough, I. (1979) *The Political Economy of the Welfare State* (London: Macmillan).

Gough, I. (2001) 'Globalization and Regional Welfare Regimes: The East Asian Case', *Global Social Policy*, 1: 2.

Gough, I. (2008) 'European Welfare States: Explanations and Lessons for Developing Countries', in A.A. Dani and A. de Haan (eds), *Inclusive States: Social Policy and Structural Inequalities* (Washington, DC: World Bank).

Gough, I. and Wood, G. with Barrientos, A., Bevan, P., Davis, P., and Room, G. (2004) *Insecurity and Welfare Regimes in Asia, Africa and Latin America: Social Policy in Development Contexts* (Cambridge: Cambridge University Press).

Gourevitch, P. (1978) 'The Second Image Reversed: The International Sources of Domestic Politics', *International Organization*, 32(4): 881–912.

Gramsci, A. (1971) *Selections from the Prison Notebooks* (London: Lawrence & Wishart).

Grant, W. (1985) 'Introduction', in W. Grant (ed.), *The Political Economy of Corporatism* (London: Macmillan).

Grant, W. (1989) *Pressure Groups, Politics and Democracy in Britain* (Hemel Hempstead: Philip Allen).

Grant, W. (2002) *Economic Policy in Britain* (Basingstoke: Palgrave Macmillan).

Gray, J. (1998) *False Dawn: The Delusions of Global Capitalism* (New York: New Press).

Graziano, P.R. (2011) 'Europeanization and Domestic Employment Policy Change: Conceptual and Methodological Background', *Governance*, 24(3), 583–605.

Green, A. (1990) *Education and State Formation: The Rise of Education Systems in England, France and the USA* (London: Macmillan).

Green, A. (1997) *Education, Globalisation and the Nation State* (London: Macmillan).

Green, D. and Shapiro, I. (1994) *Pathologies of Rational Choice Theories: A Critique of Applications in Political Science* (New Haven, CT: Yale University Press).

Greer, S. (2004) *Territorial Politics and Health Policy* (Manchester: Manchester University Press).

Grunwald, M. (2009) 'How Obama Is Using the Science of Change', *Time Magazine*, 2 April.

Gunningham, N. and Grabovsky, P. (1998) *Smart Regulation: Designing Environmental Policy* (Oxford: Clarendon Press).

Gunningham, N. and Rees, J. (1997) 'Industry Self-Regulation: An Institutional Perspective', *Law and Policy*, 10: 363.

Gwiazda, A. (2011) 'The Europeanization of Flexicurity: The Lisbon Strategy's Impact on Employment Policies in Italy and Poland', *Journal of European Public Policy*, 18(4): 546–65.

Haas, E.B. (1958) *The Uniting of Europe* (Stanford, CA: Stanford University Press).

Haas, E.B. (1961) 'International Integration: The European and the Universal Process', *International Organization*, 15(3): 366–92.

Haas, P.M. (1992) 'Introduction: Epistemic Communities and International Policy Coordination', *International Organization*, 46: 1–36.

Hacker, J.S. (2002) *The Divided Welfare State: The Battle over Public and Private Social Benefits in the United States* (New York: Cambridge University Press).

Hacker, J.S. (2004) 'Dismantling the Health Care State? Political Institutions, Public Policies and the Comparative Politics of Health Reform', *British Journal of Political Science*, 34(4): 693–724.

Hacker, J.S. (2005) 'Policy Drift: The Hidden Politics of US Welfare State Retrenchment', in W. Streeck and K. Thelen, *Beyond Continuity: Institutional Change in Advanced Political Economies* (Oxford: Oxford University Press).

Hajer, M. and Wagenaar, H. (2003) 'Introduction', in M. Hajer and H. Wagenaar (eds), *Deliberative Policy Analysis. Understanding Governance in the Network Society* (Cambridge: Cambridge University Press).

Hakim, C. (2002) *Research Design: Successful Designs for Social and Economic Research*, 2nd edn (London: Routledge).

Hall, P. (1989) 'Conclusion: The Political Power of Economic Ideas', in P.A. Hall (ed.), *The Political Power of Economic Ideas: Keynesianism across Nations* (Princeton, NJ: Princeton University Press): 361–92.

Hall, P.A. (1986) *Governing the Economy: The Politics of State Intervention in Britain and France* (New York: Oxford University Press).

Hall, P. and Soskice, D. (2003) 'Varieties of Capitalism and Institutional Change: A Response to Three Critics', *Comparative European Politics*, 1(1), 241–50.

Hall, P. and Taylor, R.C.R. (1996) 'Political Science and the Three New Institutionalisms', *Political Studies*, 44(5): 936–57.

Hall, P.A. (1993) 'Policy Paradigms, Social Learning, and the State: The Case of Economic Policymaking in Britain', *Comparative Politics*, 25(3): 275–96.

Hall, P.A. and Gingerich, D.W. (2004) 'Varieties of Capitalism and Institutional Complementarities in the Macroeconomy: An Empirical Analysis', MPlfG Discussion Paper 4/5, Max Planck Institute: Cologne.

Hall, P.A. and Soskice, D. (2001) *Varieties of Capitalism: The Institutional Foundations of Comparative Advantage* (Oxford: Oxford University Press).

Halpin, D. (2011) 'Explaining Policy Bandwagons: Organized Interest Mobilization and Cascades of Attention', *Governance: An International Journal of Policy, Administration, and Institutions*, 24(2): 205–30.

Halsey, A.H. (1992) *Decline of Donnish Dominion: The British Academic Professions in the Twentieth Century* (Oxford: Clarendon Press).

Hamblin, R. (2008) 'Regulation, Measurements and Incentives. The Experience in the US and UK: Does Context Matter?', *Journal of the Royal Society for the Promotion of Health*, 128: 291.

Hancké, B. (2002) *Large Firms and Institutional Change: Industrial Renewal and Economic Restructuring in France* (Oxford: Oxford University Press).

Hancock, A.M. (2004) *The Politics of Disgust: The Public Identity of the Welfare Queen* (New York: New York University Press).

Hanley, N. and Whitby, M. (2003) 'Alternative Criteria for Judging the Success of Agro-Environmental Policy in the UK', in D.E. Ervin, J.R. Kahn and M.L. Livingston (eds), *Does Environmental Policy Work? The Theory and Practice of Outcomes Assessment* (Cheltenham: Edward Elgar): 145–68.

Hans, N.A. (1949) *Comparative Education: A Study of Educational Factors and Traditions* (London: Routledge & Kegan Paul).

Hantrais, L. (1995) 'Comparative Research Methods', *Social Research Update*, 13, accessed at http://sru.soc.surrey.ac.uk/SRU13.html, June 2011.

Hantrais, L. and Mangen, S. (1996a) 'Preface', in L. Hantrais and S. Mangen (eds), *Cross-National Research Methods in the Social Sciences* (London and New York: Pinter).

Hantrais, L. and Mangen, S. (1996b) 'Method and Management of Cross-National Social Research', in L. Hatrais and S. Mangen (eds), *Cross-National Research Methods in the Social Sciences* (London and New York: Pinter).

Hardin, F. (1968) 'The Tragedy of the Commons', *Science*, 162: 1243–8.

Harper, S. (2009) 'How Canada Survived the Recession', Speech to New York Business Leaders, 21 September.

Harrison, K. (ed.) (2006) *Racing to The Bottom? Provincial Interdependence in the Canadian Federation* (Vancouver: University of British California Press).

Harrison, M. (2004) *Implementing Change in Health Systems: Market Reforms in Health Systems in the United Kingdom, Sweden and the Netherlands* (London: Sage).

Hartlapp, M. and Rauh, C. (2011) 'Is There a Re-Regulatory Capacity in the European Commission? Market Efficiency and Wider Social Goals in the Regulation of Financial Services in Europe', Paper presented at the 2011 SOG Workshop 'The Future of the Regulatory State: Adaptation, Transformation, or Demise?', Oslo.

Harvey, D. (1989a) 'Transformations in Urban Governance in Late Capitalism', *Geografiska Annaler*, Series B, Human Geography, 71(1): 3–17.

Harvey, D. (1989b) *The Conditions of Post-Modernity: An Enquiry into the Origins of Cultural Change* (Oxford: Blackwell).

Harvey, D. (2006) 'Neo-liberalism as Creative Destruction', *Geographical Annals*, 88B, 2.

Hassenteufel, P. (1997) *Les Médecins face à l'Etat. Une comparaison Europeenne* (Paris: Presses de Sciences Po).

Hassenteufel, P. (2008) *Sociologie politique: l'action publique* (Paris: Armand Colin).

Hausmann, R., Tyson, L.D. and Zahidi, S. (2010) *Global Gender Gap Report* (Geneva: World Economic Forum).

Haverland, M. (2005) 'Does the EU Cause Domestic Developments? The Problem of Case Selection in Europeanization Research', *European Integration online Papers* (EIoP), 9: 2.

Hay, C. (2011) 'Interpreting Interpretivism Interpreting Interpretations: The New Hermeneutics of Public Administration', *Public Administration*, 89(1): 167–82.

Hay, C. and Rosamond, B. (2002) 'Globalization, European Integration and the Discursive Construction of Economic Imperatives', *Journal of European Public Policy*, 9(2): 147–67.

Hay, C. and Smith, N.J. (2010) 'How Policy-Makers (Really) Understand Globalization: The Internal Architecture of Anglophone Globalisation Discourse', *Public Administration*, 88(4): 903–927.

Hayden, M., Thompson, J. and Walker, G. (eds) (2002) *International Education in Practice: Dimensions for National and International Schools* (London: Kogan Page).

Hayek, F. (1988) *The Fatal Conceit: The Errors of Socialism*, W.W. Bartley III (ed.) (Chicago, IL: University of Chicago Press).

Heclo, H. (1974) *Modern Social Politics in Britain and Sweden: From Relief to Income Maintenance* (New Haven, CT: Yale University Press).

Heidenheimer, A.J. (1973) 'The Politics of Public Education, Health and Welfare in the USA and Western Europe: How Growth and Reform Potentials Have Differed', *British Journal of Political Science*, 3(3): 315–40.

Heidenheimer, A.J. (1981) 'Education and Social Security Entitlements in Europe and America', in P. Flora and A.J. Heidenheimer (eds) *The Development of Welfare States in Europe and America* (New Brunswick, NJ: Transaction Books).

Heidenheimer, A.J., Heclo, H. and Adams, C. (1983) *Comparative Public Policy* (New York: St Martin's Press).

Heidenheimer A.J., Heclo, H., Adams, T.C. (1990) *Comparative Public Policy: The Politics of Social Choice in America, Europe and Japan*, 3rd edn (New York: St Martin's Press).

Heinz, J.P., Laumann, E.O., Nelson, R.L., and Salisbury, R.H. (1993) *The Hollow Core: Private Interests in National Policy Making* (Cambridge, MA: Harvard University Press).

Helgøy, I. and Homme, A. (2006) 'Policy Tools and Institutional Change: Comparing Education Policies in Norway, Sweden and England', *Journal of Public Policy*, 26(2): 141–65.

Helleiner, E. (2011) 'International Financial Reform after the Crisis: The Costs of Failure', *Socioeconomic Review*, 9(3): 567–96.

Helleiner, E. and S. Pagliari (2011) 'The End of an Era in International Financial Regulation? A Post-Crisis Research Agenda', *International Organization*, 65(3): 169–200.

Helm, D. and Tindall, T. (2009) 'The Evolution of Infrastructure and Utility Ownership and its Implications', *Oxford Review of Economic Policy*, 25: 3, 411–434.

Helmke, G and Levitsky, S. (2004) 'Informal Institutions and Comparative Politics: A Research Agenda', *Perspectives on Politics*, 2(4): 725–40.

Hennis, M. (2001) 'Europeanization and Globalization: The Missing Link', *Journal of Common Market Studies*, 39(5): 829–50.

Hertin, J. and Berkhout, F. (2003) 'Analysing Institutional Strategies for Environmental Policy Integration', *Journal of Environmental Policy and Planning*, 5(1): 39–56.

Heyes, A.G. (1998) 'Making Things Stick: Enforcement and Compliance', *Oxford Review of Economic Policy*, 14(4): 50–63.

Higgins W. and Apple, N. (1981) *Class Mobilisation and Economic Policy: Struggles over Full Employment in Britain and Sweden* (Stockholm: Arbetslivcentrum).

Hill, M. (2006) *Social Policy in the Modern World: A Comparative Text* (Oxford: Blackwell).

Hirschman, A.O. (1970) *Exit, Voice and Loyalty: Responses to Decline in Firms, Organizations, and States* (London: Harvard University Press).

Hirst, P. and Thompson, G. (1996) 'Can the Welfare State Survive Globalization?', in P. Hirst and G. Thompson, *Globalization in Question* (Cambridge: Polity).

Hirst, P. and Thompson, G. (1999) *Globalization in Question: The International Economy and the Possibilities of Governance* (Cambridge: Polity).

Hiscox, M.J. (2001) 'Class versus Industry Cleavages: Inter-Industry Factor Mobility and the Politics of Trade', *International Organization*, 55(1): 1–46.

Hiscox, M.J. (2003) *International Trade and Political Conflict: Commerce, Coalitions, and Mobility* (Princeton, NJ: Princeton University Press).

HMRC/National Statistics (2011) 'Child and Working Tax Credits Statistics', UK, December.

Hoberg, G. (1991) 'Sleeping with an Elephant: The American Influence on Canadian Environmental Regulation', *Journal of Public Policy*, 11(1): 107–32.

Hodge, G.A. and Bowman, D.M. (2010) 'Engaging in Small Talk: Nanotechnology Policy and Dialogue Processes in the UK and Australia', *Australian Journal of Public Administration*, 66(2): 223–37.

Hoekman, B.M. (2002) 'The WTO: Functions and Basic Principles', in B.M. Hoekman, A. Mattoo and P. English, *Development, Trade, and the WTO: A Handbook, Part 1*, World Bank Publications: 41–9.

Hoffman, D.L. (2000) 'Mothers in the Motherland: Stalinist Pronatalism in its Pan-European Context', *Journal of Social History*, 34(1): 35–54.

Holliday, I. (2005) 'East Asian Social Policy in the Wake of the Financial Crisis: Farewell to Productivism?', *Policy and Politics*, 33(1): 145–62.

Hollingsworth, J.R. and Boyer, R. (1997) *Contemporary Capitalism: The Embeddedness of Institutions* (Cambridge: Cambridge University Press).

Holmes, B. (1965) *Problems in Education: A Comparative Approach* (London: Routledge).

Holzinger, K. and Knill, C. (2004) 'Competition and Cooperation in Environmental Policy: Individual and Interaction Effects', *Journal of Public Policy*, 24(1): 25–47.

Holzinger, K., Knill, C. and Arts, B. (eds) (2008) *Environmental Governance in Europe. The Impact of International Institutions and Trade* (Cambridge: Cambridge University Press).

Holzinger, K., Knill, C. and Shafer, A. (2006) 'Rhetoric or Reality? "New Governance" in EU Environmental Policy', *European Law Journal*, 12(3): 403–20.

Holzinger, K., Knill, C. and Sommerer, T. (2011) 'Is There Convergence of National Environmental Policies? An Analysis of Policy Outputs in 24 OECD Countries', *Environmental Politics*, 20(1): 20–41.

Holzner, B. and Marx, J.H. (1979) *Knowledge Application: The Knowledge System in Society* (Boston, MA: Allyn & Bacon).

Hood, C. (1986) *The Tools of Government* (Chatham: Chatham House).

Hood, C. (1998) *The Art of the State* (Oxford and New York: Oxford University Press).

Hood, C. (2007) 'Intellectual Obsolescence and Intellectual Makeovers: Reflections on the Tools of Government after Two Decades', *Governance*, 20(1): 127–44.

Hopkins, N. (2002) 'Five-Year Jail Terms Mooted on Gun Crime', *The Guardian*, 20 December.

Horowitz, D.L. (1989) 'Is There a Third-World Policy Process?', *Policy Sciences*, 22(3-4): 197–212.

Howard, P. (1993) 'The Hidden Side of the American Welfare State', *Political Science Quarterly*, 108(3): 403–36.

Howarth, D. (2010) 'Power, Discourse, and Policy: Articulating a Hegemony Approach to Critical Policy Studies', *Critical Policy Studies*, 3(3–4): 309–35.

Howell, C. (2003) 'Varieties of Capitalism: And Then There Was One?', *Comparative Politics*, October: 103–24.

Howlett, M. (2000) 'Beyond Legalism? Policy Ideas, Implementation Styles and Emulation-Based Convergence in Canadian and U.S. Environmental Policy', *Journal of Public Policy*, 20(3): 305–29.

Howlett, M. and Ramesh, R. (2003) *Studying Public Policy: Policy Cycles and Policy Subsystems*, 2nd edn (Oxford: Oxford University Press).

Htun, M. and Weldon, S.L. (2010) 'When Do Governments Promote Women's Rights? A Framework for the Comparative Analysis of Sex Equality Policy', *Perspectives on Politics*, 8(1): 207–16.

Huber, E. (2001) *Development and Crisis of the Welfare State: Parties and Politics in Global Markets* (Chicago and London: University of Chicago Press).

Huber, E. and Stephens, J.D. (2001) *Development and Crisis of the Welfare State: Parties and Politics in Global Markets* (Chicago, IL: University of Chicago Press).

Hudson, C. and Lidström, A. (2002a) 'Introduction', in C. Hudson and A. Lidström (eds), *Local Education Policies: Comparing Sweden and Britain* (Basingstoke: Palgrave Macmillan): 1–26.

Hudson, C. and Lidström, A. (2002b) 'National School Policy Changes in Britain and Sweden', in C. Hudson and A. Lidström (eds), *Local Education Policies: Comparing Sweden and Britain* (Basingstoke: Palgrave Macmillan): 27–64.

Humphreys, M., Sachs, J.D. and Stiglitz, J.E. (2007) 'What is the Problem with Natural Resource Wealth?', in M. Humphreys, J.D. Sachs and J.E. Stiglitz (eds), *Escaping the Resource Curse* (New York: Colombia University Press).

Huneeus, C. (2000) 'Technocrats and Politicians in an Authoritarian Regime. The "ODEPLAN Boys" and the "Gremialists" in Pinochet's Chile', *Journal of Latin American Studies* , 32(2): 461–501.

Hussey, P.S. (2007) 'International Migration Patterns of Physicians to the United States: A Cross-National Panel Analysis', *Health Policy*, 84(2–3): 298–307.

Hutter, B. (1997) *Compliance: Regulation and Environment* (Oxford: Oxford University Press).

Immergut, E. (1992) *Health Politics: Interests and Institutions in Western Europe* (New York: Cambridge University Press).

Inglehart, R. (undated) 'World Values Survey', available at www.worldvaluessurvey.org

Inglehart, R. (1984) 'The Changing Structure of Political Cleavages in Western Society', in R.J. Dalton, S.C. Flanagan and P.A. Beck (eds), *Electoral Change in Advanced Industrial Democracies: Realignment or Dealignment?* (Princeton, NJ: Princeton University Press).

Inglehart, R. and Norris, P. (2000) 'The Developmental Theory of the Gender Gap: Women and Men's Voting Behaviour in Global Perspective', *International Political Science Review*, 21(4): 441–62.

Institute of Development Studies (2007) *Id21 Insights*. (Brighton: Institute of Development Studies, University of Sussex).

Irwin, D. (2010) 'Trade Restrictiveness and Deadweight Losses from US Tariffs', *American Economic Journal: Economic Policy*, 2: 111–33.

Iversen, T. and Cusack, T.R. (2000) 'The Causes of Welfare State Expansion: Deindustrialization or Globalization?', *World Politics*, 52(3): 313–49.

Iversen, T. and Soskice, D. (2009) 'Distribution and Redistribution: The Shadow of the Nineteenth Century', *World Politics*, 61(3): 438–86.

Iversen, T. and Stephens, J.D. (2008) 'Partisan Politics, the Welfare State, and Three Worlds of Human Capital Formation', *Comparative Political Studies*, 41: 600–37.

Iyengar, S. (1993) 'Social Research in Developing Countries', in M. Bulmer and D. Warwick (eds), *Social Research in Developing Countries* (London: UCL Press).

Jacob, K. and Volkery, A. (2006) 'Modelling Capacities for Environmental Policy-Making in Global Environmental Politics', in M. Jänicke and K. Jacob (eds), *Environmental Governance in Perspective. New Approaches to Ecological and Political Modernisation* (Berlin: Free University): 67–94.

Jacob, S. and Genard, J.-L. (2004) 'En guise de conclusion. Les metamorphoses de l'expertise', in S. Jacob and J.-L. Genard, *Expertise et action publique* (Brussels: Editions de l'université de Bruxelles).

Jacobs, S. (1985) 'Race, Empire and the Welfare State: Council Housing and Racism', *Critical Social Policy*, 5–6(13): 6–40.

Jakobsen, M.L.F. (2010) 'Untangling the Impact of Europeanization and Globalization on National Utility Liberalization: A Systematic Process Analysis of two Danish Reforms', *Journal of European Public Policy*, 17(6): 891–908.

James, O. and Lodge, M. (2003) 'The Limitations of "Policy Transfer" and "Lesson Drawing" for Public Policy Research', *Political Studies Review*, 1: 179–93.

James, S. (2010) 'Adapting to Brussels: Europeanization of the Core Executive and the "Strategic-Projection" Model', *Journal of European Public Policy*, 17(6): 818–35.

Jänicke, M. (1990) *State Failure: The Impotence of Politics in Industrial Society* (Cambridge: Polity Press).

Jänicke, M. (2006) 'The Environmental State and Environmental Flows: The Need to Reinvent the Nation-State', in G. Spaargaren, A.P.J. Mol and F.H. Buttel (eds), *Governing Environmental Flows: Global Challenges to Social Theory* (Cambridge, MA: MIT Press): 83–106.

Jänicke, M. (2007) 'Ecological Modernization: New Perspectives', *Journal of Cleaner Production*, 16(2008): 557–65.

Jarman, H. and Greer, S. (2010) 'Crossborder Trade in Health Services: Lessons from the European Laboratory', *Health Policy*, 94(2): 158–63.

Jarvis, P. (2007) 'Continuing Education in a Late-Modern or Global Society: Towards a Theoretical Framework for Comparative Analysis', in M. Crossley, P. Broadfoot and M. Schweisfurth (eds), *Changing Educational Contexts, Issues and Identities: 40 Years of Comparative Education* (London: Routledge): 175–90.

Jelen, T., Thomas, S. and Wilcox, C. (1994) 'The Gender Gap in Comparative Perspective: Gender Differences in Abstract Ideology and Concrete Issues in Western Europe', *European Journal of Political Research*, 25: 171–86.

Jennings, W., Bevan, S., Timmermans, A., Breeman, G., Brouard, S., Chaqués-Bonafont, L., Green-Pedersen, C., John, P., Mortensen, P.B. and Palau, A.M. (2011) 'Effects of the Core Functions of Government on the Diversity of Executive Agendas', *Comparative Political Studies*, 44(8): 1001–30.

Jensen, C. (2009) 'Policy Punctuations in Mature Welfare States', *Journal of Public Policy*, 29(3): 287–303.

Jessop, B. (2000) 'From KWNS to SWPR', in G. Lewis, S. Gewirtz and J. Clarke (eds), *Rethinking Social Policy* (London: Sage/Open University Press): 171–84.

Jessop, B. (2003) *Narrating the Future of the National Economy and the National State? Remarks on Remapping Regulation and Reinventing Governance* (Lancaster: Lancaster University of Sociology).

Jobert, B. and Muller, P. (1987) *L'Etat en action: politiques publiques et corporatismes* (Paris: Presses Universitaires de France).

John, P. (1998) *Analysing Public Policy* (London: Continuum).

Join-Lambert, M.-T., Bolot-Gittler, A., Daniel, C., Lenoir, D., Méda, D. (1994) *Politique Sociale* (Paris: Presses de la Fondation Nationale des Sciences Politiques).

Jónasdóttir, A.G. (1988) 'On the Concept of Interest, Women's Interest, and the Limitations of Interest Theory', in K.B. Jones and A.G. Jónasdóttir (eds), *The Political Interests of Gender: Developing Theory and Research with a Feminist Face* (London, Newbury Park, and New Delhi: Sage).

Jones, B.D., Baumgartner, F.D., Breunig, C., Wlezien, C., Soroka, S., Foucault, M., François, A., Green-Pedersen, C., Koski James, C., John, P., Mortensen, P.B., Varone, F., Walgrave, S., (2009) 'A General Empirical Law of Public Budgets: A Comparative Analysis', *American Journal of Political Science*, 53(4): 855–73.

Jones, C. (1990) 'Hong Kong, Singapore, South Korea and Taiwan: Oikonomic Welfare States', *Government and Opposition*, 25: 446–62.

Jones, C. (1993) 'The Pacific Challenge: Confucian Welfare States', in C. Jones, *New Perspectives on the Welfare State in Europe* (London: Routledge).

Jones, M. (1996) *The Australian Welfare State* (Sydney: Allen & Unwin).

Jones, P.W. (1998) 'Globalization and Internationalism: Democratic Prospects for World Education', *Comparative Education*, 34(2): 143–55.

Jones, T. and Newburn, T. (2007) *Policy Transfer and Criminal Justice* (Buckingham: Open University Press).

Jordan, A., Wurzel, R. and Zito, A. (2003a) '"New" Instruments of Environmental Governance: Patterns and Pathways of Change', *Environmental Politics*, 12(1): 1–24.

Jordan, A., Wurzel, R. and Zito, A. (2005) 'The Rise of "New" Policy Instruments in Comparative Perspective: Has Governance Eclipsed Government?', *Political Studies*, 53(3): 477–96.

Jordan, A., Wurzel, R. Zito, A. and Brückner, L. (2003b) 'European Governance and the Transfer of "New" Environmental Policy Instruments (NEPIs) in the European Union', *Public Administration*, 81(3): 555–74.

Jordan, G. (1990) 'Sub-Governments, Policy Communities and Networks: Refilling the Old Bottles?', *Journal of Theoretical Politics*, 2: 319–38.

Jordan, J. (2011) 'Health Care Politics in the Age of Retrenchment', *Journal of Social Policy*, 40(1): 113–34.

Jost, T.S. (2003) 'Private or Public Approaches to Insuring the Uninsured: Lessons from International Experience with Private Insurance', *New York University Law Review*, 76: 419–92.

Jowell, R. (1998) 'How Comparative is Comparative Research?', *American Behavioural Scientist*, 42(2): 168–77.

Kalnins, V. (2005) *Parliamentary Lobbying: Between Civil Rights and Corruption* (Latvia: Centre for Public Policy 'Providus'.

Kandel, I. (1954) *The New Era in Education* (London: George Harrap & Co.).

Kangas, O. (1991) *The Politics of Social Rights; Studies on the Dimensions of Sickness Insurance in OECD Countries* (Stockholm: Swedish Institute for Social Research).

Kangas, O., Lundberg, U. and Ploug, N. (2010) 'Three Routes to Pension Reform: Politics and Institutions in Reforming Pensions in Denmark, Finland and Sweden', *Social Policy and Administration*, 44(3): 265–84.

Karelis, C. (2007) *The Persistence of Poverty: Why the Economics of the Well-Off Can't Help The Poor* (New Haven, CT: Yale University Press).

Kassim, H. and Le Galès, P. (2010) 'Exploring Governance in a Multi-Level Polity: A Policy Instruments Approach', *West European Politics*, 33(1): 1–21.

Kasza, G.J. (2002) 'The Illusion of Welfare "Regimes"', *Journal of Social Policy*, 31(2): 271–87.

Kasza, G.J. (2006) *One World of Welfare: Japan in Comparative Perspective* (Ithaca, NY: Cornell University Press).

Katzenstein, P.J. (1985) *Small States in World Markets: Industrial Policy in Europe* (Ithaca, NY: Cornell University Press).

Kay, A. (2005) 'A Critique of the Use of Path Dependency in Policy Studies', *Public Administration*, 83: 3.

Kay, S.J. (2009) 'Political Risk and Pension Privatization: The Case of Argentina (1994–2008)', *International Social Security Review*, 62(3): 1–21.

Kaye, R.P. (2006) 'Regulated (Self-)Regulation: A New Paradigm for Controlling the Professions?', *Public Policy and Administration*, 21: 105–19.

Keech, W.R. (1980) 'Elections and Macroeconomic Policy Optimization', *American Journal of Political Science*, 24: 345–67.

Kelemen, R.D. (2000) 'Regulatory Federalism: EU Environmental Regulation in Comparative Perspective', *Journal of Public Policy*, 20(3): 133–67.

Kelemen, R.D. (2010) 'Globalizing European Union Environmental Policy', *Journal of European Public Policy*, 17(3): 335–49.

Kelemen, R.D. and Vogel, D. (2010) 'Trading Places: The Role of the United States and the European Union in International Environmental Politics', *Comparative Political Studies*, 43(4): 427–56.

Kellermann, A.L., Rivara, F.P., Rushforth, N.B., *et al.* (1993) 'Gun Ownership as a Risk Factor for Homicide in the Home', *New England Journal of Medicine*, 329(15): 1084–91.

Kelly, D., Rajan, R.S. and Goh, G. (eds) (2006) *Managing Globalization: Lessons from China and India* (Singapore: World Scientific Publishing).

Kelly, N.J. (2005) 'Political Choice, Public Policy, and Distributional Outcomes', *American Journal of Political Science*, 49(4): 865–80.

Kelman, S. and Friedman, J.N. (2009) 'Performance Improvement and Performance Dysfunction: An Empirical Examination of Distortionary Impacts of the Emergency Room Wait-Time Target in the English National Health Service', *Journal of Public Administration Research and Theory*, 19: 917–46.

Kemmerling, A. (2010) 'Does Europeanization Lead to Policy Convergence? The Role of the Single Market in Shaping National Tax Policies', *Journal of European Public Policy*, 17(7): 1058–73.

Kennedy, I. (2001) *The Bristol Royal Infirmary Inquiry* (London, Department of Health: HMSO).

Kennett, P. (2001) *Comparative Social Policy: Theory and Research* (Buckingham: Open University Press).

Keohane, R.O. (1984) *After Hegemony: Cooperation and Discord in the World Political Economy* (Princeton, NJ: Princeton University Press).

Keohane, R.O. (1998) 'International Institutions: Can Interdependence Work?', *Foreign Policy*, 82–96.

King, E. (2007) 'The Purpose of Comparative Education', in M. Crossley, P. Broadfoot and M. Schweisfurth (eds), *Changing Educational Contexts, Issues and Identities, 40 Years of Comparative Education* (London: Routledge): 2, 21–36.

King, G., Keohane, R.O. and Verba, S. (1994) *Designing Social Inquiry: Scientific Inference in Qualitative Research* (Princeton, NJ: Princeton University Press).

King, K. (2007) 'Mutilateral Agencies in the Construction of the Global Agenda on Education', *Comparative Education*, 43(3): 377–91.

King, R. (undated) 'Globalization and Higher Education', available at www.acu.ac. uk/yearbook/may2003/kingfull.pdf (accessed October 2005).

Kingdon, J. (1984) *Agendas, Alternatives, and Public Policies* (New York: University of Michigan).

Kingdon, J.W. (1995) *Agendas, Alternatives, and Public Policies*, 2nd edn (New York: Harper Collins).

Kirby, P. and Murphy, M. (2010) 'Globalisation and Models of State: Debates and Evidence from Ireland', *New Political Economy*, 16(1): 19–39.

Kirschen, E.S. and associates (1964) *Economic Policy in Our Time, Volume I: General Theory* (Chicago, IL: Rand McNally).

Kitschelt, H. (1994) *The Transformation of European Social Democracy* (Cambridge: Cambridge University Press).

Kitschelt, H. (2000) 'Partisan Competition and Welfare State Retrenchment: When Do Politicians Choose Unpopular Policies?', in P. Pierson (ed.), *The New Politics of the Welfare State* (New York: Oxford University Press).

Kjaer, A.M. (2011) Rhodes' Contribution to Governance Theory: Praise, Criticism and the Future Governance Debate', *Public Administration*, 89(1): 101–13.

Kling, A. (2010) 'The Financial Crisis: Moral Failure or Cognitive Failure?', *Harvard Journal of Law and Public Policy*, 33: 507–18.

Knill, C. (2005) 'Introduction: Cross-National Policy Convergence: Concepts, Approaches and Explanatory Factors', *Journal of European Public Policy*, 12(5): 764–74.

Knill, C. and Lehmkuhl, D. (2002a) 'Private Actors and the State: Internationalization and Changing Patterns of Governance', *Governance*, 15(1): 41–63.

Knill, C. and Lehmkuhl, D. (2002b) 'The National Impact of European Union Regulatory Policy: Three Europeanization Mechanisms', *European Journal of Political Research*, 41(2): 255–80.

Knill, C. and Lenschow, A. (2005) 'Compliance, Communication and Competition: Patterns of EU Environmental Policy Making and Their Impact on Policy Convergence', *European Environment*, 15: 114–28.

Knill, C. and Tosun, J. (2009) 'Hierarchy, Networks, or Markets: How Does the EU Shape

Environmental Policy Adoptions Within and Beyond its Borders?', *Journal of European Public Policy*, 16(6): 873–94.

Knill, C. and Tosun, J. (2012) *Public Policy: A New Introduction* (Basingstoke: Palgrave Macmillan).

Knoepfel, P., Larrue, C., Varone, F. and Hill, M. (2007) *Public Policy Analysis* (Bristol: Policy Press).

Kono, M. (2005) 'The Welfare Regime in Japan', in A. Walker and C. Wong (eds), *East Asian Welfare Regimes in Transition: From Confucianism to Globalization* (Bristol: Policy Press).

Korpi, W. (1983) 'The Social Democratic Model and Beyond: Two "Generations" of Comparative Research on the Welfare State', *Comparative Social Research*, 6: 315–51.

Kovács, J.M. (2002) 'Approaching the EU and Reaching the US? Rival Narratives on Transforming Welfare Regimes in East-Central Europe', *West European Politics*, 25(2): 175–204.

Krasner, S.D. (1978) *Defending the National Interest* (Princeton, NJ: Princeton University Press).

Kratchowil, F. and Ruggie, J.G. (1986) 'International Organization: A State of the Art on the Art of the State', *International Organization*, 40(4): 753–75.

Kuhn, T. (1970) *The Structure of Scientific Revolutions* (Chicago, IL: University of Chicago Press).

Kuznets, S. (1955) 'Economic Growth and Income Inequality', *American Economic Review*, 65: 1–28.

Kvist, J. and Sinfield, A. (1997) 'Comparing Tax Welfare State', in M. May, E. Brunsdon, and G. Craig (eds), *Social Policy Review*, 9 (London: Social Policy Association).

Kwon, H.-j. (1997) 'Beyond European Welfare Regimes: Comparative Perspectives on East Asian Welfare Systems', *Journal of Social Policy*, 26(4): 467–84.

Kwon, H.-j. (1998) 'Democracy and the Politics of Social Welfare: A Comparative Analysis of Welfare Systems in East Asia', in R. Goodman, G. White and Huck-ju Kwon (eds), *The East Asian Welfare Model: Welfare Orientalism and the State* (London: Routledge).

Lane, J.-E. (2000) *New Public Management* (London: Routledge).

Langan, M. and Ostner, I. (1991) 'Gender and Welfare. Towards a Comparative Framework', in G. Room (ed.), *Towards a European Welfare State* (Bristol: SAUS, University of Bristol).

Lange, P. and Garrett, G. (1987) 'The Politics of Growth Reconsidered', *Journal of Politics*, 49: 257–274.

Larsen, C.A. (2008) 'The Institutional Logic of Welfare Attitudes: How Welfare Regimes Influence Public Support', *Comparative Political Studies*, 41(2): 145–68.

Larsson, L., Sundén. A. and Settergren, O. (2008) 'Pension Information: The Annual Statement at a Glance', *OECD Journal: General Papers*, 3: 131–71.

Lascoumes, P. and Le Galès, P. (2004) *Gouverner par les Instruments* (Paris : Presses de Sciences Po).

Lascoumes, P. and Le Galès, P. (2007) 'Introduction: Understanding Public Policy through Its Instruments – From the Nature of Instruments to the Sociology of Public Policy Instrumentation', *Governance*, 20(1): 1–21.

Lash, S. and Urry, J. (1987) *The End of Organized Capitalism* (Madison, WI: University of Wisconsin Press).

Lasswell, H.D. (1950) *Politics: Who Gets What, When, How* (New York: Peter Smith).

Latour, B. (1993) *We Have Never Been Modern* (Cambridge, MA: Harvard University Press).

Latour, B. (2004) *Politics of Nature: How to Bring the Sciences into Democracy* (Cambridge, MA: Harvard University Press).

Latour, B. (2007) *Politics of Nature: How to Bring the Sciences into Democracy* (Cambridge, MA: Harvard University Press).

Latour, B. and Woolgard, S. (1979) *Laboratory Life: The Social Construction of Scientific Facts* (Princeton, NJ: Princeton University Press).

Lauth, H.-J. (2000) 'Informal Institutions and Democracy', *Democratization*, 7(4): 21–50.

Lavenex, S., Lehmkuhl, D. and Wichmann, N. (2009) 'Modes of External Governance: A Cross-National and Cross-Sectoral Comparison', *Journal of European Public Policy*, 16(6): 813–33.

Lavoie, J., Boulton, A. and Dwyer, J. (2010) 'Analysing Contractual Environments: Lessons from Indigeneous Health in Canada, Australia and New Zealand', *Public Administration*, 88(3): 665–79.

Law, J. (1999) 'After ANT: Complexity, Naming and Topology', in J. Law and J. Hasard, *Actor Network Theory and After* (Oxford: Blackwell Publishing): 1–14.

Law, J. (2004) *After Method. Mess in Social Science Research* (London and New York: Routledge).

Le Galès, P. (1995) 'Politique de la ville en France et en Grande-Bretagne: volontarisme et ambiguities de l'Etat', *Sociologie du travail*, 2: 249–75.

Le Galès, P. and Thatcher, M. (eds) (1995) *Les réseaux de politique publique, Débat autour des policy networks* (Paris: Editions L'Harmattan).

Lees, C. (2006) 'We Are All Comparativists Now: Why and How Single-Country Scholarship Must Adapt and Incorporate the Comparative Politics Approach', *Comparative Political Studies*, 39: 1084–108.

Legro, J.W. (2000) 'The Transformation of Policy Ideas', *American Journal of Political Science*, 44(3): 419–32.

Leibfried, S. (1991) *Towards a European Welfare State? On Integrating Poverty Regimes in the European Community* (Bremen, Germany: Centre for Social Policy Research, Bremen University).

Leibfried, S. (1992) 'Towards a European Welfare State? On Integrating Poverty Regimes in the European Community', in Z. Ferge and J.E. Kollberg (eds), *Social Policy in a Changing Europe* (Frankfurt: Campus Verlag).

Leibfried, S. (1993) 'Towards a European Welfare State?', in C. Jones (ed.), *New Perspectives on the Welfare State in Europe* (London: Routledge).

Leichter, H.M. (1979) *A Comparative Approach to Policy Analysis: Health Care Policy in Four Nations* (Cambridge: Cambridge University Press).

Leisering, L., (2009) 'Germany: A Centrist Welfare State at the Crossroads', in P. Alcock and G. Craig (eds), *International Social Policy: Welfare Regimes in the Developed World*, 2nd edn (Basingstoke: Palgrave Macmillan).

Lerner, D., Pool, I. and Lasswell, H.D. (1951–52) 'Comparative Analysis of Political Ideologies: A Preliminary Statement', *Public Opinion Quarterly*, 15(4): 715–33.

Levi-Faur, D. (2006) 'A Question of Size? A Heuristics for Stepwise Comparative Research Design', in B. Rihoux and H. Grimm (eds), *Innovative Comparative Methods for Policy Analysis: Beyond the Quantitative–Qualitative Divide* (New York: Springer): 43–66.

Levi-Faur, D. and Gilardi, F. (2004) 'The Rise of the British Regulatory State', *Comparative Politics*, 37(1), October: 105–24.

Levin, B. (1998) 'An Epidemic of Education Policy: (What) Can We Learn From Each Other?', *Comparative Education*, 34: 131–41.

Levitsky, S. and Way, L.A. (2010) *Competitive Authoritarianism: Hybrid Regimes after the Cold War* (Cambridge: Cambridge University Press).

Lewis, J. (1992) 'Gender and the Development of Welfare Regimes', *Journal of European Social Policy*, 2(3): 159–73.

Lewis, J. (1999) 'The "Problem" of Lone Motherhood in Comparative Perspective', in J. Clasen (ed.), *Comparative Social Policy: Concepts, Theories and Methods* (London: Blackwell).

Lewis, J. and Knijn, T. (2002) 'The Politics of Sex Education Policy in England and Wales and The Netherlands since the 1980s', *Journal of Social Policy*, 31(4): 669–94.

Lewis, M. (2007) 'Informal Payments and the Financing of Health Care in Developing and Transition Countries', *Health Affairs*, 26(4): 984–97.

Lewis, M.P. (ed.) (2009) *Ethnologue: Languages of the World*, 16th edn (Dallas, TX: SIL International).

Lieberman, R.C. (2002) 'Ideas, Institutions, and Political Order: Explaining Political Change', *American Political Science Review*, 96(4): 697–712.

Liebowitz, S. and Margolis, S.E. (1990) 'The Fable of the Keys', *Journal of Law and Economics*, 33(1): 1–26.

Liefferink, D., Arts, B., Kamstra, J. and Ooijevaar, J. (2009) 'Leaders and Laggards in Environmental Policy: A Quantitative Analysis of Domestic Policy Outputs', *Journal of European Public Policy*, 16(5): 677–700.

Lightman, E.S. and Riches, G. (2009) 'Canada: One Step Forward, Two Steps Back?', in P. Alcock and G. Craig (eds), *International Social Policy: Welfare Regimes in the Developed World*, 2nd edn (Basingstoke: Palgrave Macmillan).

Lijphart, A. (1971) 'Comparative Politics and the Comparative Method', *American Political Science Review*, 65: 682–93.

Lijphart, A. (1975) 'The Comparable-Cases Strategy in Comparative Research', *Comparative Political Studies*, 8: 158–77.

Lijphart, A. (1984) *Democracies: Patterns of Majoritarian and Consensus Government in Twenty-One Countries* (New Haven, CT: Yale University Press).

Lijphart, A. (1994) *Electoral Systems and Party Systems: A Study of Twenty-Seven Democracies* (Oxford: Oxford University Press).

Limerick, M. (2009) 'What Makes an Aboriginal Council Successful? Case Studies of Aboriginal Community Government Performance in Far North Queensland', *Australian Journal of Public Administration*, 68(4): 414–28.

Lind, J. (2008) *Sorry States: Apologies in International Politics* (Ithaca, NY: Cornell University Press).

Lindblom, C. (1977) *Politics and Markets: The World's Political-Economic Systems* (New York: Basic Books).

Linder, S.H. and Peters, B.G. (1984) 'From Social Theory to Policy Design', *Journal of Public Policy*, 4(3): 237–59.

Linder, S.H. and Peters, B.G. (1989) 'Instruments of Government: Perceptions and Contexts', *Journal of Public Policy*, 9(1): 35–58.

Linz, J.J. and Stepan, A.C. (1978) *The Breakdown of Democratic Regimes* (Baltimore, MD: Johns Hopkins University Press).

Lipset, S.M. and Rokkan. S. (eds) (1967) *Party Systems and Voter Alignments* (New York: Free Press).

Lipson, L. (1957) 'The Comparative Method in Political Studies', *Political Quarterly*, 68(1): 372–82.

Lister, R. (1994) '"She Has Other Duties" – Women, Citizenship and Social Security', in S. Baldwin and J. Falkingham (eds), *Social Security and Social Change: New Challenges to the Beveridge Model* (Hemel Hempstead: Harvester Wheatsheaf).

Loder, J. (2011) 'The Lisbon Strategy and the Politicization of EU Policy-Making: The Case of the Services Directive', *Journal of European Public Policy*, 18(4): 566–83.

Lodge, M. (2002) 'Varieties of Europeanisation and the National Regulatory State', *Public Policy and Administration*, 17(2): 43–67.

Lodge, M. and Stirton, L. (2006) 'Withering in the Heat? In Search of the Regulatory State in the Commonwealth Caribbean', *Governance*, 19(3): 465–95.

Lodge, M., Wegrich, K., and McElroy, G. (2010) 'Dodgy Kebabs Everywhere? Variety of Worldviews and Regulatory Change', *Public Administration*, 88(1): 247–66.

Louzek, M. (2008) 'Pension System Reform in Central and Eastern Europe', *Post-Communist Economies*, 20(1): 119–31.

Lovenduski, J. (ed.) (2005) *State Feminism and Political Representation* (Cambridge: Cambridge University Press).

Lowi, T). (1964) 'Review: American Business, Public Policy, Case-Studies, and Political Theory', *World Politics*, 16(4): 677–715.

Lowi, T. (1972) 'Four Systems of Politics, Policy and Choice', *Public Administration Review*, 32(4): 298–311.

Lukes, S. (1974) *Power: A Radical View* (London: Macmillan).

Lynch, D. (2004) *Engaging Eurasia's Separatist States: Unresolved Conflicts and De Facto States* (Washington, DC: United States Institute for Peace).

Lynch, J. (2006) *Age in the Welfare State: The Origins of Social Spending on Pensioners, Workers, and Children* (Cambridge: Cambridge University Press).

Lynggaard, K. (2011) 'Domestic Change in the Face of European Integration and Globalization: Methodological Pitfalls and Pathways', *Comparative European Politics*, 9: 18–37.

Lyotard, J.-F. (1984) *The Postmodern Condition: A Report on Knowledge* (Manchester: Manchester University Press).

MacFarlane, S.N. and Foong-Khong, Y. (2006) *Human Security and the UN: A Critical History* (Bloomington, IN: Indiana University Press).

Macintyre, A. (1984) 'Is a Science of Comparative Politics Possible?', in A. Macintyre, *Against the Self-Images of the Age: Essays on Ideology and Philosophy* (Notre Dame: Notre Dame University Press).

Mackie, V. (1988) 'Feminist Politics in Japan', *New Left Review*, 167: 53–76.

Mackintosh, N. and Sandall, J. (2008) 'Failure to Rescue: Problems and Solutions', NIHR King's Patient Safety and Service Quality Centre (PSSQ), *Innovations Programme*, Working Paper 1.

MacPherson, S. and Midgley, J. (1987) *Comparative Social Policy and the Third World* (Sussex: Wheatsheaf Books).

Maddison, A. (1991) *Dynamic Forces in Capitalist Development* (Oxford: Oxford University Press).

Mahoney, C. and Beckstrand, M.J. (2011) 'Following the Money: European Union Funding of Civil Society Organizations', *Journal of Common Market Studies*, 49: 1339–61.

Mahoney, J. (2000) 'Strategies of Causal Inference in Small-N Analysis', *Sociological Methods and Research*, 28(4): 387–424.

Mahoney, J. and Goertz, G. (2004) 'The Possibility Principle: Choosing Negative Cases in Comparative Research', *American Political Science Review*, 98: 653–69.

Mahoney, J. and Thelen, K. (2010) 'A Theory of Gradual Institutional Change', in J. Mahoney and K. Thelen (eds), *Explaining Institutional Change: Ambiguity, Agency, and Power* (Cambridge: Cambridge University Press): 1–37.

Maioni, A. (1998) *Parting at the Crossroads: The Emergence of Health Insurance in the United States and Canada* (Princeton, NJ: Princeton University Press).

Mair, P. (1996) 'Comparative Politics: An Overview', in Robert E. Goodin and H.-D. Klingemann, *A New Handbook of Political Science* (Oxford: Oxford University Press): 309–35.

Majone, G. (1989) *Evidence, Argument and Persuasion in the Policy Process* (New Haven, CT: Yale University Press).

Majone, G. (1997) 'From the Positive to the Regulatory State: Causes and Consequences of Changes in the Mode of Governance', *Journal of Public Policy*, 17: 139–67.

Majone, G. (2002) 'What Price Safety? The Precautionary Principle and its Policy Implications', *Journal of Common Market Studies*, 40: 89.

Malone, D.M. (ed.) (2004) *The UN Security Council: From the Cold War to the 21st Century* (Boulder, CO: Lynne Rienner).

Maloney, W.A., Jordan, G. and McLaughlin, A.M. (1994) 'Interest Groups and Public Policy: The Insider/Outsider Model Revisited', *Journal of Public Policy*, 14(1): 17–38.

Maor, M. (2010) 'Organisational Reputation and Jurisdictional Claims: The Case of the US Food and Drug Administration', *Governance*, 23(1): 133–60.

March, J.G. and Olsen, J.P. (1984) 'The New Institutionalism: Organizational Factors in Political Life', *American Political Science Review*, 78: 734–49.

March, J. and Olsen, J. (1989) *Rediscovering Institutions: The Organizational Basis of Politics* (New York: Free Press).

Mares, I. (2003) *The Politics of Social Risk: Business and Welfare State Development* (Cambridge: Cambridge University Press).

Margetts, H.Z. (1999) *Information Technology in Government: Britain and America* (London: Routledge).

Marier, P. (2008) 'The Changing Conception of Pension Rights in Canada, Mexico and the United States', *Social Policy and Administration*, 42(4): 418–33.

Marin, B. and Mayntz, R. (eds) (1991) *Policy Networks: Empirical Evidence and Theoretical Considerations* (Frankfurt am Main: Campus Verlag).

Marín, G. and Marín, B.V.O. (1991) *Research with Hispanic Populations* (Newbury Park, CA: Sage Publications).

Marinakou, M. (1998) 'Welfare States in the European Periphery: The Case of Greece', in R. Sykes and P. Alcock (eds), *Developments in European Social Policy: Convergence and Diversity* (Bristol: Policy Press).

Marmor, T.R. and Lieberman, E.S. (2004) 'Tobacco Control in Comparative Perspective: Eight Nations in Search of an Explanation', in E.A. Feldman and R. Bayer (eds), *Unfiltered: Conflicts over Tobacco Policy and Public Health* (Cambridge, MA: Harvard University Press).

Marsh, D. (ed.) (1998) *Comparing Policy Networks* (Buckingham: Open University Press).

Marsh, D. and Rhodes, R.A.W. (eds) (1992) *Policy Networks in British Government* (Oxford: Oxford University Press).

Marsh, D. and Smith, M. (2000) 'Understanding Policy Networks: Towards a Dialectical Approach', *Political Studies*, 48: 4–21.

Marshall, T.H. (1963) *Sociology at the Crossroads* (London: Heinemann).

Martin, C.J. and Swank, D. (2009) 'Gonna Party like it's 1899: Party Systems and the Origins of Varieties of Coordination', paper available at http://www.mu.edu/polisci/documents/GonnaParty Like1899.pdf

Martinsen, D.S. (2005) 'Towards an Internal Health Market with the European Court', *West European Politics*, 28(5): 1035–56.

May, M. (2006) 'Employment Policy', in M. Hill, *Social Policy in the Modern World: A Comparative Text* (Oxford: Blackwell): 93–115.

May, T. (1997) *Social Research: Issues, Methods and Process* (Buckingham: Open University Press).

May, T. (2003) *Social Research: Issues, Methods and Process*, 3rd edn (Buckingham: Open University Press).

McGillivray, F. (2004) *Privileging Industry: The Comparative Politics of Trade and Industrial Policy* (Princeton, NJ: Princeton University Press).

McKinney, S. (1991) 'International Crime Policy and Efficient Resource Allocation', in S.S. Nagel, (ed.), *Global Policy Studies: International Interaction toward Improving Public Policy* (London: Macmillan): 243–58.

McLaughlin, E. (2001) 'Ireland: From Catholic Corporatism to Social Partnership', in A. Cochrane, J., Clarke, and S. Gewirtz (eds), *Comparing Welfare States*, 2nd edn (London: Sage/Open University Press): 223–60.

McLean, C., Campbell, C. and Cornish, F. (2003) 'African-Caribbean Interactions with Mental Health Services in the UK: Experiences and Expectations of Exclusion as (Re)Productive of Health Inequalities', *Social Science and Medicine*, 56: 657–69.

McNamara, K. (1998) *The Currency of Ideas: Monetary Politics in the European Union* (Ithaca, NY: Cornell University Press).

McNamara, K. (2002) 'Rational Fictions: Central Bank Independence and the Social Logic of Delegation', *West European Politics*, 25(1): 47–76.

McNulty, T. (2009) 'Response to Question on Jobseeker's Allowance', UK Hansard, 2 Apr 2009: Column 1401W.

Meadows, D.H., Meadows, D.L., Randcers, J. and Behrens III, W.W. (1972) *Limits to Growth* (London: Pan).

Mechanic, D. and Rochefort, D.A. (1996) 'Comparative Medical Systems', *Annual Review of Sociology*, 22: 239–70.

Mele, V. and Compagni, A. (2010) 'Explaining the Unexpected Success of the Smoking Ban in Italy: Political Strategy and Transition to Practice, 2000–2004', *Public Administration*, 88(3): 819–35.

Menon, A. and Sedelmeier, U. (2010) 'Instruments and Intentionality: Civilian Crisis Management and Enlargement Conditionality in EU Security Policy', *West European Politics*, 33(1): 75–92.

Mény, Y. and Thoenig, J.C. (1989) *Politics Publiques* (Paris: Presses Universitaires de France).

Mercer, J. (2010) 'Emotional Beliefs', *International Organization*, 64: 1–31.

Meseguer, C. (2006) 'Learning and Economic Policy Choices', *European Journal of Political Economy*, 22: 156–78.

Middleton, S. (1998) *Disciplining Sexualities* (New York: Teachers College Press).

Miliband, R. (1977) *Marxism and Politics* (Oxford: Oxford University Press).

Mill, J.S. (1974) *The Collected Works of John Stuart Mill, Volume VII – A System of Logic Ratiocinative and Inductive, Being a Connected View of the Principles of Evidence and the Methods of Scientific Investigation (Books I–III)*, (ed.) John M. Robson, Introduction by R.F. McRae (London: Routledge & Kegan Paul).

Minns, J. (2006) *The Politics of Developmentalism: The Midas States of Mexico, South Korea and Taiwan* (Basingstoke: Palgrave Macmillan).

Mintz, A. and Huang, C. (1991) 'Guns versus Butter: The Indirect Link', *American Journal of Political Science*, 35(3): 738–57.

Mishra, R. (1999) *Globalization and the Welfare State* (Cheltenham: Edward Elgar).

Mitchell, A. (1995) *Election '45: Reflections on the Revolution in Britain* (London: Bellew Publishing).

Mitchell, D. (1991) *Income Transfers in Ten Welfare States* (Aldershot: Avebury).

Mol, A. (2002) *The Body Multiple. Ontology in Medical Practice* (Durham, NC and London: Duke University Press).

Mol, A. (2008) *The Logic of Care. Healthcare and the Problem of Patient Choice* (London and New York: Routledge).

Mol, A.P.J. and Buttel, F.H. (eds) (2002) *The Environmental State under Pressure* (Oxford: Elsevier).

Mol, A.P.J. and Sonnenfeld, D.A. (2000) 'Ecological Modernization around the World: An Introduction', *Environmental Politics*, 9(1): 3–16.

Mol, A.P.J. and Spaargaren, G. (2006) 'Toward a Sociology of Environmental Flows: A New Agenda for 21st Century Environmental Sociology', in G. Spaargaren, A.P.J. Mol and F.H. Buttel (eds), *Governing Environmental Flows: Global Challenges to Social Theory* (Cambridge, MA: MIT Press): 39–83.

Monière, D. (1999) *Démocratie médiatique et représentation politique: analyse comparative de quatre journaux télévisés: Radio-Canada, France 2, RTBF (Belgique) et TSR (Suisse)* (Montréal: Les Presses de l'Université de Montréal).

Montesquieu, Charles de Secondat, Baron de (1989) Trans. and ed. by A.M. Cohler, B.C. Miller and H.S. Stone, *The Spirit of the Laws* (Cambridge: Cambridge University Press).

Montpetit, E). (2002) 'Policy Networks, Federal Arrangements, and the Development of Environmental Regulations: A Comparison of the Canadian and American Agricultural Sectors', *Governance*, 15(1): 1–20.

Moran, M. (1997) *The British Regulatory State: High Modernism and Hyper-Innovation* (Oxford: Oxford University Press).

Moran, M. (1999) *Governing the Health Care State: A Comparative Study of the United Kingdom, the United States and Germany* (Manchester: Manchester University Press).

Moran, M. (2007) *The British Regulatory State: High Modernism and Hyper-Innovation* (Oxford: Oxford University Press).

Moran, M. and Wood, B. (1993) *States, Regulation and the Medical Profession* (Buckingham: Open University Press).

Moran, M. and Wood, B. (1996) 'The Globalization of Health Care Policy?' in P. Gummett (ed.), *Globalization and Public Policy* (Cheltenham: Edward Elgar).

Morey, A.I. (2003) 'Major Trends Impacting Faculty Roles and Rewards: An International Perspective', in H. Eggins (ed.), *Globalization and Reform in Higher Education* (Buckingham: Society for Research in Higher Education and Open University Press).

Morris, L. (1998) 'Legitimate Membership of the Welfare Community', in M. Langan (ed.), *Welfare: Needs, Rights and Risks* (London: Routledge/Open University Press).

Moser, I. (2008) 'Making Alzheimer's Disease Matter. Enacting, Interfering and Doing the Politics of Nature', *Geoforum*, 39: 98–110.

Mosher, F. (1980) 'The Changing Responsibilities and Tactics of the Federal Government', *Public Administration Review*, 40: 541–8.

Mossialos, E., Mrazek, M. and Walley, T. (2004) *Regulating Pharmaceuticals in Europe: Striving for Efficiency, Equity, and Quality* (Maidenhead: McGraw-Hill International).

Mueller, H.-E. (1984) *Bureaucracy, Education, and Monopoly: Civil Service Reforms in Prussia and England* (Berkeley, CA: University of California Press).

Muller, P. (2000) 'L'analyse cognitive des politiques: vers une sociologie politique de l'action publique', *Revue Française de Science Politique*, 50(2): 189–207.

Muller, P. and Surel, Y. (1998) *L'analyse des politiques publiques* (Paris: Montchrestien).

Münchener Merkur (2007) 'Wovor es Ude in London graust', *Münchener Merkur*, 3 April: 3.

Mur-Veeman, I., van Raak, A., and Paulus, A. (2008) 'Comparing Integrated Care Policy in Europe: Does Policy Matter?', *Health Policy*, 85(2): 172–83.

Nagel, S.S. (1991) 'Introduction to Global Policy Studies', in S.S. Nagel, (ed.), *Global Policy Studies: International Interaction toward Improving Public Policy* (London: Macmillan).

Naroll, R. (1965) 'Galton's Problem: The Logic of Cross-Cultural Analysis', *Social Research*, 32: 428–51.

National Archives (1944) HO 187/828, Note of discussion with Mr G L Swan, National Board of Fire Underwriters (Kew: National Archives).

National Center for Education Statistics (undated (a)) *Digest of Education Statistics*, US Department of Education and Institute of Education Sciences.

National Center for Education Statistics (undated (b)) *Early Childhood Longitudinal Survey of Kindergarten Children (ECLS-K)*, US Department of Education and Institute of Education Sciences.

National School of Government (2011) *An Interactive Guide to our Courses, 2011–12*, Spring (London: National School of Government).

Neave, G. (2003) 'The Bologna Declaration: Some of the Historic Dilemmas posed by the Reconstruction of the Community in Europe's Systems of Higher Education', *Educational Policy*, 17: 141–64.

Neave, G. and Van Vught, F.A. (1991a) 'Introduction', in G. Neave and F.A. Van Vught (eds), *Prometheus Bound: The Changing Relationship between Government and Higher Education in Western Europe* (Oxford: Pergamon): ix–xv.

Neave, G. and Van Vught, F.A. (1991b) 'Conclusion', in G. Neave and F.A. Van Vught (eds), *Prometheus Bound: The Changing Relationship between Government and Higher Education in Western Europe* (Oxford: Pergamon): 239–56.

Nettl, J.P. (1968) 'The State as a Conceptual Variable', *World Politics*, 20(4): 559–92.

Neumann, S. (1957) 'Comparative Politics: A Half-Century Appraisal', *Journal of Politics*, 19: 369–90.

Niskanen, W. (1971) *Bureaucracy and Representative Government* (Chicago, IL: Aldine).

Noah, H.J. and Eckstein, M.A. (1969) *Toward a Science of Comparative Education* (New York: Macmillan).

Nordhaus, W.D. (1975) 'The Political Business Cycle', *Review of Economic Studies*, 62: 169–90.

North, D. (1986) 'The New Institutional Economics', *Journal of Institutional and Theoretical Economics*, 142: 230–7.

North, D.C. (1990) *Institutions, Institutional Change and Economic Performance* (Cambridge: Cambridge University Press).

Nóvoa, A. and Yariv-mashal, T. (2007) 'Comparative Research in Education: A Mode of Governance or a Historical Journey?', in M. Crossley, P. Broadfoot and M. Schweisfurth (eds), *Changing Educational Contexts, Issues and Identities: 40 Years of Comparative Education* (London: Routledge): 350–69.

Nye, J. (1971) *Peace in Parts: Integration and Conflict in Regional Organization* (Boston, MA: Little Brown).

O'Connor, D. (2008) 'Governing the Global Commons: Linking Carbon Sequestration and Biodiversity Conservation in Tropical Forests', *Global Environmental Change*, 18: 368–74.

O'Connor, J. (1993) 'Gender, Class and Citizenship in the Comparative Analysis of Welfare State Regimes: Theoretical and Methodological Issues', *British Journal of Sociology*, 44(3): 501–18.

O'Connor, J.S., Orloff, A.S. and Shaver, S. (1999) *States, Markets, Families: Gender, Liberalism and Social Policy in Australia, Canada, Great Britain and the United States* (Cambridge: Cambridge University Press).

O'Neill, F. (2000) 'Health, the Internal Market and the Reform of the National Health Service', in D. Dolowitz (ed.), *Policy Transfer and British Social Policy. Learning from the USA?* (Buckingham, PA: Open University Press): 59–76.

O'Neill, K. (2002) *Experiments in Living: The Fatherless Family* (London: Civitas).

Oakley, A. (1981) 'Interviewing Women: A Contradiction in Terms', in H. Roberts (ed.), *Doing Feminist Research* (London: Routledge): 243–62.

Ochs, K. and Phillips, D. (2002) 'Comparative Studies and "Cross-National Attraction" in Education: A Typology for the Analysis of English Interest in Educational Policy and Provision in Germany', *Educational Studies*, 28(4): 325–39.

OECD (2006) *OECD Employment Outlook 2006* (Paris: OECD).

OECD (2007) *OECD Environmental Data: Compendium 2006–7* (Paris: OECD).

OECD (2008) *Pharmaceutical Pricing Policies in a Global Market* (Paris: OECD).

OECD (2009a) *Pensions at a Glance 2009* (Paris: OECD).

OECD (2009b) *OECD Health at a Glance 2009* (Paris: OECD).

OECD (2010a) *Factbook: Economic, Environmental and Social Statistics* (Paris: OECD).

OECD (2010b) *Pension Database*, version updated June 2010 (Paris: OECD).

OECD (2010c) *Education at a Glance* (Paris: OECD).

OECD (2011a) *Economic Policy Reforms 2011: Going for Growth* (Paris: OECD).

OECD (2011b) 'Housing and the Economy: Policies for Renovation', *Economic Policy Reforms 2011: Going for Growth* (Paris: OECD): 181–203.

OECD (2011c) *International Migration Outlook* (Paris: OECD).

OECD/EEA (2011) *OECD/EEA Database on Instruments used for Environmental Policy and Natural Resources Management* (Paris: OECD).

Offe, C. (2005) 'The European Model of 'Social' Capitalism: Can it Survive European Integration?', in M. Miller (ed.), *Worlds of Capitalism* (London: Routledge): 146–78.

Ogus, A. (1994) *Regulation: Legal Form and Economic Theory* (Oxford: Clarendon Press).

Ohmae, K. (1995) *The End of the Nation State: The Rise of Regional Economics* (New York: Free Press).

Okun, A. (1975) *Equality and Efficiency: The Big Trade-Off* (Washington, DC: Brookings Institution).

Olson, M. (1963) *The Logic of Collective Action: Public Goods and the Theory of Groups* (Cambridge, MA: Harvard University Press).

Olson, M ((1982) *The Rise and Decline of Nations: Economic Growth, Stagflation, and Social Rigidities* (New Haven, CT: Yale University Press).

Olsson, O. (2004) 'Unbundling Ex-Colonies: A Comment on Acemoglu, Johnson, and Robinson', *Working Papers in Economics* 146, Göteborg University.

Omi, M. and Winant, H. (1994) *Racial Formation in the United States: From the 1960s to the 1990s* (New York: Routledge).

Orenstein, M.A. (2008) 'Out-Liberalizing the EU: Pension Privatization in Central and Eastern Europe', *Journal of European Public Policy*, 15(6): 899–917.

Osborne, D. and Gaebler, T. (1992) *Reinventing Government: How the Entrepreneurial Spirit is Transforming the Public Sector* (New York: Penguin).

Osborne, G. (2010) 'Spending Review Statement', Presented to the UK House of Commons, 20 October.

Ostrom, E. (1990) *Governing the Commons: The Evolution of Institutions for Collective Action* (Cambridge: Cambridge University Press).

Ostrom, E. (2009) 'A Polycentric Approach for Coping with Climate Change', Policy Research Working Paper 5095 (Washington, DC: World Bank).

Øyen, E. (ed.) (1990) *Comparative Methodology: Theory and Practice in International Social Research* (London: Sage).

Page, E.C. and Mark-Lawson, J. (2007) 'Outward-Looking Policy Making', in H. Bochel and S. Duncan (eds), *Making Policy in Theory and Practice* (Bristol: Policy Press): 47–64.

Pahl, J. and Vaile, M. (1988) 'Health and Health Care Among Travellers', *Journal of Social Policy*, 17(2): 195–213.

Palier, B. (2007) 'Tracking the Evolution of a Single Instrument Can Reveal Profound Changes: The Case of Funded Pensions in France', *Governance*, 20(1): 85–107.

Palier, B. and Surel, Y. (2005) 'Les "trois I" et l'analyse de l'etat en action', *Revue Française de Science Politique*, 55(1): 7–32.

Panke, D. (2010) 'Small States in the European Union: Structural Disadvantages in EU Policy-Making and Counter-Strategies', *Journal of European Public Policy*, 17(6): 799–817.

Parkyn, G.W. (2007) 'Comparative Education Research and Development Education', in M. Crossley, P. Broadfoot and M. Schweisfurth (eds), *Changing Educational Contexts, Issues and Identities, 40 Years of Comparative Education* (London: Routledge): 37–45.

Parsons, T. (1949) *The Structure of Social Action* (New York: Free Press).

Parsons, W. (1996) *Understanding Public Policy: An Introduction to the Theory and Practice of Policy Analysis* (Cheltenham: Edward Elgar).

Peck, J. (2001) *Workfare States* (New York: Guilford Press).

Peck, J. and Theodore, N. (2007) 'Variegated Capitalism', *Progress in Human Geography*, 31(6): 731–72.

Pedersen S. (1993) *Family Dependence and the Origin of the Welfare State: Britain and France, 1914-45* (Cambridge: Cambridge University Press).

Penhale, B. and Manthorpe, J. (2004) 'Older People, Institutional Abuse and Inquiries', in N. Stanley and J. Manthorpe (eds), *The Age of Inquiry: Learning and Blaming in Health and Social Care* (London and New York: Routledge): 257–72.

Pennycook, A. (1994) *The Cultural Politics of English as an International Language* (Harlow: Longman).

Pépin, L. (2007) 'The History of EU Cooperation in the Field of Education and Training: How Lifelong Learning Became a Strategic Objective', *European Journal of Education*, 42: 121–32.

Perez, S.A. and Westrup, J. (2010) 'Finance and the Macroeconomy: The Politics of Regulatory Reform in Europe', *Journal of European Public Policy*, 17(8): 1171–92.

Permanand, G. and Mossialos, E. (2005) 'Constitutional Asymmetry and Pharmaceutical Policy-Making in the European Union', *Journal of European Public Policy*, 12(4): 687–709.

Perrings, C., Mooney, H. and Williamson, M. (eds) (2010) *Bioinvasions and Globalization: Ecology, Economics, Management, and Policy* (Oxford: Oxford University Press).

Perrow, C. (1984) *Normal Accidents: Living with High-Risk Technologies* (New York: Basic Books).

Perrow, C. (1986) *Complex Organizations: A Critical Essay*, 3rd edn (New York: Random House).

Persson, T. and Tabellini, G. (2004) 'Fiscal Effects of Constitutions', *American Economic Review*, 94: 25–46.

Peters, B.G. (1988) *Comparing Public Bureaucracies: Problems of Theory and Method* (Tuscaloosa, AL: University of Alabama Press).

Peters, B.G. (2002) 'The Politics of Tool Choice', in L. Salamon (ed.), *The Tools of Government: A Guide to the New Governance* (Oxford: Oxford University Press): 552–64.

Petitville, F. and Smith, A. (2006) 'Analyser les politiques publiques internationales', *Revue Française de Science Politique*, 56(3): 357–66.

Phillips, D. (1989) 'Neither a Borrower nor a Lender be? The Problems of Cross-National Attraction in Education', *Comparative Education*, 25(3): 267–74.

Phillips, D. and Ochs, K. (2003) 'Processes of Policy Borrowing in Education: Some Explanatory and Analytical Devices', *Comparative Education*, 39(4): 451–64.

Phillips, N. (2006) 'States and Modes of Regulation in the Global Political Economy', in M. Minogue and L. Carino, *Regulatory Governance in Developing Countries* (Aldershot: Edward Elgar): 17–38.

Philpott, D. (1996) 'The Possibilities of Ideas', *Security Studies*, 5: 183–96.

Pickvance, C.G. (1986) 'Comparative Urban Analysis and Assumptions about Causality', *International Journal of Urban and Regional Research*, 10(2): 162–84.

Pierson, P. (1994) *Dismantling the Welfare State? Reagan, Thatcher, and the Politics of Retrenchment* (Cambridge: Cambridge University Press).

Pierson, P. (1998) 'Irresistible Forces, Immovable Objects: Post-Industrial States Confront Permanent Austerity', *Journal of European Public Policy*, 5(4): 539–60.

Piven, F.F. and Cloward, R. (1993) *Regulating the Poor: The Functions of Public Welfare*, 2nd edn (New York and Toronto: Random House).

Polanyi, K. (2001) *The Great Transformation* (Boston, MA: Beacon Press).

Pollak, M.A. (1997) 'Delegation, Agency, and Agenda Setting in the European Community', *International Organization*, 51(1): 99–134.

Pollitt, C. (2011) 'Not Odious but Onerous: Comparative Public Administration', *Public Administration*, 89(1): 114–27.

Pollitt, C., Caulfield, J., Smullen, A. and Talbot, C. (2001) 'Agency Fever? Analysis of an International Fashion', *Journal of Comparative Policy Analysis*, 3: 271–90.

Polsby, N W. (1960) 'How to Study Community Power: The Pluralist Alternative', *Journal of Politics*, 22(30; 474–84.

Polanyi, K. (2001 [1944]) *The Great Transformation: The Political and Economic Origins of Our Time* (Boston, MA: Beacon Press).

Poncelet, E.C. (2001) 'A Kiss Here and a Kiss There: Conflict and Collaboration in Environmental Partnerships', *Environmental Management*, 27(1): 13–25.

Popper, K. (2002) *The Logic of Scientific Discovery* (London: Routledge Classics).

Population Division, Department of Economic and Social Affairs, United Nations (2002) *World Population Ageing: 1950–2050* (New York: United Nations).

Porter, T. (2005) *Globalization and Finance* (Cambridge: Polity).

Potoski, M. and Prakash, A. (2005) 'Green Clubs and Voluntary Governance: ISO 14001 and Firms' Regulatory Compliance', *American Journal of Political Science*, 49(2): 235–48.

Powell, M. (2007) *Understanding the Mixed Economy of Welfare* (Bristol: Policy Press).

Powell, M. and Barrientos, A. (2004) 'Welfare Regimes and the Welfare Mix', *European Journal of Political Research*, 43: 83–105.

Powell, W.W. and DiMaggio, P. (eds) (1991) *The New Institutionalism in Organizational Analysis* (Chicago, IL: University of Chicago Press).

Powell, F.D. and Wesson, A.F. (eds) (1999) *Health Care Systems in Transition: An International Perspective* (London: Sage).

Prakash, A and Potoski, M. (2006) 'Racing to the Bottom? Trade, Environmental Governance, and ISO 14001', *American Journal of Political Science*, 50(2): 350–64.

Przeworski, A. (1987) 'Methods of Cross-National Research 1970-83', in M. Dierkes, H.N. Weiler and A.B. Antal (eds), *Comparative Policy Research: Learning from Experience* (Aldershot: Gower).

Przeworski, A. and Teune, H. (1966) 'Equivalence in Cross-National Research', *Public Opinion Quarterly*, 30(4): 551–68.

Przeworski, A. and Teune, H. (1970) *The Logic of Comparative Social Inquiry* (New York: Wiley).

Putnam, R.D. (1988) 'Diplomacy and Domestic Politics: The Logic of Two-Level Games', *International Organization*, 42(3): 427–60.

Putnam, T.L. (2009) 'Courts without Borders: Domestic Sources of U.S. Extraterritoriality in the Regulatory Sphere', *International Organization*, 63: 459–90.

Quadagno, J. (1994) *The Colour of Welfare: How Racism Undermined the War on Poverty* (Oxford: Oxford University Press).

Rabe, B.G. (2010) 'The Aversion to Direct Cost Imposition: Selecting Climate Policy Tools in the United States', *Governance*, 23(4): 583–608.

Radaelli, C. (2003) 'The Europeanization of Public Policy', in K. Featherstone and C. Radaelli (eds), *The Politics of Europeanization* (Oxford: Oxford University Press): 27–56.

Radaelli, C.M. (2004) 'The Puzzle of Regulatory Competition', *Journal of Public Policy*, 24(1): 1–23.

Raffe, D., Brannen, K., Croxford, L. and Martin, C. (1999) 'Comparing England, Scotland, Wales and Northern Ireland: The Case for "Home Internationals" in Comparative Research', *Comparative Education*, 35(1): 9–25.

Ragin, C. (1987) *The Comparative Method: Moving Beyond Qualitative and Quantitative Strategies* (Berkley and Los Angeles, CA: University of California Press).

Rainey, H.G. and Bozeman, B. (2000) 'Comparing Public and Private Organizations: Empirical Research and the Power of the A Priori', *Journal of Public Administration Research and Theory*, 10(2): 447–70.

Ram, R. (1995) 'Defence Expenditure and Economic Growth', in K. Hartley and T. Sandler (eds), *Handbook of Defence Economics, Volume 1* (Amsterdam: Elsevier Science): 251–74.

Ramcharan, B.G. (2008) *Preventive Diplomacy at the UN* (Bloomington: Indiana University Press).

Raphael, S. and Winter-Ebmer, R. (1999) *Identifying the Effect of Unemployment on Crime* (London: Centre for Economic Policy Research).

Raven, J., Achterberg, P., Van der Veen, R. and Yerkes, M. (2011) 'An Institutional Embeddedness of Welfare Opinions? The Link between Public Opinion and Social Policy in the Netherlands (1970–2004)', *Journal of Social Policy*, 40(2): 369–86.

Reeves, W.P. (1969) *State Experiments in Australia and New Zealand* (South Melbourne, Australia: Macmillan of Australia).

Rein, M. and Schon, D. (1991) 'Frame-Reflective Policy Discourse', in Peter Wagner, B. Wittock and H. Wollman (eds), *Social Science and Modern States: National Experiences and Theoretical Crossroads* (Cambridge: Cambridge University Press): 262–89.

Rhodes, M. and Thatcher, M. (eds) (2007) *Beyond Varieties of Capitalism: Conflict, Contradictions, and Complementarities in the European Economy* (Oxford: Oxford University Press).

Rhodes, R.A.W. (1997) *Understanding Governance. Policy Networks, Governance, Reflexivity and Accountability* (Buckingham: Open University Press).

Richardson, J. (1982) 'Convergent Policy Styles in Europe?', in J. Richardson (ed.), *Policy Styles in Western Europe* (London: Allen & Unwin): 197–209.

Richardson, J., Gustafsson, G., and Jordan, G. (1982) 'The Concept of Policy Style', in J. Richardson (ed.), *Policy Styles in Western Europe* (London: Allen & Unwin): 1–16.

Richter, M. (1969) 'Comparative Political Analysis in Montesquieu and Tocqueville', *Comparative Politics*, 1: 129–60.

Rieger, E. and Leibfried, S. (1998) 'Welfare State Limits to Globalization', *Politics and Society*, 26(3): 363–90.

Rihoux, B. and Grimm, H. (2006a) 'Introduction. Beyond the 'Qualitative–Quantitative' Divide: Innovative Comparative Methods for Policy Analysis', in B. Rihoux and H. Grimm (eds), *Innovative Comparative Methods for Policy Analysis: Beyond the Quantitative–Qualitative Divide* (New York: Springer): 1–12.

Rihoux, B. and Grimm, H. (2006b) 'Conclusion: Innovative Comparative Methods for Policy Analysis: Milestones to Bridge Different Worlds', in B. Rihoux and H. Grimm (eds), *Innovative Comparative Methods for Policy Analysis: Beyond the Quantitative–Qualitative Divide* (New York: Springer): 287–96.

Riker, W.H. (1980) 'Implications from the Disequilibrium of Majority Rule for the Study of Institutions', *American Political Science Review*, 74(2): 432–46.

Ringeling, A.B. (2002) 'European Experience with Tools of Government', in L. Salamon (ed.), *The Tools of Government: A Guide to the New Governance* (Oxford: Oxford University Press): 585–99.

Ringer, F.K. (1979) *Education and Society in Modern Europe* (Bloomington, IN: Indiana University Press).

Ringquist, E.J. and Kostadinova, T. (2005) 'Assessing the Effectiveness of International Environmental Agreements: The Case of the 1985 Helsinki Protocol', *American Journal of Political Science*, 49(1): 86–102.

Risse, T., Green Cowles, M. and Caporaso, J. (2001) 'Europeanization and Domestic Change: Introduction', in M. Green Cowles, J. Caporaso and T. Risse (eds), *Transforming Europe. Europeanization and Domestic Change* (Ithaca, NY: Cornell University Press): 1–20.

Rittberger, B. and Richardson, J. (2003) 'Old Wine in New Bottles? The Commission and the Use of Environmental Policy Instruments', *Public Administration*, 81(3): 575–605.

Rizvi, F. and Lingard, B. (2010) *Globalizing Education Policy* (London: Routledge).

Roberts, A. (2009) 'The Politics of Healthcare Reform in Postcommunist Europe: The Importance of Access', *Journal of Public Policy*, 29: 305–25.

Roberts, A. (2010) *The Logic of Discipline: Global Capitalism and the Architecture of Government* (New York: Oxford University Press).

Roberts, S. and Bolderson, H. (1999) 'Inside Out: Migrants' Disentitlement to Social Security Benefits in the EU', in J. Clasen (ed.), *Comparative Social Policy: Concepts, Theories and Methods* (Oxford: Blackwell): 200–19.

Robinson, W.I. (2004) *A Theory of Global Capitalism* (Baltimore: Johns Hopkins University Press).

Rodgers, J. (2000) *From a Welfare State to a Welfare Society* (London: Macmillan).

Rodrik, D. (1997) *Has Globalization Gone Too Far?* (Washington, DC: Peterson Institute for International Economics).

Rodrik, D. (1998) 'Why Do More Open Economies Have Bigger Governments?', *Journal of Political Economy*, 106: 997–1032.

Rodrik, D. (2006) 'Goodbye Washington Consensus, Hello Washington Confusion? A Review of the World Bank's *Economic Growth in the 1990s: Learning from a Decade of Reform*', *Journal of Economic Literature*, 44(4): 973–87.

Roe, E. (1994) *Narrative Policy Analysis: Theory and Practice* (Durham, NC and London: Duke University Press).

Rogowski, R. (1986) *Commerce and Coalitions: How Trade Affects Domestic Political Alignments* (Princeton, NJ: Princeton University Press).

Rogowski, R. (1987) 'Political Cleavages and Changing Exposure to Trade', *American Political Science Review*: 1121–37.

Ronit, K. and Schneider, V. (eds) (2000) *Private Organizations in Global Politics* (Abingdon: Routledge).

Rose, H. (1985) 'Women and the Restructuring of the Welfare State', in E. Oyen (ed.), *Comparing Welfare States and their Futures* (Aldershot: Gower).

Rose, R. (1991a) 'Comparing Forms of Comparative Analysis', *Political Studies*, 39: 446–62.

Rose, R. (1991b) 'What Is Lesson-Drawing', *Journal of Public Policy*, 11: 3–30.

Rose, R. (1993) *Lesson-Drawing in Public Policy. A Guide to Learning across Time and Space* (Chatham, NJ: Chatham House).

Rose, R. (2005) *Learning from Comparative Public Policy: A Practical Guide* (Routledge, Abingdon).

Ross, F. (2008) 'The Politics of Path-Breaking Change: The Transformation of the Welfare State in Britain and Germany', *Journal of Comparative Policy Analysis: Research and Practice*, 10(4): 365–84.

Rostow, W. (1960) *The Stages of Economic Growth: A Non-Communist Manifesto* (Cambridge: Cambridge University Press).

Rotberger, R.I. (2008) *China into Africa: Trade, Aid and Influence* (Baltimore: Brookings Institute).

Rothgang, H., Cacace, M., Grimmeisen, S. and Wendt, C. (2005) 'The Changing Role of the State in Healthcare Systems', *European Review*, 13(suppl. 1): 187–212.

Rothman, S. (1963) 'The Politics of Catholic Parochial Schools: An Historical and Comparative Analysis', *Journal of Politics*, 25: 49–71.

Rudra, N. (2007) 'Welfare States in Developing Countries: Unique or Universal?', *Journal of Politics*, 69(2): 378–96.

Rueda, D. (2005) 'Insider-Outsider Politics in Industrialised Democracies: The Challenge to ', *American Political Science Review*, 99(1): 61–74.

Rueda, D. and Pontusson, J. (2000) 'Wage Inequality and Varieties of Capitalism', *World Politics*, 52: 350–83.

Rutter, M., Maughan, B., Mortimore, P. and Ouston, J. (1979) *Fifteen Thousand Hours: Secondary Schools and their Effects on Children* (London: Open Books).

Sabatier, P. (1987) 'Knowledge, Policy-Oriented Learning, and Policy Change: An Advocacy Coalition Framework', *Science Communication*, 8: 649–92.

Sabatier, P. (1993) 'Policy Change over a Decade or More', in P. Sabatier and H. Jenkins-Smith (eds), *Policy Learning and Policy Change: An Advocacy Coalition Approach* (Boulder, CO: Westview).

Sabatier, P. and Jenkins-Smith, H.C. (eds) (1993) *Policy Change and Learning* (Boulder, CO.: Westview).

Sabatier, P. and Schlager, E. (2000) 'Les approaches cognitive des politiques publiques: perspectives américaines', *Revue Française de Science Politique*, 50(2): 209–34.

Sachs, J. (1994) *Poland's Jump to a Free Market Economy* (Cambridge, MA: MIT Press).

Sachs, J.D. and Warner, A.M. (2001) 'The Curse of Natural Resources', *European Economic Review*, 45: 4–6.

Sadler, M. (1979) 'How Far Can We Learn Anything of Practical Value from the Study of Foreign Systems of Education?', in J.H. Higginston (ed.), *Selections From Michael Sadler* (Liverpool: Dejall & Meyorre) 48–51; Guilford Lecture: 49.

Saffär, M. (1992) *Disorienting Encounters: Travels of a Moroccan Scholar in France in 1845–1846*, trans. and ed. S.G. Miller (Berkeley, CA: University of California Press).

Sage, A. (2011) 'Millions of Weapons to Remain in Homes as Voters Reject Ban', *The Times*, 14 February: 26.

Sainsbury, D. (1996) *Gender, Equality and Welfare States* (Cambridge: Cambridge University Press).

Salamon, L. (2002) 'The New Governance and the Tools of Public Action: An Introduction', in L. Salamon (ed.), *The Tools of Government: A Guide to the New Governance* (Oxford: Oxford University Press): 1–47.

Salditt, F., Whiteford, P. and Adema, W. (2008) 'Pension Reform in China', *International Social Security Review*, 61(3): 47–71.

Salonen, T. (2009) 'Sweden: Between Model and Reality', in P. Alcock and G. Craig (eds), *International Social Policy: Welfare Regimes in the Developed World*, 2nd edn (Basingstoke: Palgrave Macmillan).

Samoff, J. (2007) 'Institutionalizing International Influence', in R.F. Arnove and C.A. Torres, *Comparative Education: The Dialectic of the Global and the Local*, 3rd edn (Lanham, MD: Rowman & Littlefield: 47–78.

Sandiford, P. (ed.) (1918) *Comparative Education: Studies of the Educational Systems of Six Modern Nations* (London: Dent).

Saraceno, C. (1997) 'The Importance of the Concept of Social Exclusion', in W. Beck, L. Van der Maesen and A. Walker (eds), *The Social Quality of Europe* (Bristol: Policy Press).

Sartori, G. (1970) 'Concept Misformation in Comparative Politics', *American Political Science Review*, 64(4): 1033–53.

Scanlon, K. and Whitehead, C. (2004) *International Trends in Housing Tenure and Mortgage Finance* (London: Council for Mortgage Lenders).

Scharpf, F.W. (1988) 'The Joint-Decision Trap: Lessons from German Federalism and European Integration', *Public Administration*, 66: 239–78.

Scharpf, F.W. (1999) *Governing in Europe. Effective and Democratic?* (Oxford: Oxford University Press).

Scharpf, F.W. (2005) 'No Exit from the Joint Decision Trap? Can German Federalism Reform Itself?', MPIfG Working Paper 05/8.

Schattschneider, E.E. (1975) *The Semi-Sovereign People: A Realist's View of Democracy in America* (Boston, MA: Wadsworth Press).

Scherrer, C. (2005) 'GATS: Long-Term Strategy for the Commodification of Education', *Review of International Political Economy*, 12: 484–510.

Schiellerup, P. and Atanasiu, B. (2011) *Innovations for a Low-Carbon Economy – An Overview and Assessment of the EU Policy Landscape. A Report for WWF Sweden – Final Report* (Brussels: Institute for European Environmental Policy).

Schlager, E. (1995) 'Policy Making and Collective Action: Defining Coalitions within the Advocacy Coalition Framework,' *Policy Sciences*, 28: 242–70.

Schmähl, W. (2007) 'Dismantling an Earnings-Related Social Pension Scheme: Germany's New Pension Policy', *Journal of Social Policy*, 36: 319–40.

Schmidt, V.A. (2002a) 'Europeanization and the Mechanics of Economic Policy Adjustment', *Journal of European Public Policy*, 9(6): 894–912.

Schmidt, V.A. (2002b) *The Futures of European Capitalism* (Oxford: Oxford University Press).

Schmidt, V.A. (2003) 'How, Where, and When Does Discourse Matter in Small States' Welfare Adjustment?', *New Political Economy*, 8(1): 127–46.

Schmidt, V.A. (2008) 'Discursive Institutionalism: The Explanatory Power of Ideas and Discourse', *Annual Review of Political Science*, 11: 303–26.

Schmidt, V.A. (2009) 'Putting the Political Back into Political Economy by Bringing the State Back in Yet Again', *World Politics*, 61(3): 516–46.

Schmidt, V.A. (2010) 'Taking Ideas and Discourse Seriously: Explaining Change through Discursive Institutionalism as the Fourth "New Institutionalism"', *European Political Science Review*, 2(1): 1–2.

Schmitter, P. (1974) 'Still the Century of Corporatism?', *Review of Politics*, 36(1): 85–131.

Schmitter, P. (1979) 'Still the Century of Corporatism?' in P. Schmitter and G. Lehmbruch (eds), *Trends towards Corporatism Intermediation* (London: Sage).

Schneider, A. and Ingram, H. (1990) 'Behavioral Assumptions of Policy Tools', *Journal of Politics*, 52(2): 510–29.

Schneider, A. and Ingram, H. (1991) 'Behavioral Assumptions of Policy Tools', *Political Science and Politics*, 24(2): 147–56.

Schneider, A. and Ingram, H. (1993) 'Social Construction of Target Populations: Implications for Politics and Policy', *American Political Science Review*, 87(2): 334–47.

Schneider, A. and Ingram, H. (1998) 'Systematically Pinching Ideas: A Comparative Approach to Policy Design', *Journal of Public Policy*, 8(1): 61–80.

Schneider, M., Scholz, J., Lubell, M., Mindruta, D. and Edwardsen, M. (2003) 'Building Consensual Institutions: Networks and the National Estuary Program', *American Journal of Political Science*, 47(1): 143–58.

Schneider, V. and Häge, F.M. (2008) 'Europeanization and the Retreat of the State', *Journal of European Public Policy*, 15(1): 1–19.

Scholte, J.A. (2005) *Globalization: A Critical Introduction* (Basingstoke: Palgrave Macmillan).

Schram, S.F. and Soss, J. (1998) 'Making Something Out of Nothing: Welfare Reform and a New Race to the Bottom', *Publius*, 28(3): 67–88.

Schumpeter, J. (1939) *Business Cycles: A Theoretical, Historical, and Statistical Analysis of the Capitalist Process* (New York: McGraw Hill).

Scott, J.C. (1985) *Weapons of the Weak: Everyday Forms of Peasant Resistance* (New Haven, CT: Yale University Press).

Scott, P. (1998) 'Massification, Internationalisation and Globalization', in P. Scott (ed.), *The Globalization of Higher Education* (Buckingham: Society for Research in Higher Education/Open University Press): 108–29.

Scruggs L. (2004) 'Welfare State Entitlements Data Set: A Comparative Institutional Analysis of Eighteen Welfare States', Version 1.1, available at http://sp.uconn.edu/~scruggs/wp.htm

Scruggs, L. and J.P. Allan (2006) 'Welfare State Decommodification in Eighteen OECD Countries: A Replication and Revision', *Journal of European Social Policy*, 16(1): 55–72.

Scruggs, L. and P. Lange (2002) 'Where Have All the Members Gone? Globalization, Institutions, and Union Density', *Journal of Politics*, 64(1): 126–53.

Segura-Ubriego, A. (2007) *The Political Economy of the Welfare State in Latin America: Globalization, Democracy, and Development* (New York: Cambridge University Press).

Shalev, M. (1999) *Limits of and Alternatives to Multiple Regression in Macro-Comparative Research* (Florence: European University Institute).

Sheahan, J. (2002) 'Alternative Models of Capitalism in Latin America', in E. Huber (ed.), *Models of Capitalism: Lessons for Latin America* (Pennsylvania, PA: Pennsylvania State University Press): 25–52.

Shefter, M. (1977) 'Party and Patronage: Germany, England and Italy', *Politics and Society*, 7(4), December: 403–51.

Shepsle, K.A. (1986) 'Institutional Equilibrium and Equilibrium Institutions', in H. Weisberg (ed.) *Political Science: The Science of Politics* (New York: Agathon).

Shepsle, K. and Weingast, B. (1981) 'Structure-Induced Equilibrium and Legislative Choice', *Public Choice*, 37: 503–19.

Shibata, M. (2010) 'Re-thinking the Context of International Politics in Comparative Education: An Analysis of Japanese Educational Policy in Search for a Modern Self', in M. Larsen (ed.), *New Thinking in Comparative Education: Honouring Robert Cowen* (Rotterdam: Sense Publishers): 163–76.

Shonfield, A. (1965) *Modern Capitalism: The Changing Balance of Public and Private Power* (Oxford: Oxford University Press).

Sica, A. (2006) 'Editor's Introduction: Comparative Methodology: Its Origins and Prospects, Comparative Methods in the Social Sciences', *Sage Benchmarks in Social Science Methods*, 1 (London: Sage).

Silber, W.L. (2009) 'Why Did FDR's Bank Holiday Succeed?', *Federal Reserve Bank of New York Economic Policy Review*, July: 19–30.

Simmons, B. and Elkins, Z. (2004) 'The Globalization of Liberalization: Policy Diffusion in the International Political Economy', *American Political Science Review*, 98: 171–89.

Simmons, B.A. and Danner, A. (2010) 'Credible Commitments and the International Criminal Court', *International Organization*, 64: 225–56.

Simmons, B.A., Dobbin, F. and Garrett, G. (2006) 'Introduction: The International Diffusion of Liberalism', *International Organization*, 60(3): 781–810.

Sinclair, D. (1997) 'Self Regulation versus Command and Control? Beyond False Dichotomies', *Law and Policy*, 20: 529–41.

Sklair, L. (1997) *The Transnational Capitalist Class* (Malden, MA: Blackwell).

Skocpol, T. (1979) *States and Social Revolutions: A Comparative Analysis of France, Russia, and China* (Cambridge: Cambridge University Press).

Skocpol, T. (1985) 'Bringing the State Back In: Strategies of Analysis in Current Research', in P.B. Evans, D. Rueschmeyer and T. Skocpol (eds), *Bringing the State Back In* (Cambridge: Cambridge University Press): 3–37.

Skocpol, T. (1992) *Protecting Soldiers and Mothers: The Political Origins of Social Policy in the United States* (Cambridge, MA: Harvard University Press).

Slaughter, S. and Leslie, L.L. (1997) *Academic Capitalism: Politics, Policies, and the Entrepreneurial University* (Baltimore, MD: Johns Hopkins University Press).

Smelser, N.J. (1976) *Comparative Methods in the Social Sciences* (Englewood Cliffs, NJ: Prentice Hall).

Smith, J. (2005) *The Shipman Enquiry* (London: Department of Health, The Shipman Enquiry).

Smith, M. (1991) 'From Policy Community to Issue Network: Salmonella in Eggs and the New Politics of Food', *Public Administration*, 69: 235–55.

Smith, N. and Hay, C. (2008) 'Mapping the Political Discourse of Globalisation and European Integration in the United Kingdom and Ireland Empirically', *European Journal of Political Research*, 47(3): 359–82.

Smith, T. (1979) 'The Underdevelopment of Development Literature: The Case of Dependency Theory', *World Politics*, 31(2): 247–88.

Smith, T. and Noble, M. (1995) *Education Divides: Poverty and Schooling in the 1990s* (London: Child Poverty Action Group).

Soroos, M.S. (1991) 'A Theoretical Framework for Global Policy Studies', in S.S. Nagel, (ed.), *Global Policy Studies: International Interaction toward Improving Public Policy* (London: Macmillan): 1–21.

Spaargaren, G., Mol, A.P.J. and Bruyninckx, H. (2006) 'Introduction: Governing Environmental Flows in Global Modernity', in G. Spaargaren, A.P.J. Mol and F.H. Buttel (eds), *Governing Environmental Flows: Global Challenges to Social Theory* (Cambridge, MA: MIT Press): 1–36.

Stanley, N. and Manthorpe, J. (2004) 'Introduction: The Inquiry as Janus', in J. Manthorpe and N. Stanley, *The Age of the Inquiry. Learning and Blaming in Health and Social Care* (Basingstoke: Routledge): 1–15.

Starr, P. (1982) *The Social Transformation of American Medicine* (New York: Basic Books).

Steel, B.S., Clinton, R.L. and Lovrich, N.P. (2003) *Environmental Politics and Policy: A Comparative Approach* (New York: McGraw Hill).

Steffen, M. (2010) 'Social Health Insurance Systems: What Makes the Difference? The Bismarckian Case in France and Germany', *Journal of Comparative Policy Analysis*, 12(1–2): 141–61.

Steiner-Khamsi, G. (2002) 'Reterritorializing Educational Import: Explorations into the Politics of Educational Borrowing', in A. Novoa and M. Lawn (eds), *Fabricating Europe: The Formation of an Educational Space* (Dordrecht: Kluwer).

Stepan, A. (1988) *Rethinking Military Politics: Brazil and the Southern Cone* (Princeton, NJ: Princeton University Press).

Stephens, J.D. (1979) *The Transition from Capitalism to Socialism* (Chicago, IL: University of Illinois Press).

Stern, N. (2007) *Stern Review on the Economics of Climate Change* (Cambridge: Cambridge University Press).

Stewart, J. (2009) *Public Policy Values* (Basingstoke: Palgrave Macmillan).

Stiglitz, J.E., Ocampo, J.O., Spiegel, S., Ffrench-Davis, R. and Nayyar, D. (2006) *Stability with Growth: Macroeconomics, Liberalization, and Development* (Oxford: Oxford University Press).

Stone Sweet, A. (2000) *Governing with Judges* (Oxford: Oxford University Press).

Stone Sweet, A. and Sandholtz, W. (1997) 'European Integration and Supranational Governance', *Journal of European Public Policy*, 4(3): 297–317.

Stone, D. (1989) *Policy Paradox and Political Reason* (Glenview, IL: Scott Forestman & Co).

Stone, D. (1999) Learning Lessons and Transferring Policy across Time, Space and Disciplines', *Politics*, 19(1): 51–9.

Stone, D. (2004) 'Transfer Agents and Global Networks in the "Transnationalization" of Policy', *Journal of European Public Policy*, 11(3): 545–66.

Strange, S. (1994) *States and Markets*, 2nd edn (London: Continuum).

Streeck, W. (1992) *Social Institutions and Economic Performance: Studies of Industrial Relations in Advanced Capitalist Economies* (London: Sage).

Streeck, W. and Thelen, K. (2005) *Beyond Continuity: Institutional Change in Advanced Political Economies* (Oxford: Oxford University Press).

Streeck, W. and Thelen, K. (2005) 'Introduction: Institutional Change in Advanced Capitalist Economies', in W. Streeck and K. Thelen (eds), *Beyond Continuity: Institutional Change in Advanced Capitalist Economies* (Oxford: Oxford University Press).

Streeck, W. and Yamamura, K. (2001) *The Origins of Nonliberal Capitalism: Germany and Japan in Comparison* (Ithaca, NY: Cornell University Press).

Stromquist, N.P. (2007) 'Women's Education in the Twenty-First Century: Balance and Prospects', in R.F. Arnove and C.A. Torres, *Comparative Education: The Dialectic of the Global and the Local*, 3rd edn (Lanham, MD: Rowman & Littlefield) 151–74.

Studlar, D.T. (2002) *Tobacco Control: Comparative Politics in the United States and Canada* (Peterborough, Ontario: Broadview Press).

Studlar, D.T. (2004) 'Tobacco Control Policy Instruments in a Shrinking World: How Much Policy Learning?', in D. Levi-Faur and E. Vigoda-Gadot (eds), *Public Policy and Public Management in a Globalized World: Policy Learning and Policy Emulation Across Countries and Regions*. (New York: Marcel Dekker): 189–209.

Swank, D. (2002) *Global Capital, Political Institutions, and Policy Change in Developed Welfare States* (New York: Cambridge University Press).

Swenson, P. (2002) *Capitalists against Markets: The Making of Labour Markets and Welfare States in the US and Sweden* (Oxford: Oxford University Press).

Taschner, K. (1998) 'Environmental Management Systems: The European Regulation', in J. Golub (ed.), *New Instruments for Environmental Policy in the EU* (London: Routledge): 215–44.

Terris, M. (1978) 'The Three World Systems of Medical Care: Trends and Prospects'. *American Journal of Public Health*, 68(11): 1125–31.

Thaler, R.H. and Sunstein, C.R. (2008) *Nudge: Improving Decisions about Health, Wealth, and Happiness* (New Haven and London: Yale University Press).

Thatcher, M. (2007) *Internationalisation and Economic Institutions: Comparing the European Experience* (Oxford: Oxford University Press).

Thatcher, M. and Stone Sweet, A. (2002) 'Theory and Practice of Delegation to Non-Majoritarian Institutions', *West European Politics*, 25(1): 1–22.

Thelen, K. (2004) *How Institutions Evolve: The Political Economy of Skills in Germany, Britain, the United States and Japan* (Cambridge: Cambridge University Press).

Thelen, K. and Steinmo, S. (1992) 'Historical Institutionalism in Comparative Politics', in S. Steinmo, K. Thelen and F. Longstreth (eds), *Structuring Politics: Historical Institutionalism in Comparative Analysis* (Cambridge: Cambridge University Press).

Therborn, G. and Roebroek, J. (1986) 'The Irreversible Welfare State', *International Journal of the Health Sciences*, 16(3): 319–38.

Tinbergen, J. (1954) *International Economic Integration* (Amsterdam: Elsevier).

Titmuss, R. (1958) *Essays on the Welfare State* (London: Allen & Unwin).

Titmuss, R. (1970) *The Gift Relationship – From Human Blood to Social Policy* (London: Allen & Unwin).

Titmuss, R.M. (1974) 'Social Policy: An Introduction', in B. Abel-Smith and K. Titmuss (eds), *Social Policy: An Introduction* (New York: Pantheon).

Torfing, J. (2005) 'Discourse Theory', in D. Howarth and J. Torfing (eds), *Discourse Theory in European Politics* (Basingstoke: Palgrave Macmillan).

Trampusch, C. (2005) 'Institutional Resettlement: The Case of Early Retirement in Germany', in W. Streeck and K. Thelen, *Beyond Continuity: Institutional Change in Advanced Political Economies* (Oxford: Oxford University Press): 203–28.

Trampusch, C. (2009) 'Europeanization and Institutional Change in Vocational Education and Training in Germany and Austria', *Governance*, 22: 371–97.

Trifiletti, R. (1999) 'Southern European Welfare Regimes and the Worsening Position of Women', *Journal of European Social Policy*, 9(1): 49–64.

Trimberger, E.K. (1978) *Revolution from Above: Military Bureaucrats and Development in Japan, Turkey, Egypt and Peru* (New Brunswick: Transaction Books).

Tripp, A.M. (2002) 'Combining Intercontinental Parenting and Research: Dilemmas and Strategies for Women', *Signs: Journal of Women in Culture and Society*, 27(3): 793–811.

Truman, D.B. (1951) *The Governmental Process: Political Interests and Public Opinion* (New York: Knopf).

Tuohy, C. (1999) *Accidental Logics. The Dynamics of Change in the Health Care Arena in the United States, Britain and Canada* (Oxford: Oxford University Press).

Turner, E. (2011) *When Parties Matter: Political Parties and Public Policy in the German Länder* (Basingstoke: Palgrave Macmillan).

Tzannatos, Z. (1999) 'Women and Labor Market Changes in the Global Economy: Growth Helps, Inequalities Hurt and Public Policy Matters', *World Development*, 27(3): 551–69.

Unger, B. and van Waarden, F. (1995) 'Introduction: An Interdisciplinary Approach to Convergence', in B. Unger and F. van Waarden (eds), *Convergence or Diversity?* (Aldershot: Avebury): 1–35.

Upton, S. (1991) *Your Health and the Public Health* (Wellington: New Zealand Government.

Urry, J. (2003) *Global Complexity* (Cambridge: Polity Press).

van Deth, J. W. (1998) 'Equivalence in Comparative Political Research', in J.W. van Deth (ed.), *Comparative Politics: The Problem of Equivalence* (London and NY: Routledge): 1–19.

van Kersbergen, K. (1995) *Social Capitalism: A Study of Christian Democracy and the Welfare State* (London: Routledge).

van Kersbergen, K. and Manow, P. (2008) 'The Welfare State', in D. Caramani (ed.), *Comparative Politics* (Oxford: Oxford University Press): 520–46.

Vaughan, D. (1999) 'The Dark Side of Organizations: Mistake, Misconduct, and Disaster', *Annual Review of Sociology*, 25: 271–305.

Vedung, E. (1998) 'Policy Instruments: Typologies and Theories', in M.-L. Bemelmans-Videc, R.C. Rist and E. Vedung (eds), *Carrots, Sticks and Sermons: Policy Instruments and Their Evaluation* (New Brunswick and London: Transaction Publishers): 21–58.

Verdier, D. and Breen, R. (2001) 'Europeanization and Globalization: Politics against Markets in the European Union', *Comparative Political Studies*, 34:3, 227–62.

Verner, J.G. (1979) 'Socioeconomic Environment, Political System, and Educational Policy Outcomes: A Comparative Analysis of 102 Countries', *Comparative Politics*, 11(2): 165–87.

Verweij, M. and Thompson, M. (eds) (2006) *Clumsy Solutions for a Complex World: Governance, Politics and Plural Perceptions* (Basingstoke: Palgrave Macmillan).

Vial, J. and Melguizo, A. (2008) Moving from Pay-as-You-Go to privately Managed Individual Pension Accounts: What Have We Learned after 25 years of the Chilean Pension Reform?', *Pensions*, 14(1): 14–27.

Vickers, G. (1965) *The Art of Judgement* (London: Sage).

Vis, B., van Kersbergen, K. and Hylands, T. (2011) 'To What Extent Did the Financial Crisis Intensify the Pressure to Reform the Welfare State?', *Social Policy and Administration*, 45(4): 338–53.

Visser, J. and Hemerijck, A. (1997) *A Dutch Miracle: Job Growth, Welfare Reform and Corporatism in the Netherlands* (Amsterdam: Amsterdam University Press).

Voeten, E. (2004) 'Resisting the Lonely Superpower: Responses of States in the United Nations to U.S. Dominance', *Journal of Politics*, 66(3): 729–54.

Vogel, D. (1986) *National Styles of Regulation: Environmental Policy in Great Britain and the United States* (Ithaca, NY: Cornell University Press).

Vogel, D. (1997) *Trading Up: Consumer and Environmental Regulation in a Global Economy* (Harvard: Harvard University Press).

Vogel, D. (2003a) *National Styles of Business Regulation: A Case Study of Environmental Protection* (Washington, DC: Beard Books).

Vogel, D. (2003b) 'The Hare and the Tortoise Revisited: The New Politics of Consumer and Environmental Regulation in Europe', *British Journal of Political Science*, 33(4): 557–80.

Vogel, D. (2004) 'The New Politics of Risk Regulation in Europe and the US', in M. Levin and M. Shapiro (eds), *Trans-Atlantic Policymaking in an Age of Austerity* (Washington, DC: Georgetown University Press).

Vogel, D. and Kagan, R.A. (eds) (2004) *Dynamics of Regulatory Change: How Globalization Affects National Regulatory Policies* (London: University of California Press).

von Beyme, K. (1984) 'Do Parties Matter? The Impact of Parties on the Key Decisions in the Political System', *World Politics*, 19(4): 5–29.

Vreeland, J.R. (2003) *The IMF and Economic Growth* (New York: Cambridge University Press).

Waine, B. (2006) 'Ownership and Security: Individualised Pensions and Pension Policy in the United Kingdom and the United States', *Competition and Change*, 10(3): 321–37.

Waine, B. (2008) 'Rules for the Rich? Contemporary Trends in Executive Pensions', *Competition and Change*, 12(3): 281–6.

Walkenhorst, H. (2008) 'Explaining Change in EU Education Policy', *Journal of European Public Policy*, 15: 567–87.

Walker, A. and Maltby, T. (2008) 'Older People', in P. Alcock, M. May and K. Rowlingson (eds), *The Student's Companion to Social Policy* (Oxford: Blackwell): 394–401.

Wallace, H. and Wallace, W. (eds) (2000) Policy-Making in the European Union, 4th edn (Oxford: Oxford University Press).

Walker, A. and Wong, C.-K. (1996) 'Rethinking the Western Construction of the Welfare State', *International Journal of Health Services*, 26(1): 67–92.

Wallace, H. and Young, A. (1997) *Participation and Policy-Making in the European Union* (Oxford: Clarendon Press).

Wallerstein, I. (1974) 'Dependence in an Interdependent World: The Limited Possibilities of Transformation within the Capitalist World Order', *African Studies Review*, 17(1), April: xvii, 2.

Walt, G. (1994) *Health Policy: An Introduction to Process and Power* (London: Zed Books).

Walter, S. (2010) 'Globalization and the Welfare State: Testing the Microfoundations of the Compensation Hypothesis', *International Studies Quarterly*, 54: 403–26.

Walters, W. (1997) 'The Active Society', *Policy and Politics*, 25: 221–34.

Waltz, K. (1954) *Man, the State, and War: A Theoretical Analysis* (New York: Columbia University Press).

Waters, M. (1995) *Globalisation* (London: Routledge).

Weale, A. (1992) *The New Politics of Pollution* (Manchester: Manchester University Press).

Weaver, K. (2010) 'Paths and Forks or Chutes and Ladders?: Negative Feedbacks and Policy Regime Change', *Journal of Public Policy*, 30(2): 137–62.

Weaver, R.K. (2004) 'Pension Reform in Canada: Lessons for the United States', *Ohio State Law Journal*, 65(45): 45–74.

Weber, M. (1918) 'Politics as a Vocation', Speech at Munich University.

Weber, M. (1930) *The Protestant Ethic and the Spirit of Capitalism*, trans. T. Parsons (London: Allen & Unwin).

Weber, M. (1946 [1920]) *From Max Weber* (New York: Oxford University Press).

Weber, M. (1947) *The Theory of Social and Economic Organization*, trans. A.M. Henderson and T. Parsons (London: Collier Macmillan Publishers).

Weber, M. (1948a) 'Politics as a Vocation', in H.H. Gerth and C.W. Mills (eds), *From Max Weber: Essays in Sociology* (London: Routledge & Kegan Paul).

Weber, M. (1948b) 'Science as a Vocation', in H.H. Gerth and C.W. Mills (eds), *From Max Weber: Essays in Sociology* (London: Routledge & Kegan Paul).

Weber, M. (1961) *The Three Types of Legitimate Rule*, trans. H. Certh, in A. Etzioni (ed.), *Complex Organizations* (New York: Holt, Rinehart & Winston).

Weber, M. (1980 [1925]) *Wirtschaft und Gesellschaft: Grundriss der verstehenden soziologie* (Baden-Württemberg: Mohr Siebeck).

Weir, M. (1992) *Politics and Jobs: The Boundaries of Employment Policy in the United States* (Princeton, NJ: Princeton University Press).

Weir, M. and Skocpol, T. (1985) 'State Structures and the Possibilities for "Keynesian" Responses to the Great Depression in Sweden, Britain, and the US', in P.B. Evans, D. Rueschmeyer and T. Skocpol (eds), *Bringing the State Back In* (Cambridge: Cambridge University Press): 107–68.

Weiser, T.G., Regenbogen, S.E., Thompson, K.D., Haynes, A.B., Lipsitz, S.R., Berry, W.R., and Gawande, A.A. (2008) 'An Estimation of the Global Volume of Surgery: A Modelling Strategy based on Available Data', *The Lancet*, 372(9633): 139–44.

Weiss, L. and Hobson, J. (1995) *States and Economic Development* (Cambridge: Polity Press).

Wendt, A. (1999) *Social Theory of International Politics* (Cambridge: Cambridge University Press).

Wendt, C., Frisina, L. and Rothgang, H. (2009) 'Healthcare System Types: A Conceptual Framework for Comparison', *Social Policy and Administration*, 43(1): 70–90.

West, K. (2011a) 'Articulating Discursive and Materialist Conceptions of Practice in the Logics Approach to Critical Policy Analysis', *Critical Policy Studies*, 5(4): 414–33.

West, K. (2011b) 'Fanning the Flames of Intergenerational Hatred', Letter published on the Guardian Society website, 21 August.

Westle, B. (1998) 'Tolerance', in J.W. van Deth (ed.), *Comparative Politics: The Problem of Equivalence* (London and New York: Routledge).

Weyland, K. (ed.) (2000) *Learning from Foreign Models in Latin America Policy Reform* (Washington, DC: Woodrow Wilson Center).

Weyland, K. (2005) 'The Diffusion of Innovations: How Cognitive Heuristics Shaped Bolivian Pension Reform', *Comparative Politics*, 38(1): 21–42.

Weyland, K. (2006) *Bounded Rationality and Policy Diffusion: Social Sector Reform in Latin America* (Princeton, NJ: Princeton University Press).

White, B.W. (1996) 'Talk about School: Education and the Colonial Project in French and British West Africa, 1860–1960', *Comparative Education*, 32: 9–25.

White, J. (2010) 'National Case Studies and Cross-National Learning: US Health Care, 1993–2006', *Journal of Comparative Policy Analysis*, 12(1–2): 115–39.

Whitehead, C. and Scanlon, K. (eds) (2007) *Social Housing in Europe* (London: London School of Economics).

Whitty, G., Power, S. and Halpin, D. (1998) *Devolution and Choice in Education: The School, the State and the Market* (Buckingham: Open University Press).

Wickham-Crowley, T.P. (1992) *Guerrillas and Revolution in Latin America: A Comparative Study of Insurgents and Regimes since 1956* (Princeton, NJ: Princeton University Press).

Wildavsky, A. (1974) *The Politics of the Budgetary Process* (Boston, MA: Little, Brown).

Wilensky, H.L. (1975) *The Welfare State and Equality: Structural and Ideological Roots of Public Expenditures* (Berkeley, CA: University of California Press).

Wilensky, H.L. and Lebeaux, C.N. (1958) *Industrial Society and Social Welfare: The Impact of Industrialisation on the Supply and Organization of Social Welfare Services in the United States* (New York: Sage).

Wilensky, H.L. and Turner, L. (1987) *Democratic Corporatism and Policy Linkages* (Berkeley, CA: Institute of International Studies).

Wilkinson, K. (2011) 'Organised Chaos: An Interpretive Approach to Evidence-Based Policy Making in Defra', *Political Studies*, 59: 959–77.

Wilkinson, R.G. (1996) *Unhealthy Societies: The Affliction of Inequality* (London: Routledge).

Willetts, D. (2011) *The Pinch: How the Baby Boomers Took Their Children's Future – And Why They Should Give it Back* (London: Atlantic Books).

Williams, F. (2008) 'Culture and Nationhood', in P. Alcock, M. May and K. Rowlingson (eds), *The Student's Companion to Social Policy* (Oxford: Blackwell): 159–65.

Williamson, J. (ed.) (1990) *Latin American Adjustment: How Much Has It Happened?* (Washington, DC: Institute for International Economics).

Williamson, O.E. (1975) *Markets and Hierarchies, Analysis and Antitrust Implications: A Study in the Economics of Internal Organization* (New York: Free Press).

Williamson, O.E. (1985) *The Economic Institutions of Capitalism* (New York: Free Press).

Wilsford, D. (1991) *Doctors and the State: The Politics of Health Care in France and the United States* (Durham, NC: Duke University Press).

Wilson, J.Q. (1980) *The Politics of Regulation* (New York: Basic Books).

Wincott, D. (2003) 'Beyond Social Regulation? New Instruments and/or a New Agenda for Social Policy at Lisbon?', *Public Administration*, 81(3): 533–54.

Witko, C. and Newmark, A.J. (2009) 'The Strange Disappearance of Investment in Human and Physical Capital in the United States', *Journal of Public Administration Research and Theory*, 20: 215–32.

Witte, J. (2006) 'Change of Degrees and Degrees of Change: Comparing Adaptations of European Higher Education Systems in the Context of the Bologna Process', CHEOS/ Universiteit Twente.

Woll, C. (2008) *Firm Interests: How Governments Shape Business Lobbying on Global Trade* (Ithaca, NY: Cornell University Press).

Wolman, H. and Page, E. (2002) 'Policy Transfer among Local Governments: An Information-Theory Approach', *Governance*, 15(4): 477–501.

Wood, G. and Gough, I. (2006) 'A Comparative Welfare Regime Approach to Global Social Policy', *World Development*, 34(10): 1696–712.

World Bank (2011) *World Development Indicators* (Washington, DC: World Bank).

World Health Organization (2008) *World Health Statistics* (Geneva: World Health Organization).

Yanow, D. (1996) *How Does a Policy Mean?* (Washington, DC: Georgetown University Press).

Yeates, N. (1999) 'Social Politics and Policy in an Era of Globalization: Critical Reflections', *Social Policy and Administration*, 33(4): 372–93.

Yeates, N. (2001) *Globalization and Social Policy* (London: Sage).

Yeates, N. (2010) 'The Globalization of Nurse Migration: Policy Issues and Responses', *International Labour Review*, 149(4): 423–40.

Yetano, A. (2010) 'Managing Performance at Local Government Level: The Cases of the City of Brisbane and the City of Melbourne', *Australian Journal of Public Administration*, 68(2): 167–81.

Young, A. (2000) *Women Who Become Men: Albanian Sworn Virgins* (Oxford: Berg).

Young, K., Ashby, D., Boaz, A. and Grayson, L. (2002) 'Social Science and the Evidence-Based Policy Movement', *Social Policy and Society*, 1: 215–24.

Young, O. (1994) *International Governance: Protecting the Environment in a Stateless Society* (Ithaca, NY: Cornell University Press).

Zahariadis, N. (2010) 'Discretion by the Rules: European State Aid Policy and the 1999 Procedural Regulation', *Journal of European Public Policy*, 17(7): 954–70.

100 people (undated) '100 People: A World Project', www.100people.org, accessed December 2011.

Index